Leiths

SIMPLE COOKERY BIBLE

Also in the Leiths series

Leiths Cookery Bible
Leiths Techniques Bible
Leiths Vegetarian Bible
Leiths Fish Bible
Leiths Baking Bible

Leiths

SIMPLE COOKERY BIBLE

**VIV PIDGEON and
JENNY STRINGER**

BLOOMSBURY

LONDON · NEW DELHI · NEW YORK · SYDNEY

For Amelia, Luca, Lily and Kit. And Thomas, Ben, Emily and Adam.

First published in Great Britain in 2008
This paperback edition published 2013

Copyright © Leiths School of Food and Wine, 2008

The moral right of the authors has been asserted.

Bloomsbury Publishing Plc, 50 Bedford Square, London WC1B 3DP

A CIP catalogue record for this book is available from the British Library.

ISBN: 9781408842171

Photographs by Jason Lowe
Home Economy by Susan Spaull
Edited by Helen Campbell
Indexed by Christine Bernstein
Plate section design by Polly Napper

10 9 8 7 6 5 4 3 2 1

Typeset by Hewer Text UK Ltd, Edinburgh
Printed in China by C&C Offset Printing Co., Ltd

All papers used by Bloomsbury Publishing are natural,
recyclable products made from wood grown in well-managed
forests. The manufacturing processes conform to the
environmental regulations of the country of origin.

www.bloomsbury.com

Contents

Acknowledgements

We would particularly like to thank all our colleagues at Leiths School of Food and Wine, past and present, for cooking and eating these recipes and giving us valuable feedback and ideas. We are especially indebted to those who have allowed us to use their recipes in this book and to Caroline Waldegrave for her unfailing support and advice.

We would also like to thank the team at Bloomsbury, particularly Natalie Hunt for her incredible dedication to this project and for having such a great eye for detail, and Lisa Fiske for her work on the production; Helen Campbell for her editing; Jason Lowe for the wonderful photos; Sue Spaull, Hélène Robinson Moltke and Marianne Lumb for all their terrific work on the photoshoot; and the Leiths students of 2007 who also helped on the photoshoot during their holidays.

Viv would like to thank her family: her parents who, between them, from the very beginning, taught her to grow and to cook food; her brothers for being her early gastronomic guinea pigs; and James for his apparent enthusiasm to eat anything that is cooked for him.

Jenny also owes her love of food and cooking to her family, particularly her mother. She would also like to thank her husband James for his support and his help with childcare while working on the manuscript, as well as for the recipe ideas he has contributed.

Viv Pidgeon and Jenny Stringer

Foreword

This is the cookery book that I have been waiting for. We can all have grand ideas about cooking elegant and complicated dishes, but when it comes to the end of the working day, few of us have the time or inclination to be in the kitchen when we would rather be with our family or friends.

This book has been written specifically so that you can cook real food simply. By using the word 'simple', we mean either that the recipe is quick and easy to prepare, or that it is simple to make and can be prepared in advance and cooked at the last minute. There are times when we all may be tempted to go and buy ready meals from the supermarkets; this collection of recipes, which is the first Leiths cookery book to include convenience ingredients, aims to avoid that temptation.

I have very much enjoyed eating the results of all the recipe testing at the School and recommend this book to you.

Caroline Waldegrave, OBE

Authors' Introduction

The seed of inspiration for this book was sown when we started writing the recipe of the day in the *Daily Mail*. The simpler style of recipe proved extremely popular, and we received floods of emails and telephone calls asking for more ideas for simple menus. Leiths School contributed to this column for six years, and many of the recipes in this book were written at that time.

Leiths Simple Cookery Bible is a collection of recipes and helpful information for people who do not usually have time to spend on elaborate recipes or who lack skills or confidence but would like to eat well and to try new ideas on a daily basis.

Here you will find recipes that are suitable for quick after-work cooking, and easy entertaining, that can be cooked in advance and frozen for whenever they are needed. In short, this is a collection of recipes for real life. Many of us wish we had more time to spend lovingly preparing dishes for ourselves, family and friends, but in reality cooking is often rushed and the dishes we cook can become repetitive. This book will give you lots of ideas that will take the strain out of continually coming up with new ideas.

The recipe sections are more flexible than in many cookbooks. It is unlikely that you will cook a three-course meal every day of the week, but a chapter of recipes that would make delicious first courses is included as these dishes are often light and speedy, ideal for a quick supper. Salads today are imaginative and make a perfect first course for entertaining, or a meal in themselves, so there is a whole chapter dedicated to them. Some of the dishes take 10 minutes to prepare from start to finish, some may take a couple of hours. All are clearly marked with the preparation time, cooking time and any chilling or marinating time in between, so you will be able to find a dish that fits in with the time you have available to cook.

At Leiths School of Food and Wine we spend nine months of the year teaching people with a passion for food to change their careers and become professional chefs. During that time we do not teach short cuts or use convenience foods or ready-made ingredients such as shortcrust pastry or mayonnaise. However, for the rest of the year we teach enthusiastic amateurs, who we know may not have the time or energy to make their own stock or pizza bases when they get home. This book is for them. However, recognizing that occasionally even the busiest person may find they do have some time to spare, or would just prefer to make a particular recipe from scratch, we have also included a section of basic recipes such as shortcrust pastry, hollandaise sauce, chicken stock – everything that in the rest of the book we suggest you buy to save time. We have also given advice on what brands we have found to be reliable or the most delicious. Many of our students ask for our advice on how they should equip and stock their kitchens, so this advice is included here too.

Leiths Simple Cookery Bible is a collection of dishes we have created to fit in with our own busy lives. We hope you will find the recipes simple to make, but no less delicious.

Part One
BASICS

How to Use This Book

Measurements

The purpose of this book is to make life simpler and to reduce stress when cooking. Where possible, the lists of ingredients will require actual pack sizes, but of course this varies from shop to shop. We would advise you to weigh carefully and follow the recipe exactly when cooking recipes from the baking section, but all the other recipes will work if you do not have exactly the right amount of one or more of the ingredients. An extra teaspoon of Parmesan, 20 g too few rocket leaves, or an onion sweated in a knob of butter instead of the specified 20 g will make precious little difference to the result.

Standard Ingredients

In this book, it is assumed that all eggs are medium size. Sugar is caster sugar, flour is plain flour and butter is salted. Onions and garlic are peeled. General oil is sunflower oil. As far as possible we would urge you to buy locally.

Substituting Ingredients

Sometimes an ingredient required in a recipe is unavailable or you may dislike it. Below is some advice about substitutions:

Herbs

One herb can easily be substituted for another. Try to match the strength of flavour when choosing. Robust herbs such as rosemary and thyme can be used interchangeably, whereas coriander could be replaced by dill, parsley or chervil. The other thing to bear in mind is the style of the dish. For example, the basil required in a Mediterranean-style dish could be replaced by marjoram or oregano.

Vegetables

Substitution of one vegetable for another is usually possible in most dishes. For example, a basic soup recipe can be followed using the same weight of a similar vegetable, such as celeriac in place of parsnip, carrot or potato. Leftover cooked vegetables can be added to a casserole as long as they are heated to a high temperature. Leeks, spring onions and garlic can all be used where regular onions are not available.

Fruit

Where one type of fruit is unavailable, or there is a glut of a particular type of fruit, one soft fruit can be readily substituted for another. Raspberries, strawberries, blackberries and mulberries can be used weight for weight in the same recipes, except in jam making. Firmer fruits, such as plums or apples, must be cooked before being used as substitutes for softer fruit. Dried fruits of a similar size are generally interchangeable. Dried cherries and cranberries are quite tart so one can be substituted for the other.

Nuts and Seeds

Types of nut or seed can be altered in most recipes according to preference. Take the flavour of the ingredient demanded by the recipe into account as well as the size. Pinenuts can be replaced by chopped almonds or even sunflower seeds, for example, and walnuts make a good substitute for pecan nuts and vice versa.

Meat and Fish

It is a good idea to use an alternative that has the same coloured flesh. Chicken can be replaced by turkey, pheasant breasts, rabbit, or even fish in some recipes. Beef can be replaced by lamb or venison. Cod can be replaced by any firm white fish.

Flavourings

Feel free to alter the flavouring ingredients in a recipe. Different-flavoured vinegars can be used, soy sauce in place of salt, mushroom ketchup instead of Worcestershire sauce.

Oils

Oils can be interchanged as long as they have a similar flash point. This is the temperature at which oil will burn. Sunflower, ground nut, vegetable and light olive oil can all be used for frying to a high temperature. A little highly flavoured oil such as sesame or walnut oil can be added for flavour but will burn if used for frying. Extra virgin olive oil should be reserved for dressings or drizzling over salads.

Sugar and Sweeteners

Baking may require a particular type of sugar, but generally in cooking brown sugar can be used in place of white, granulated in place of caster, according to taste. Maple syrup, honey or ginger syrup, along with American corn syrup, can be interchanged. Artificial sweeteners cannot all be used in the same way as sugar, so check the manufacturer's instructions.

Dairy Ingredients

Salted and unsalted butter can be used interchangeably, just by adjusting the seasoning accordingly. Skimmed, semi-skimmed or full-fat milk can usually be used in most recipes, only the final richness will be affected. Double or whipping cream can be whisked, but single cream cannot. Only double cream should be boiled, as other lower-fat creams may split. Coconut cream and synthetic creams can often be used to enrich dishes in the place of fresh cream, but not all can be heated to a high temperature. Pasteurized eggs, or pasteurized egg whites, can be used in place of the eggs in these recipes. Both are available from some supermarkets and are suitable for vulnerable groups. Use 60 g when substituting for 1 whole egg; use 30 g of pasteurized egg white in place of the white of 1 egg. When finding a replacement for an unavailable cheese, try to choose one with a similar strength of flavour. Emmental can be used in place of Gruyère, and Grana Padano is similar to Parmesan, and cheaper. Don't substitute low-fat products as they rarely work in place of the full-fat product.

Flour

It is important to use strong plain flour when making pasta or bread and self-raising flour when baking. In most situations, such as making a sauce, self-raising flour can be used in place of plain flour with no ill effects. Brown flour can be used but will give a heavier result. Gluten-free flours can be used for sauces but may need more liquid than wheat flours.

Cooking Times

Cooking times are given as a guide but depend on a variety of factors such as individual ovens, the temperature of the ingredients before cooking, the size of the ingredients and the dish used for cooking. Ovens should be preheated for 30 minutes or until the desired temperature is reached before use. Recipes will generally indicate what to look for as well as the time. Therefore if the dish is piping hot and brown on top as required, there is no need to finish the last few minutes of the suggested cooking time. Similarly, if the cooking time has expired and the dish is hot all the way through but is still not brown on the top, heat the grill and brown quickly before serving.

Chopping Sizes

Recipes will sometimes suggest chopping roughly or slicing finely. This tends to be a direction that will only affect the presentation of the dish, so if time or knife skills do not permit fine chopping, the result will just be a more rustic-looking dish.

Conversion Tables

This book is the first Leiths cookery book to specify metric measurements only. Accurately, 1 oz = 28 g, so in reality on electric scales it is easier to weigh out 25 g or 30 g. With many recipes a few grams here and there does not make too much of a difference, with the exception of baking recipes when the ingredients should be weighed accurately.

The following conversion table gives a range of grams for the equivalent in ounces.

Weights

Metric	Imperial
15–20 g	½ oz
25–30 g	1 oz
50–60 g	2 oz
80–90 g	3 oz
100–120 g	4 oz
130–150 g	5 oz
160–180 g	6 oz
200 g	7 oz
220–230 g	8 oz
250–260 g	9 oz
280–290 g	10 oz
300–320 g	11 oz
330–340 g	12 oz
360–380 g	13 oz
400 g	14 oz
410–430 g	15 oz
450 g	16 oz/1 lb
1 kg	2 lb 4 oz
1.5 kg	3 lb 5 oz

Liquid conversions

Metric	Imperial
15 ml	1 tablespoon or ½ fl oz
30 ml	2 tablespoons or 1 fl oz
150 ml	¼ pint or 5 fl oz
280–300 ml	½ pint
425–450 ml	¾ pint
570–600 ml	1 pint
1 litre	1¾ pints
1.2 litres	2 pints

Some recipes call for 142 ml, 284 ml or 568 ml of cream, depending on the container sizes. They don't need to be measured so accurately – 150 ml, 300 ml or 600 ml is fine.

Useful conversions

1 level tablespoon = approx 15 g or ½ oz
1 heaped tablespoon = approx 30 g or 1 oz
1 glass of wine = 100–150 ml
1 tablespoon = 3 teaspoons
1 lime gives about 30 ml/2 tablespoons juice
1 lemon gives about 120 ml/8 tablespoons juice

Oven Temperatures

°C	°F	Gas mark	
70	150	¼	
80	175	¼	
100	200	½	COOL
110	225	½	
130	250	1	VERY LOW
140	275	1	
150	300	2	LOW
170	325	3	MODERATE
180	350	4	
190	375	5	MODERATELY HOT
200	400	6	FAIRLY HOT
220	425	7	HOT
230	450	8	VERY HOT
240	475	8	
250	500	9	
270	525	9	EXTREMELY HOT
290	550	9	

Terms, Techniques and Tips

Al Dente

An Italian term meaning 'firm to the tooth'. It is used to describe how pasta, risotto and some vegetables are cooked, i.e. not completely soft but with some 'bite'.

Bain-marie

A roasting tin half-filled with hot water in which delicate dishes stand while cooking in the oven to protect them from direct fierce heat. A bain-marie can be used to keep sauces warm.

Basting

Sometimes it is necessary to pour stock or fat over roasting food to prevent it from drying out during cooking. Often, when a joint is roasted, the fat will drain out of the meat as it cooks. The joint can then be removed from the oven a few times during roasting, and the melted fat can be spooned over the meat.

Blanching and Refreshing

Blanching is the process of boiling vegetables until they are only part cooked, then stopping the cooking by immediately plunging them into very cold water. This preserves the colour and is a technique used when trying to avoid doing too much cooking at the last minute by preparing as much as possible in advance. To serve, the cooking can be quickly completed by boiling the vegetables briefly in boiling water, or heating up in butter.

Boiling

Cooking food submerged in liquid over a high heat, with fast, agitated bubbles.

Bouquet Garni

This consists of parsley stalks, a small bay leaf, fresh thyme, a celery stalk and (sometimes) a blade of mace, tied together with string. It is used to flavour stews, and is always removed before serving. They can be bought ready-assembled from shops.

Breadcrumbs

It is best to use bread that is slightly stale when making breadcrumbs as the crumbs form more easily, or alternatively dry out slices of fresh bread by laying them out on a baking sheet and putting into the oven at its coolest temperature. Bread-crumbs are usually made from white bread, and are good way of using up leftover French bread or ciabatta, which goes stale quickly. Brown bread will work just as well. Remove the crusts if an even colour is important. Cut the bread into even chunks and pulse in a food processor until crumbed. Dried bread crumbs are readily available in supermarkets; try to use the 'natural' colour breadcrumbs rather than 'golden' ones.

Broad Beans, Double Podding

Remove the individual beans from the large green pod. Blanch and refresh, then peel off the wrinkled grey skins and use the bright green beans within as required.

Browning

This refers to pan-frying meat, fish or vegetables until they reach a golden brown colour, to improve the appearance and flavour of certain dishes.

Caramelizing

Browning vegetables, sometimes with a little added sugar, with particular reference to onions, for onion gravy and marmalade; or boiling sugar to a caramel.

Chopping chillies

Chillies, Chopping

Try not to get the chilli oil on your fingers when chopping chillies as it will burn your eyes and does not wash off for some time. Use gloves to cut the chilli in half lengthways and scrape out and discard the seeds and white membrane.

A useful tip for cutting chillis is to use a fork to secure the chilli to the board and cut into strips lengthways, leaving the stalk end intact to keep the strips together. Then turn the chilli round with the fork and cut crossways into squares of the required size.

Chining

This is where the ribs have been cut through next to the backbone, for example on a rack of lamb. When buying meat from the butcher's, ask them to chine the joint for you, as it is very difficult to do this with domestic knives.

Citrus Fruit, Peeling, Segmenting and Slicing

Cut a slice from the top and bottom of the fruit so that the inside of the fruit can just be seen. Using a small, serrated knife, cut off the pith and the peel from top to bottom in strips, cleanly revealing the fruit below. Move round steadily clockwise, trying to follow the natural shape so that the result is a round fruit, with the dividing membranes visible, free from all pith. (a) Often recipes call for the zest and juice of a fruit. A classic mistake is to juice it before zesting. This makes zesting virtually impossible.

To remove each segment cleanly, cut each side of each membrane, getting as close as possible to the membrane as possible. Remove the segments of fruit following the angle of the segments, to avoid leaving any behind on the membrane. (b) Alternatively, slice the orange crossways and remove all the pips. (c) Cut each slice into quarters if required by the recipe.

Citrus Fruit, Zesting

The zest is just the coloured outer layer of the skin, not the bitter white pith between the zest and the fruit. Waxed fruit should be washed before use. Use a zester which creates long strips for pared zest, or a microplane grater if grated zest is required (see page 43). Otherwise use a box grater and brush out the zest from the teeth with a pastry brush. Clingfilm can be wrapped around the cutting edge of the grater before zesting. When the fruit has been zested, the clingfilm can be removed, bringing the zest away with it; this avoids zest getting stuck in the grater. Use a very good-quality clingfilm so that no pieces of plastic are shed into the zest.

Cream, Whipping

Double cream has the highest fat content of any cream and is the easiest to whip. Whipping cream is lower in fat but can also be whipped. Single cream cannot be whipped.

Cream should not be overwhipped or it will begin to look lumpy, rather like cottage cheese. Cream should be whipped to the soft peak stage so it then can be spooned on to puddings or folded into other ingredients.

A balloon whisk can be used to whip cream by hand, but electric whisks or the whisk attachment of a food mixer will be much quicker. In fact, with electric whisks it is wise to go reasonably slowly or to whisk in short blasts to avoid overwhisking. As soon as the cream holds its shape on the whisk it is ready. If it has been whisked too far, add a little milk to soften it.

Creaming

When making cakes, creaming together the butter and sugar means to beat well with a spoon or electric whisk to incorporate air. The mixture will become very pale when it has been beaten sufficiently.

Peeling citrus fruit (a)

Segmenting citrus fruit (b)

Slicing citrus fruit (c)

Cucumber, Deseeding

Cut the cucumber in half lengthways and use a teaspoon to scrape down the length, removing the seeds.

Deep Frying

It is important to keep safety in mind when deep frying. If using a deep fat fryer, follow the manufacturer's instructions carefully. Use a suitable oil, such as sunflower and vegetable oil, which will not ignite at a low temperature. If using a pan instead of a fryer, fill it only one-third full and do not leave the pan unattended while it is on the heat. Heat the pan gradually: the oil is hot enough when a cube of bread will brown in 20 seconds. It should not be allowed to get any hotter. The hot fat should not be moved until it cools down. Should a pan catch fire, turn off the heat, cut off the oxygen source by covering with a lid or a baking sheet and stand back. Do not throw on water.

Use a higher heat for small items to be fried and a lower heat for larger items, or they will burn on the outside before the inside is cooked. After cooking, drain the food on kitchen paper and sprinkle with salt or sugar depending on the dish.

Deglazing

When meat, fish or vegetables are browned in a frying pan, they leave a brown sediment on the base of the pan which can add delicious flavour to the sauce. Add liquid to the hot pan and scrape the bottom with a wooden spoon to dissolve the sediment into the liquid, then add the liquid to the sauce.

Dried Chickpeas, Beans and Pulses, How to Cook

Dried peas and beans are generally cheaper than their fresh or canned equivalents but require some preparation before they are used for cooking. Most pulses need soaking until softened and swollen before cooking. Soaking can be done overnight but not for much longer than 12 hours. After soaking, drain the pulses, place them in a saucepan and cover with cold water. Bring to the boil, then simmer for 10 minutes. Change the water and simmer until tender. Depending on the type of bean or pulse, this could take between 15 minutes and 2 hours. Cans of ready-cooked chickpeas and beans in water can be bought and do not need any treatment. They can just be drained, rinsed and used as required.

Red kidney beans must be boiled fast for at least 10 minutes to destroy the dangerous toxins they contain.

Puy and red lentils do not need any soaking and cook within 15–20 minutes so are sometimes convenient to use in place of other pulses that require lengthier treatment.

Dripping

The melted fat and juices that run from a roasting joint of meat. Canned goose fat or vegetable oils can be used as alternatives.

Eggs, Hardboiled and Semi-hardboiled

Eggs can be boiled either by putting them straight into boiling water and starting the timer straight away, or by putting them into a pan of cold water and bringing them up to the boil, starting the timer when the water starts to boil. An egg will take 12 minutes to be hardboiled by the first method but only 10 by the second method.

Whichever method is used, once the eggs are in the water and it has come to the boil, reduce the temperature so that the water simmers rather than boils, as this will prevent the white from becoming too rubbery (see below).

How the egg will be cooked	Egg goes into cold water. Number of minutes from when the water comes to the boil.	Egg goes into boiling water. Number of minutes from when the egg is immersed.
Set white and runny yolk *Suitable for breakfast boiled eggs and soldiers*	3 minutes	4½ minutes
Set white and yolk starting to set but still liquid in the centre *Suitable for peeling carefully to serve on salads or risottos*	4 minutes	6 minutes
Set white and just set yolk which is still yellow and moist *Suitable for peeling and halving to serve on salads*	6 minutes	8 minutes
Set white and dry-set yolk *Suitable for mashing*	10 minutes	12 minutes

Eggs, Poached

It is important to use very fresh eggs for poaching or they will not hold together well. Break an egg into a small cup. Bring a pan of water to the boil, turn it down to a simmer, then swirl the water round with a spoon to create a whirlpool effect. When the whirlpool has nearly disappeared, lower the cup almost to the surface of the water and gently slip the egg out, allowing it to fall through the water in the centre.

Increase the heat slightly, allowing the water to bubble gently, as it needs to be hot enough to set the egg white. Poach for 2–3 minutes, or until the white is set but the yolk is still runny. Remove from the water with a slotted spoon and dab the bottom of the spoon with kitchen paper to prevent water from being transferred to the plate.

An egg poacher can also be used, where eggs are cracked into special cups with a knob of butter, which then slot into a poaching pan. The result is not the same as the poached eggs described above, but an egg poacher is extremely simple to use and will work even when the eggs are not fresh enough for the traditional method.

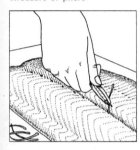

Fish, Pinboning

This is done to remove all the small bones that run along the flanks of the fish through the flesh. Fish can be pinboned either before or after cooking. Run the tips of the fingers of one hand over the surface of the flesh to locate the ends of the small bones. Pull the bones out with clean tweezers or pliers.

Flamber

This is when alcohol is set alight and poured over the pan. It is best to use alcohol from a reasonably recently opened bottle as it will flame better. A steak is sometimes flambéed, which means the harsh flavour of the raw alcohol is burnt off and the flavour of the particular spirit is imprinted on the steak. Make sure the pan containing the ingredients to be flambéed is hot before you start, but then move aside from the heat.

In order to flamber safely, make sure your arm is covered, place the alcohol in a ladle and warm over the heat of the hob. When warmed through, ignite the alcohol. If using a gas hob, tilt the ladle towards the flame at arm's length and the edge will ignite. Pour away from you over the ingredients in the pan to be flambéed. Shake the pan gently over the heat until the flames have subsided. If you do not have a gas hob, the warm ladle will need to be set alight with a match. Again, make sure it is done at arm's length and tilt and light the edge of the ladle.

Frying

Use as wide a pan as necessary, to avoid overcrowding, and use just enough oil to cover the bottom of the pan. Heat the pan before adding the food, salting it before frying to help the browning process. Fry in small batches, as the food will not brown if too much is fried at one time.

Garlic, Bruising

Place the clove of garlic on the chopping board and flatten slightly with the heel end of a large knife. The skin should split, but the clove should still remain intact. The clove can now be easily peeled for crushing, or used as necessary.

Garlic, Roasting

Roasting garlic can give a mellower flavour when used in cooking. Garlic with or without its skin can be roasted in the oven preheated to 190°C|375°F|gas mark 5 for about 15–20 minutes, or until softening and beginning to brown, then used as required. Whole bulbs of garlic can be cut in half across the middle and roasted.

Gelatine

Powdered gelatine should be sprinkled on to a minimum of 3 tablespoons cold water or other liquid in a small pan. When it has absorbed the water, it should be melted over a very low heat without stirring. On no account should it be allowed to boil. It can then be added to the liquid to be set, making sure all the gelatine is scraped out of the pan. The liquid to be set should not be too cold, or the gelatine will set in lumps before it has been mixed through properly.

Leaf gelatine should be soaked in cold water until completely soft. The leaves should then be removed and squeezed to remove any excess water. Make sure you read the packet instructions as leaves come in different sizes and therefore different brands set different amounts of liquid. For the recipes in this book, we assume that 1 leaf of gelatine = 1 teaspoon powdered gelatine.

Ginger, Peeling and Chopping

Root ginger is covered by a papery skin and due to the ginger's knobbly shape it can be difficult to remove this with a peeler. Scrape it off with the tip of the bowl of a teaspoon which can be scraped around all the nooks and crannies. Fresh young ginger can then be finely chopped or grated. Older fibrous ginger should be grated, as the fibres will be left behind. Excess chopped or grated ginger can be rolled in clingfilm in the shape of a pencil and frozen. Pieces can then be broken off and used as required, which is useful as one often has to buy a far larger piece of ginger than is actually needed.

Grilling

When grilling, it is important to preheat the grill to the highest setting or food will not brown. It may take up to 20 minutes to heat up the grill properly. If time allows, bring meat or fish that you intend to grill out of the fridge to allow it to come to room temperature for up to 30 minutes before cooking. Season at the last minute or the salt will draw out valuable juices and make the food dry. Grill the side that will be the presentation side first. If the food to be cooked is thinner than 2 cm, or does not need to be well cooked all the way through, have the grill pan as near to the element as possible so that the food is not overcooked by the time it browns. If the food to be grilled is thicker than this, or needs to be well cooked all the way through, move the grill pan a few more centimetres away from the element, or the outside of the food will be burnt before the middle is cooked.

Infusing

Heating up a liquid with a strong-flavoured ingredient and leaving it to cool results in it taking on that flavour and is called an infusion. A good use of this method would be the addition of bruised garlic cloves, robust herbs such as thyme or rosemary or chopped chillies to olive oil. This results in a delicious flavoured oil that can then be used for cooking or dressing salads. In the same way, milk can be scalded (heated almost to boiling point) with a cinnamon stick when making a cinnamon custard or pudding.

Lemon or Lime Wedges

Cut a small slice off the top and bottom of the fruit to reveal a little of the white pith beneath. Cut in half lengthways and cut each half into wedges. Cut the membrane from the middle of the wedge and remove any visible pips.

Letting Down (a sauce)

Sauces often continue to thicken after the heating has stopped or if prepared in advance. They should then be let down, or diluted, with water or another liquid that has been used in the dish, before serving.

Removing the stone (a)

Mango, Cutting into Chunks

Lay the mango on the chopping board. The stone is quite flat and will be in the middle of the fruit, so the top curve of the fruit and the bottom curve resting against the board can be sliced from the flat stone. (a)

Taking each half of the mango, and using a small, sharp knife, cut into the flesh as far as, but not into, the skin. First make some parallel cuts depending on the size of chunks required, then cut across the first lines to make squares or diamonds. (b)

Cutting through the flesh (b)

Push the flesh 'inside out', then remove the chunks by cutting as closely to the skin as possible. (c)

Marinating

To soak meat, fish or vegetables in liquid containing flavourings to give flavour. Acidic ingredients in marinades and oils also tenderize the food and keep it moist. Even marinating for as little as 10 minutes is worthwhile, but where time permits, marinating overnight will give a better flavour and result.

Dicing a mango (c)

Microwaves

Microwaves are extremely useful for reheating leftover food, defrosting frozen food and cooking vegetables and fish speedily and well.

When cooking with the microwave, put the ingredient to be cooked into a non-metal container or a specially designed microwave dish. Add a little liquid and cover with clingfilm, pierced once or twice. Cook on full power and then allow to stand for a few minutes as the food will continue to cook. Be careful when removing the clingfilm as the hot steam will escape. The cooking time required will depend on the particular microwave oven, the ingredient to be cooked, its temperature and the quantity. However, as a rough guide, 2 portions of tender green vegetables will need 2 minutes at high power and then 2 minutes' standing time. Firmer vegetables, such as carrot batons or cauliflower florets, will need 3 minutes at high power and then 3 minutes' standing time. Thin fillets of fish will need 4 minutes at high power and then 3 minutes' standing time and thicker fillets will take longer depending on their size. It is a good idea to move the dish halfway through the cooking time.

When reheating in the microwave, cook the food for a few minutes on full power, covered with clingfilm, then stir and repeat until piping hot all the way through. A little extra liquid may be required for soups and stews.

When defrosting, use the defrost setting but move the dish every so often and stir as soon as the mixture has defrosted sufficiently. It is important that the food defrosts evenly. Defrosting large pieces of meat in the microwave is never particularly successful as 'hotspots' occur where some areas actually cook while other areas are still frozen.

Microwaves are very useful for other cooking tasks. To soften butter, heat for just 10 seconds at a time or the centre will melt completely. To soften ice cream, again microwave for only 10 seconds at a time to achieve a perfect scooping consistency (do not refreeze once it has melted).

To sweat onions, put the onion with 1 tablespoon of oil or 2 tablespoons water in a microwave dish. Cover with clingfilm and cook on full power for 3 minutes, then allow to stand for a further 3 minutes.

Wilt washed baby leaf spinach in the bag for 2 minutes on full power, then season and serve, or toss quickly in seasoned melted butter.

Mussels, Preparation

Where possible, buying mussels that have already been well cleaned will save a considerable amount of time. When cleaning them yourself, scrub well, chipping off any barnacles and pulling away any 'beards' protruding from the shells. Discard any that are broken, that do not shut when tapped on the work surface, or that are exceptionally heavy. Cook as required and throw away any mussels that have not opened after cooking. Store raw mussels in the refrigerator in a bowl or tray covered with a damp tea towel.

Nuts and Seeds, Roasting or Toasting

Nuts and seeds have a more pronounced flavour and a golden colour when they have been cooked. They can either be briefly fried in a pan, stirring all the time, baked in the oven preheated to 190°C|375°F|gas mark 5 for an even colour, or grilled. Make sure they are turned frequently during the cooking process or they will brown unevenly. They have a tendency to burn very quickly once browned, so check on them every few minutes. They will take approximately 10–15 minutes to brown.

Onion, Chopping

Chop the onion in half through the root, but without chopping the root off completely as this will hold the onion together, making it more manageable. Peel and lay one half flat on the chopping board, then make even, vertical cuts through the onion, right down to the board. Again, leave the root intact. (a)

Cut through the width of the onion, once or twice depending on the size. Again, leave the root intact. (b)

Slice the onion across its width as finely as required. (c)

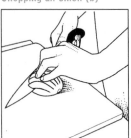

Papillote Cases, Securing the Edges

Fold over 1–2 cm of the greaseproof paper and make a crisp crease. Twist the folded edge of the 2 sheets together, working your way around the edge of the paper to make sure that the whole case is secure. Do not make the case too tight as the steam needs to circulate during cooking.

Parmesan Cheese, Shavings

Use a potato peeler on a chunk of Parmesan cheese to produce shavings for garnishing salads, pasta dishes or risottos. Vary the pressure on the cheese depending on its freshness and the thickness of shavings you require.

Pastry, Lining a Flan Ring and Blind Baking

Roll out the pastry to the thickness of a £1 coin and large enough to line the base and sides of the flan ring, with some to spare. Cut off any excess if the pastry is too large for the ring. Roll the pastry over the rolling pin, then lower it over the flan ring. (a)

Ease the pastry into the ring, not worrying about any that is hanging over the edges. Make sure the pastry goes right into the bottom corner of the ring and up the sides without being stretched. If there are any holes or cracks, just fill with some of the excess pastry. (b)

Roll the rolling pin over the top of the flan ring. Roll off all the excess pastry and then tidy the edges. (c) Chill until firm before using.

Blind baking means cooking the pastry case completely before adding a filling. To bake a pastry case blind, take a piece of greaseproof paper and make a circle large enough to cover the base of the pastry and extend up the sides, with some to extend above the top. Scrunch up the paper before lining, as this will make it easier to fit into the pastry case and right into the corners.

Put enough baking beans on top of the paper to cover the base, about 3–4 beans deep, then heap more beans up around the edges so there are enough to support the sides and prevent them from collapsing. Cook in the top third of the oven preheated to 200°C|400°F|gas mark 6 (lower if the pastry has sugar in it) for about

12–15 minutes, or until the sides are set. Then remove the beans with a spoon and carefully tweak out the paper.

Return the pastry case to the oven for 5–10 minutes, or until the base is completely cooked. It will look sandy in texture and there will be no grey patches left. If there are any holes or cracks, fill with some of the leftover raw pastry. You can buy porcelain 'beans' but dried beans or rice can be used, cooled, stored and used again and again.

Easing the pastry up the sides to avoid creases (b)

Peppers, Grilling and Skinning

Preheat the grill to the highest setting. Remove the green stalk and cut the pepper in half or into quarters lengthways. Scrape out the seeds and cut out any white membrane. Place on a baking sheet, skin side up, and paint the skin with oil. Grill until the skins have blackened. Place the peppers in a plastic bag to cool, which will help to make the skins easier to peel off. When cool, peel off the skins and use as required. The liquid in the bag is also delicious added to salad dressings and sauces.

Rolling off extra pastry (c)

Pineapple, Preparation

Cut off the top and bottom of the pineapple so that the flesh can be seen. Using a serrated knife, cut off the skin in strips from the top to the bottom, cleanly revealing the fruit below, and following the shape of the fruit so as not to waste any flesh.

Remove the sharp 'eyes' in the flesh by cutting a groove in the flesh on either side of the eyes. They form an even pattern, so can be removed in straight diagonal lines. Use the pineapple as required. Alternatively, use a pineapple corer or slicer (see page 43).

Poaching

Cooking food submerged in liquid which is set over a very low heat, where there are barely any bubbles and the liquid just trembles.

Pork Fillet, Removing the Membrane

Using a thin-bladed knife such as a fish filleting knife, slide the blade under the silver membrane surrounding the fillet. It is not necessary to remove every little piece, but try to ensure that there is not a continuous piece of membrane around the circumference as it contracts upon cooking.

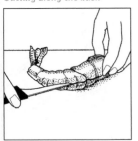

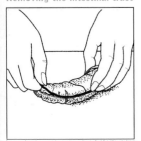

Prawns, Removing the Vein

When preparing a prawn, it may be necessary to remove the head and shell, and this should be done first. Then, using a small sharp knife, remove the vein by cutting just a few millimetres deep along the curved back of the prawn.

The intestinal tract, which may be black or transparent, runs along the length of the back. Pull it out with the tip of the knife before cooking the prawns as required.

Reducing

When a liquid is too thin or tastes too weak, it can be reduced by boiling rapidly, in order to intensify the flavour. It is best to use a wide pan with a large surface area, to accelerate the process.

Refreshing

Passing boiled green vegetables under cold running water or immersing them in iced water prevents them from cooking further in their own steam and sets their colour.

Rendering

When cooking chicken or duck portions with the skin on, or steaks with a little fat around the edges, for example, the fat must be melted away when it is fried so that it is left in the pan and no flabby fat remains attached to the meat.

When cooking chicken portions, heat the frying pan with very little oil. Salt the chicken and fry skin side down first, until the skin is beginning to brown. Then reduce the heat and cook until the fat from underneath the skin has melted away and the skin itself is golden brown. Press the chicken down on to the surface of the pan so that all the skin is browned.

When cooking steaks, again salt just before frying. Press any fat down on to the surface of the pan so that some of it melts, and the fat that is left is brown and crisp.

Scallops, Preparation

Some scallops can be bought fully prepared, but some still need some preparation. Remove the muscle found opposite the scallop roe and the membrane that runs all the way round the scallop. The orange scallop roe can be cooked with the white scallop flesh or discarded, according to preference.

Seasoned Flour

Plain flour can be seasoned with salt, pepper or dry spices and used to lightly coat ingredients, often fish, before cooking. This adds flavour and colour and protects delicate foods from intense heat. The food should be dipped in the seasoned flour, then shaken well to remove all the excess flour.

Seasoning

This usually refers to adding salt and pepper to a dish in order to balance its flavour. However, it may also involve adding sugar or an acid ingredient such as lemon juice. The ideal is to add enough to enhance and bring out the flavours of the dish without overpowering it. Adding a little sugar to fruit dishes and sauces brings out the natural flavour of the fruit and salt does the same for vegetables.

Sieving, Pushing Ingredients through a Sieve

In some recipes ingredients are required to be pushed through a sieve to give a smooth texture. It is useful to have a sieve that is not too fine or too much can be left behind in the mesh. Metal sieves are very hardwearing, but metal spoons should not be used when pushing ingredients through as metal on metal means that some will come off in the food, giving it a grey appearance and a metallic taste. It is easier to push a small amount through at a time rather than putting in everything to be sieved at once. A plastic ladle or the back of a wooden spoon is quite effective at pushing the food through the mesh.

Simmering

Cooking food submerged in liquid which is set over a low heat, with gentle bubbles just around the edge of the pan.

Slaking

An ingredient which would set firm or curdle if stirred straight into the main mixture must be slaked in. This means mixing the ingredient in a bowl with a little of the main mixture before adding it to the pan. For example, yoghurt can be slaked into a curry to prevent it from curdling. Cornflour must be mixed to a loose paste with cold water before being stirred into a mixture to thicken it, or it will set in lumps.

Steaming Vegetables

Bring some water to the boil in a pan in which a steamer, metal sieve or metal colander will fit comfortably. The water should be well below the level of the steamer. Put the vegetables into the steamer and cover with a lid. Steam until the vegetables feel tender when tested with a sharp knife. It is an easy way to cook vegetables and thought to be most healthy as vitamins are not leached into the boiling water.

Straining

Pouring a mixture of solids and liquids through a sieve into a bowl to separate the two.

Sugar, Making Caramel

Follow the directions below for a syrup. Continue to boil the syrup until it turns a caramel colour. Pour immediately onto a greased tray for caramel shards, or pour straight onto brûlées. If you want to make a caramel sauce, add liquid to the syrup (it will fizz so stand back) and allow to cool.

Sugar, Melting for a Syrup

When melting sugar to make a syrup, use a large-crystal sugar such as granulated. Make sure the pan is clean. The general rule for sugar syrups is to use 1 measure of sugar and 2 measures of water. Using boiling water can speed up the process.

Place the pan over a low heat and stir gently until the sugar has melted, taking care not to let the liquid slop up the sides of the pan. When the sugar has dissolved, stop stirring and use a pastry brush dipped in water to wash any syrup from the sides of the pan. Do not dip the brush into the syrup. Increase the heat under the pan and boil for 2 minutes. Use as required.

Sweating

This usually refers to cooking vegetables, particularly onions. The method involves cooking the chopped vegetable slowly in oil or butter until softened but not browned. It is also possible to sweat vegetables in water or stock instead of fat. A steamy atmosphere can be created by wetting a piece of greaseproof paper, scrunching it up, pressing it on to the sweating vegetables and covering the pan with a lid to prevent them from burning. Sweating can be done more quickly in the microwave (see page 16).

Tomatoes, Peeling, Deseeding and Chopping

Bring a saucepan of water to the boil and have a large bowl of very cold water to hand. Plunge the tomatoes into the boiling water, 2 at a time, and leave for about 10 seconds. An underripe tomato will take a few seconds longer, a very ripe tomato will take a few seconds less. Remove with a slotted spoon and put immediately into the cold water. Remove when cool and peel away the skin. Cut the tomatoes into quarters, scoop out the seeds with a teaspoon and chop the flesh as required. When tomatoes are out of season and lacking in colour, it is sometimes better not to peel them to keep maximum colour.

Vegetables, Burnt

If vegetables, for example onions, burn on to the bottom of the cooking pan, usually only the vegetable in direct contact with the base will have burnt and there will be plenty above that is perfectly usable. Resist the temptation to stir – just remove the pan quickly from the heat and tip the contents into another pan, leaving the burnt vegetable stuck to the original pan. Add a little more oil or butter to the second pan and continue with the recipe.

Entertaining

The essence of this book is hassle free food and this should lead effortlessly to easy entertaining. It is important to be able to enjoy the meal and the company rather than being slavishly devoted to the kitchen, so here are a few simple guidelines to make entertaining easier.

- Mise-en-place (prepare in advance). Leave yourself plenty of time for preparation the evening before. Even laying the table the night before can help. Choose dishes that can be prepared all or part of the way through in advance.
- Don't be too proud to stick a plan of action on the wall and follow it slavishly. Professional cooks often do it and it saves their sanity as well as a lot of time. Think about recipes that can be prepared ahead, such as a crumble topping that can be made and frozen in advance which, if you are busy with a main course like a Sunday roast, saves a lot of time on the day.
- A cold first course or pudding (or both) makes life easier.
- Do not cook too many types of vegetable. One or two cooked beautifully is much better than a huge variety overcooked or kept warm for too long. Blanch and refresh your vegetables in advance. They can be reheated in a microwave or plunged into boiling water just before serving up.
- Do not attempt new dishes/methods. Practise what you plan to serve first on partners or friends.
- Portion control is very important. Individual tarts, puddings, etc. look better for presentation and are easier to plate. This way, you can also be sure you have enough servings.
- Do any cooking that creates a smell, such as chargrilling or frying, beforehand. You do not want your kitchen (or yourself!) to smell of food when your guests arrive.
- Do not worry about the results of your cooking. Good ingredients and preparation speak for themselves.
- Think about presentation before you start serving up. Make sure you know how you would like the food to look in advance. For details on food presentation, see page 25.
- Plan your menu carefully – see page 24.
- If it all goes wrong: don't panic and remember your guests came to see you. Open another bottle of wine and put out some more crisps!

Menu Planning

The most obvious but important rule must be to keep the menu simple. There is no point in attempting so many dishes that the quality of execution is threatened.

You need to bear the following in mind when planning a menu:

- **Season of year: hot or cold:** Although hearty soups are delicious, you would probably want to keep a chowder to a winter menu and serve cucumber soup in a summer one.
- **Availability of ingredients, and seasonal constraints:** For example, baked peaches and strawberry cream will only work well in the summer when the fruits are in season.
- **Cost/budget:** Entertaining need not be prohibitively expensive. Choosing recipes wisely, with ingredients that you already have in your store cupboard and/or that are in season, makes it a cost-effective way of meeting up with friends.
- **Special diets:** The most obvious example of this is vegetarians, but increasingly people exclude ingredients from their diet for health or religious reasons.
- **Style of occasion:** The menu you plan for a special birthday will be quite different from the one that you serve for an informal light supper.
- **Size and equipment of kitchen.**
- **Size of dining table and serving dishes available.**
- **Holding ability:** If you are short of time or want to prepare ahead, choosing a cold starter or pudding is sensible.
- **Balancing a menu:** If a menu is not balanced properly, your guests may feel bloated and overfull. The commonest mistake is to serve too much rich food. The secret is not to abandon creamy or buttery dishes altogether but to limit their size and number. The main thing to aim for is plenty of fresh fruit and vegetables, some starch, but not too many fatty or meaty foods.

Avoid Repetition of:

Ingredients: For example, tomato salad followed by prawn and tomato pasta would not be a good idea. Check that the first or main course and the pudding are not predominantly fruit-based, for example melon to start, meat, poultry or fish with a fruity sauce as a main course, and fruit salad to finish.

Colours: Think about the colours of the different courses. For example, parsnip soup followed by smoked haddock rarebit with mashed potato, and bread and butter pudding to finish would not look very attractive or appetizing. Also think about the colour of the main course plate and what you are serving on it. Aim for a colour contrast.

Method of cooking: For example, a first course of griddled red pepper salad followed by a main course of chargrilled lamb would be best avoided.

Texture: If the main course is a tender casserole served with mashed potatoes to mop up the gravy, provide something crunchy such as a crisp French beans to go with it. A smooth pâté, followed by lasagne, with a custard pudding to finish, can leave guests longing for something they can quite literally get their teeth into.

Food Presentation

If food looks delicious, people are predisposed to find that it tastes delicious too. If you have spent time organizing, preparing and cooking a meal, it seems a shame just to throw the food on a plate. At Leiths School we have developed a set of rules which can be used as guidelines when presenting food. Fashion may dictate the presentation, be it stylish, nouvelle cuisine or chunky 'real' food, but the guidelines are the same. The following is a summary.

- **Keep it simple:** Overdecorated food often looks messed about. The more cluttered the plate, the less attractive it becomes.
- **The right plate:** A dish will look at its best on a plate that is big enough for it. Too big a plate and it can look rather mean and like an unsuccessful attempt at nouvelle cuisine, but too small a plate will look overcrowded and clumsy. Make sure the plate is sufficiently big so that the food does not need to sit on the rim. The rim should be left empty, like the frame of a painting. If the dish is very colourful, use a plain plate. For more simple food a more decorative plate can look stunning.
- **Centre height:** Whilst it is important not to overload a plate, it is a good idea to arrange food so that it is highest in the middle of the plate or slightly off centre. This draws the eye upwards and looks much more professional than food laid out flat on the plate. Overlapping slices will also improve the presentation, rather than leaving slices flat on the plate.
- **Uneven numbers:** As a rule, uneven numbers look better on a plate than even numbers: 3 fillets of lemon sole rather than 2 or 4, for example.
- **Keep it fresh:** Nothing looks more offputting than tired food. Use sprigs of herbs to garnish, making sure they are absolutely fresh. Pot herbs are now widely available in supermarkets. Use herbs for garnishing that appear in the recipe, if possible, to keep the garnish relevant and avoid clashing flavours. Dress salads at the last minute, and don't fry food too far in advance as it can look dull.
- **Colour:** Try not to have too many colours on a plate, other than when presenting a colourful mixed salad, for example. Conversely, try to serve a colourful vegetable to accompany a bland-looking main course. Where possible, keep particular colours in blocks and ensure adjacent blocks of colour complement each other.
- **Best side uppermost:** Usually the side of a steak or cutlet that is fried or grilled first looks the best, and should be placed uppermost.

Catering Quantities

Few people weigh or measure quantities as accurately as a control-conscious chef must do, but when catering for large numbers it is useful to know how much food to allow per person. As a general rule, the more guests you are catering for, the less food per head you need to provide, for example, 225 g stewing beef per head is essential for 4 people, but 170 g per head would feed 60 people. These quantities are fairly generous. Per head individual portions need to be more generous than those served on large platters.

Soup

Allow 250–300 ml soup per head, depending on the size of the bowl.

Poultry

Chicken: When cooking a whole bird, allow 350 g per person. An average chicken serves 4 people on the bone and 6 people off the bone. Allow 1 chicken breast per person.
Duck: A 2.7 kg bird will feed 3–4 people; a 1.8 kg bird will feed 2 people.
Turkey: Allow 450 g on the bone per person.

Meat

Lamb or Mutton
Casseroled (off the bone): 225 g per person.
On the bone: 340 g per person.
Grilled best end cutlets: 3–4 per person.
Grilled loin chops: 2 per person.

Beef
Stewed (off the bone): 225 g per person.
Roast (off the bone): 225 g per person.
Roast (on the bone): 340 g per person.
Roast whole fillet: 1.8 kg piece for 10 people.
Grilled steaks: 170–225 g per person.

Pork
Casseroled: 170 g per person
Roast leg or loin, off the bone: 200 g per person.
Roast leg or loin, on the bone: 340 g per person.
2 average fillets: Will feed 3–4 people.
Grilled: 1 × 170 g chop or cutlet per person.

Minced meat

110–170 g per person, depending on use.

Fish

Whole large fish (e.g. sea bass, salmon, whole haddock) weighed unclean, with head on: 340–450 g per person.
Cutlets and steaks: 170 g per person.
Fillets (e.g. sole, lemon sole, plaice): 3 fillets per person.
Fish off the bone (in fish pie, with sauce, etc.): 170 g per person.

Shellfish

Prawns: 60–90 g per person as a first course; 150 g per person as a main course.

Vegetables

Weighed before preparation and cooking, and assuming 3 vegetables, including potatoes, served with a main course: 110 g of each vegetable per person, except:
French beans: 60 g per person.
Peas: 60 g per person.
Spinach: 200 g per person. (250 g raw spinach gives approx 150 g cooked.)
Potatoes: 3 small (roast) per person; 170 g (mashed) per person; 1 large or 2 small (baked) per person; 110 g (new) per person.

Rice

Plain, boiled or fried: 60 g (weighed before cooking) per person.
In risotto or pilaf: 30 g per person (weighed before cooking) for first course; 60 g per person for main course.
40 g uncooked rice gives approx 100 g cooked rice.

Pasta

For a starter: 50–80 g per person.
For a main course: 80–120 g per person.

Couscous

50–70 g per person.

Salads

Allow 1–1½ servings of salad, in total, per head – for example, if only one salad is served, make sure there is enough for 1 generous helping each. If 100 guests are to choose from 5 different salads, allow a total of 150 portions, i.e. 30 portions of each salad.

Tomato salad: 450 g tomatoes (average 6 tomatoes), sliced, serves 4 people.
Coleslaw: 1 small cabbage, finely shredded, serves 10–12 people.
Grated carrot salad: 450 g carrots, grated, serves 6 people.
Potato salad: 450 g potatoes (weighed before cooking) serves 5 people.
Green salad: Allow a loose handful of leaves for each person.

Sandwiches

2 slices of bread makes 1 round of sandwiches. Allow 1½ rounds per head.
Butter: 30 g soft butter will cover 8 large bread slices.
Cucumber: 1 cucumber makes 15 rounds.
Egg: 1 hardboiled egg makes 1 round.
Ham: Allow 20 g for each round.
Tomato: 450 g makes 9 rounds.
Smoked salmon: Allow 20 g for each round.

Cocktail parties

Allow 10 cocktail canapés per head (or about 4–6 per hour).
Allow 14 cocktail canapés per head if served at lunchtime when guests are unlikely to go on to a meal.
Allow 4–5 cocktail canapés with pre-lunch or pre-dinner drinks.

Miscellaneous

French bread: 1 large loaf for 8 people; 1 small loaf for 4 people.
Cheese: After a meal, if serving one blue-veined, one hard and one soft cheese: 75–90 g per person for up to 8 people; 60 g per person for over 20 people.
Biscuits: 3 each for up to 10 people; 2 each for up to 30 people; 1 each for over 30 people.
Butter: 20 g per person if bread is served with the meal; 40 g per person if cheese is served as well.
Cream: 1 tablespoon per person for coffee; 3 tablespoons per person for pudding or dessert.
Milk: 600 ml for 18–20 cups of tea.
Strawberries: 110 g per person for pudding.

Preparing Ahead

Many of the recipes in this book can be prepared ahead, some completely and some in part. Cooking and entertaining are most stress free when much of the cooking has been done in advance, and dishes either just need to be mixed together and served, or put into the oven to heat through, leaving the cook able to relax.

In some of the recipes the cooking time may seem prohibitively long, but on closer reading, only 5 minutes may need to be spent stirring over the stove while for the rest of the time the dish sits cooking in the oven. Therefore we advise reading the recipe in full to get a complete picture of the time involved. The estimated preparation time includes any chopping or slicing that needs to be done before starting to cook. These times are obviously estimates as everyone cooks at different speeds, but all the recipes have been tested, so we hope they give a realistic idea. After cooking a few recipes from the book you will be in a position to know whether you work a little faster or slower than generally advised, and plan accordingly.

Where advice is given to prepare some of the stages in advance, the final quality of the dish will not be affected by it being tackled in two stages. Some dishes, like stews or marinated dishes, will positively improve by being prepared in advance when possible, and reheated when there is little time for cooking. These dishes will appeal to people who like to be organized, but there are also plenty of recipes for those who never seem to have the time even to plan, but who would like ideas for instant meals that can be put together in minutes.

Some of the recipes are very good ways of using up leftover ingredients such as roast chicken or mashed potato. Ensure that the leftovers have been chilled as soon as they have cooled and that they are used up quickly, ideally within 24 hours. Take particular care with cooked rice, as this can harbour bacteria.

Food Safety

Preparing food in advance can be done safely, but as many foods contain harmful organisms, care must be taken when cooking food to be eaten at a later stage. Vulnerable groups who are particularly at risk include pregnant women, babies, the elderly and those with medical conditions which result in impaired resistance to infection. These special groups are advised to avoid pâtés and soft ripened cheeses such as Brie, Camembert and blue-vein cheeses, and to reheat cooked chilled meals until piping hot rather than eat them cold. They should also avoid lightly cooked eggs. The advice given below will ensure all that you cook can be eaten with confidence:

- **Initial cooking:** Make sure all food is cooked to a high temperature initially, which will kill any bacteria. It is wise to take particular care with raw chicken, stewing meat and minced beef and lamb.

- **Raw foods:** Some meat and fish is eaten raw, or nearly raw, such as steak tartare or salmon gravad lax. In this case make sure it is absolutely fresh and of the highest quality.
- **Reheating food:** When reheating food, make sure it is piping hot all the way through and not just tepid. Stir regularly where possible to ensure that all the food is heated sufficiently throughout.
- **Stock rotation:** Keep older food separate from fresh food. Do not add the leftovers of today's dinner to yesterday's leftovers, or the remains of one carton of milk to a new full one.
- **Keeping food warm:** When keeping food warm, make sure it was piping hot initially and has not cooled in the meantime. It should not be cooked in advance, cooled to store and then reheated until just warm.
- **Cooling food down:** When cooking ahead, cool food down as quickly as possible and then put into the refrigerator or freezer as soon as it is cool. Where possible, spread it out over a tray as the large surface area will allow it to cool more quickly. Stand pans of food in a sink of cold water, giving the occasional stir to speed things up, but do not cover cooling food with a lid.
- **Storage in the refrigerator:** Different food groups should be kept apart. Raw meat or fish should be kept on the bottom shelf of the refrigerator so that there is no chance of it dripping on to cooked food. Eggs keep better if stored with the pointed end downwards. Supermarket eggs have the 'use by' date stamped on them, but an effort should be made always to eat the oldest eggs first. Eggs have porous shells, so don't store with a cut onion, for example, or it could affect the taste of your cakes!
- **Milk and cream** should be kept covered or their flavour will be tainted. Similarly, butter and cheese must be well wrapped. Vegetables and fruit keep better if unwrapped, or any plastic wrapping pierced and stored in the vegetable tray or above any raw meat or fish.
- **Freezing:** Food should be cooked to a high temperature, cooled and then frozen as soon as possible. Frozen food that has been defrosted must be heated to a very high temperature before refreezing. Food should be left to defrost on a plate in the refrigerator overnight, depending on its size. The microwave can be used to defrost, but the food should then be cooked immediately, as microwaving will warm it up. Frozen food must be defrosted completely before recooking and then checked carefully to ensure it is very hot all the way through.
- **Wrapping:** Cooked food should be only loosely covered when cooling, but once it is cold it should be very well wrapped for chilling or freezing.
- **Cross-contamination:** To avoid cross-contamination, make sure utensils, chopping boards and kitchen cloths are washed well between tasks, particularly when dealing with raw and then cooked food.

Storecupboard Ingredients and Convenience Foods

Many of the ingredients used in the recipes are very useful to have in your store cupboard. In this section we also give advice on how to choose some of the convenience products that will cut your cooking time down to a minimum. (See the section on Leiths Basic Recipes if you would prefer to make these yourself.) Obviously this is a huge list, but buying a selection from each category will enable you to create lots of flavoursome combinations. See 'How to Use This Book' for ideas on substituting one ingredient for another.

Many supermarkets now have their own ranges of excellent products for cooks. Waitrose in particular has an excellent range of 'Cook's Ingredients', Sainsburys have 'Special Selection' and 'Taste the Difference' ranges and Tesco have 'Ingredients' and 'Finest' ranges, which are worth investigating.

Mustards

- Dijon mustard
- English mustard
- Wholegrain mustard

Vinegars

- Aged balsamic vinegar: This can be expensive; you can instead reduce ordinary balsamic vinegar to a syrupy consistency
- Chilli vinegar
- Chinese rice wine vinegar
- Red wine vinegar
- Sherry vinegar
- White wine vinegar

Flours

- Cornflour: For thickening and coating
- Plain flour
- Self-raising flour: For baking

Oils

- Chilli oil
- Hazelnut oil
- Olive oil
- Extra virgin olive oil
- Sesame oil
- Sunflower oil
- Walnut oil

Pasta, noodles, rice, grains and lentils

- Shaped pastas such as penne (quills), conchiglie (shells), farfalle (bows)
- Spaghetti
- Tagliatelle
- Medium egg noodles
- Rice noodles
- Straight-to-wok noodles: Good for saving time
- Arborio rice
- Basmati rice
- Jasmine rice
- Long-grain rice
- Sushi rice
- Wild rice
- Bulghur wheat
- Couscous
- Gnocchi
- Polenta
- Puy lentils
- Red lentils

Dried Herbs and Spices

- Allspice, ground
- Bay leaves
- Cardamom, whole and ground
- Cayenne pepper
- Chilli powder
- Cinnamon, whole and ground
- Cloves
- Coriander
- Cumin
- English mustard powder
- Herbes de Provence

- Mixed spice
- Nutmeg, whole and ground
- Oregano
- Paprika
- Rosemary
- Tarragon
- Thyme
- Turmeric
- Vanilla pods
- Fresh herbs: Supermarket pots for the window sill, bay trees for the garden
- Black pepper: Buy whole black peppercorns and use in a grinder for the best flavour
- Sea salt: Cooking salt and sea salt crystals, such as Maldon

Bottles and Jars

- Preserved chillies: Avoid getting chilli juices on your hands, and save chopping time
- Easy garlic: Avoid having to crush a clove of garlic or buy a whole bulb when only one clove is needed
- Easy ginger: Avoid having to buy a large piece of ginger when only a couple of centimetres are needed
- Preserved kaffir lime leaves
- Preserved lemons: Use in or serve with Moroccan recipes
- Preserved lemon grass
- Lemon juice, long-life
- Olives
- Peanut butter: Great for quick satay sauces with chilli sauce and lime
- Red peppers, skinned and in oil: Use in place of grilled, skinned peppers in a variety of recipes for speed, and use the oil in salad dressings
- Caramelized onions, onion marmalade, or onion chutney: Bay Tree is a good brand
- Chestnut purée, sweetened: Makes a quick pudding stirred into fromage frais
- Dulche de Leche: A delicious thick sticky caramel sauce, used in banoffee pie. We would recommend Merchant Gourmet
- Jam, strawberry, raspberry and apricot: Bonne Maman or Tiptree are good
- Lemon curd: Makes a quick pudding stirred into Greek yoghurt. Duchy of Cornwall is good. Try to avoid fluorescent yellow jelly types.
- Marmite: Useful for adding a savoury flavour to stews and sauces, but use in small quantities
- Mincemeat: A quick tart filling, mixed with some slices of cooking apple. Makes a delicious sauce when heated up with water and a little brandy to serve with ice cream, or use to stuff baked apples
- Preserved ginger in syrup: The ginger is delicious used in recipes or chopped and sprinkled over ice cream with some of its syrup
- Vanilla extract

Cans

- Anchovies
- Baked beans
- Chickpeas
- Coconut milk
- Crabmeat
- Flageolet beans
- Green peppercorns
- Kidney beans
- Plum tomatoes, chopped
- Sweetcorn
- Tuna fish
- Water chestnuts

Nuts and Seeds

- Almonds, ground and blanched
- Cashew nuts
- Hazelnuts
- Mustard seeds
- Nigella seeds
- Peanuts
- Pecan nuts
- Pinenuts
- Poppy seeds
- Pumpkin seeds
- Sesame seeds
- Sunflower seeds
- Walnuts

Sugars and Sweeteners

- Caster sugar
- Demerara sugar
- Golden syrup
- Granulated sugar
- Honey
- Maple syrup
- Soft dark brown sugar
- Soft light brown sugar

Other Storecupboard Ingredients

- Dark chocolate: A good-quality chocolate is best for cooking
- Coconut cream/milk
- Coffee, good-quality, ground
- Dried fruit, such as sultanas, raisins, dates, cherries, blueberries, apricots and cranberries
- Miso pastes and soup: Flavour varies a great deal between varieties, so keep trying until you find one you like. Yutaka is a very good brand that works well in most dishes
- Dried mushrooms: Ceps or porcini have an excellent strong flavour, so although they are expensive, just a few grams can make a huge difference to the flavour of a dish. Less expensive mixed mushrooms and wild mushrooms are often available
- Lemons and limes
- Stock: Liquid stock such as Knorr's liquid variety, 'A Touch of Taste', works well. Add a little dry white wine at the same time as adding the stock for a more homemade taste. Marigold vegetable bouillon is also good, and Marks and Spencer make a jar of concentrated chicken stock, much the same consistency as Marmite, which is good (although we prefer to dilute it rather more than it says in the instructions). Fresh stock can be found in the chilling cabinet with the meat in supermarkets, which is great for making soup and gravy, but is very expensive for a very dilute, cloudy stock. For a really good-flavoured sauce, buy two or more cartons and reduce by rapid boiling until strong enough in flavour. Cans of beef consommé can be used in place of stock, as can Japanese miso soup sachets
- Sundried tomatoes: Very useful for adding intense flavour to soups, stews and sauces. Where they are preserved in oil, the oil can be used to make delicious dressings
- Sunblush tomatoes: Still slightly moist and very good for adding to salads
- Tomato purée
- Dry vermouth, such as Noilly Prat: Can be used in place of wine and does not go off as soon as it is opened
- Wasabi paste

Savoury Sauces

- Black bean sauce
- Black olive tapenade
- Bread sauce sachet
- Cranberry sauce
- Fish sauce, Thai (nam pla)
- Hoisin sauce
- Horseradish sauce
- Indian curry paste: Patak's is a good brand
- Mint jelly
- Mushroom ketchup
- Oyster sauce
- Pesto sauce

- Plum sauce
- Redcurrant jelly
- Sweet chilli dipping sauce: This is different from other chilli sauces
- Soy sauce
- Tandoori paste
- Teriyaki sauce
- Thai curry pastes, red and green: Thai Taste is a good brand
- Tomato ketchup
- Tomato passata: Sieved tomatoes, which can also be used instead of a tomato sauce
- Tomato sauce: Choose an organic plain tomato pasta sauce such as Seeds of Change. Try to avoid those with extra flavourings such as basil or garlic and add your own as it is often these that give the sauce its 'bought' flavour
- White sauce: Available in dried packet form or ready-made in a jar
- Worcestershire sauce
- Yellow bean sauce

Sweet Sauces

- Chocolate sauce
- Custard: Bird's Custard Powder is the mix that everyone remembers from childhood. Banana custard wouldn't be the same without it! Alternatively, buy good-quality supermarket fresh custard made with real vanilla pods
- Fruit sauces: Very good-quality raspberry, apricot, passion fruit and mango sauces, otherwise known as coulis, can be bought
- Ginger syrup: This is the same as the syrup from a bottle of preserved ginger but can be bought separately

Pastry

Many types of pastry can be bought and frozen for future use:
- Danish pastry and croissant dough
- Filo pastry
- Pre-baked pastry cases: Where possible, make or buy pastry, roll out and blind-bake (see page 18) as the result is better than using pre-baked cases
- Puff pastry, block or rolled
- Shortcrust pastry, block or rolled
- Sweet pastry, block or rolled

Refrigerated Food

- Cheddar cheese
- Cream: Double cream is the most versatile as it can be whipped and boiled without splitting
- Crème fraîche: Use full-fat for cooking, half-fat for serving with puddings

- Eggs
- Mozzarella cheese: Try to use balls of buffalo mozzarella as they are far superior to the blocks
- Parmesan cheese or Grana Padano: These can be bought either in blocks or freshly grated. Beware of some tubs of rather dry, grated Parmesan as the flavour can be completely altered
- Yoghurt

Frozen Food

- Baby broad beans: Broad beans take a while to pod, which means they do not feature very often in this book. However, defrosted frozen beans can be quickly podded and keep most of their colour and flavour, and are great for adding to salads
- Ice cream: A good-quality vanilla will be made with real vanilla pods, cream, milk, eggs and sugar and not much more. Cheaper varieties will be made with synthetic ingredients, contain mainly air, and may not have a particularly good flavour
- Peas: Petits pois are smaller than normal-sized peas and sweeter. Bird's Eye peas have the best flavour, we have found
- Spinach: Either chopped, which is useful for pasta sauces and soups, or leaf, which can be added to curries and stews
- Summer fruits: Bags of mixed summer fruits or individual varieties can be defrosted as required and make quick puddings, stirred into yoghurt with honey, or into whipped cream with a fruit liqueur. Also good served still semi-frozen, with hot chocolate sauce

Bread and Bread Mixes

- Part-baked baguettes
- Part-baked ciabatta
- Pizza bases or pizza base mix: Top with a combination of fresh cheese, sliced meats, sliced tomato or bought pasta sauce, sundried tomato, olives and rocket, drizzle with olive oil, or pesto and oil mixed, and bake
- Scone mix: Add dried fruits, citrus fruit zest, grated cheeses or seeds to liven up a packet mix

Seasonal Table

This table is only intended as a guide to the seasons of fruit and vegetables as they vary year on year according to the weather, and the use of greenhouses and polytunnels for growing fruit and vegetables makes the seasons longer. Most salad vegetables are available throughout the summer, and different varieties of lettuce are available year-round.

Although in fact most fruit and vegetables are available year-round these days (as much of it is grown overseas and imported), it is still best to use local produce in season where possible as it has fewer food miles to travel, so is fresher and generally has a better flavour. It is also a good way of supporting local producers. We have, nevertheless, included some fruit and vegetables that are *always* imported, such as bananas, as it gives a better picture of what is available each month.

January		February	
Fruits	**Vegetables**	**Fruits**	**Vegetables**
apples	broccoli	apples	beetroots
bananas	Brussels sprouts	bananas	broccoli
clementines	cabbages	dates	Brussels sprouts
cranberries	carrots	early rhubarb	cabbages
dates	celeriac	grapefruits	carrots
grapefruits	celery	grapes	celeriac
grapes	fennel	lemons	celery
kiwi fruits	Jerusalem artichokes	oranges	Jerusalem artichockes
lemons	leeks	tangerines	leeks
mangoes	mushrooms		mushrooms
oranges	parsnips		parsnips
pears	potatoes		potatoes
pomegranates	salsify		swedes
Seville oranges	swedes		turnips
tangerines	sweet potatoes		
	turnips		

March	
Fruits	**Vegetables**
apples	asparagus
bananas	Brussels sprouts
grapefruits	cabbages
grapes	carrots
lemons	cauliflowers
mangoes	celeriac
melons	chicory
pears	Jerusalem artichokes
pineapples	leeks
rhubarb	mushrooms
tangerines	parsnips
	spring greens
	sprouting broccoli
	swedes
	turnips

April	
Fruits	**Vegetables**
apples	aubergines
bananas	beetroot
elderflowers	broccoli
grapefruits	cabbages
grapes	carrots
lemons	cauliflowers
limes	celery
mangoes	cucumbers
melons	leeks
oranges	mushrooms
pears	onions
pineapples	parsnips
rhubarb	peppers
	potatoes – early
	radishes
	sweet potatoes
	turnips

May	
Fruits	**Vegetables**
apples	asparagus
apricots	aubergines
avocados	beans
bananas	broccoli
elderflowers	cauliflowers
gooseberries	courgettes
grapes	fennel
kiwi fruit	leeks
lemons	lettuces
limes	mushrooms
mangoes	peppers
melons	potatoes – early
oranges	spinach
pears	sweet potatoes
strawberries	radishes

June	
Fruits	**Vegetables**
apricots	asparagus
avocados	aubergines
bananas	beans
cherries	beetroots
grapes	broccoli
kiwi fruit	cauliflowers
lemons	courgettes
oranges	cucumbers
peaches	fennel
plums	lettuces/rocket
strawberries	mangetout
	mushrooms
	peas
	peppers
	potatoes – early
	radishes
	spinach
	spring onions
	sweet potatoes
	sweetcorn
	tomatoes

July	
Fruits	**Vegetables**
apricots	artichokes
avocados	aubergines
bananas	beans
blackcurrants	beetroot
blueberries	broccoli
cherries	carrots
gooseberries	cauliflowers
grapes	courgettes
figs	cucumbers
melons	lettuce
nectarines	mushrooms
peaches	okra
raspberries	peppers
redcurrants	potatoes – 2nd early
strawberries	radishes
	spinach
	spring onions
	tomatoes

August	
Fruits	**Vegetables**
apples	artichokes
avocados	aubergines
bananas	beans
blackberries	potatoes – 2nd early
blueberries	broccoli
damsons	carrots
grapefruits	celery
grapes	Chinese leaves
greengages	courgettes
kiwi fruits	fennel
lemons	spring onions
melons	lettuces
nectarines	mangetout
peaches	marrows
pears	tomatoes
plums	sweetcorn
raspberries	mushrooms
redcurrants	onions
strawberries	peppers
	radishes

September	
Fruits	**Vegetables**
avocados	artichokes
bananas	aubergines
dates	beans
figs	beetroot
grapefruits	broccoli
grapes	cabbages
kiwi fruits	carrots
melons	cauliflowers
nectarines	celery
passion fruits	courgettes
peaches	fennel
pears	lettuces
plums	mangetout
quinces	marrows
raspberries	mushrooms
strawberries	onions
hazelnuts	parsnips
walnuts	potatoes – 2nd early
	pumpkins
	squash
	sweetcorn
	tomatoes
	turnips

October	
Fruit	**Vegetables**
apples	aubergines
bananas	beans
coconuts	broccoli
dates	Brussels sprouts
grapefruits	cabbages
grapes	carrots
lemons	cauliflower
pears	celery
pineapples	leeks
plums	lettuces
pomegranates	marrows
satsumas	onions
hazelnuts	parsnips
pecan nuts	peppers
walnuts	potatoes – maincrop
	pumpkin
	spinach
	squash
	sweetcorn
	tomatoes

November	
Fruit	**Vegetables**
apples	broccoli
bananas	Brussels sprouts
coconuts	cabbages
cranberries	carrots
grapes	celery
pecan nuts	Jerusalem artichokes
kiwi fruits	leeks
lemons	lettuces
mangoes	mangetout
melons	mushrooms
nuts	okra
oranges	onions
pears	parsnips
pineapples	potatoes – maincrop
pomegranates	swedes
satsumas	turnips
tangerine	
Brazil nuts	
chestnuts	

December	
Fruit	**Vegetables**
apples	broccoli
avocados	Brussels sprouts
bananas	cabbages
clementines	carrots
coconuts	celery
pears	cucumbers
cranberries	Jerusalem artichokes
dates	leeks
grapefruit	lettuces
grapes	mushrooms
kiwi fruit	onions
lemons	parsnips
mangoes	potatoes – maincrop
melons	spring onions
nuts	
oranges	
pineapples	
satsumas	
Brazil nuts	
chestnuts	

Essential Equipment

Most cooking can be done with a fairly small amount of basic cooking equipment. It is worth making sure you have a good set of sharp knives, as by having the right tools for each job you will find preparation quick and easy. We have included some recommendations for other equipment that we find useful.

Basic Equipment

- 1 large chopping knife with a 10–25 cm blade, whatever feels comfortable
- 1 small paring knife
- 1 serrated fruit knife
- 1 serrated bread knife
- 1 palette knife
- 1 spatula
- wooden spoons
- 1 fish slice
- 1 slotted spoon
- 1 metal basting spoon
- tongs
- 1 vegetable peeler
- 1 garlic press: Try to buy one that means the garlic does not need to be peeled
- 1 ladle
- 1 potato masher
- 1 lemon squeezer
- 1 sieve
- 1 colander
- 1 measuring jug with ½ litre capacity
- 1 grater
- 1 set of scales: Electronic ones are the easiest to read
- Sauce whisk: Very useful for combining small amounts of ingredients in dressings as well as for whisking any lumps out of sauces
- 1 rolling pin
- 1 pastry brush
- 1 set of measuring spoons: It is important to use these and not cutlery spoons when measuring
- 1 balloon whisk
- kitchen scissors
- 2 chopping boards, one for raw food, one for cooked

- 2 baking sheets
- 1 roasting pan
- a selection of ovenproof dishes in different sizes
- a selection of mixing bowls in different sizes
- 1 wire rack
- 1 × 24 cm flan ring
- 1 large saucepan
- 2 medium saucepans
- 1 small saucepan
- Salad spinner
- Oven gloves

Other Useful Equipment

- Apple corer: Saves time when baking apples, or preparing them for pies or crumbles
- Cake tins and loaf tins for baking: It is important to have the right-sized tin for a particular recipe. Muffin tins are useful for muffins, fairy cakes and Yorkshire puddings
- Flexible fish filleting knife: Obviously useful for filleting fish, but because of its very thin blade it is also very good for removing fine membranes from meat
- Griddle pan: Used with very little oil, or none at all if non-stick, this can be a healthy way of cooking, an alternative to grilling and a way of creating attractive decorative lines on food
- Microplane grater: This produces far finer zest than a grater and is much easier to clean
- Mouli: This is quite an old-fashioned piece of equipment, but is great for puréeing soups and vegetables by turning the handle attached to a large sieve
- Pineapple corer: Removes the core and also the flesh from the skin of the pineapple in a manageable spiral of slices
- Poultry shears: These are so strong they will cut though meat bones and prove very useful about the kitchen
- Pressure cooker: These have developed over the years and have now lost their rather dangerous and explosive image. They can cut down cooking times of soups, stews, dried pulses and even marmalade dramatically. The base can also come in useful as another big pan for kitchen use
- Ramekins: Very useful when serving individual portions or for dips
- Ricer: Looks like a giant garlic crusher and is fantastic for mashing potatoes without lumps and without overworking, which can lead to gluey potatoes
- Steamers: Useful but not essential for steaming vegetables (see the Terms, Techniques and Tips section (page 9)
- Tweezers or pliers: Useful for pinboning fish
- Vegetable scourer: Using a scourer means that thin-skinned vegetables, such as baby carrots, will not need to be peeled
- Wok: Useful firstly for the stir-frying for which it was designed, but also because it doubles as another very large pan for kitchen use

Electrical Equipment

Many electric mixers do the same jobs. You need to work out what you are likely to cook most often when making a choice.

- Blender or liquidizer: Processes mixtures until extremely smooth, very useful for soups and sauces as well as smoothies and milkshakes
- Breadmaker: Can be timed to produce bread when you wake up in the morning, but the shape of the loaves is limited
- Deep fat fryer: Often safer than using a saucepan of oil, and it is easier to control the temperature. However, it takes up a lot of space on the work surface if you are not going to deep-fry very often
- Food mixer: The two most popular brands are the Kenwood Chef and the American Kitchen Aid. You can expect both to have a long life and to make good pastry, cakes and meringues. Some of the attachments such as a blender, dough hook for bread or pasta roller may be useful, depending on what you intend to cook. They can combine several 'gadgets' in one
- Food processor: Very good for chopping, grating, blending, liquidizing and pastry making. Not so good however, for whisking and cake making
- Hand blender: Reasonably priced, easy to store, and great for whizzing soups and sauces while still in the pan, avoiding extra washing up
- Hand mixer/Electric whisk: Reasonably priced and invaluable for whisking cream and egg whites and making cakes
- Ice cream machine: Incredibly useful as you can just throw in a mixture of sweetened fruit purée and cream and end up with delicious homemade ice cream, or add fruit purée by itself and end up with sorbet. However, choose carefully as some brands do take up a lot of space in the freezer, or have quite small capacities
- Microwave oven: Very useful for many cooking tasks (see Terms, Techniques and Tips, page 16) but the conventional cook often finds it is rarely used and so just takes up work surface. Excellent for reheating dishes prepared in advance. Some also have grills and convection oven modes. It may take some time to adapt traditional cooking skills, but many people who have mastered the art of microwaving feel it saves a huge amount of time
- Rice cooker: Cooks perfect rice every time. Used extensively in areas of the world where rice is a staple foodstuff, but can take up valuable space if you don't eat rice often

Lakeland Limited supplies much of the equipment on this list (www.lakelandlimited.co.uk). For professional cooking equipment and knives, we recommend Nisbets (www.nisbets.com).

Choosing Wine to Match Food

Most wines taste different when tasted on their own or drunk with food. Different elements in the wine and the food react with one another. Strong-tasting food will kill a light wine, just as a rich, full-bodied wine will overwhelm light food. A wine with good acidity and dryness can be a perfect match for oily food.

When selecting wine to match a specific dish, it is important to remember that it is not just a question of choosing the wine to complement the particular type of meat or fish; the sauce in which they are cooked can have greater effect on the wine. Cream- or butter-based sauces demand wines with acidity rather than alcohol to help cut the richness.

If you are serving different wines during a meal, it is important to serve them in the right order; dry before sweet, light before full-bodied, young before old.

Food	Style of Wine	Suggestion
Fish Dishes		
Terrine	Light dry white	Chablis
Soups	Crisp dry white	Sancerre/Pouilly-Fumé
Mayonnaise		New Zealand Sauvignon
Buttery sauce		Burgundy
Smoked	Spicy white	
Chinese-style		Alsace
Barbecued		Tokay/Riesling
Chicken Dishes		
Mayonnaise	Clean, dry white	Soave
Buttery sauce		
Chinese-style	Full white	Mâcon, Australian Chardonnay
Roast	Light, fruity red	Beaujolais
Casseroled		
Barbecued/Indian/ Tandoori	Fuller red	Côtes du Rhône

Food		Style of Wine	Suggestion
Veal			
Buttery sauce	}	Light, fruity red	Valpolicella
Roast			
Casserole		Fuller red	Chianti Classico
Pork			
Buttery sauce	}	Light red	Beaujolais Villages
Spicy/			
Chinese style			
Stewed/Cassoulet		Full red	Corbières
Roast	}	Medium red	Burgundy
Barbecued			
Lamb			
With a rich sauce		Light to medium red	Chinon/Bourgueil
Stewed	}	Fuller red	Claret/Rioja
Roast			
Spiced/curried/		Spicy red	Crozes-Hermitage
barbecued			
Beef			
With hollandaise		Medium red	Burgundy
Casserole	}	Fuller red	Rhône/Châteauneuf du Pape
Roast			
Spiced/barbecued		Full, spicy red	Australian Shiraz Australian/Californian Cabernet
Venison		Rich red	Australian Shiraz
Duck		Medium red	Burgundy
Game birds		Full red	Claret

Food	Style of Wine	Suggestion
Cold Collations/ Salamis	Rosé or light red	Tavel Rosé Valpolicella
Pâtés/terrines	Spicy red	Côtes du Rhône
Foie gras	Sweet white	Sauternes Alsace Gewurztraminer/Tokay
Soups Light	Fortified	Dry sherry/Madeira
Creamy	Dry white	Burgundy
Vegetable dishes	Light dry wine	Soave
Cheese Soufflé Soft, creamy Blue	Light, sweet wine	Alsace Tokay Loire (Coteaux du Layon)
Hard	Medium red	Burgundy
Puddings Plain fruit	Slightly sweet white	German Spätlese/Auslese
Light fruit puddings Ice creams/sorbets	Sweet white	Coteaux du Layon Italian Moscato
Rich creamy puddings Hot soufflés	Rich, sweet, white Sweet	Sauternes Champagne
Chocolate puddings	Fortified	Muscat de Beaumes de Venise Australian Liqueur Muscat

Wine Style	Style of Food
Very dry white (Muscadet, Sauvignon grape wines, Chablis)	Shellfish, salmon, oily fish
Dry white (Soave, Frascati, Chardonnay wines, Burgundy)	White fish
Spicy dry white (Alsace, some dry German and English wines)	Smoked fish
Medium dry white (Moselle, Vouvray, Vinho Verde)	Chicken
Medium sweet white (German Spätlese/Auslese, Italian Moscato)	Soft, creamy cheese Fruit and fruit puddings
Sweet white (Sauternes, Barsac, Muscat de Beaumes de Venise)	Foie gras Rich puddings Chocolate puddings
Rosé (Tavel, Provence)	Bouillabaisse Cold meats
Light red (Beaujolais, Valpolicella)	Chicken, veal Pork
Soft red (Burgundy)	Pork, duck
Medium red (Claret, Côtes du Rhône, Chianti, Rioja)	Lamb Game birds
Full red (Châteauneuf du Pape, Cabernet-Sauvignon wines)	Beef
Very full red (Crozes-Hermitage, Barolo, Australian Shiraz)	Rich stews Venison

Part Two
RECIPES

First Courses and Light Meals

These recipes were originally designed as first courses for relaxed entertaining. However, we found when testing them that they were just the kind of dishes that make perfect midweek suppers, often just served with a green salad and some crusty bread.

Asparagus with Parmesan and Soft-boiled Eggs

Preparation time: 5 minutes
Cooking time: 10 minutes

SERVES 2

340 g asparagus
2 eggs
Parmesan cheese shavings
Maldon sea salt flakes and freshly ground black
   pepper

To serve

crusty white bread

1 Break off the woody ends from the asparagus and discard. (If you bend the stems they tend to snap into two, leaving you with one piece to discard – the root end – and one to keep.)
2 Place the eggs in a saucepan of water and bring to the boil. Simmer for 3 minutes.
3 Using a slotted spoon, remove the eggs from the pan and place in a bowl of cold water.
4 Bring the pan of water back to the boil, add the asparagus and simmer for 2–4 minutes, or until tender.
5 Meanwhile, using the handle of a teaspoon, very carefully peel the eggs. Drain the asparagus and divide between 2 individual plates, keeping the spears pointing in the same direction. Season with salt and pepper and scatter over the Parmesan shavings.
6 Place an egg on top of each serving of asparagus, and gently cut open. Serve immediately with crusty white bread.

NOTE: This can be made with poached eggs (see page 13) instead of soft-boiled eggs.

Asparagus with Parma Ham and Herby Hollandaise

Preparation time: 15 minutes
Cooking time: 10 minutes

SERVES 6

900 g asparagus

6 slices of Parma ham

olive oil, for brushing

1 × 200 g jar of good-quality hollandaise

1 tablespoon chopped fresh dill

1 Preheat the oven to 200°C|400°F|gas mark 6.
2 Break off the woody ends from the asparagus and discard. Wash well. Simmer for 2 minutes, or until just tender, in boiling salted water. Drain well and refresh under cold running water.
3 Trim the asparagus into equal lengths.
4 Divide the asparagus into 6 bundles and wrap each bundle in a piece of Parma ham. Place in a roasting tin, drizzle with a little oil and bake in the oven for 8 minutes.
5 Meanwhile, heat the hollandaise according to the manufacturer's instructions and add the dill. Serve with the hot asparagus bundles.

Baked Mushrooms

Preparation time: 10 minutes
Cooking time: 20 minutes

SERVES 4

4 large field mushrooms, stalks removed

olive oil

1 × 150 g packet of garlic and herb soft cheese

a small bunch of chives, finely chopped

grated zest of 1 lemon

60 g fresh white breadcrumbs

salt and freshly ground black pepper

To garnish

8 slices of pancetta

Serving suggestion: Green salad (see page 381)

1 Preheat the oven to 200°C|400°F|gas mark 6.
2 Place the mushrooms, skin side down, in a roasting tin. Drizzle with oil and season.
3 Mix together the garlic and herb soft cheese, the chives, lemon zest and breadcrumbs and season lightly. Divide the mixture between the 4 mushrooms.
4 Bake in the oven for 20 minutes, or until tender.
5 Meanwhile, preheat the grill to the highest setting and grill the pancetta until crisp.
6 Divide the mushrooms between 4 individual plates, garnish with the pancetta and serve.

Asparagus with Parmesan and Poached Eggs

Baked Figs with Gorgonzola and Parma Ham

Potato Cakes with Smoked Salmon

Smoked Trout Cakes with Mustard Sauce

Thai Mussels

Crab and Prawn Cocktail

Smoked Salmon and Pea Tart

Tom Yum Soup

Courgette Soup with
Crisp Prosciutto and Parmesan

Smoked Haddock and Spinach Soup

Bloody Mary Soup

Courgettes with Leeks and Ham

Preparation time: 15 minutes
Cooking time: 25 minutes

SERVES 4

4 large courgettes

15 g butter

2 leeks, finely sliced

4 slices of cooked ham, chopped

400 ml cheese sauce (see page 503)

3 teaspoons English mustard

2 tablespoons grated Cheddar cheese

2 tablespoons dried breadcrumbs

salt and freshly ground black pepper

To prepare ahead: Make in advance to the end of stage 4, then refrigerate.
Serving suggestion: Green salad (see page 381)

1 Preheat the oven to 200°C|400°F|gas mark 6.

2 Cut the courgettes in half lengthways and scoop out the seeds with a teaspoon.

3 Place the courgettes, hollow side up, in an ovenproof dish. Season well with salt and pepper and bake in the oven for 15 minutes.

4 Melt the butter in a heavy pan, add the leeks and cook over a low heat until soft. Add the ham and stir in the cheese sauce and mustard. Season well with salt and pepper and divide between the hollowed-out courgettes.

5 Preheat the grill to the highest setting.

6 Scatter the Cheddar cheese and breadcrumbs over the courgettes and place under a grill until lightly browned. Serve immediately.

VARIATIONS: Leftover cooked rice can also be added. Leftover bolognese or chilli sauce is a good stuffing for the courgettes.

Tortilla

This is a good recipe for using up leftover cooked potatoes.

Preparation time: 10 minutes
Cooking time: 40 minutes

SERVES 8

oil

about 500 g floury potatoes, peeled and sliced

2 medium onions, thickly sliced

10 eggs

salt and freshly ground black pepper

To prepare ahead: If the tortilla is to be served cold, it can be made a day in advance.
Serving suggestion: Green salad (see page 381)

1 Preheat the grill to the medium setting.
2 Heat about 1 cm oil in a large, heavy frying pan (25 cm diameter). Add the potatoes and onions. Season with salt and pepper and fry slowly until soft but not coloured.
3 Break the eggs into a large mixing bowl, beat well and add the onion and potato mixture. Season with salt and pepper.
4 Add more oil to the pan if necessary to coat the bottom and sides with a thin film of oil. Place over a direct heat. Tip the egg mixture into the pan and cook over a medium heat until the tortilla is nearly set. This may take 10 minutes – be careful not to let the bottom of the tortilla get too dark.
5 Transfer the pan to the grill and continue to cook until the egg has set.
6 Turn on to a serving plate and serve warm or cold, cut into wedges.

VARIATIONS: Other leftovers such as peas or cooked courgettes can be added to the tortilla, and other ingredients such as chopped red pepper and bacon can be fried with the onions.

Camembert Tempura

Preparation time: 10 minutes
Cooking time: 5 minutes

SERVES 2–4

2 slightly under-ripe Camembert cheeses
1 × 150 g packet of tempura batter mix
oil, for deep frying

To serve
cranberry sauce
crusty bread
green salad (see page 381)

1 Cut each Camembert into 8 wedges.
2 Make up the tempura batter according to the manufacturer's instructions.
3 Heat the oil in a deep fryer or a large pan until a cube of bread will sizzle in it in 20 seconds (see page 12).
4 Coat the wedges of Camembert in the batter and immediately deep-fry them until puffed up and golden brown. Drain well on kitchen paper and serve immediately with the cranberry sauce, bread and salad.

Baked Figs with Gorgonzola and Parma Ham

Preparation time: 10 minutes
Cooking time: 10 minutes

SERVES 4

8 fresh figs
150 g Gorgonzola cheese
4 slices of Parma ham, cut in half lengthways

To prepare ahead: Make in advance to the end of stage 4, then refrigerate.
Serving suggestion: Rocket salad (see page 381)

1 Preheat the oven to 190°C|375°F|gas mark 5.
2 Cut the figs almost into quarters to the root end and gently push upwards with finger and thumb to open up the fig.
3 Place a quarter of the Gorgonzola in the centre of each fig.
4 Wrap a length of Parma ham loosely around the bulb of each fig and place on a baking sheet. Bake the figs in the oven for about 10 minutes, or until the cheese begins to melt and the ham is crisp.

Marinated Halloumi

Preparation time: 5 minutes
Marinating time: at least 1 hour
Cooking time: 10 minutes

SERVES 4

pared zest and juice of 1 lemon

5 tablespoons olive oil

5 fresh basil leaves, torn

1 × 250 g pack of halloumi cheese, cut into slices
 1 cm thick

1 large ripe tomato, peeled, deseeded and chopped
 (see page 22)

salt and freshly ground black pepper

To serve

green salad (see page 381)

To prepare ahead: Leave to marinate until required.

1 Mix the lemon zest and juice together with the oil, basil and pepper. Place the halloumi in a shallow dish and pour over the dressing. Leave to marinate for at least 1 hour or as long as possible.
2 When ready to serve, remove the halloumi from the dressing. Taste the dressing and adjust the seasoning as required, then stir the chopped tomato through the dressing.
3 Heat a heavy frying pan, add the halloumi and fry on both sides until golden brown.
4 Arrange the green salad on 4 individual plates, place the halloumi slices over the top and drizzle over the dressing.

NOTE: Serve this as a first course. Alternatively, arranged on one large plate without salad, it can be served as part of a selection of tapas with other dishes such as salted almonds, marinated anchovies and black olives.

Baked Mozzarella in Prosciutto

Preparation time: 10 minutes
Chilling time: 30 minutes
Cooking time: 5–10 minutes

SERVES 4

2 balls of buffalo mozzarella

4 slices of prosciutto or Parma ham

8 large fresh basil leaves

2 tablespoons extra virgin olive oil

salt and freshly ground black pepper

To prepare ahead: Make in advance to the end of stage 4, then refrigerate.
Serving suggestions: Mixed salad (see page 381), crusty bread

1 Preheat the oven to 200°C|400°F|gas mark 6.
2 Drain the mozzarella and cut each ball in half.
3 Lay out the slices of prosciutto and arrange 2 basil leaves in the centre of each slice. Season with pepper.
4 Place a piece of mozzarella on the basil and wrap up into a parcel, making sure the mozzarella is completely covered. Repeat with the remaining mozzarella. Chill for 30 minutes.
5 Put the parcels seam side down on a baking sheet, drizzle 1 teaspoon oil over each and season with pepper.
6 Bake in the oven for 5–10 minutes, or until the prosciutto is slightly crisp and the mozzarella warmed through. Serve immediately.

VARIATION: You can use different cheeses such as Brie or Camembert in this recipe. But you will require more slices of ham as you'll need to make sure the cheese is well wrapped in the ham to stop the melted cheese escaping whilst baking.

Baked Eggs with Smoked Haddock and Spinach

Preparation time: 20 minutes
Cooking time: 15 minutes

SERVES 4

butter, for greasing	4 eggs
140 g baby spinach leaves	4 tablespoons single cream
170 g smoked haddock fillet, poached and flaked (see page 19)	2 tablespoons freshly grated Parmesan cheese salt and freshly ground black pepper

To prepare ahead: Make in advance to the end of stage 4, then refrigerate.

1 Preheat the oven to 180°C|350°F|gas mark 4. Lightly butter 4 ramekins.
2 Place the spinach in a large colander and pour over a kettle of boiling water. Drain well and squeeze dry. Chop roughly.
3 Divide the smoked haddock between the ramekins. Season with a little pepper and then place the spinach on top. Make a hollow in the centre of the spinach.
4 Break an egg into each ramekin so that the yolk sits in the centre of the spinach. Spoon 1 tablespoon of the cream on to each egg and sprinkle with the Parmesan.
5 Stand the dishes in a roasting pan half filled with hot water (a bain-marie) and bake in the oven for 15 minutes, or until the egg whites are just set and the yolks are still runny.

VARIATIONS: Strips of smoked salmon or crisp cooked bacon lardons can be used in place of the smoked haddock.

Souffléd Crab Bread and Butter Puddings

Preparation time: 50 minutes
Chilling time: at least 30 minutes
Cooking time: 25 minutes

SERVES 4

8 slices of white or brown bread

60 g butter

1 × 170 g tin crabmeat, drained

2 spring onions, finely chopped

½ tablespoon chopped fresh parsley

2 tablespoons freshly grated Parmesan cheese

cayenne pepper

40 g Gruyère cheese, grated

75 ml milk

75 ml double cream

1 egg

salt and freshly ground black pepper

To prepare ahead: Prepare to the end of stage 6 and leave the sandwiches to soak in the egg mixture overnight.

1 Cut the bread into 8 circles to fit snugly into 4 ramekins.
2 Butter the ramekins, then butter both sides of the bread circles.
3 Mix the crab meat with the spring onions, parsley, Parmesan and a pinch of cayenne pepper.
4 Make 4 sandwiches with the bread circles and crab filling. Put one in each ramekin and sprinkle the Gruyère on top of each sandwich.
5 Mix together the milk, cream and egg and beat well. Season well with salt and pepper.
6 Pour the mixture on to the sandwiches, dividing it evenly between the 4 ramekins. Chill for 30 minutes or overnight.
7 Place a baking sheet in the oven and preheat the oven to 180°C|350°F|gas mark 4. Place the ramekins on the preheated baking sheet and bake for 25 minutes, or until slightly risen and browning on top.

Game and Brandy Terrine

Preparation time: 30 minutes
Cooking time: 1 hour 25 minutes

SERVES 6–8

60 g rindless streaky bacon, cut into small pieces

225 g uncooked mixed game flesh, minced

225 g rindless belly of pork, minced

110 g pheasant, duck or chicken livers, cleaned and finely chopped

2 shallots, finely chopped

1 clove of garlic, crushed

2 teaspoons brandy

a pinch of ground allspice

225 g thin rashers of rindless streaky bacon, to line the terrine

3 bay leaves

salt and freshly ground black pepper

To serve

bread or toast and green salad (see page 381)

1 Preheat the oven to 170°C|325°F|gas mark 3.
2 Mix together all the ingredients except for the rashers of bacon and the bay leaves. Season well with salt and black pepper.
3 Line a medium terrine or loaf tin with the bacon rashers.
4 Tip in the prepared mixture and spread it flat. Cover with the overhanging bacon. Lay the bay leaves on the surface.
5 Cover with a piece of greaseproof paper. Stand the terrine in a roasting pan half-filled with hot water and bake in the oven for 1¼ hours. The mixture should feel fairly firm to the touch.
6 Remove from the roasting pan, place a weight on the terrine (a second terrine or loaf tin with a tin of fruit in it will do) and leave to cool and firm up. Refrigerate until required. Turn out on to a plate to serve.

NOTE: If you do not have a mincer ask the butcher to mince the meat for you.

Smoked Mackerel Pâté

Preparation time: 10 minutes
Chilling time: at least 15 minutes

SERVES 4

4 smoked mackerel fillets

6 tablespoons crème fraîche

2 teaspoons lemon juice

30 g capers, rinsed, drained and chopped

30 g gherkins, rinsed, drained and chopped

salt and freshly ground black pepper

To serve

melba toast (see page 380)

green salad (see page 381)

To prepare ahead: Make the pâté and refrigerate, well covered, for 2–3 days.

1 Check over the mackerel, removing any bones and the skin. Place the mackerel fillets, crème fraîche and lemon juice in a food processor and whizz until smooth.
2 Turn into a bowl and add the capers and gherkins. Season with salt and pepper. Combine well and turn into 4 ramekins. Keep covered and chilled until ready to serve.
3 Serve with melba toast and green salad.

VARIATIONS: This is a basic recipe that can be made using other smoked fish such as kippers, trout, salmon or eel. If you don't like gherkins and capers, use a little creamed horseradish instead.

Seared Loin of Tuna with Soy and Lime

Preparation time: 10 minutes
Cooking time: 5 minutes

SERVES 4

350 g very fresh loin of tuna
1 tablespoon oil
6 tablespoons light soy sauce
juice of 2 limes

freshly ground black pepper

To garnish
pared zest of 1 lime

1 Season the loin of tuna well with pepper.

2 Heat the oil in a heavy frying pan, add the tuna and fry for 1–2 minutes on each side: the outside should be browned and the inside raw in the middle. Remove from the pan and allow to cool completely.

3 Meanwhile, mix together the soy sauce and the lime juice. Flood 4 plates with the sauce.

4 Cut the tuna into 3 mm slices and lay overlapping in a circle in the centre of each plate. Place the lime zest garnish in the centre and serve immediately.

NOTE: It is very important to buy absolutely fresh tuna fish for this dish. If it is possible to buy a piece of fish that is almost rectangular in shape it will produce an attractive seared effect.

Salmon Ceviche

Preparation time: 5 minutes
Marinating time: at least 1 hour

SERVES 4

grated zest and juice of 2 limes
2 tablespoons fresh orange juice
1 small red chilli, deseeded and finely chopped
400 g salmon fillet
2 spring onions, finely sliced on the diagonal
1 tomato, peeled, deseeded and chopped (see page 22)
freshly ground black pepper

To garnish
coriander leaves

To serve
green salad with avocado (see page 381)
crusty bread

To prepare ahead: The salmon can be left to marinate for several hours.

1 In a shallow dish mix together the lime zest and juice, orange juice and red chilli and season with pepper.

2 Cut the salmon into very thin slices. Lay the salmon slices in the marinade, cover and chill for at least 1 hour, turning occasionally.

3 To serve: remove the salmon from the dish, arrange the slices overlapping on a serving plate, pour over some of the marinade and sprinkle over the spring onions and tomato. Garnish with the coriander leaves. Serve immediately with the salad and bread.

NOTE: If you place the salmon piece in the freezer for 15 minutes it will be easier to cut into thin slices.

Duck Liver and Cointreau Pâté

Preparation time: 10 minutes
Cooking time: 20 minutes
Chilling time: 4 hours

SERVES 6–8

250 g butter
1 large onion, very finely chopped
1 large clove of garlic, crushed
450 g duck livers
3 tablespoons Cointreau
grated zest of 2 oranges
melted butter, to seal
salt and freshly ground black pepper

To serve
toasted brioche or melba toast (see page 380)

To prepare ahead: Make up to 72 hours before serving. Seal with a layer of butter and keep refrigerated.

1 Melt a quarter of the butter in a large, heavy frying pan, add the onion and sweat over a low heat until soft and transparent.
2 Add the garlic and cook for 1 further minute. Remove the onion and garlic from the pan and set aside. Wipe out the pan with kitchen paper.
3 Discard any discoloured pieces of liver as they will be bitter. Rinse well and pat dry.
4 Heat a third of the remaining butter in the pan and add the livers. Brown the livers lightly on all sides and continue to cook until firm but still pink in the middle. Flamber the Cointreau (see page 14) and add to the livers. Shake the pan well.
5 When the flames subside, scrape the mixture into a bowl, allow to cool, then add the orange zest and season with salt and plenty of pepper.
6 Whizz the onion and liver mixtures in a food processor with the remaining butter and push through a sieve into an earthenware dish or pot. Melted butter may then be poured over the pâté to seal it (see note below). Serve with toasted brioche or melba toast.

NOTE: Pâté is often covered with a layer of clarified butter to preserve it. This is butter that has had the milk solids removed, meaning it will keep longer. To make it, melt some butter in a pan and leave until all the milk solids have sunk to the bottom. Carefully pour off the melted butter on top. Pour a little on to the top of each pot of pâté. Alternatively, if the pâté is to be served within 24 hours, cover with ordinary melted butter.

Fillet of Beef Carpaccio

Freezing time: 30 minutes–1 hour
Preparation time: 20 minutes

SERVES 6–8 AS A FIRST COURSE, 4 AS A MAIN COURSE

675 g fillet of beef

To garnish

Parmesan cheese shavings

For the sauce

3 tablespoons plain yoghurt

3 tablespoons double cream

3 tablespoons mayonnaise

1 tablespoon made English mustard

½ teaspoon horseradish cream

a little lemon juice

salt and freshly ground black pepper

To serve

Salad with rocket and beetroot (see page 381)

1 Wrap the beef in clingfilm and place in the freezer for 30 minutes–1 hour, until just beginning to freeze.

2 Slice the beef against the grain of the meat into the thinnest slices possible.

3 Flatten the slices of beef between 2 sheets of clingfilm or damp greaseproof paper, using a mallet or the end of a rolling pin. Carefully remove all the sinews.

4 When the slices are as thin as possible, spread them over individual plates without letting them overlap.

5 Mix together the sauce ingredients and season well with salt and pepper. Add a little lemon juice to taste.

6 Drizzle the sauce over the beef and garnish with the Parmesan shavings.

7 Serve with a rocket and beetroot salad dressed with lemon juice and olive oil.

NOTE: The beef is partially frozen here to make it possible to cut very thin slices. These are then further flattened as they should be almost paper-thin when served.

Crab Cakes

This is a good recipe for using up leftover mashed potato.

Preparation time: 30 minutes
Cooking time: 5 minutes

SERVES 4

2 tablespoons oil
5 spring onions, finely sliced on the diagonal
1 × 2.5 cm piece of fresh root ginger, peeled and grated
1 clove of garlic, crushed
grated zest and juice of 1 lime
2 × 170 g cans of crabmeat, drained
90 g mashed potato
1 tablespoon chopped fresh coriander

a few drops of Tabasco (optional)
plain flour
1 egg, beaten
dried white breadcrumbs
salt and freshly ground black pepper

To garnish
lime wedges
fresh coriander
sweet chilli dipping sauce

To prepare ahead: Make the cakes in advance, then refrigerate or freeze. If frozen, defrost thoroughly before cooking.

Serving suggestions: Avocado and spring onion salad (see page 332), green salad (see page 381), new potato, red onion, parsley and pepper salad (see page 335)

1 Heat 1 tablespoon of the oil in a pan, add the spring onions and cook for 1–2 minutes until beginning to soften.
2 Add the ginger and garlic and cook for 1 further minute. Add the lime juice to the pan. Remove from the heat.
3 Put the crabmeat and potato into a bowl. Add the onion mixture, lime zest, coriander and the Tabasco, if using. Season with salt and pepper. Mix together with a fork. Flour your hands and shape into 4 large or 8 small cakes.
4 Dust the crab cakes with flour, then roll in the beaten egg and coat with the breadcrumbs.
5 Heat the remaining oil in a frying pan, add the crab cakes and fry for about 2 minutes on each side until golden brown.
6 Serve garnished with lime wedges and coriander, with sweet chilli sauce on the side.

Smoked Haddock and Caper Cakes

This is a good recipe for using up leftover mashed potato, in which case omit stages 2 and 3.

Preparation time: 20 minutes
Cooking time: 30 minutes

SERVES 4

250 g floury potatoes

30 g butter

300 g smoked haddock, poached and flaked, bones
  removed (see page 181)

200 ml milk, reserved from cooking the fish

1 hardboiled egg, roughly chopped (see page 13)

1 tablespoon chopped fresh parsley

1 tablespoon capers, drained and rinsed

beaten egg, to bind

dried white breadcrumbs

oil, for frying

salt and freshly ground black pepper

To prepare ahead: Make the cakes, then refrigerate or freeze. If frozen, defrost thoroughly before cooking.
Serving suggestions: Green salad (see page 381), Italian tomato salad (see page 334)

1 Preheat the oven to 190°C|375°F|gas mark 5.
2 Bring the potatoes to the boil in a saucepan of cold water. Reduce the heat and simmer until tender. Do not salt the water.
3 Drain the potatoes thoroughly, then mash with the butter and some of the milk the haddock was cooked in. The mash should not be too wet.
4 Mix together the haddock, mashed potato, hardboiled egg, parsley and capers. Season with plenty of pepper and salt (taste first, as you may not need the salt).
5 Add enough beaten egg to bind the mixture so that it is soft but not sloppy.
6 Flour your hands and shape the mixture into 8 small or 4 large cakes, 2.5 cm thick. Brush with more of the beaten egg and coat in the breadcrumbs.
7 Heat the oil in a heavy frying pan, add the cakes and fry until brown on all sides.

Thai Fish Cakes

Preparation time: 10 minutes
Cooking time: 15 minutes

MAKES 12

450 g monkfish fillet or other firm white fish

2 teaspoons Thai red curry paste

2 kaffir lime leaves, finely shredded

2–3 tablespoons nam pla (fish sauce)

55 g French beans, topped and tailed, finely chopped

beaten egg, to bind

oil, for frying (see page 14)

To serve

sweet chilli dipping sauce

To prepare ahead: Make in advance to the end of stage 1, then refrigerate. Alternatively, complete to the end of stage 2 and reheat thoroughly in a hot oven.

Serving suggestions: Salad including beansprouts, mangetout and cashew nuts

1 Mince the fish and add the curry paste and lime leaves. Transfer to a bowl and stir in the nam pla and beans. Add enough beaten egg to bind. Shape the mixture into small, flat cakes, no more than 1.5 cm thick.

2 Pour the oil into a frying pan until it is 1 cm deep. Heat the oil and fry the cakes in batches until golden brown. Drain on kitchen paper and sprinkle with a little salt.

3 Serve with sweet chilli dipping sauce.

Smoked Trout Cakes with Mustard Sauce

This is a good recipe for using up leftover mashed potato.

Preparation time: 15 minutes
Cooking time: 15 minutes

SERVES 4

225 g smoked trout, skinned, boned and flaked	**For the sauce**
170 g mashed potato	3 tablespoons crème fraîche
1 tablespoon chopped fresh dill	1 tablespoon wholegrain mustard
plain flour	lemon juice
1 egg, beaten	a pinch of sugar (optional)
dried white breadcrumbs	salt and freshly ground black pepper
oil, for frying	
salt and freshly ground black pepper	

To prepare ahead: Make in advance to the end of stage 2, then refrigerate and fry as required. Alternatively, fry and then refrigerate, and reheat thoroughly in a hot oven.

1 Stir the trout into the potato with the dill. Season well with salt and pepper.

2 Flour your hands lightly and shape the mixture into 8 small or 4 large cakes, 2.5 cm thick. Brush with beaten egg and coat with the breadcrumbs. Chill.

3 In a small bowl, stir together the crème fraîche and mustard and season to taste with lemon juice, salt, pepper and the sugar, if using.

4 Heat the oil in a frying pan, add the fish cakes and fry until brown on all sides and hot all the way through (it may be necessary to put them into a hot oven for an extra 5–10 minutes). Serve with a spoonful of the mustard sauce.

Potato Cakes with Smoked Salmon

This is a good recipe for using up leftover mashed potato.

Preparation time: 15 minutes
Cooking time: 15 minutes

SERVES 4

200 g mashed potato
2 spring onions, finely chopped
1 tablespoon chopped fresh parsley
55 g self-raising flour
½ egg, beaten
oil or butter, for frying

freshly ground black pepper

To serve
3 tablespoons crème fraîche
1 tablespoon horseradish sauce
8 slices of smoked salmon
rocket leaves

To prepare ahead: Make in advance to the end of stage 3, then refrigerate or freeze. If frozen, defrost thoroughly before cooking.

1 Preheat the oven to 200°C|400°F|gas mark 6.
2 Mix together the potato, spring onions, parsley and black pepper. Sift in the flour and combine well.
3 Make a well in the centre and gradually add the beaten egg. Shape the cakes into 8 patties with floured hands.
4 Heat the oil or butter in a frying pan.
5 Add the potato cakes and fry for 2 minutes on each side or until golden brown.
6 Transfer to a baking sheet and put into the oven for 5–10 minutes or until hot all the way through.
7 Meanwhile, mix the crème fraîche with the horseradish sauce.
8 Place 2 cakes on each plate and cover with a slice of smoked salmon. Serve with the crème fraîche mixture and the rocket.

Ham, Leek and Potato Cakes

This is a very good recipe for using up leftover mashed potato, in which case omit stages 1 and 2.

Preparation time: 5 minutes
Cooking time: 30 minutes

SERVES 4

500 g floury potatoes, peeled and cut into large
   chunks
about 75 ml milk
30 g butter
3 leeks, sliced and washed

75 g cooked ham, sliced
85 g Stilton cheese, slightly crumbled
½ tablespoon oil
butter, for frying
salt and freshly ground black pepper

To prepare ahead: Make the potato cakes in advance, then refrigerate or freeze. If frozen, defrost thoroughly before reheating.

Serving suggestions: Green salad (see page 381), poached or fried eggs, Parmesan baked tomatoes (see page 349)

1 Place the potatoes in a saucepan of salted water. Bring to the boil, then simmer for about 15 minutes, or until tender. Mash the potatoes. Beat in the milk and half of the butter. Do not make the mash too wet. Season to taste with salt and pepper.

2 Cook the leeks slowly in the rest of the butter until soft but not coloured. Cool.

3 Mix together the leeks, ham and potato. Gently stir in the Stilton. Season lightly with salt and pepper. Shape the mixture into 8 round cakes and chill to allow them to firm up, about 20 minutes.

4 Preheat the oven to 180°C|350°F|gas mark 4.

5 Heat the oil and a knob of butter together in a large, heavy frying pan. Add the potato cakes and fry until golden brown on each side. Place on a baking sheet and put into the oven for 10 minutes or until they are hot all the way through.

VARIATIONS: Substitute 200 g frozen peas for the leeks. Boil the peas for 2 minutes, then lightly crush before stirring into the potato mixture. Use chopped cold cooked sausage in place of the ham.

Crab and Prawn Cocktail

Preparation time: 25 minutes

SERVES 4

250 g cooked tiger prawns, peeled

2 × 170 g cans of crabmeat

100 ml mayonnaise

1–2 tablespoons sweet chilli sauce

grated zest and juice of 2 limes

1 × 2.5 cm piece of fresh root ginger, peeled and
   finely grated

2 spring onions, thinly sliced on the diagonal

salad leaves, such as rocket and watercress

salt and freshly ground black pepper

To garnish

1 tablespoon chopped fresh coriander

lime wedges

To prepare ahead: Make in advance to the end of stage 2, then refrigerate.

1 Chop all but 4 of the prawns.
2 Mix together all the remaining ingredients except for the spring onions and salad leaves and stir in the chopped prawns. Season with salt and pepper, adding more chilli sauce to taste if necessary.
3 Make a bed of salad leaves on 4 individual plates. Divide the crabmeat and prawn mixture between the plates. Scatter over the spring onions and garnish with the reserved prawns and coriander. Serve with the lime wedges.

Grilled Oysters

Preparation time: 10 minutes
Cooking time: 2 minutes

SERVES 2

12 oysters, shucked

6 tablespoons double cream

30–50 g grated Cheddar cheese

freshly ground black pepper

1 Preheat the grill to the highest setting.
2 Put the oysters in their half shells on a baking sheet.
3 Pour ½ tablespoon of the cream into each oyster, season with pepper and sprinkle over a little cheese.
4 Place the baking sheet under the grill until the cheese melts and browns lightly.
5 Serve immediately.

Mussels with Leeks and Cider

Preparation time: 10 minutes
Cooking time: 15 minutes

SERVES 4

2 kg mussels

50 g butter

1 large leek, finely chopped and carefully washed

2 cloves of garlic, chopped

300 ml dry cider

2 tablespoons double cream (optional)

salt and freshly ground black pepper

To serve

crusty bread

To prepare ahead: Make in advance to the end of stage 2, then refrigerate. Reheat the broth and add the mussels and continue from stage 3.

1 Clean the mussels by scrubbing them well under cold running water. Pull away the 'beards' (seaweed-like threads). Throw away any mussels that are cracked or that remain open when tapped: they may take some time to respond if they have been kept in the refrigerator, so place to one side and check again when you have prepared the others before discarding.

2 Melt one-third of the butter in a large saucepan with a tight-fitting lid. Add the leek and sweat until beginning to soften. Add the garlic and cook for 1 further minute. Add the cider and bring to the boil, then reduce the heat and allow to simmer for 2 minutes.

3 Add the mussels, then cover the pan and leave to steam over a low heat until the shells are open, shaking the pan occasionally (about 5 minutes). Tip the mussels into a colander set over a bowl.

4 Throw away any mussels that have not opened. Pour the mussel liquid from the bowl into a saucepan. Boil and reduce well. Lower the heat and whisk in the remaining butter, then season to taste with salt and pepper. If desired, a little cream can be added to the sauce at the end.

5 Transfer the mussels to a warmed soup tureen or warmed wide soup bowls, and pour over the sauce.

NOTE: Before cooking, store mussels in the refrigerator in a bowl or on a tray, not in a sealed bag.

Thai Mussels

Preparation time: 15 minutes
Cooking time: 10 minutes

SERVES 4

2 kg mussels

2 tablespoons oil

2 medium onions, very finely chopped

1 clove of garlic, crushed

1–2 teaspoons Thai red curry paste

150 ml water

150 ml coconut milk

1 tablespoon chopped fresh coriander

salt and freshly ground black pepper

To garnish

2 tablespoons roughly chopped fresh coriander

To serve

French bread

To prepare ahead: Make in advance to the end of stage 2. When ready to finish the dish, make sure that the broth is brought back to simmering point before adding the mussels.

1 Clean the mussels by scrubbing them well under cold running water. Pull away the 'beards' (seaweed-like threads). Throw away any mussels that are cracked or that remain open when tapped: they may take some time to respond if they have been kept in the refrigerator, so place to one side and check again when you have prepared the others before discarding.

2 Heat the oil in a large deep pan, add the onions and sweat until soft but not coloured. Add the garlic and curry paste and cook for a further 45 seconds, then add the water, coconut milk and coriander and bring up to simmering point.

3 Add the mussels to the pan, cover with a lid and leave to steam over a low heat until the shells are open, shaking the pan occasionally (about 5 minutes). Tip the mussels into a colander set over a bowl.

4 Throw away any mussels that have not opened. Pour the mussel liquid from the bowl back into a saucepan. Boil to reduce well, then season to taste with salt and pepper. If the sauce is too spicy, add a little more coconut milk.

4 Transfer the mussels to a warmed soup tureen or warmed wide soup bowl. Pour over the sauce and sprinkle with the fresh coriander.

5 Serve immediately with French bread.

NOTE: Store mussels in the refrigerator in a bowl or on a tray, not in a sealed bag. Add more or less curry paste depending on taste.

Spicy Prawn Kebabs

Preparation time: 25 minutes
Marinating time: up to 24 hours
Cooking time: 6–8 minutes

SERVES 4

4 tablespoons oil

2 tablespoons ginger wine

½ red chilli, finely chopped

1 kaffir lime leaf, bruised (optional)

1 stick of lemon grass, bruised

½ tablespoon chopped fresh coriander

1 clove of garlic, crushed

16 raw tiger prawns, peeled and deveined but
  tail left on

juice of ½ lime

freshly ground black pepper

4 wooden skewers, soaked in water

To garnish

fresh coriander sprigs

lime wedges

To prepare ahead: The prawns can be left to marinate for 24 hours.
Serving suggestions: Thai rice salad (see page 354), pineapple rice (see page 376)

1 Put the oil, ginger wine, chilli, lime leaf, lemon grass, coriander, garlic, and pepper into a bowl. Add the prawns, stir well and leave to marinate for as long as possible, up to 24 hours, basting occasionally.

2 Preheat the grill to the highest setting.

3 Squeeze the lime juice over the prawns and stir, then thread 4 prawns on to each skewer. Place the skewers on a baking sheet. Cook under the grill for about 3 minutes on each side, basting with the marinade as necessary.

4 When the prawns are pink and cooked, serve immediately, garnished with the coriander and lime wedges.

NOTE: If you do not have ginger wine use 1 × 2.5 cm piece of peeled and grated fresh root ginger in its place and increase the amount of oil used. The marinade can also be used for chicken.

Filo-wrapped Prawns

Preparation time: 30 minutes
Cooking time: 10 minutes

SERVES 4

20 raw shell-on king prawns
1–2 teaspoons wasabi paste
60 g butter, melted
4 sheets of filo pastry
oil, for deep frying (see page 12)
salt

To serve
soy sauce
sweet chilli dipping sauce

To prepare ahead: Make in advance to the end of stage 4, then refrigerate.

1 Take the head off each prawn and peel the shell from the body, leaving the tail intact. Make a shallow cut along the back of each prawn and remove the black intestine.
2 Mix the wasabi paste into the melted butter (it will stay in lumps but don't worry).
3 Take 1 sheet of filo and brush all over with the melted butter mixture. Cut into 5 strips and wrap each prawn in a filo strip, leaving the tail shell exposed. Repeat with the remaining sheets of filo and prawns.
4 Lay out separately on a large tray, ready to deep-fry.
5 Pour the oil into a large pan. It should not be more than one-third full. Heat the oil until a cube of bread will sizzle and brown in 30 seconds.
6 Deep-fry the prawns a few at a time until golden brown (be careful they do not brown too quickly or they may not be cooked through). Drain on kitchen paper and sprinkle with salt.
7 Serve with soy sauce and sweet chilli dipping sauce.

Chicken Kebabs

Preparation time: 10 minutes
Marinating time: at least 1 hour
Cooking time: 10–15 minutes

SERVES 4

4 chicken breasts, skinned, boned and cut into cubes
8 wooden skewers, soaked in water

For the marinade
1 × 2.5 cm piece of fresh root ginger, peeled and grated

2 cloves of garlic, crushed
2 tablespoons dark soy sauce
2 tablespoons orange juice
1 teaspoon soft dark brown sugar

To prepare ahead: Marinate the chicken overnight.

Serving suggestions: Rice or noodles, stir-fried vegetables (see page 351), steamed bok choi with soy and ginger (see page 350), roast butternut squash (see page 179), quick raita (see page 495), fruit couscous (see page 355)

1 Mix the marinade ingredients together. Add the chicken to the marinade and leave for at least 1 hour.
2 Preheat the grill to the highest setting or light the barbecue.
3 Thread the chicken on to the skewers. Cook under the grill or on a barbecue, turning occasionally and basting with any remaining marinade.
4 Serve immediately.

Chicken Tikka Kebabs

Preparation time: 5 minutes
Marinating time: 24 hours
Cooking time: 10 minutes

SERVES 4

4 chicken breasts, skinned, boned and cut into cubes
8 wooden skewers, soaked in water

To garnish

chopped fresh coriander

For the marinade

4 tablespoons tikka curry paste
grated zest and juice of 1 lime
1 small carton of plain yoghurt
1 small red chilli, very finely chopped

To prepare ahead: Marinate the chicken overnight.

Serving suggestions: Quick raita (see page 495), grilled pitta bread, pineapple rice (see page 376)

1 Place the chicken in a bowl.
2 Mix together the curry paste, lime zest and juice, yoghurt and chilli. Pour the mixture over the chicken, mix well, cover and chill for 24 hours.
3 Preheat the grill to the highest setting.
4 Divide the chicken between the skewers and grill, turning as necessary, until the chicken is lightly browned and cooked all the way through.
5 Arrange the skewers on a plate and garnish with the coriander.

Soups

Soup can be made from a huge range of ingredients. The basic method is to sweat some vegetables (see page 22) and this is the key skill. If you do this over a low heat and take your time, the vegetables will be really soft and their flavour will intensify, providing a delicious base with which to make your soup. Ideally the vegetables should not brown at this stage as this will affect the flavour, but if they do, as long as they have not burnt, you will simply have made a soup with a caramelized flavour which you may enjoy just as much!

Most soups depend on a good-quality stock for much of their flavour. A homemade stock made from vegetables or leftover bones from a roast chicken (see page 500) will give the best result, but if this is not possible use bought liquid vegetable or chicken stock. (We wouldn't recommend stock cubes as they can be very salty.) A little white wine added to shop-bought stock also improves the flavour. (For recommended brands of stock, see page 35.)

Some of these soups require liquidizing in a blender or food processor for a very smooth result. Alternatively, use a hand blender, which has the added advantage of being used in the pan, thus avoiding more washing up. The texture of the soup is a matter of personal preference. Most of the soups in this section are intended to be smooth, to make a good first course for a dinner party as well as a quick lunch or light supper. If you prefer soup with a more chunky texture, use a potato masher to break up the vegetables rather than liquidizing, or only liquidize half of the soup so that some of the texture remains.

Take care when liquidizing hot soup as occasionally the hot liquid can escape the blender or food processor and cause burns. Allow the soup to cool slightly before blending, liquidizing it in batches to avoid overfilling the blender or food processor. Make sure that the lid is securely in place before turning on the blender. Hold the lid down and cover with a tea towel whilst the machine is on.

Smooth soups should be the consistency of single or double cream and can be marbled with cream to serve. To do this, pour a little cream over the back of a teaspoon held low over the bowl of soup and drizzle over the surface. Using the end of a teaspoon, stir through the soup a few times to create a marbled effect.

Most soups can be made in advance and frozen. They may need a little extra liquid when being reheated to serve. Serve the soups with crusty bread or croûtons (see page 380).

Artichoke Soup

Preparation time: 15 minutes
Cooking time: 30 minutes

SERVES 4–6

50 g butter

1 medium onion, sliced

700 g Jerusalem artichokes

600 ml chicken or vegetable stock

600 ml milk

salt and freshly ground white pepper

To garnish

double cream (optional)

toasted flaked almonds (see page 17)

To prepare ahead: Make the soup to the end of stage 5, then refrigerate or freeze.

1 Melt the butter in a saucepan, add the onion and sweat over a low heat until soft but not coloured.

2 Scrub the artichokes well and slice. Add to the pan with the onion. Continue cooking, covered, for a further 10 minutes, giving an occasional stir.

4 Add the stock, season well with salt and pepper and simmer for a further 20 minutes, or until the artichokes are soft.

5 Liquidize in a food processor or blender, adding the milk as you go (you might not need it all) and push through a sieve. Check for seasoning – this soup needs plenty of salt and pepper.

6 To serve: reheat the soup and pour into warmed soup bowls. Swirl cream, if using, on the top and sprinkle with the almonds.

Mexican Bean Soup

Preparation time: 10 minutes
Cooking time: 15 minutes

SERVES 4

1 tablespoon oil
1 onion, roughly chopped
1 red chilli, finely chopped
1 clove of garlic, crushed
1 × 400 g can of chopped tomatoes
a pinch of sugar
1 × 400 g can of cooked mixed beans, drained and rinsed

500 ml chicken or vegetable stock
salt and freshly ground black pepper

To garnish
grated cheese
tortilla chips
1 tablespoon chopped fresh coriander

To prepare ahead: Make the soup in advance, then refrigerate or freeze.

1 Heat the oil in a large, heavy saucepan. Add the onion and sweat over a low heat until beginning to soften, then add the chilli and cook for a further 2 minutes. Add the garlic and cook for 1 further minute.
2 Add the tomatoes, sugar and beans to the onion and heat through. Add the stock and bring up to the boil, then simmer for 5 minutes. Season to taste with salt and pepper.
3 Serve in warmed soup bowls, garnished with grated cheese, a couple of tortilla chips and the coriander.

Tuscan White Bean Soup

Preparation time: 10 minutes
Cooking time: 25 minutes

SERVES 6

30 g unsalted butter
1 large onion, finely chopped
2 sticks of celery, finely chopped
2 cloves of garlic, crushed
2 × 400 g cans of butterbeans, drained and rinsed
2 × 400 g cans of cannellini beans, drained and rinsed
900 ml chicken stock

200 ml milk
freshly grated nutmeg
2 tablespoons crème fraîche
salt and freshly ground white pepper

To garnish
chilli oil or olive oil
crisp bacon pieces (optional)

To prepare ahead: Make the soup in advance, then refrigerate or freeze.

1 Melt the butter in a large, heavy saucepan. Add the onion and celery and sweat over a very low heat until soft but not coloured. Add the garlic and cook for 1 further minute, ensuring that it takes on no colour.

2 Add the beans to the pan with the stock and bring to the boil, then simmer for 5 minutes. Remove from the heat, add the milk and liquidize thoroughly in a blender or food processor.

3 Push the soup through a fine sieve and return to the pan. Add a little more stock or milk if the soup is too thick, and season to taste with salt, pepper and freshly grated nutmeg.

4 Reheat the soup gently, without boiling, stir in the crème fraîche and check the seasoning. To serve, pour into warmed soup bowls, drizzle over a little chilli oil and scatter over the bacon pieces, if using.

NOTE: For a more rustic texture, liquidize only half the soup and mix with the unblended soup.

Broccoli and Stilton Soup

Leftover cooked broccoli can be used to make this soup. Add it to the sweated onion and reheat in the stock.

Preparation time: 10 minutes
Cooking time: 10 minutes

SERVES 4

1 tablespoon oil	6 tablespoons crème fraîche
1 onion, chopped	170 g Stilton cheese, crumbled
450 g broccoli	salt and freshly ground white pepper
500 ml chicken or vegetable stock	

To prepare ahead: Make the soup in advance, then refrigerate or freeze.

1 Heat the oil in a large, heavy saucepan, add the onion and sweat over a low heat until soft but not coloured.

2 Break the broccoli into florets. Discard any tough woody stalks and slice the tender stems thinly. Add to the onion with the stock and cook until tender.

3 Add the crème fraîche and Stilton and whizz in a blender or food processor until smooth.

4 Strain the soup into a clean saucepan.

5 Reheat gently without boiling. Season with salt and pepper if necessary. Serve in warmed soup bowls.

Cauliflower Cheese Soup

Leftover cauliflower cheese can be used in this recipe. Add it to the sweated onion with the stock and heat through well. Continue from stage 4.

Preparation time: 15 minutes
Cooking time: 10 minutes

SERVES 4–6

1 tablespoon oil
1 onion, chopped
450 g cauliflower
600 ml chicken or vegetable stock
200 g strong Cheddar cheese, grated

6 tablespoons double cream or crème fraîche
salt and freshly ground white pepper

To garnish
croûtons (see page 380)

To prepare ahead: Make the soup in advance, then refrigerate or freeze.

1 Heat the oil in a large, heavy saucepan, add the onion and sweat over a low heat until soft but not coloured.
2 Break the cauliflower into florets. Discard any tough woody stalks and slice the tender stems finely.
3 Add the stock and cauliflower to the onion and cook until tender. Remove from the heat and stir in the cheese.
4 Add the cream or crème fraîche and whizz in a blender until very smooth.
5 Pour into a clean saucepan and reheat gently without boiling. Season with salt and pepper. To serve, pour into warmed soup bowls and garnish with the croûtons.

Spiced Lentil and Cauliflower Soup

Preparation time: 5 minutes
Cooking time: 25 minutes

SERVES 4–6

1 tablespoon oil
1 onion, finely chopped
1 tablespoon medium curry powder
1 litre chicken or vegetable stock
170 g red lentils

250 g cauliflower florets
salt and freshly ground black pepper

To garnish
4 tablespoons plain yoghurt
2 tablespoons chopped fresh coriander

To prepare ahead: Make the soup in advance, then refrigerate or freeze.

1 Heat the oil in a large, heavy saucepan, add the onion and sweat over a low heat until soft but not coloured.

2 Add the curry powder and cook for 30 seconds. Add the stock and lentils. Bring to the boil, then simmer for 10 minutes and season with salt and pepper.

3 Add the cauliflower and simmer for a further 10 minutes, or until tender. You may need to add more stock or water.

4 Whizz the soup in a blender or food processor until smooth, then return to the rinsed-out saucepan. This may have to be done in batches and more water may need to be added to reach the desired consistency.

5 Reheat the soup, pour into warmed soup bowls and swirl in the yoghurt. Sprinkle with the coriander.

Celery and Ginger Soup

Preparation time: 10 minutes
Cooking time: 30 minutes

SERVES 4–6

2 tablespoons oil

1 onion, roughly chopped

1 head of celery, roughly chopped

1 × 1.5 cm piece of fresh root ginger, peeled and finely chopped

900 ml vegetable stock

salt and freshly ground black pepper

To garnish

3 tablespoons roughly chopped fresh parsley

To prepare ahead: This soup can be made in advance and frozen. Whizz again once defrosted if the soup has separated.

1 Heat the oil in a large, heavy saucepan. Add the onion to the pan and sweat over a low heat until soft but not coloured. Add the celery and ginger and cook for a further 10 minutes.

2 Add the stock and bring slowly to the boil, then reduce the heat and allow to simmer for 15 minutes.

3 Remove the pan from the heat and allow to cool slightly. Whizz the soup in a blender or food processor until smooth. For an extra smooth soup strain through a sieve.

4 Return the soup to the pan and reheat gently without boiling. Season to taste with salt and pepper and serve immediately in warmed soup bowls, sprinkled with the parsley.

Chestnut and Mushroom Soup

Preparation time: 20 minutes
Cooking time: 30 minutes

SERVES 4–6

30 g butter
1 onion, finely chopped
225 g flat mushrooms, chopped
400 g vacuum-packed chestnuts, chopped
900 ml chicken or vegetable stock

grated zest of ½ grated lemon
salt and freshly ground black pepper

To garnish
crème fraîche
chopped fresh parsley

To prepare ahead: Make the soup to the end of stage 3, then refrigerate or freeze.

1 Melt the butter in a large, heavy saucepan, add the onion and sweat over a low heat until soft but not coloured. Add the mushrooms and cook until the moisture has evaporated.
2 Add the chestnuts and stock and bring slowly to the boil. Add the lemon zest, salt and pepper and simmer for 15 minutes.
3 Whizz the soup in a blender or food processor until smooth, then return to the rinsed-out pan, adding more water if required.
4 Reheat, check the seasoning, and serve in warmed soup bowls with a spoonful of crème fraîche on each serving, sprinkled with the parsley.

Corn Chowder

Preparation time: 10 minutes
Cooking time: 30 minutes

SERVES 4–6

150 g rindless streaky bacon, chopped
30 g butter
1 large onion, chopped
3 sticks of celery, chopped
1 bay leaf
1 large potato, peeled and diced
30 g plain flour

550 ml milk
340 g cooked sweetcorn
salt and freshly ground black pepper

To garnish
chopped fresh parsley

To prepare ahead: Make the soup to the end of stage 4 and refrigerate or freeze, then reheat gently to prevent the vegetables from breaking up.

1 In a large, heavy saucepan, fry the bacon in the butter until brown, but not crisp. Add the onion, celery and bay leaf. Reduce the heat and cook slowly until the onion is soft, then add the potato.
2 Remove the pan from the heat. Stir in the flour and cook for 1 minute, then add the milk.
3 Return the pan to the heat and stir until boiling.
4 Add the sweetcorn and season to taste with salt and pepper. Simmer for 10 minutes or until the vegetables are soft but not broken. Remove and discard the bay leaf.
5 Serve in warmed soup bowls, sprinkled with the parsley.

Sweetcorn Soup

Preparation time: 10 minutes
Cooking time: 15 minutes

SERVES 4

1 tablespoon oil
1 onion, chopped
500 ml chicken stock
150 ml milk
1 large potato, peeled and cut into chunks
1 × 375 g can of creamed sweetcorn
salt and freshly ground black pepper

To garnish

crispy bacon, crumbled
finely chopped fresh parsley

To prepare ahead: Make the soup in advance, then refrigerate or freeze.

1 Heat the oil in a large, heavy saucepan. Add the onion and sweat over a low heat until soft but not coloured.
2 Add the stock and milk and bring to the boil. Add the potato and sweetcorn and continue to simmer for about 10 minutes or until the potato is cooked.
3 Remove the pan from the heat and allow to cool slightly. Whizz the soup in a blender or food processor, in batches if necessary, until smooth, then return to the rinsed-out pan and reheat. Season well with salt and pepper.
4 Serve immediately in warmed soup bowls, garnished with the bacon and parsley.

Courgette Soup with Crisp Prosciutto and Parmesan

Preparation time: 5 minutes
Cooking time: 20 minutes

SERVES 4–6

1 tablespoon oil
1 clove of garlic, crushed
800 g courgettes, sliced
1.2 litres chicken stock
1 tablespoon chopped fresh thyme

juice of 1 lemon
salt and freshly ground black pepper

To garnish
6 slices of prosciutto
50 g Parmesan cheese, shaved

To prepare ahead: Make the soup to the end of stage 4, then refrigerate or freeze.

1 Preheat the grill to the highest setting.
2 Heat the oil in a large heavy saucepan, add the garlic and sweat over a low heat for 1 minute. Add the courgettes and sweat for a further 8–10 minutes.
3 Add the stock and thyme. Bring up to the boil, then simmer for 5 minutes, or until the courgettes are just soft. Season to taste with salt and pepper.
4 Whizz the soup in batches, if necessary, in a blender or food processor until smooth, then return to the rinsed-out pan. Stir in the lemon juice and check the seasoning.
5 Grill the prosciutto until crisp and chop into small pieces.
6 Reheat the soup. Serve in warmed soup bowls with the prosciutto and Parmesan scattered on top.

Leek and Carrot Soup

Preparation time: 10 minutes
Cooking time: 15 minutes

SERVES 4

30 g butter
2 leeks, finely chopped
4 carrots, peeled and sliced
750 ml chicken stock
2 tablespoons crème fraîche
salt and freshly ground black pepper

To garnish
Gruyère cheese, grated
croûtons (see page 380)

To prepare ahead: Make the soup to the end of stage 4, then refrigerate or freeze.

1 Melt the butter in a large, heavy saucepan. Add the leeks and cover the pan with a tight-fitting lid. Allow the leek to sweat over a low heat until soft (about 4 minutes).

2 Add the carrots and stock and simmer for 10 minutes, or until the carrots are cooked. Season to taste with salt and pepper and allow to cool slightly.

3 Whizz the soup in a blender or food processor until smooth, then pass through a sieve if desired.

4 Return the soup to the rinsed-out pan, reheat gently and stir through the crème fraîche.

5 To serve: ladle into warmed soup bowls and scatter over the grated cheese and croûtons.

NOTE: This recipe specifies whizzing the soup until smooth, but it can also be served unpuréed, in which case slice the leeks very finely and dice rather than slice the carrots.

Lentil Soup

Preparation time: 10 minutes
Cooking time: 30 minutes

SERVES 4

350 g orange lentils

1 litre chicken stock

4 rashers of good-quality dry-cure smoked bacon

1 bay leaf

1 onion, sliced

parsley stalks

3–4 tablespoons single cream

salt and freshly ground black pepper

To garnish

chopped fresh parsley

To prepare ahead: Make the soup to the end of stage 3, then refrigerate or freeze.

1 Wash and drain the lentils. Put them into a large, heavy saucepan with the stock, bacon, bay leaf, onion and parsley stalks, and boil for about 30 minutes, or until the lentils are completely cooked.

2 When the lentils are soft, remove the bacon, bay leaf and parsley stalks.

3 Whizz the lentils with the cooking liquid in a blender or food processor until very smooth. Season to taste with salt and pepper.

4 Return the soup to the rinsed-out pan with the cream and heat through. Serve in warmed soup bowls, sprinkled with the parsley.

Lettuce Soup

This is a great recipe to use up a bowl of leftover dressed salad, which won't keep. It is best if made with a pure green salad – one including radicchio, for example, will give a rather murky colour. The quantities are approximate as it depends on the amount of salad you are using.

Preparation time: 5 minutes
Cooking time: 15 minutes

SERVES 4

1 tablespoon oil
1 onion, chopped
1 clove of garlic, crushed
1 dressed (wilted) leftover lettuce salad

about 600 ml chicken or vegetable stock
1 × 142 ml pot of double cream
salt and freshly ground black pepper

To prepare ahead: Make the soup in advance, then refrigerate or freeze.

1 Heat the oil in a large, heavy saucepan. Add the onion and sweat over a low heat until soft but not coloured. Add the garlic and cook for a further 45 seconds.
2 Add the wilted lettuce salad and enough stock to half cover. Bring to the boil, then cover with a lid and allow to simmer for 5 minutes. Remove from the heat and allow to cool slightly, then whizz in a blender or food processor until smooth and return to the rinsed-out pan.
3 Add the cream and season to taste with salt and pepper.
4 Reheat and serve immediately in warmed soup bowls.

Mushroom Soup

Preparation time: 10 minutes
Cooking time: 25 minutes

SERVES 4

60 g butter
350 g flat mushrooms, chopped
3 tablespoons chopped fresh parsley
½ clove of garlic, crushed
2 large slices of bread, crusts removed, crumbled

850 ml chicken or vegetable stock
a pinch of freshly grated nutmeg
1 × 142 ml pot of single cream
salt and freshly ground black pepper

To prepare ahead: Make the soup to the end of stage 3, then refrigerate or freeze. If frozen, it may need to be whizzed again once defrosted if it has separated.

1 Melt the butter in a large, heavy saucepan.

2 Add the mushrooms and most of the parsley. Cook over a low heat, stirring, until soft. Add the garlic and the bread. Stir until the bread and mushrooms are well mixed, then add the stock, nutmeg and salt and plenty of pepper to taste. Bring to simmering point, then cook slowly for 10 minutes.

3 Whizz the soup in a blender or food processor with the cream until smooth.

4 Serve in warmed soup bowls, sprinkled with the remaining parsley.

NOTE: This soup can also be served chilled. Add the parsley and cream just before serving.

Pea and Lemon Soup

Preparation time: 20 minutes
Cooking time: 15 minutes

SERVES 4

20 g butter

1 onion, finely chopped

1 rasher of dry-cure smoked streaky bacon

250 g potatoes, peeled and diced

350 g frozen peas or petits pois

1 litre chicken stock

grated zest of 1 lemon

salt and freshly ground black pepper

To garnish

2 tablespoons double cream (optional)

To prepare ahead: Make the soup to the end of stage 3, then refrigerate or freeze.

1 Melt the butter in a large, heavy saucepan. Add the onion and bacon. Cook over a low heat until the onion is very soft. Add the potato and cook for a further 2 minutes, stirring.

2 Add the peas, stock and half the lemon zest. Bring to the boil, then simmer for 15 minutes or until the potato is cooked through.

3 Remove the soup from the heat and discard the bacon. Season to taste with salt and pepper. Stir in the remaining lemon zest. Whizz in a blender or food processor until very smooth.

4 Reheat and serve in warmed soup bowls, marbled with the cream, if using.

Pea and Mint Soup

Preparation time: 10 minutes
Cooking time: 10 minutes

SERVES 4

oil

1 onion, finely chopped

900 ml chicken stock

500 g peas, fresh and podded or frozen

150 ml crème fraîche

1 tablespoon very finely chopped fresh mint

salt and freshly ground black pepper

To prepare ahead: Make the soup to the end of stage 4, then refrigerate or freeze.

1 Heat the oil in a large heavy saucepan, add the onion and sweat over a low heat until soft but not coloured. Add the stock, bring to a simmer and add the peas.

2 Simmer for 3–5 minutes until the peas are cooked.

3 Remove the soup from the heat and allow to cool for a minute or two, then whizz in a blender or food processor until smooth and push through a sieve into a rinsed-out saucepan. If it is a little thick add extra stock or water.

4 Reheat, add the crème fraîche and mint and season to taste with salt and pepper. Serve in warmed soup bowls.

VARIATIONS: For a milder mint flavour, cook the peas with a couple of sprigs of mint and remove before whizzing. Scatter shredded ham on the soup before serving. Alternatively, stir through cooked flaked smoked haddock.

Spanish Red Pepper and Rice Soup

This is a good way of using up leftover rice – but do make sure it is no more than 1 day old, has been stored correctly in a refrigerator and is fully heated through in stage 4. Alternatively, you can use uncooked rice and cook fully in stage 4, although you will need to add more stock or water to the pan.

Preparation time: 20 minutes
Cooking time: 40 minutes

SERVES 4–6

4 tablespoons olive oil

4 red peppers, grilled, skinned (see page 19) and cut into strips

1 Spanish onion, finely chopped

1 stick of celery, finely sliced

1 carrot, finely sliced

1 × 400 g can of chopped tomatoes

800 ml chicken stock

1 wine glass of medium-dry sherry

85 g long-grain rice, cooked

salt and freshly ground black pepper

To garnish

fresh basil leaves, torn

To prepare ahead: If you are using cooked rice, make the soup to the end of stage 3 and only add the rice when you are finally reheating. If you are cooking the rice in the soup, prepare ahead to the end of stage 5. Reheat thoroughly.

1 Heat the oil in a large, heavy saucepan. Add half the peppers to the pan with the onion, celery and carrot. Cook over a low heat until soft but not coloured, stirring occasionally (about 20 minutes).
2 Add the tomatoes, stock and sherry. Bring to the boil, then simmer for 5 minutes.
3 Whizz the soup in a blender or food processor until smooth and pass through a sieve. Return to the rinsed-out pan.
4 Add the rice and the remaining peppers and simmer until the rice is hot through. You may need to add more water or stock to the pan if the soup becomes too thick.
5 Season well with salt and pepper.
6 Stir the basil through the soup just before serving.

NOTE: It is possible to buy roasted and skinned peppers in jars from most supermarkets.

Bloody Mary Soup

Preparation time: 10 minutes
Cooking time: 35 minutes

SERVES 4–6

1 tablespoon oil	6–10 drops Tabasco, to taste
1 onion, roughly chopped	1 teaspoon sugar
1 clove of garlic	vodka
1 teaspoon crushed chillies	freshly ground black pepper
600 ml tomato passata	
600 ml chicken stock	**To garnish**
2–3 teaspoons Worcestershire sauce	celery leaves

To prepare ahead: Make the soup to the end of stage 3, then refrigerate or freeze.

1 Heat the oil in a large, heavy saucepan, add the onion and sweat over a low heat until soft but not coloured. Add the garlic and cook for 1 further minute.
2 Add the remaining ingredients except for the vodka. Season with pepper and bring to the boil, then simmer for 25 minutes. Allow to cool slightly, then whizz in a blender or food processor until smooth.
3 Strain through a sieve into the rinsed-out pan.
4 Reheat. Add the vodka just before serving, allowing up to a shot per serving. Serve in warmed soup bowls, garnished with the celery leaves.

NOTE: If passata is not available, use 2 × 400 g cans of chopped tomatoes.

Smoky Aubergine and Tomato Soup

Preparation time: 10 minutes
Cooking time: 40 minutes

SERVES 6

2 large aubergines, cut into 2.5 cm cubes
3 tablespoons olive oil
2 large pinches of smoked paprika
3 cloves of garlic
4 tomatoes, quartered

1.2 litres vegetable stock
salt and freshly ground black pepper

To garnish
50g Parmesan cheese, freshly grated
2 tablespoons shredded fresh basil

To prepare ahead: Make the soup to the end of stage 4, then refrigerate or freeze.

1 Preheat the oven to 190°C│375°F│gas mark 5.
2 Place the aubergines in a roasting pan, drizzle with half the oil and sprinkle over the paprika. Bake in the oven for 15 minutes. Turn the aubergines in the oil, add the garlic and tomatoes and bake for a further 10–15 minutes, or until the aubergines are soft.
3 Place the roast vegetables in a large, heavy saucepan with the stock and season with salt and pepper. Bring slowly to the boil, then simmer for 10 minutes.
4 Allow the soup to cool slightly, then whizz in a blender or food processor, in batches if necessary, until smooth. Return to the rinsed-out pan.
5 To serve: reheat, ladle into warmed soup bowls, and add the Parmesan and basil.

Tomato and Carrot Soup

Preparation time: 15 minutes
Cooking time: 25 minutes

SERVES 4–6

30 g butter
1 onion, chopped
4 carrots, peeled and sliced
6 tomatoes, roughly chopped

750 ml chicken stock
2 tablespoons crème fraîche or double cream
salt and freshly ground black pepper

To prepare ahead: Make the soup to the end of stage 3, then refrigerate or freeze.

1 Melt the butter in a large, heavy saucepan. Add the onions and carrots and sweat over a low heat for about 10–15 minutes, or until soft.
2 Add the tomatoes and stock and simmer for 5 minutes or until the carrots are cooked through. Season to taste with salt and pepper and allow to cool slightly.

3 Whizz the soup in a blender or food processor until smooth, then pass through a sieve.

4 Reheat, stir though the crème fraîche and serve in warmed soup bowls.

Cherry Tomato Soup with Basil Crème Fraîche

This soup can be served hot or cold.

Preparation time: 15 minutes
Cooking time: 20 minutes

SERVES 4

30 g butter

1 small red onion, finely chopped

1 clove of garlic, crushed

6 fresh basil stalks

680 g cherry tomatoes

300 ml chicken or vegetable stock

¼ teaspoon caster sugar

salt and freshly ground black pepper

For the basil cream

4 tablespoons crème fraîche

8 fresh basil leaves, shredded

salt and freshly ground black pepper

To prepare ahead: Make the soup to the end of stage 4, then refrigerate or freeze.

1 Melt the butter in a large, heavy saucepan. Add the onion and sweat over a low heat until soft but not coloured. Add the garlic and cook for 1 further minute. Add the basil stalks.

2 Add the tomatoes and cook over a low heat until they have softened and are releasing their juices.

3 Add the stock and bring to the boil, then simmer for 5 minutes.

4 Allow the soup to cool a little before whizzing in a blender or food processor until smooth. Push through a sieve into the rinsed-out pan.

5 Season the crème fraîche well with salt and pepper and stir the basil through it.

6 Season the soup with the sugar, salt and pepper and pour into warmed soup bowls. Spoon some of the basil cream into each bowl of soup just before serving.

Carrot and Chickpea Soup

Preparation time: 15 minutes
Cooking time: 40 minutes

SERVES 4

700 g carrots, peeled and sliced

1 onion, finely chopped

20 g butter

1 bunch of fresh coriander, leaves roughly chopped,
    stalks tied together

1 litre chicken stock

1 × 400 g can of chickpeas, drained and rinsed

salt and freshly ground black pepper

To garnish

Greek yoghurt

To prepare ahead: Make the soup in advance, then refrigerate or freeze.

1 Put the carrots and onion into a large, heavy saucepan with the butter. Sweat over a low heat for 10 minutes, or until beginning to soften. Add the coriander stalks (reserving the leaves), stock, salt and pepper. Bring to the boil, then simmer as slowly as possible for 25 minutes. Remove and discard the coriander stalks.

2 Whizz the soup in a food processor or blender until smooth, then push through a sieve into the rinsed-out pan. Adjust the seasoning and add the chickpeas.

3 Reheat and pour into warmed soup bowls. Place a spoonful of the yoghurt on each serving and scatter over the coriander leaves.

Carrot and Coriander Soup

Preparation time: 15 minutes
Cooking time: 30 minutes

SERVES 4

700 g carrots, peeled and sliced

1 onion, finely chopped

15 g butter

1 bay leaf

1 litre chicken or vegetable stock or water

1 tablespoon chopped fresh parsley

1 tablespoon chopped fresh coriander

4 tablespoons double cream

salt and freshly ground black pepper

To garnish

chopped fresh coriander

To prepare ahead: Make the soup in advance, then refrigerate or freeze.

1 Put the carrots and onion into a large, heavy saucepan with the butter. Sweat over a low heat for 10 minutes, or until beginning to soften. Add the bay leaf, stock, salt and

pepper. Bring to the boil, then simmer for 20 minutes, or until the carrots are tender. Remove the bay leaf.

2 Whizz the soup with the parsley and coriander in a blender or food processor until smooth, then push through a sieve into a clean saucepan. Check the consistency. If the soup is a little thin, reduce by rapid boiling; if a little thick, add extra water.

3 Add the cream and season to taste with salt and pepper.

4 Pour into warmed soup bowls and garnish with the coriander.

Celeriac and Stilton Soup

Preparation time: 15 minutes
Cooking time: 35 minutes

SERVES 6–8

1 tablespoon oil	1 × 142 ml pot of double cream
1 onion, finely chopped	120 g Stilton cheese, crumbled
1 small celeriac, peeled and cut into 1 cm cubes	salt and freshly ground black pepper
1.5 litres vegetable stock	

To prepare ahead: This soup can be prepared in advance, but do not allow it to boil when reheating as this can affect the texture.

1 Heat the oil in a large, heavy saucepan, add the onion and sweat over a low heat until soft but not coloured. Add the celeriac and mix well.

2 Add the stock and season with salt and pepper. Bring to the boil, then simmer for 25 minutes, or until the celeriac is soft.

3 Add the cream and Stilton, remove from the heat and stir until the Stilton has melted.

4 Whizz in a blender or food processor, in batches if necessary, until smooth, then return to the rinsed-out pan.

5 Reheat and adjust the seasoning to taste. Serve in warmed soup bowls.

Spiced Parsnip Soup

Preparation time: 10 minutes
Cooking time: 25 minutes

SERVES 4

2 tablespoons olive oil
1 medium onion, finely chopped
350 g parsnips, peeled and diced
1 teaspoon ground coriander
1 teaspoon ground cumin

½ teaspoon chilli flakes
850 ml chicken stock
1 × 142 ml pot of single cream
salt and freshly ground black pepper

To prepare ahead: Make the soup to the end of stage 4, then refrigerate or freeze.

1 Heat the oil in a large, heavy saucepan, add the onion and sweat over a low heat until beginning to soften, then add the parsnips and cook, covered, until just soft.
2 Add the coriander, cumin and chilli flakes and cook for 1 minute.
3 Add the stock, salt and pepper and bring to the boil, then simmer for 20 minutes. Allow to cool slightly.
4 Whizz the soup in a blender or food processor until smooth and return to the rinsed-out pan. Add the cream and reheat without boiling. Season to taste with salt and pepper and serve in warmed soup bowls.

Thai Butternut Squash Soup

Preparation time: 5 minutes
Cooking time: 30 minutes

SERVES 4–6

1 tablespoon oil
1 onion, finely chopped
½–1 tablespoon Thai green curry paste
2 medium butternut squash, peeled, deseeded and
   cut into chunks
500 ml chicken stock
1 × 400 ml can of coconut milk

2 tablespoons shredded Thai basil
salt and freshly ground black pepper

To garnish
crème fraîche or coconut cream
coriander leaves

To prepare ahead: Make the soup to the end of stage 4, then refrigerate or freeze.

1 Heat the oil in a large, heavy saucepan, add the onion and sweat over a low heat for 10 minutes.

2 Add the Thai curry paste and cook over a low heat for 1 minute.

3 Add the butternut squash, stock and coconut milk. Bring to the boil, then season with salt and pepper and simmer for up to 20 minutes, or until the squash is soft.

4 Remove from the heat and whizz the soup in a blender or food processor, in batches if necessary, until smooth. Return to the rinsed-out pan. Check the seasoning.

5 Reheat the soup and add the basil just before serving.

6 Pour into warmed soup bowls and serve with a spoonful of crème fraîche or swirl in the coconut cream and scatter over the coriander.

Butternut Squash and Thyme Soup

Preparation time: 10 minutes
Cooking time: 40 minutes.

SERVES 4

700 g butternut squash, peeled, deseeded and cut into chunks

1 onion, finely chopped

20 g butter

1 bay leaf (optional)

900 ml chicken or vegetable stock

½ tablespoon chopped fresh thyme

4 tablespoons double cream (optional)

salt and freshly ground black pepper

To prepare ahead: Make the soup in advance, then refrigerate or freeze.

1 Put the squash and onion into a large, heavy saucepan with the butter. Sweat over a low heat for 10 minutes, or until beginning to soften. Add the bay leaf, stock and a little salt and pepper.

2 Bring to the boil, then simmer as slowly as possible for 25 minutes, or until the squash is soft.

3 Whizz the soup in a blender or food processor, in batches if necessary, until smooth. Return to the rinsed-out pan. Stir in the thyme and the cream, if using, and check the consistency. If the soup is too thin, reduce by boiling rapidly; if too thick, add extra stock or water.

4 Season to taste with salt and pepper and serve in warmed soup bowls.

Spiced Roast Squash and Carrot Soup

Preparation time: 10 minutes
Cooking time: 40 minutes

SERVES 4

1 butternut squash, peeled and deseeded

5 carrots, peeled

chilli oil

1 onion, finely chopped

600 ml chicken or vegetable stock

salt and freshly ground black pepper

To garnish

crème fraîche

chopped fresh chives

To prepare ahead: Make the soup to the end of stage 4, then refrigerate or freeze.

1 Preheat the oven to 200°C│400°F│gas mark 6.
2 Chop the butternut squash and carrots into cubes. Place in a roasting pan and drizzle over some chilli oil, then season with salt and pepper. Roast in the oven, turning occasionally, for 20–30 minutes, or until soft.
3 Meanwhile, heat a little more chilli oil in a heavy pan, add the onion and sweat until soft but not coloured. Add the stock and vegetables and bring to the boil.
4 Whizz the soup in a blender or food processor until smooth. Return to the rinsed-out pan. Reheat, add a little more stock if too thick, and adjust the seasoning if necessary.
5 Pour into warmed soup bowls and place a teaspoon of crème fraîche in the centre of each. Scatter the chives on top.

Sweet Potato, Chilli and Lime Soup

Preparation time: 10 minutes
Cooking time: 35 minutes

SERVES 6

1 tablespoon oil

1 small onion, finely chopped

1–2 red chillies, chopped

2 sweet potatoes, peeled and cut into chunks

grated zest and juice of 2 limes

1.2 litres chicken or vegetable stock

salt and freshly ground black pepper

To garnish

double cream, crème fraîche or plain yoghurt

To prepare ahead: Make the soup to the end of stage 4, then refrigerate or freeze.

1 Heat the oil in a large, heavy saucepan. Add the onion and sweat over a low heat until soft but not coloured. Add the chilli and cook for 1 further minute.

2 Add the sweet potatoes and lime zest and cook with the onion and chilli for 1 further minute. Add the stock. Bring to the boil, then simmer slowly for about 15–20 minutes, until the sweet potatoes are cooked through.

3 Remove from the heat and allow the soup to cool slightly. Whizz in a blender or food processor until smooth, then strain through a sieve back into the rinsed-out pan.

4 Season to taste with salt, pepper and lime juice.

5 Reheat and serve in warmed soup bowls with a spoonful of cream, crème fraîche or yoghurt on each serving.

Maple Roast Parsnip Soup

Preparation time: 10 minutes
Cooking time: 40 minutes

SERVES 4–6

700 g parsnips, peeled and cubed
olive oil
1 large onion, chopped
4 tablespoons maple syrup

1 litre hot chicken or vegetable stock
3 tablespoons crème fraîche
salt and freshly ground black pepper

To prepare ahead: Make the soup to the end of stage 4, then refrigerate or freeze.

1 Preheat the oven to 190°C|375°F|gas mark 5.

2 Place the parsnips in a large roasting pan, drizzle with a little oil and season with salt and pepper. Roast in the oven for 15 minutes.

3 Turn the parsnips and add the onion, then return to the oven for a further 15 minutes, or until the vegetables are beginning to soften and brown. Drizzle over the maple syrup and continue to roast for a further 10 minutes. Do not allow the vegetables to burn.

4 Remove the vegetables from the oven and whizz in a blender or food processor, in batches if necessary, with the stock. Pass through a sieve into a pan.

5 To serve: reheat the soup and stir in the crème fraîche, adjust the seasoning as necessary and serve immediately in warmed soup bowls.

Sweet Potato and Pea Soup with Bacon

Preparation time: 15 minutes
Cooking time: 35 minutes

SERVES 4–6

1 tablespoon oil

8 rashers of dry-cure bacon, finely diced, or a piece of pancetta cut into small cubes

1 onion, finely chopped

1 medium sweet potato, peeled and diced

1.2 litres vegetable, chicken or ham stock

250 g frozen peas or petits pois

salt and freshly ground black pepper

To garnish

1 tablespoon chopped fresh parsley

To prepare ahead: Make the soup in advance, then refrigerate or freeze.

1 Heat the oil in a large, heavy saucepan, add the bacon and fry over a medium heat until just beginning to brown.
2 Remove half of the bacon with a slotted spoon and set aside.
3 Add the onion and potato to the bacon in the pan. Reduce the heat and sweat over a low heat for about 10 minutes, until the onion is soft but not coloured.
4 Add the stock to the pan and bring to the boil, then simmer for about 20 minutes, depending on the size of the dice, until the sweet potato is soft.
5 Add all but 2 tablespoons of the peas. Bring to the boil, then simmer for 2 minutes. Cool slightly, then whizz the mixture in a blender or food processor, in batches if necessary, until completely smooth.
6 Return the soup to the rinsed-out pan. Add more water if necessary. The soup should lightly coat the back of a spoon. Stir in the reserved peas and bacon and season to taste with salt and pepper.
7 Reheat and add the parsley. Serve in warmed soup bowls.

NOTE: If you have any leftover ham from a joint this can be used in place of the bacon.

Pumpkin Soup

Preparation time: 10 minutes
Cooking time: 35 minutes

SERVES 6–8

oil

1 onion, peeled and chopped

1 leek, sliced and washed

1 tablespoon masala curry paste

900 g pumpkin, peeled, deseeded and chopped

1.2 litres chicken stock

salt and freshly ground black pepper

To garnish

6 slices of white bread

To prepare ahead: Make the soup to the end of stage 3, then refrigerate or freeze.

1 Heat the oil in a large, heavy saucepan. Add the onion and leek and sweat over a low heat, until soft but not coloured. Add the curry paste and cook for 1 further minute.
2 Add the pumpkin and stock. Bring to the boil, then simmer for 25 minutes, or until the pumpkin is cooked through. Remove from the heat and allow to cool slightly.
3 Whizz the soup in a blender or food processor in batches. Return to the rinsed-out pan. Reheat and season to taste with salt and pepper.
4 Toast the bread, remove the crusts and stamp out into crescents using a pastry cutter.
5 Pour the soup into warmed soup bowls and float the croûtons on top.

NOTE: This is a good soup for Hallowe'en and Bonfire Night, hence the moon-shaped croûtons. Otherwise just use ordinary croûtons (see page 380).

White Winter Vegetable Soup

Preparation time: 15 minutes
Cooking time: 40 minutes

SERVES 6–8

1 medium onion, finely chopped
60 g butter
white part of 1 leek, finely sliced and washed
1 parsnip, peeled and finely diced
½ small cauliflower, cut into small florets
2 sticks of celery, finely sliced

½ small celeriac, peeled and finely diced
1.2 litres vegetable stock
300 ml milk
salt and freshly ground black pepper

To garnish
2 tablespoons finely chopped fresh parsley

To prepare ahead: Make the soup to the end of stage 4, then refrigerate or freeze.

1 Place the onion in a large, heavy saucepan with the butter and sweat over a low heat until the onion begins to soften.
2 Add the remaining vegetables and cook, covered, until just softening (about 10 minutes).
3 Add the stock and season to taste with salt and pepper. Bring to the boil, then reduce the heat and simmer for 20 minutes. Allow to cool slightly.
4 Whizz the soup in a blender or food processor until smooth, then return to the rinsed-out pan. Add the milk. Check the seasoning.
5 Reheat the soup and serve in warmed soup bowls, with the parsley scattered on top.

Simple Vegetable Soup

Preparation time: 10 minutes
Cooking time: 35 minutes

SERVES 4

30 g butter
1 onion, chopped
200 g carrots, chopped
1 stick of celery, chopped
100 g potatoes, chopped

450 ml vegetable stock or water
200 ml milk
salt and freshly ground black pepper

To prepare ahead: Make the soup to the end of stage 3, then refrigerate or freeze.

1 Melt the butter in a large, heavy saucepan. Stir in the onion, carrots and celery. Sweat over a low heat for about 20 minutes, or until soft but not coloured, stirring occasionally.
2 Add the potatoes and stock or water. Season with salt and pepper and simmer, uncovered, for 15 minutes.
3 Whizz the soup in a blender or food processor, with the milk, until smooth, then sieve. Pour into the rinsed-out pan. Check the seasoning and add water as required if the soup is too thick.
4 Reheat without boiling and serve in warmed soup bowls.

VARIATION: The vegetable selection used in this recipe can be varied according to availability.

Watercress and Potato Soup

Preparation time: 15 minutes
Cooking time: 20 minutes

SERVES 4

30 g butter
1 medium onion, chopped
225 g potatoes, diced
600 ml chicken or vegetable stock
2 bunches of watercress, chopped
300 ml milk

a pinch of freshly grated nutmeg
salt and freshly ground black pepper

To garnish
chopped fresh chives

To prepare ahead: Make the soup to the end of stage 3, then refrigerate or freeze. If frozen, it may need to be whizzed again once it has defrosted if it has separated.

1 Melt the butter in a large, heavy saucepan, add the onion and sweat over a low heat until soft but not coloured. Add the potatoes and stock and simmer for 10 minutes, or until the potatoes are tender. Stir in the watercress, then remove immediately from the heat.

2 Whizz the soup in a blender or food processor until smooth, then push it through a sieve. Pour into the rinsed-out pan.

3 Add enough of the milk to achieve the required consistency and season to taste with salt, pepper and nutmeg.

4 Reheat until the soup is just below boiling point. Serve in warmed soup bowls, garnished with the chives.

VARIATION: This soup can be made with rocket instead of watercress.

Beetroot Soup with Soured Cream

Preparation time: 20 minutes

SERVES 4

675 g cooked beetroots

900 ml chicken or vegetable stock

1–2 teaspoons ground cumin or caraway seeds
  (optional)

caster sugar

salt and freshly ground black pepper

To garnish

soured cream

chopped fresh chives

To prepare ahead: This soup improves if prepared a day in advance and kept chilled in the refrigerator.

1 Peel the beetroots, cut roughly into small pieces and whizz in a food processor or blender (use a little of the stock to help reduce the beetroot to a purée).

2 Push the purée through a fine sieve, then add the remaining stock to give a thick consistency which will still easily run from a spoon.

3 Season the soup to taste with cumin or caraway if using, sugar, salt and pepper. Chill.

4 Ladle the beetroot soup into ice-cold soup plates. Place a spoonful of soured cream on the top of each serving and scatter with the chives.

NOTE: This soup can also be served hot. If preferred, use raw beetroot, but they can take up to 1 hour to cook. For added piquancy, stir in 2 tablespoons creamed horseradish after blending.

Cold Cucumber Soup

Preparation time: 25 minutes

SERVES 4

1 large cucumber

300 ml plain yoghurt

1 × 142 ml pot of double cream

2 tablespoons white wine vinegar

2 tablespoons olive oil

salt and freshly ground white pepper

To garnish

chopped fresh mint (optional)

1 Peel, deseed and chop the cucumber (see page 12). Sprinkle with salt and leave for 15 minutes.

2 Rinse the cucumber and place in a blender or food processor with the remaining soup ingredients.

3 Whizz until smooth. If necessary, add a little more cream or some milk to achieve the desired consistency.

4 Chill in the refrigerator and stir in the mint, if using, just before serving.

Vichyssoise

Preparation time: 15 minutes
Cooking time: 30 minutes

SERVES 4

60 g butter

1 medium onion, finely chopped

white part of 3 large or 5 small leeks, washed and
  chopped

110 g potatoes, peeled and sliced

300 ml chicken stock

300 ml milk

2 tablespoons single cream

salt and freshly ground white pepper

To garnish

chopped fresh chives

extra cream (optional)

To prepare ahead: Make the soup to the end of stage 5, then refrigerate or freeze.

1 Melt the butter in a large, heavy saucepan, add the onion and leek and sweat over a low heat for 15 minutes, or until soft but not brown.

2 Add the potatotes, salt and pepper and the stock. Simmer until the potatoes are soft.

3 Whizz the soup in a blender or food processor until smooth, then push it through a sieve.

4 Add the milk and cream. (Check the consistency before adding all the milk.)

5 Check the seasoning, then chill. Add the chives just before serving in chilled soup bowls, with an extra swirl of cream on each serving if desired. Alternatively, serve this hot.

Gazpacho

Preparation time: 30 minutes

SERVES 6

1 kg fresh, very ripe tomatoes, peeled (see page 22)

1 Spanish onion

2 red peppers

1 small cucumber

1 thick slice of white bread, crust removed

1 egg yolk

2 large cloves of garlic

6 tablespoons olive oil

1 tablespoon tarragon vinegar

1 × 400 g can of tomatoes

1 tablespoon tomato purée

salt and freshly ground black pepper

To garnish

croûtons (see page 380)

1 Chop or dice finely a small amount of the fresh tomato, onion, red pepper and cucumber and set aside for the garnish. Roughly chop the remaining vegetables.

2 Put the bread, egg yolk and garlic into a blender or food processor. Turn it on and add the oil in a thin steady stream while the motor is running. You should end up with a thick, mayonnaise-like emulsion.

3 Add the vinegar and then gradually add all the soup ingredients in batches and whizz until smooth.

4 Sieve the soup to remove the tomato seeds, if preferred, and add salt and pepper to taste. Chill well.

5 To serve: Check the seasoning and ladle into chilled bowls. Sprinkle the croûtons and reserved vegetables on top, or if preferred hand them separately.

NOTE: There is quite a lot of chopping to be done to make this version of the classic Spanish soup. The garnish needs careful chopping, but the rest can be roughly chopped, then whizzed in a blender or food processor. Gazpacho should be served icy cold. Sometimes crushed ice is added to the soup at the last minute. If you prefer a thinner soup, dilute it with iced water or tomato juice.

Chicken and Tarragon Soup

This recipe calls for roast chicken. Use leftover roast chicken or alternatively roast chicken breasts are available in many supermarkets.

Preparation time: 10 minutes
Cooking time: 30 minutes

SERVES 4–6

50 g butter	600 ml milk
80 g button mushrooms, sliced	225 g roast chicken, cut into small pieces
50 g plain flour	1 teaspoon chopped fresh tarragon
½ glass of dry white wine	salt and freshly ground black pepper
500 ml chicken stock	

To prepare ahead: Make the soup to the end of stage 3, then refrigerate or freeze.

1 Melt the butter in a large, heavy saucepan. Stir in the mushrooms and cook over a low heat until soft. Add the flour and cook for 1 minute over a medium heat.
2 Gradually add the wine and stock, stirring to incorporate the flour. Stir in the milk, add the chicken and bring to the boil. Season to taste with salt and pepper.
3 Simmer for 15 minutes. Adjust the consistency, adding more milk if necessary.
4 Stir in the tarragon and serve in warmed soup bowls.

Chicken Noodle Soup

This is a good recipe for using up leftover roast chicken.

Preparation time: 15 minutes
Cooking time: 10 minutes

SERVES 4

1.2 litres chicken stock	225 g cooked chicken or turkey, shredded
1 × 2.5 cm piece of stem ginger, peeled and finely chopped	2 tablespoons light soy sauce
	1 tablespoon nam pla (Thai fish sauce)
2 cloves of garlic, finely chopped	salt and freshly ground black pepper
1 red chilli, deseeded and finely chopped	
85 g fine egg noodles	**To garnish**
1 × 200 g can of sweetcorn, drained and rinsed	chopped fresh coriander

To prepare ahead: Make the soup to the end of stage 3, then refrigerate or freeze.

1 Put the stock, ginger, garlic and chilli into a large, heavy saucepan. Bring to the boil, then simmer for 5 minutes.
2 Cook the noodles according to the manufacturer's instructions. Drain and cut into small lengths, using kitchen scissors.
3 Add the sweetcorn, chicken or turkey and the noodles to the pan. Season with the soy sauce, nam pla, salt and pepper, and bring back to a simmer.
4 Ladle into warmed soup bowls and sprinkle generously with coriander.

NOTE: If nam pla is not available, use more soy sauce instead.

Pasta and Bacon Soup

Preparation time: 10 minutes
Cooking time: 20 minutes

SERVES 4

oil, for frying
1 onion, finely chopped
4 carrots, diced
80 g bacon lardons
1 clove of garlic, crushed
1 × 500 ml bottle of tomato passata
700 ml vegetable stock

60 g small pasta for soup
salt and freshly ground black pepper

To garnish
freshly grated Gruyère cheese
chopped fresh chives

To prepare ahead: Make the soup to the end of stage 2, then refrigerate or freeze.

1 Heat the oil in a large, heavy saucepan, add the onion and carrots and sweat over a low heat until soft. Increase the heat, add the bacon and cook until golden brown. Add the garlic and cook for 1 further minute.
2 Add the passata and stock, season to taste with salt and pepper and bring to boil. Add the pasta and cook until al dente. Check the seasoning.
3 Pour into warmed soup bowls and sprinkle with the Gruyère cheese and chives.

NOTE: If you can't find pasta specifically labelled for soup, use the smallest shapes you can find.

Smoked Bacon and Lentil Soup

Preparation time: 20 minutes
Cooking time: 20 minutes

SERVES 4

20 g butter

1 onion, chopped

225 g smoked bacon lardons

1 clove of garlic, crushed

1 × 400 g can of green lentils, drained and
   rinsed

250 ml tomato passata

6 tomatoes, peeled, deseeded and roughly chopped
   (see page 22)

750 ml chicken stock

salt and freshly ground black pepper

To prepare ahead: Make up to 24 hours in advance to the end of stage 3, then reheat as required. This soup can also be frozen but the lentils may break up on reheating.

1 Melt the butter in a large, heavy saucepan. Add the onion and sweat over a low heat until soft but not coloured.
2 Add the bacon to the pan and cook until the fat has rendered down and the bacon is becoming golden. Add the garlic and cook for 1 minute.
3 Add the lentils, passata, tomatoes and stock and simmer for 10 minutes. Season to taste with salt and pepper. Serve in warmed soup bowls.

Smoked Haddock and Spinach Soup

Preparation time: 10 minutes
Cooking time: 30 minutes

SERVES 4–6

1 tablespoon oil

300 g potatoes, peeled and cut into small cubes

3 cloves of garlic, crushed

1.7 litres fish or vegetable stock

freshly grated nutmeg

1 × 200 g bag of spinach leaves

350 g smoked haddock, skinned and cut into pieces

salt and freshly ground black pepper

To prepare ahead: Make the soup to the end of stage 4, then refrigerate or freeze.

1 Heat the oil in a large, heavy saucepan. Add the potatoes and garlic and cook over a low heat for 2–3 minutes.
2 Add the stock and bring up to the boil. Season with nutmeg, salt and pepper and simmer slowly until the potatoes are cooked.
3 Add the spinach and cook for a further 2 minutes.

4 Whizz the soup in a blender or food processor, in batches if necessary, until smooth. Return the soup to the rinsed-out pan.

5 Reheat, add the haddock pieces and cook over a low heat for 3 minutes or until the fish is just cooked. Adjust the seasoning to taste and serve in warmed soup bowls.

Smoked Haddock Chowder

Preparation time: 10 minutes
Cooking time: 25 minutes

SERVES 4

30 g butter	150 ml milk
1 large onion, chopped	1 × 142 ml pot of double cream or crème fraîche
125 g bacon lardons	350 g smoked haddock, skinned and cut into pieces
1 large potato, peeled and cut into small chunks	60 g peas, fresh or frozen
450 ml fish or vegetable stock	salt and freshly ground black pepper

To prepare ahead: Make the soup to the end of stage 4, then refrigerate or freeze.

1 Melt the butter in a large, heavy saucepan, add the onions and sweat over a low heat until soft but not coloured.

2 Add the bacon and cook until golden.

3 Add the potato and stock and bring to the boil. Allow to simmer until the potato is cooked.

4 Add the milk and cream or crème fraîche and bring to a gentle simmer.

5 Add the haddock and peas and continue to cook until the haddock is cooked through. Try not to stir too much or the fish will break up. Add more stock if necessary.

6 Season to taste with salt and pepper. Serve immediately in warmed soup bowls.

Tom Yum Soup

Preparation time: 10 minutes
Cooking time: 5–10 minutes

3–4 tablespoons tom yum paste
800 ml boiling water
2 tomatoes, deseeded and chopped (see page 22) or
  6 cherry tomatoes, quartered
6 mushrooms, sliced or quartered

fresh lime juice
nam pla (Thai fish sauce) (optional)
200 g raw tiger prawns, peeled and deveined
50 g mangetout, finely sliced on the diagonal
roughly chopped fresh coriander

To prepare ahead: Make the soup to the end of stage 2 then refrigerate or freeze.

1 Place the tom yum paste in a large, heavy saucepan and add the boiling water. Stir well to dissolve the paste.
2 Place over a medium heat and add the tomatoes and mushrooms. Simmer for 3 minutes. Taste and, if desired, add more tom yum paste. Season to taste with the lime juice and fish sauce.
3 Add the prawns and cook for a further 1–2 minutes or until they turn pink.
4 Stir in the mangetout and coriander and serve in warmed soup bowls.

NOTES: Cooked shredded chicken can be added in place of the prawns and the soup can be made more substantial with the addition of rice noodles.

    The amount of tom yum paste added to the soup varies according to taste. If you are unsure, start cautiously and gradually add more while making the soup. Try to use an authentic Thai brand.

Tarts and Parcels

The tarts and parcels in this section can be made in different sizes for different appetites and can also make delicious and different picnic food. Most busy cooks will use bought pastry, but for those who would prefer to make it themselves, all the recipes are in the Leiths Basic Recipes section (see page 516).

Camembert and Onion Parcels

Preparation time: 15 minutes
Cooking time: 10 minutes

SERVES 4–8

1 × 220 g ripe Camembert cheese
3 tablespoons caramelized onions or onion marmalade (see page 508)
24 sheets of filo pastry

melted butter
beaten egg, to glaze

To serve
green salad (see page 381)

To prepare ahead: Make in advance to the end of stage 6, then refrigerate, well covered, so that the parcels will not dry out, and bake as required.

1 Preheat the oven to 200°C|400°F|gas mark 6.
2 Cut the Camembert into 8 equal wedges.
3 Cut the filo sheets into 20 cm squares and brush with melted butter. Arrange 3 squares on top of one another, overlapping to give a star shape.
4 Place a wedge of Camembert in the centre and spoon half a tablespoon of the caramelized onions or marmalade on the top. Repeat, using up the remaining pastry and cheese.
5 Draw the sides of the pastry up around the cheese and pinch together at the top.
6 Brush with beaten egg.
7 Place the parcels on a baking sheet and bake in the oven for 10 minutes, or until golden brown.
8 Serve immediately with a green salad.

Chicken, Mushroom and Garden Pea Puffs

Cooked leftover chicken can be used in this recipe in place of the chicken breasts.

Preparation time: 30 minutes, plus cooling time
Cooking time: 30–35 minutes

SERVES 4

30 g butter	30 g plain flour
1 leek, finely chopped and washed	150 ml chicken stock
2 chicken breast fillets, skinned and cubed	500 g puff pastry
80 g brown cap mushrooms, chopped	beaten egg, to glaze
60 g frozen garden peas	salt and freshly ground black pepper

To prepare ahead: The puffs can be assembled in advance, then baked as required. Alternatively they can be frozen, then defrosted in the refrigerator and baked as required.

Serving suggestions: Green salad (see page 381), borlotti bean and fennel salad (see page 335), spring onion and radish salad (see page 333)

1 Preheat the oven to 200°C|400°F|gas mark 6.

2 Heat the butter in a heavy saucepan, add the leek and sweat over a low heat until soft. Add the chicken and fry for 5 minutes, or until the chicken is cooked.

3 Add the mushrooms and peas and cook for a further 2 minutes. Add the flour, stir and cook for 30 seconds. Remove from the heat, then add the stock and mix well. Return to the heat and simmer for 2 minutes. Season to taste with salt and pepper, then allow to cool.

4 On a floured surface, roll out the puff pastry to the thickness of a £1 coin and cut into 4 × 18 cm diameter circles. Divide the filling mixture into 4 and place a portion on one half of each circle. Fold over the other edge of the circle and seal the edges with a little water. Press down firmly so they are well sealed, then lightly score a pattern on the sealed edges, using either a sharp knife or the prongs of a fork.

5 Place the puffs on a baking sheet and brush with beaten egg. Bake on the top shelf of the oven for 30–35 minutes, or until they are well risen and golden brown. Serve immediately.

Crab and Asparagus Tart

Preparation time: 20 minutes
Cooking time: 25 minutes

SERVES 6

375 g ready-rolled shortcrust pastry

1 tablespoon oil

2 shallots, finely chopped

6–8 asparagus spears

2 eggs, beaten

150 ml crab or lobster bisque

1½ tablespoons finely chopped fresh dill

1 × 170g can of crabmeat, drained

1 tablespoon lemon juice

salt and freshly ground black pepper

To prepare ahead: Complete to the end of stage 6. Assemble and cook as required.

Serving suggestions: Green salad (see page 381), Italian tomato salad (see page 334), new potato, dill and caper salad (see page 337), soda bread (see page 462)

1 Line a 24 cm flan ring with the pastry, chill for 15 minutes and bake blind (see page 18).

2 Preheat the oven to 190°C|375°F|gas mark 5.

3 Heat the oil in a heavy saucepan, add the shallots and sweat until soft but not coloured.

4 Prepare the asparagus: trim off the woody ends – if you bend the stems they tend to snap into two, leaving you with one end to discard (the root end) and one to keep. Trim the spears from the tip into 10 cm lengths and reserve. Cut the remaining stems into slices, add to the onion mix and allow to soften. Remove from the heat and allow to cool.

5 Very lightly blanch and refresh the 10 cm long asparagus tips in boiling water (see page 9).

6 Beat together the eggs and add the bisque, the asparagus and onion mixture, the dill, crabmeat, lemon juice and plenty of salt and pepper. Pour the mixture into the pastry case and arrange the reserved asparagus tips on the top. Bake in the oven for 25–30 minutes, or until just set and lightly browned.

NOTE: This tart can be served warm or cold. Crab or lobster bisque is available in cans from the soup section of most supermarkets.

Crab and Prawn Rolls

Preparation time: 30 minutes
Cooking time: 2 minutes

MAKES 12–15

20 g butter

3 spring onions, finely sliced on the diagonal

1 small red chilli, finely chopped

2 teaspoons pickled ginger, finely chopped

2 × 170 g cans of crabmeat, drained

120 g cooked prawns

grated zest of 1 lime

1 packet of spring roll wrappers

oil, for deep frying (see page 12)

salt and freshly ground black pepper

To serve

sweet chilli dipping sauce

1 Melt the butter in a small frying pan, add the spring onions and sweat over a low heat until soft. In a bowl, mix together the chilli, ginger, crabmeat, prawns and lime zest and season to taste with salt and pepper. Stir in the spring onions.

2 Put a portion of the filling in the centre of each spring roll wrapper and fold the 2 opposite corners on top of it. Then roll up from one of the exposed corners to form rolls. Seal the ends with a little water.

3 Heat the oil in a deep fryer or large, heavy saucepan until a crumb will sizzle vigorously in it in 20 seconds, and add the spring rolls. Fry until golden brown, then drain well on kitchen paper. Sprinkle lightly with salt and serve immediately with the dipping sauce.

VARIATION: Use strips of filo pastry in place of spring roll wrappers. Bake brushed in oil at 200°C|400°F|gas mark 6 for 20 minutes instead of frying.

Blue Cheese and Leek Tartlets

Preparation time: 15 minutes
Chilling time: at least 15 minutes
Cooking time: 30 minutes

SERVES 4

30 g butter

2 medium leeks, outer leaves discarded, then finely chopped and well washed

375 g ready-rolled puff pastry

50 g ham, shredded

170 g strong blue cheese, crumbled

1 tablespoon Dijon mustard

beaten egg, to glaze

freshly ground black pepper

To prepare ahead: Make in advance to the end of stage 5, then refrigerate.

1 Preheat the oven to 200°C | 400°F | gas mark 6. Heat the butter in a heavy saucepan, add the leeks and sweat over a low heat until soft, allowing any liquid to evaporate. Remove from the heat and allow to cool.

2 On a floured surface, cut the pastry into 4 × 11 cm squares. Using a sharp knife, score a 1 cm border around the sides of each square. Prick the centre of the pastry case all over with a fork. Place the squares on a baking sheet and chill for at least 15 minutes.

3 Add the ham and 110 g of the cheese to the leeks. Season with pepper.

4 Remove the pastry cases from the refrigerator and spread the mustard over the centre of each. Then pile on the leek and cheese mixture, keeping it within the border and making sure it covers the mustard. Sprinkle over the remaining cheese.

5 Brush the borders with beaten egg and chill for 15 minutes.

6 Bake in the oven for 20 minutes, or until the pastry is golden brown and cooked through.

Fig and Goat's Cheese Parcels

Preparation time: 10 minutes
Cooking time: 15 minutes

SERVES 4

8 sheets of filo pastry, cut into 16 cm squares

melted butter

2 crottin cheeses, cut in half horizontally

2 ripe figs, quartered

2 teaspoons clear honey

grated zest of 1 lime

beaten egg, to glaze

To serve

green salad (see page 381)

To prepare ahead: Make in advance to the end of stage 6, then refrigerate, well covered.

1 Preheat the oven to 190°C | 375°F | gas mark 5.

2 For each parcel take 1 square of filo pastry, brush with melted butter and place another sheet on top at an angle.

3 Arrange the crottin halves in the centre of each square.

4 Place 2 fig quarters on each crottin half, drizzle over the honey and scatter over the lime zest.

5 Draw up the edges of each square to form a pouch and place on a baking sheet.

6 Brush the parcels with beaten egg.

7 Bake in the oven for 15 minutes, or until golden brown. Allow to cool slightly, then serve with a green salad.

Caramelized Onion and Goat's Cheese Tarts

Preparation time: 15 minutes
Chilling time: 15 minutes
Cooking time: 45 minutes

SERVES 4

2 tablespoons oil

700 g onions, very finely sliced

1 tablespoon chopped fresh thyme

2 tablespoons soft dark brown sugar

2 tablespoons balsamic vinegar

flour, for rolling

375 g ready-rolled puff pastry

60 g goat's cheese, crumbled

salt and freshly ground black pepper

To prepare ahead: Make in advance to the end of stage 5 but allow the onions to cool completely before filling the cases. Reheat for 10–15 minutes or until the tarts are hot through and the cheese is melting.

1 Preheat the oven to 200°C|400°F|gas mark 6.
2 Put the oil, onions, thyme, sugar and vinegar into a large roasting pan and season with salt and pepper. Stir to cover the onions in the seasonings, then place in the oven for 15 minutes. Stir again and continue to cook until the onions are soft and caramelized, about 30 minutes.
3 Meanwhile, on a floured surface, cut the pastry into 4 even-sized rectangles. Mark a border around the sides of each rectangle and prick the centre of the rectangle all over with a fork. Chill for 15 minutes.
4 Bake the pastry cases on the top shelf of the oven for 15–20 minutes, or until brown and crisp.
5 Remove the pastry cases from the oven. Fill with the onions and sprinkle over the goat's cheese.
6 Return to the oven for 5 minutes, or until the goat's cheese is just beginning to melt. Serve immediately.

NOTE: It is possible to buy caramelized onions, which you can use to fill the tarts instead of caramelizing the onions as above. This can also be made as one large tart.

VARIATION: A blue cheese such as Stilton also works well in this recipe in place of the goat's cheese.

Egg Florentine Tarts

Preparation time: 15 minutes
Chilling time: 15 minutes
Cooking time: 20 minutes

SERVES 4

flour, for rolling

375 g ready-rolled puff pastry

450 g fresh spinach, well washed and large stalks
   removed

4 tablespoons crème fraîche

freshly grated nutmeg

4 eggs

salt and freshly ground black pepper

To prepare ahead: Cook the pastry and spinach, then refrigerate and assemble and bake as required, increasing the cooking time in stage 5 to 8 minutes.

1 Preheat the oven to 200°C|400°F|gas mark 6.

2 On a floured surface, cut the pastry into 4 even-sized rectangles. Mark a 1 cm border around the sides of each square and prick the centre all over with a fork. Chill for 15 minutes.

3 Place the puff pastry rectangles on a baking sheet. Bake in the oven for 15 minutes.

4 Meanwhile, place the spinach in a large pan over a low heat and allow it to wilt. Alternatively, place the spinach in a colander and pour over a kettle full of boiling water. When wilted, squeeze as much water as possible from the spinach by pressing between 2 plates. Chop the spinach and stir in the crème fraîche, then season well with nutmeg, salt and pepper.

5 Remove the pastry cases from the oven. Pile the spinach mixture into each case, leaving a slight dip in the centre, and return to the oven for 3 minutes.

6 Remove the tarts from the oven and crack an egg into the middle of each. Return to the oven for 5–7 minutes, or until the egg is just set. Serve immediately, seasoned with salt and pepper.

VARIATION: A mixture of sautéed mushrooms works well in place of the spinach.

Pear and Roquefort Tart

Preparation time: 15 minutes, plus chilling time
Cooking time: 25 minutes

SERVES 4

375 g ready-rolled puff pastry

2 pears

60 g Roquefort cheese, crumbled

Serving suggestion: Watercress salad with French dressing made with walnut oil

1 Preheat the oven to 200°C│400°F│gas mark 6.
2 On a floured surface cut the pastry into 4 × 11 cm diameter circles. Place on a baking sheet. Using a sharp knife, score a border about 1 cm from the edge of each pastry circle. Do not cut all the way through the pastry.
3 Peel, core and thinly slice the pears and arrange in circles fanning out from the centre (rather like spokes on a wheel) within the border of each pastry tart, trimming the pear slices if necessary. Crumble over the Roquefort. Then, using a sharp knife, mark a pattern on the pastry border. Chill for 15 minutes.
4 Bake in the oven for 25 minutes. Remove from the oven and leave to cool slightly.

Spinach and Jarlsberg Flan

Preparation time: 10 minutes
Chilling time: 20 minutes
Cooking time: 40 minutes

SERVES 6

375 g ready-rolled shortcrust pastry

1 egg

2 egg yolks

1 × 142 ml pot of single cream

200g fresh spinach, well washed and large stalks removed

110 g Jarlsberg cheese, grated

freshly grated nutmeg

salt and freshly ground black pepper

To prepare ahead: Make the flan in advance and refrigerate – it will reheat well.

1 Preheat the oven to 200°C│400°F│gas mark 6. Line a 24 cm flan ring with the pastry. Chill for 15 minutes then bake blind (see page 18).
2 Reduce the oven temperature to 150°C│300°F│gas mark 3.
3 Place the spinach in a colander and pour over boiling water. Drain well (press between 2 plates) and chop well.
4 Beat the egg and egg yolks together with the cream.
5 Mix well with the spinach and cheese. Season well with salt, pepper and nutmeg.
6 Pour into the flan case and bake in the oven for 30–40 minutes, or until set.

Beetroot and Goat's Cheese Tarts with a Pesto Dressing

Preparation time: 10 minutes
Chilling time: 15 minutes
Cooking time: 20 minutes

SERVES 6

375 g ready-rolled puff pastry

250 g ready-cooked beetroot (vacuum-packed, not in preserved vinegar)

2 × 200 g rolled goat's cheeses with skin

2 tablespoons olive oil

salt and freshly ground black pepper

For the dressing

3 tablespoons ready-made pesto (or see page 512)

1 tablespoon balsamic vinegar

3 tablespoons olive oil

To garnish

rocket leaves

To prepare ahead: Make in advance to the end of stage 3, then refrigerate

1 Preheat the oven to 200°C|400°F|gas mark 6.
2 On a floured surface, cut out 6 × 8 cm diameter circles from the pastry and place on a baking sheet.
3 Slice the beetroot and goat's cheese into 5 mm slices and arrange on the top of the pastry, starting with a layer of goat's cheese, followed by a layer of beetroot. Chill for 15 minutes.
4 Drizzle the oil over the top of the tarts and sprinkle with salt and pepper. Bake in the oven for about 20 minutes, or until golden brown.
5 Mix together the dressing ingredients.
6 Put each tart on a plate and serve garnished with the rocket leaves and a drizzle of the dressing.

Tomato and Mozzarella Tarts

Preparation time: 5 minutes
Chilling time: 30 minutes
Cooking time: 25 minutes

SERVES 4

375g ready-rolled puff pastry

4 teaspoons ready-made basil pesto or black olive tapenade (or see page 513)

2 plum tomatoes, sliced

1 × 125 g mozzarella cheese, sliced

olive oil

salt and freshly ground black pepper

To garnish

fresh basil leaves

To prepare ahead: Make in advance to the end of stage 4 then refrigerate.

1 Preheat the oven to 200°C|400°F|gas mark 6.
2 Cut the pastry into either 4 × 7.5 cm squares or 4 × 10 cm diameter circles.
3 With a sharp knife, mark a 1 cm border around the edges of each piece of pastry. Prick the centre of the pastry all over with a fork.
4 Spread the pesto or tapenade over the central piece of the pastry, cover and chill for 15 minutes.
5 Arrange the tomato and mozzarella slices overlapping over the pesto or tapenade.
6 Drizzle over a little oil and season with salt and pepper.
7 Bake for 20–25 minutes, or until golden brown. Garnish with basil and serve.

Smoked Salmon and Pea Tart

Preparation time: 10 minutes
Cooking time: 35 minutes

SERVES 6

375 g ready-rolled shortcrust pastry

1 tablespoon oil

½ onion, finely chopped

2 egg yolks, beaten

1 × 142 ml pot of double cream

100 g smoked salmon trimmings

squeeze of lemon juice

zest of ½ lemon

100 g peas

salt and freshly ground black pepper

To prepare ahead: The tart can be served hot or cold and can be reheated as required.
Serving suggestions: Green salad (see page 381), buttered new potatoes, potato salad (see page 337)

Tomato and Mozzarella Tarts

Chicken, Mushroom and Garden Pea Puffs

Pesto Pizza

Bacon and Cheese Puff

Pork and Green Olive Burger in Ciabatta with Roast Peppers

Jerk Chicken Sandwich

Lamb Pitta Kebab

Steak Sandwich with Mustard Butter

Chorizo Quesadillas with Coriander and Chilli Salad

Hummus and Salad Burritos

Baked Potatoes Lorraine

1 Preheat the oven to 190°C|375°F|gas mark 5. Line a 24cm flan ring with the pastry. Chill for 15 minutes, then bake blind in the preheated oven (see page 18).

2 Meanwhile, heat the oil in a heavy-based saucepan and sweat the onion until soft but not coloured.

3 Mix together the egg yolks, onion, cream, smoked salmon, lemon juice and zest, and plenty of salt and pepper. Stir in the peas. Pour the mixture into the pastry case. Bake in the preheated oven for 25–35 minutes until just set and beginning to brown.

NOTE: If using fresh peas they will need to be blanched (see page 9); if using frozen, simply pour boiling water over them to allow them to defrost, drain very well and add to the filling.

Spicy Crab and Coriander Pancakes

Preparation time: 5 minutes
Cooking time: 30 minutes

MAKES 8

8 ready-made pancakes

2 tablespoons chopped fresh coriander
salt and freshly ground black pepper

For the filling

½ tablespoon oil

1–2 red chillies, finely chopped

1 stick of lemon grass, finely sliced

4 spring onions, finely sliced on the diagonal

2 × 170 g cans of crabmeat, very well drained

To garnish
fresh coriander
lime wedges

To serve
sweet chilli dipping sauce

1 Make the filling: heat the oil in a frying pan; add the chilli, lemon grass and spring onions and fry over a low heat until beginning to soften.

2 Add the crabmeat with the coriander, fork well to separate the flesh and season with salt and pepper.

3 Meanwhile, heat the pancakes in a microwave or oven according to the manufacturer's instructions.

4 Divide the hot crab filling between the pancakes. Roll up or fold into triangles and place 2 pancakes on each plate. Garnish with coriander and lime wedges. Serve with the sauce.

NOTE: If you want to make your own pancake batter (see page 519), coconut milk can be used in place of regular milk to make the batter, and chopped coriander can also be added to the batter.

Creamy Fish Flan with Burnt Hollandaise

Preparation time: 30 minutes
Cooking time: 30 minutes

SERVES 6–8

375 g ready-rolled shortcrust pastry
30 g butter
1 small onion, finely chopped
30 g plain flour
1 bay leaf
300 ml milk
1 egg, separated

250 g white fish, cooked, skinned and flaked (see page 180)
1 tablespoon chopped fresh parsley
a squeeze of lemon juice
1 × 175 g jar of good-quality hollandaise sauce
salt and freshly ground black pepper

To prepare ahead: Cook completely in advance and warm through, or serve cold.
Serving suggestions: Green salad (see page 381), new potatoes, cherry tomato salad

1 Preheat the oven to 200°C|400°F|gas mark 6. Line a 24 cm flan ring with the pastry, chill for 15 minutes and bake blind (see page 18). Reduce the oven temperature to 180°C|350°F|gas mark 4.
2 Melt the butter in a heavy saucepan, add the onion and sweat over a low heat until soft but not coloured. Add the flour and bay leaf. Cook, stirring, for 1 minute. Remove from the heat and stir in the milk, then bring slowly to the boil, stirring continuously. Season to taste with salt and pepper. Simmer for 2 minutes, then remove the bay leaf and allow the sauce to cool for 5 minutes.
3 Beat the egg yolk into the mixture. Stir in the fish, parsley and lemon juice to taste. Whisk the egg white until stiff but not dry and fold into the mixture. Pour into the pastry case. Bake in the centre of the preheated oven for about 25 minutes, until set.
4 Preheat the grill to the highest setting 10 minutes before the flan is cooked.
5 Heat the hollandaise in a small saucepan and spoon it over the flan. Put the flan under the hot grill until the top is nicely browned.
6 Serve immediately.

VARIATION: This is also delicious made with crab. Try to use good-quality crab meat.

Smoked Fish Pasties

Preparation time: 10 minutes
Chilling time: 20 minutes
Cooking time: 25 minutes

MAKES 4

500 g puff pastry

beaten egg, to glaze

For the filling

125 g smoked cod or haddock, cut into 2.5 cm pieces

125 g hot-smoked trout, cut into 2.5 cm pieces

3 spring onions, finely sliced on the diagonal

6 new potatoes, boiled and diced

3 tablespoons double cream

a squeeze of lemon juice

salt and freshly ground black pepper

To prepare ahead: Prepare to the end of stage 5, keep covered in the refrigerator and bake when required.
Serving suggestion: Green salad (see page 381)

1 Preheat the oven to 200°C|400°F|gas mark 6.
2 Gently mix together all the filling ingredients in a large bowl. Season with salt and pepper.
3 On a floured surface, roll out the pastry to the thickness of a £1 coin and cut into 4 × 18 cm diameter circles.
4 Divide the filling between the pastry circles. Moisten the edges with a little water, draw up the edges over the top of the filling and crimp them together. Place on a baking sheet.
5 Brush with a little beaten egg and chill, covered, for 20 minutes.
6 Bake in the oven for 20–25 minutes, or until golden brown.
7 Serve hot or warm.

VARIATION: Add a little extra cream and pile the filling into a pie dish, top with a layer of puff pastry and bake as a pie instead of pasties.

Snacks and Sandwiches

Sometimes we want to get away from more formal eating and just have something that can be eaten with the fingers.

Hot sandwiches made with well-seasoned interesting ingredients are perfect for a snack or for Saturday lunch, and can be made quite easily for large groups. Often sandwiches at delicatessens or restaurants are disappointing when the chefs are mean with the tastiest of the ingredients. With the ideas in this section you can fill them as full as you like and vary the quantities to taste.

Apple and Stilton Toasts

Preparation time: 5 minutes
Cooking time: 5 minutes

SERVES 4

4 medium-thick slices of bread
1½ eating apples, cored and thinly sliced
100 g Stilton cheese, crumbled

85 g walnuts, roughly chopped
100 g strong Cheddar cheese, grated

1 Preheat the grill to the medium setting.
2 Toast the bread slices on one side. Arrange the apple slices on the uncooked side of the bread. Scatter over the Stilton and walnuts and finally the Cheddar cheese.
3 Arrange on the grill rack and grill for about 3–5 minutes, or until the cheese has melted and browned.
4 Serve immediately.

Avocado Toast

Preparation time: 5 minutes

SERVES 2–4

4 slices of wheaten or soda bread
2 ripe avocados

aged balsamic vinegar
sea salt flakes and freshly ground black pepper

1 Lightly toast the bread on both sides.
2 Peel the avocados and remove the stones.

3 Roughly mash the avocados over the toast.

4 Sprinkle with salt and pepper. Drizzle over the balsamic vinegar.

NOTE: Aged balsamic vinegar is much sweeter and thicker than ordinary balsamic. Alternatively, pour 300 ml balsamic vinegar into a saucepan and boil and reduce. If you reduce it too much, add a little water to the pan. Allow to cool, then use as above or drizzled over salad. Store in a well-sealed bottle.

Cranberry and Brie Crostini

Preparation time: 5 minutes
Cooking time: 5 minutes

SERVES 4–8

1 French stick or flute
90 g cranberry sauce

300 g Brie cheese, sliced
freshly ground black pepper

1 Heat the grill to the medium setting. Cut the bread on the diagonal into 8 × 1.5 cm slices. Place the bread slices on a grill rack and toast on both sides under the grill.

2 Spread the toast with the cranberry sauce and put the slices of Brie over the top, making sure none of the toast is left exposed. Sprinkle with a little pepper. Put the grill rack back under the grill until the Brie has melted. Serve immediately.

Mozzarella in Carrozza

Preparation time: 15 minutes
Cooking time: 5 minutes

SERVES 4

8 slices of white bread, crusts removed
8 large slices of mozzarella cheese
2 eggs

oil, for frying
salt

1 Make 4 rounds of mozzarella sandwiches. Press the edges together.

2 Beat the eggs together with a pinch of salt in a shallow dish, place the sandwiches in the egg and leave for 5–10 minutes, turning once to make sure they are completely saturated.

3 Heat the oil in a frying pan and fry the sandwiches in the hot pan until golden brown.

4 Drain well on kitchen paper, sprinkle with a little salt and serve immediately.

Swiss Croûte

Preparation time: 5 minutes
Cooking time: 10 minutes

SERVES 2

butter, for greasing

1 clove of garlic

2 thick slices of bread

2 tablespoons dry white wine or kirsch

2 thick slices ham

300 g Gruyère or Emmental cheese, grated

To prepare ahead: Assemble to the end of stage 4.

1 Preheat the oven to 220°C|425°F|gas mark 7.
2 Lightly grease 1 large or 2 small shallow ovenproof dishes (such as gratin or eared dishes).
3 Cut the garlic clove in half and rub the cut side over the bread.
4 Sprinkle a little wine or kirsch over the bread and place a slice of ham on top. Sprinkle over the cheese.
5 Bake in the oven for 20–25 minutes, or until the cheese has melted completely and is beginning to bubble.
6 Serve immediately in the dish.

NOTE: This dish is very rich, so it is good served with pickled onions or gherkins. You can also spread a layer of mustard on the bread before the ham. Jarlsberg or any other good melting cheese can also be used.

Welsh Rarebit

Preparation time: 5 minutes
Cooking time: 5 minutes

SERVES 2

100 g Gruyère cheese, grated

100 g Cheddar cheese, grated

2 teaspoons French mustard

pinch of cayenne pepper

½ egg, beaten

1 tablespoon beer

2 slices of bread

butter, for spreading

salt and freshly ground black pepper

To prepare ahead: Make the rarebit mixture in stage 2, then refrigerate.

1 Preheat the grill to the highest setting.
2 Combine the cheeses and mix all but 1 tablespoon with the mustard, cayenne, egg, beer, salt and pepper.

3 Toast the bread on both sides and spread on one side with butter.

4 Spoon the rarebit mixture on to the toast and spread it neatly, making sure that all the edges are covered.

5 Sprinkle over the remaining cheese and grill until nicely browned. Serve immediately.

Mushroom Burgers with Cheese

Preparation time: 10 minutes
Cooking time: 20 minutes

SERVES 4

8 Portobello or field mushrooms
2 cloves of garlic, crushed
2 tablespoons olive oil
4 floury baps
120 g Cambozola cheese, cut into 8 slices

1 small bag of rocket
1 tablespoon balsamic vinegar
4 cherry or sunblush tomatoes, quartered
salt and freshly ground black pepper

To prepare ahead: Make in advance to the end of stage 3. Reheat the mushrooms with the Cambozola.

1 Preheat the oven to 200°C│400°F│gas mark 6.

2 Lay the mushrooms on a baking sheet. Mix the garlic and oil together and drizzle over the mushrooms. Season with salt and pepper.

3 Bake in the oven for about 20 minutes, or until tender.

4 About 5 minutes before the end of the cooking time, remove the mushrooms from the oven and lay the slices of Cambozola over the top of each mushroom. Return to the oven to allow the cheese to melt. Place the baps in the oven to warm through.

5 Toss the rocket gently in the balsamic vinegar.

6 Slice the baps in half and place most of the rocket on the bottom half of each bap. Stack two mushrooms on top of each other and place on the bed of rocket.

7 Arrange the tomato quarters and remaining rocket on the top and cover with the top half of the bap. Serve immediately.

NOTE: If preferred, use 1 salad or beef tomato sliced horizontally in place of the cherry or sunblush tomatoes.

Indian Spiced Burgers

Preparation time: 10 minutes
Cooking time: 25 minutes

SERVES 4

1 tablespoon sunflower oil

1 medium onion, chopped

5 tablespoons tikka masala curry paste

3 tablespoons chopped fresh coriander

2 spring onions, finely chopped

450 g lean minced beef

salt and freshly ground black pepper

To serve

warm mini naan bread or baps

raita (see page 495)

mango chutney

To prepare ahead: Make the burgers to the end of stage 3, then refrigerate or freeze. If frozen, defrost thoroughly before cooking.

Serving suggestions: Chilli potato wedges (see page 368), green salad (see page 381)

1 Heat the oil in a heavy saucepan, add the onion and sweat over a low heat until soft. Add the curry paste and fry for 30–45 seconds. Remove from the heat and allow to cool.

2 In a large bowl, combine the cooled cooked onions with the remaining ingredients. Preheat the grill to the medium setting.

3 Make the hamburgers: with wet hands, shape the meat into 4 flattish rounds, making sure that they are equal in size. Make a slight dip in the centre. They will shrink and thicken when they cook.

4 Grill steadily, turning once. Allow 3 minutes on each side for rare burgers, 5 for well done. Alternatively, brown in a ovenproof frying pan and then cook through in a hot oven.

5 Serve in the naan bread or baps with the raita and mango chutney.

Open Italian Burgers on Ciabatta

Preparation time: 10 minutes
Cooking time: 25 minutes

SERVES 4

1 onion, finely chopped

700 g good-quality minced beef

a handful of fresh basil leaves, roughly chopped

60 g sundried tomatoes, drained and sliced

60 g black olives, pitted and chopped

beaten egg, to bind

1 ciabatta loaf

1 clove of garlic

olive oil

4 tablespoons ready-made red or green pesto (or see page 512)

1 buffalo mozzarella cheese

To prepare ahead: Make the burgers to the end of stage 2, then refrigerate or freeze. If frozen, defrost thoroughly before cooking.

1 Mix together the onion, beef, basil, tomatoes and olives, and add enough egg to bind the mixture together. With wet hands, shape the meat into 8 equal flattish rounds. Make a slight dip in the centre. They will shrink and thicken when they cook.

2 Preheat the grill to the medium setting. Cut the ciabatta in half horizontally, then cut each half in half. Cut the garlic clove in half and rub the cut side over the ciabatta. Drizzle with a little oil and toast lightly under the grill. Set aside.

3 Grill the burgers for 3–5 minutes on each side, depending on the thickness and how well cooked you like them.

4 Spread the ciabatta pieces with the pesto and put 2 burgers and some mozzarella slices on the top of each. Place under the grill for a minute until the mozzarella begins to melt. Serve immediately.

Thai-spiced Burgers

Preparation time: 20 minutes
Cooking time: 6–10 minutes

SERVES 4

1 tablespoon sunflower oil
1 medium red onion, chopped
1 tablespoon Thai green curry paste
1 red chilli, finely chopped
3 tablespoons chopped fresh coriander
4 spring onions, finely chopped
450 g lean minced beef
salt and freshly ground black pepper

To serve
baps or pitta bread
soured cream mixed with chopped fresh coriander
   and the grated zest of 1 lime
sweet chilli sauce

To prepare ahead: Make the burgers to the end of stage 3, then refrigerate or freeze. If frozen, defrost thoroughly before cooking.

Serving suggestions: Chilli potato wedges (see page 368), green salad (see page 381)

1 Heat the oil in a heavy saucepan, add the onion and sweat over a low heat until soft. Add the curry paste and fry for 30–45 seconds. Remove from the heat and allow to cool.

2 In a large bowl, combine the cooled cooked onion with all the remaining ingredients. Season well with salt and pepper. Preheat the grill to the medium setting.

3 Make the hamburgers: with wet hands, shape the meat into 4 flattish rounds, making sure that they are equal in size. Make a slight dip in the centre. They will shrink and thicken when they cook.

4 Grill or fry, turning once. Allow 3 minutes each side for rare burgers, 5 for well done.

5 Serve in a bap or pitta bread with the soured cream mixture and sweet chilli sauce.

Pork and Apple Burgers

Preparation time: 15 minutes
Cooking time: 30 minutes

SERVES 4

1 small onion, finely chopped
450 g minced pork
1 large Bramley apple, peeled, cored and grated
60 g fresh white breadcrumbs
2 teaspoons finely chopped fresh sage
1 egg, beaten
oil, for frying
salt and freshly ground black pepper

To serve
floury baps
ready-made onion marmalade (or see page 508) or
   relish
green salad (see page 381)

To prepare ahead: Make the burgers to the end of stage 4, then refrigerate or freeze. If frozen, defrost thoroughly before cooking.

1 Preheat the oven to 200°C|400°F|gas mark 6.
2 Mix together the onion, minced pork, apple, breadcrumbs and sage. Season with plenty of salt and pepper.
3 Bind the mixture together with the egg.
4 Using wet hands, shape the mixture into 4 burgers. Make a slight dip in the centre. They will shrink and thicken when they cook.
5 To cook the burgers: heat a little oil in a heavy frying pan and cook the burgers for 5 minutes on each side or until brown. Transfer the pan to the oven for 20 minutes, or until completely cooked through.
6 To serve: split the baps, place a little salad on the bottom half of each and top with the burger and relish. Serve immediately.

Pork and Green Olive Burgers in Ciabatta with Roast Peppers

Preparation time: 15 minutes
Cooking time: 30 minutes

SERVES 4

450 g minced pork

80 g green olives, pitted and roughly chopped

1 clove of garlic, crushed

5 tablespoons roughly chopped fresh coriander

½ red chilli, finely chopped

1 egg, beaten

2 red peppers, cored, deseeded and quartered

2 yellow peppers, cored, deseeded and quartered

balsamic vinegar

olive oil

4 ciabatta rolls, 1 ciabatta loaf cut into quarters or floury baps

salt and freshly ground black pepper

To prepare ahead: Make the burgers to the end of stage 2, then refrigerate or freeze. If frozen, defrost thoroughly before cooking.

Serving suggestions: Chilli potato wedges (see page 368), green salad (see page 381)

1 Preheat the grill to the highest setting.
2 Make the pork burgers: mix together the minced pork, olives, garlic, coriander and chilli. Use as much of the egg as necessary to bind the mixture together and season well with salt and pepper. Using wet hands, shape the mixture into 4 burgers. Make a slight dip in the centre of each. They will shrink and thicken when they cook. Chill until required.
3 Grill the peppers skin side up until the skin begins to blacken. When cool enough to handle, peel off the skins, drizzle the peppers with balsamic vinegar, salt and pepper and set aside.
4 Brush the burgers with oil and grill on both sides until golden brown, then reduce the heat and continue grilling for about 8 minutes, or until completely cooked through.
5 Split the ciabatta or baps and warm through. Assemble the burgers in the ciabatta or baps with the peppers and a little of the salad.

NOTE: Ready-roasted and peeled peppers can be bought in jars or at the deli section of supermarkets.

Jerk Chicken Sandwiches

Preparation time: 5 minutes
Cooking time: 20 minutes

SERVES 2

olive oil

2 chicken breasts, skinned and boned

2 tablespoons Jerk seasoning

1 French baton, ciabatta or submarine rolls

mayonnaise

1 tomato, sliced, or 4 cherry tomatoes, halved

1 Little Gem lettuce

1 Preheat the oven to 200°C|400°F|gas mark 6.

2 Pour a little oil on each chicken breast and spread with your fingers so the breast is coated.

3 Sprinkle over the Jerk seasoning so it coats the breasts evenly. Place on a baking sheet and bake in the oven for 20 minutes.

4 Slice the bread in half horizontally and spread a layer of mayonnaise on the top half.

5 Place the tomato slices on the bottom half of the rolls and then add a couple of lettuce leaves.

6 When the chicken is cooked, slice each breast into about 7 slices on the diagonal and lay on top of the lettuce. Cover with the top of the roll and cut in half. Serve warm.

Balsamic Chicken and Red Onion Ciabatta

Preparation time: 5 minutes
Cooking time: 30 minutes

SERVES 4

olive oil, for frying

4 chicken breasts, skinned and boned

8 Portobello mushrooms

3 large red onions, sliced

4 half-sized ciabatta loaves, ready to bake

8 tablespoons balsamic vinegar

170 g hummus

100 g rocket or watercress, washed and picked over

salt and freshly ground black pepper

To prepare ahead: Cook the onion and mushrooms, then reheat in the oven while cooking the chicken.

1 Preheat the oven to 200°C|400°F|gas mark 6.

2 Heat 2 tablespoons of the oil in a large frying pan. When the pan is hot, fry the chicken breasts on each side until brown. Remove the chicken from the pan and place on a baking sheet with the mushrooms, stalk side up. Drizzle the mushrooms with a little more oil. Season with salt and pepper. Bake in the oven for about 20 minutes, or until the mushrooms are soft and the chicken cooked.

3 Meanwhile, reduce the heat of the frying pan and add the onions (you may need to add a little more oil). Cover with a lid and sweat over a low heat, stirring occasionally, until very soft.

4 When the chicken breasts and mushrooms are cooked, remove from the oven and sprinkle them with half the vinegar. Add the remaining vinegar to the onions and continue to fry until the vinegar is reduced and the onions are brown and sticky.

5 Place the ciabatta loaves on a baking sheet and bake in the oven for 8 minutes.

6 Split the ciabatta loaves in half and spread with the hummus. Top with the chicken, red onion, mushrooms and rocket or watercress.

7 Cover with the tops of the loaves and serve immediately.

Lamb Pitta Kebabs

Preparation time: 5 minutes
Marinating time: 2 hours–overnight
Cooking time: 10 minutes

SERVES 4

4 lamb steaks, trimmed
3 tablespoons olive oil
½ tablespoon chopped fresh rosemary
grated zest of ½ lemon
1 small bag of bistro salad
2 tablespoons salad dressing (see page 382)

4 pitta breads
salt and freshly ground black pepper

To serve (optional)
sweet chilli dipping sauce
soured cream

To prepare ahead: The lamb can be marinated overnight.

1 Preheat the grill to the highest setting.

2 Put the lamb steaks into a shallow bowl, pour over the oil, rosemary and lemon zest and season with pepper. Allow to marinate overnight or for as long as possible.

3 Dress the salad with your choice of dressing: French dressing or one made with chilli oil is particularly good.

4 Season the lamb steaks with a little salt and grill for about 4 minutes on either side, depending on the thickness of the steaks, until cooked.

5 Remove from the grill and slice the steaks into thin strips.

6 Toast or grill the pitta breads. Open them up and half fill with the salad. Place the lamb slices on top.

7 Top with sweet chilli dipping sauce or soured cream, if using. Serve immediately.

Steak Sandwich with Mustard Butter

Preparation time: 10 minutes
Cooking time: 5 minutes

SERVES 4

1 ciabatta loaf or French stick
60 g unsalted butter, softened
1½ tablespoons wholegrain mustard
2 heaped teaspoons made English mustard

1 tablespoon oil
4 × 140 g sirloin steaks, trimmed
mixed salad leaves
salt and freshly ground black pepper

1 Preheat the oven to 200°C|400°F|gas mark 6. Heat the bread in the oven.
2 Meanwhile, make the mustard butter: put the butter and mustards into a small bowl and beat together. Season with pepper. Set aside.
3 Heat the oil in a frying pan. Season the steaks with salt and pepper. Brown on both sides, then cook for a further 2 minutes on each side (see page 240).
4 Meanwhile, cut the ciabatta or French stick into 4 pieces. Cut each piece in half horizontally and spread the mustard butter on the base of each piece of bread.
5 Place the steak on top and cover with the salad leaves. Serve immediately.

NOTE: If you have time, fry some onions beforehand. Reheat in the steak pan and add to the sandwich. Alternatively, use caramelized onions from a jar. If preferred, slice the steak before placing on the bread.

Pan Bagna

Preparation time: 10 minutes
Standing time: 1–4 hours

1 French stick or ciabatta loaf
1 clove of garlic, peeled and halved
2 tablespoons extra virgin olive oil
1 mozzarella cheese, sliced
peeled tomatoes, sliced (see page 22)

pitted black olives
anchovy fillets, chopped
artichoke hearts, sliced
fresh basil leaves
salt and freshly ground black pepper

1 Cut the bread in half horizontally and remove a little of the soft crumb in the centre. Rub each piece with the cut side of the garlic and sprinkle liberally with oil.
2 Scatter the remaining ingredients over the base. Season with salt and pepper.
3 Sandwich together. Wrap tightly in clingfilm or foil and weight with a chopping board for at least 1 hour to compress slightly.
4 Cut into 5 cm slices on the diagonal to serve.

Tuna Melt

Preparation time: 5 minutes
Cooking time: 5 minutes

SERVES 2

½ red onion, finely chopped

1 × 170 g can of tuna, drained

2 tablespoons mayonnaise

1 Irish soda farl

60 g Cheddar cheese, sliced

salt and freshly ground black pepper

To serve

green salad (see page 381)

1 Mix together the onion, tuna and mayonnaise and season to taste with salt and pepper.
2 Heat the grill to the medium setting.
3 Split the soda farl in half horizontally and toast lightly.
4 Divide the tuna mixture in half and spread over the farl. Lay the cheese over the top and place under the grill for 3–5 minutes, or until the cheese has melted and is beginning to brown slightly. Remove and serve immediately with green salad.

NOTE: If you can't find soda farl, a soft bap, breakfast muffin or a thick slice of bread would work well too.

Muffin Pizza Snacks

Preparation time: 10 minutes
Cooking time: 5 minutes

SERVES 4

4 English breakfast muffins

4 tablespoons ready-made pesto (or see page 512)

1–2 beef tomatoes, cut horizontally to give 8 slices ½ cm thick

1 large ball buffalo mozzarella cheese, sliced or torn into strips

10 black olives, pitted and roughly chopped

1 Preheat the grill to the medium setting.
2 Cut the muffins in half horizontally and toast lightly on both sides.
3 Spread the cut sides of the muffins with the pesto.
4 Place the muffins on a baking sheet. Place a slice of tomato on top of each and scatter over the cheese and olives.
5 Place under the grill for about 5 minutes, until the cheese has melted and is beginning to brown. Serve immediately.

VARIATIONS: Other cheeses such Cheddar can be used in place of mozzarella. Add other ingredients to the topping, such as cooked ham or canned anchovies.

Pesto Pizzas

Preparation time: 25 minutes
Cooking time: 25 minutes

MAKES 2 LARGE OR 4 SMALL PIZZAS

1 × 280 g packet of pizza mix

5 tablespoons ready-made pesto

170 g sunblush tomatoes in oil, drained and chopped
  (reserve the oil)

110 g Gorgonzola cheese, sliced

110 g mozzarella cheese, sliced

5 slices of Parma ham, cut into strips

1 × 200 g bag of rocket

olive oil

balsamic vinegar

salt and freshly ground black pepper

To prepare ahead: Complete to the end of stage 4 and allow to cool on a wire rack. Reheat for 15 minutes.

1 Preheat the oven to 220°C|425°F|gas mark 7.

2 Make up the pizza dough following the manufacturer's instructions, but using the pesto in place of 5 tablespoons of the water called for.

3 Divide the dough into 2 or 4 equal pieces. Roll each into a circle, place on non-stick baking sheets and drizzle with half of the reserved tomato oil, and leave to rise in a warm place for 20 minutes.

4 Cook the pizza bases in the oven for 15–20 minutes, or until cooked through.

5 As soon as the bases are cooked, layer the tomatoes and cheeses over the top and cover loosely with the ham. Drizzle over some more of the tomato oil and season with pepper. Return to the oven for 5–7 minutes.

6 Meanwhile, dress the rocket salad with the oil and vinegar and season.

7 Remove the pizzas from the oven and place a large handful of the rocket salad on top of each. Serve immediately.

Caramelized Red Onion, Fig and Goat's Cheese Pizza

Preparation time: 5 minutes
Cooking time: 35 minutes

SERVES 2

1 tablespoon oil

2 large red onions, sliced

5 tablespoons balsamic vinegar

½ tablespoon soft light brown sugar

1 tablespoon chopped fresh thyme

1 × 150 g pizza base

110 g goat's cheese log, crumbled

4 ripe figs, cut into quarters

freshly ground black pepper

To prepare ahead: Assemble the pizza to the end of stage 4, then refrigerate until required.

Serving suggestion: Rocket salad or Italian tomato salad (see page 334)

1 Preheat the oven to 200°C|400°F|gas mark 6.
2 Heat the oil in a heavy frying pan for about 10 minutes, over a low to medium heat. Add the onions and sweat until soft.
3 Increase the heat and allow the onions to become caramelized and start to brown. Add the vinegar and sugar, stir gently and continue cooking over a medium heat so that the vinegar begins to reduce. When the vinegar has become thick and sticky, add the thyme and remove the onions from the heat. Allow to cool.
4 Place the pizza base on a baking sheet and spread over the onion mixture. Scatter over the cheese and season with a little pepper.
5 Bake the pizza in the oven for 10 minutes, or until the cheese is beginning to melt.
6 Place the figs on top of the pizza and return to the oven for a further 10 minutes, until heated through. Serve immediately.

VARIATION: Use caramelized onion relish instead of caramelizing the onions in stages 2 and 3.

Bacon and Cheese Puffs

Preparation time: 15 minutes
Chilling time: 20–30 minutes
Cooking time: 20 minutes

SERVES 4

375 g ready-rolled puff pastry	110 g strong hard cheese such as Cheddar, grated
1 tablespoon wholegrain mustard	beaten egg, to glaze
8 rashers of bacon, cooked	freshly ground black pepper

To prepare ahead: Make in advance to the end of stage 3, then refrigerate.

1 Preheat the oven to 200°C|400°F|gas mark 6.
2 On a floured surface, cut the pastry into 4 × 13 cm squares. Spread a quarter of the mustard on each square, then lay 2 slices of bacon across each square on the diagonal. Sprinkle the grated cheese over the bacon and season with a little pepper.
3 Fold the other 2 corners up so that they just overlap in the centre of the square, and push down lightly. Place the puffs on a baking sheet and brush each one with beaten egg. Chill for 20–30 minutes.
4 Bake in the oven for 20 minutes, or until the cheese has melted and the pastry is well risen and golden brown.

VARIATIONS: A slice of tomato can be placed between the bacon and cheese, or use tomato ketchup in place of the mustard.

Sausage and Mustard Rolls

Preparation time: 15 minutes
Chilling time: 10 minutes
Cooking time: 25 minutes

MAKES 12

400 g sausagemeat

375 g ready-rolled shortcrust or puff pastry

2 tablespoons wholegrain mustard

85 g strong Cheddar cheese, finely grated

1 egg, beaten, to glaze

salt and freshly ground black pepper

To prepare ahead: Make in advance to the end of stage 6, then freeze. Defrost well before baking.

1 Preheat the oven to 200°C|400°F|gas mark 6.

2 Season the sausagemeat with salt and pepper.

3 If necessary roll out the pastry further to get a large rectangle about 3 mm thick and cut in half lengthways.

4 With wet or floured hands, roll the sausagemeat mixture into 2 long sausages the same length as the pastry. The pastry should be wide enough to wrap around the sausagemeat.

5 Spread the mustard over the pastry, sprinkle the cheese over the mustard and press down gently. Place a roll of sausagemeat down the centre of each strip of pastry.

6 Dampen one edge of each strip and bring the pastry over the sausagemeat, pressing the edges together and making sure that the join is underneath the roll. Chill for 10 minutes.

7 Brush the sausage rolls with beaten egg. Cut into 5 cm lengths. Using a pair of kitchen scissors, snip a small 'V' in the top of each sausage roll.

8 Place on a baking sheet and bake in the preheated oven for 25–30 minutes, or until the pastry is golden brown.

VARIATIONS: Good-quality onion relish and sundried tomatoes can be used in place of the mustard and cheese if preferred.

Ham and Cheese Quesadillas

Preparation time: 5 minutes
Cooking time: 10 minutes

SERVES 4

1 jar of spicy salsa (or see page 368)

6 flour tortillas

200 g Cheddar cheese, grated

100 g shredded smoked ham

butter, for frying

1 Spread some of the salsa over 3 of the tortillas so that there is a good covering. Scatter over the cheese and ham and place the remaining tortillas on top to make sandwiches.

2 Heat a frying pan over a medium heat and melt a little butter in it. Place one of the quesadillas in the pan and cook for about 2 minutes on each side, or until golden brown. Repeat with the remaining quesadillas.

3 Cut into wedges to serve. Use any remaining salsa as a dip or accompaniment.

NOTE: The quesadillas can be made with a wide variety of fillings. Using extra filling, they can be layered up as a 3–4-layer stack rather than a sandwich, topped with extra cheese and baked in a medium oven for 10–15 minutes. They are also good as a canapé, served with more salsa as a dipping sauce.

Chorizo Quesadillas with Coriander and Chilli Salad

Preparation time: 10 minutes
Cooking time: 10 minutes

SERVES 4

For the salad dressing
100 ml mayonnaise
½ green chilli, finely chopped
grated zest and juice of 1 lime
½ small bunch of coriander, roughly chopped
salt and freshly ground black pepper

For the salad
110 g canned black-eyed beans, drained and rinsed
60 g canned sweetcorn, drained and rinsed

1 iceberg lettuce, torn into bite-sized pieces
½ small bunch of coriander

For the quesadillas
8 soft flour tortillas
4 tablespoons ready-made spicy salsa (or see page 368)
100 g strong Cheddar cheese, grated
1 chorizo sausage, thinly sliced
3 tablespoons olive oil

1 Prepare the salad dressing: put all the ingredients into a blender and whizz until smooth. Season to taste with salt and pepper.

2 Toss all the salad ingredients together with the dressing.

3 Make the quesadillas: spread each tortilla with a thin layer of the salsa, then sprinkle 4 of them with the cheese and the sausage. Top with the remaining tortillas to make sandwiches.

4 Heat 1 tablespoon of the oil in a heavy frying pan and fry 1 quesadilla on both sides until the cheese has melted and the quesadilla is golden brown. Repeat with the remaining quesadillas, adding more oil when necessary.

5 Cut the quesadillas into triangles or wedges. Toss the salad in the dressing, pile on to plates and serve with the quesadillas.

Burritos

Preparation time: 10 minutes

SERVES 4

200 g hummus

4 flour tortillas

1 large ripe avocado, peeled, stoned and sliced

12 cherry tomatoes, quartered, or sunblush tomatoes

30 g pinenuts, toasted (see page 17)

1 × 110 g bag of rocket or herb salad

1 Spread a quarter of the hummus down the centre of each tortilla.

2 Place the avocado slices on top.

3 Scatter over the tomatoes and pinenuts and top with a small handful of salad.

4 Roll one end of the tortilla over about 2 cm. Turn the tortilla 90° and roll up like a pancake.

NOTE: This adaptation of the Mexican recipe is perfect for picnics. The burritos can be secured together with a cocktail stick for transporting. They can be made with a wide variety of fillings, using the salad as a base. Popular alternatives are: tuna and hardboiled egg; mozzarella, red pepper and pesto; shredded chicken and mango chutney; smoked ham and Gruyère cheese; shredded chicken, guacamole and red onion.

Oven-baked Tortilla

This is a delicious way to use up leftover roast chicken or turkey.

Preparation time: 20 minutes
Cooking time: 25 minutes

SERVES 4–6

225 g cooked chicken or turkey, shredded

a handful of chopped fresh coriander

1 × 142 ml pot of soured cream

1 avocado, peeled, stoned and diced

2 tomatoes, cored and diced

½ red chilli, deseeded and finely chopped

6 spring onions, finely sliced on the diagonal

grated zest of ½ lime

170 g Cheddar cheese, grated

oil, for brushing

6 large flour tortillas

1 small (about 200 g) can of refried beans

salt and freshly ground black pepper

Serving suggestions: Avocado and spring onion salad with lemon and soy dressing (see page 332), green salad (see page 381), Italian tomato salad (see page 334)

1 Preheat the oven to 200°C|400°F|gas mark 6.
2 Mix together the chicken or turkey, the coriander and soured cream and season with salt and pepper. Set aside.
3 Mix together the avocado, tomatoes, chilli, spring onions, lime zest, and all but a handful of the cheese. Season with salt and pepper. Set aside.
4 On an oiled baking sheet, or in an ovenproof serving dish, spread half the chicken or turkey mixture over 1 tortilla. Cover with the second tortilla and spread with half the avocado mixture. Cover with the third tortilla and spread with the refried beans. Repeat with the remaining chicken or turkey and avocado layers, ending with a tortilla on top.
5 Sprinkle with the remaining cheese.
6 Bake in the oven for 25 minutes, or until hot all the way through.

Spinach and Gruyère Soufflé Omelette

Preparation time: 5 minutes
Cooking time: 5 minutes

SERVES 2

1 × 150 g bag of baby spinach leaves, well rinsed and roughly chopped
4 eggs, separated
freshly grated nutmeg

20 g butter
90 g Gruyère cheese, grated
salt and freshly ground black pepper

Serving suggestion: Green salad (see page 381)

1 Place the spinach in a colander and pour over boiling water so that it begins to wilt. Leave to drain well.
2 Place the egg yolks in a large bowl and add the nutmeg, salt and pepper.
3 In another bowl, whisk the egg whites until they form soft peaks but are not dry. Fold the egg whites into the egg yolks.
4 Melt the butter in a large frying pan, tipping the pan so that the bottom and sides are coated. When the foaming subsides, add the egg mixture.
5 When the omelette is beginning to set, sprinkle over the cheese and the spinach and cook until the omelette is lightly set.
6 Fold in half and slide on to a warm dish. Cut in half and serve.

VARIATION: Other strongly flavoured cheeses, such as Parmesan, goat's cheese or mature Cheddar, may be substituted for the Gruyère.

Brie Soufflé Omelette with Pear and Date Chutney

Preparation time: 5 minutes
Cooking time: 5 minutes

SERVES 2

3 eggs
1 egg white
1 tablespoon finely chopped fresh chives
½ tablespoon finely chopped fresh parsley
1 tablespoon water

20 g butter
120 g Brie cheese, sliced
3 tablespoons pear and date chutney (see page 470)
salt and freshly ground black pepper

Serving suggestion: Green salad (see page 381)

1 Preheat the oven to 180°C│350°F│gas mark 4.
2 Separate one of the eggs. Reserve the white, and beat the yolk with the 2 remaining eggs, the herbs and the water. Season to taste with salt and pepper.

3 In a separate bowl, whisk the 2 egg whites until they form soft peaks. Fold into the yolk mixture.

4 Melt the butter in a frying pan with an ovenproof handle until it begins to foam. Pour in the egg mixture. Cook over a medium heat, using a palette knife to prevent it from sticking, until nearly set.

5 Cover half the omelette with the Brie and spread the chutney over the top. Fold the omelette in half and place the pan in the oven for 5 minutes, or until the cheese has just melted.

NOTE: Use a good-quality bought chutney or caramelized onion relish to save time.

Baked Potatoes Florentine

Preparation time: 15 minutes
Cooking time: 1¼ hours

SERVES 4

4 baking potatoes	250 g ricotta cheese
1 large bag of spinach, washed and any coarse stalks removed	60 g Gruyère cheese, grated
	freshly grated nutmeg
50 g butter	salt and freshly ground black pepper

To prepare ahead: Make in advance to the end of stage 4, then refrigerate. Sprinkle with the remaining cheese and return to a preheated over for 25 minutes or until heated through. There should be no need to grill.

1 Preheat the oven to 200°C│400°F│gas mark 6.

2 Prick the potatoes all over with a fork and bake in the oven for 1 hour, or until cooked all the way through.

3 Meanwhile, place the spinach in a colander and pour over a kettle of boiling water so that it wilts. Drain very well and chop roughly.

4 Cut the potatoes in half lengthways and scrape out the flesh. Mash it with a fork and add the butter, spinach, ricotta and three-quarters of the Gruyère. Mix and season lightly with salt, pepper and nutmeg.

5 Heat the grill to the highest setting.

6 Pile the mixture back into the potato shells, sprinkle with the reserved cheese and return to the oven for 10 minutes, or until hot all the way through.

7 Place under the grill until lightly browned.

VARIATIONS: Any type of cheese can be used. Fresh herbs such as parsley can also be used in place of the spinach.

Baked Potatoes Lorraine

Preparation time: 20 minutes
Cooking time: 1¼ hours

SERVES 4

4 baking potatoes

oil

8 rashers of smoked bacon, cut into lardons

50 g butter

3 spring onions, finely sliced on the diagonal

60 g Cheddar cheese, grated

60 g Gruyère cheese, grated

salt and freshly ground black pepper

To prepare ahead: Make in advance to the end of stage 4, then refrigerate. Sprinkle with the remaining cheese and return to a preheated oven for 25 minutes or until hot through. There should be no need to grill.

1 Preheat the oven to 200°C|400°F|gas mark 6.
2 Prick the potatoes all over with a fork and bake in the oven for 1 hour, or until cooked all the way though.
3 Meanwhile, heat a little oil in a frying pan, add the bacon and cook until golden brown.
4 Cut a cross into the top of the potatoes and scrape out the flesh. Mash it with a fork and add the butter, bacon, spring onions and three-quarters of the cheese. Mix together and season with salt and pepper.
5 Heat the grill to the highest setting.
6 Pile the mixture back into the potato shells, sprinkle with the reserved cheese and return to the oven for 10 minutes, or until hot all the way through.
7 Place under the grill until lightly browned.

VARIATION: Use shredded ham in place of the bacon and stir it in with the cheese.

Corn on the Cob with Chilli Butter

Preparation time: 10 minutes
Cooking time: 8–10 minutes

SERVES 4

4 corn on the cob

For the chilli butter
60 g butter, softened
½ –1 red chilli, finely chopped
grated zest of 1 lime

juice of ½ lime
2 tablespoons finely chopped fresh coriander
1 × 1.25 cm piece of fresh root ginger, peeled and
  grated (optional)
salt and freshly ground black pepper

To prepare ahead: The chilli butter can be made well in advance and stored in the refrigerator or freezer.

1 Prepare the chilli butter: put the butter into a small bowl, add the remaining ingredients and mix well together.
2 Place the mixture on a piece of greaseproof paper or clingfilm, roll into a fat cylinder and chill.
3 Bring a large saucepan of water to the boil, add the corn and cook for about 5–10 minutes, or until tender. Drain well.
4 Cut the butter into slices and serve it separately so that guests may put the butter on top of their corn. As the butter melts it will flavour the corn.

NOTE: Do not salt the water as this can toughen the corn. The corn can also be microwaved. Place in a covered dish with a little water and cook for about 4 minutes.

Salads

It is not just a desire to eat healthily that has led to the increase in popularity of a salad as a first course, a main course or the only course of a meal. Salads offer the opportunity to combine interesting ingredients and flavours from around the world without having to work too hard at the presentation, as the naturally attractive colours of the different ingredients do not need fancy garnishes.

Many of the salads in this section are suitable as both first and main courses, so approximate servings have been given for each where relevant. Most will benefit from being served with crusty bread to soak up the dressings.

All the dressings in these recipes can be used as a change from a basic French dressing to dress a simple green salad to serve with plain grilled or barbecued meat or fish.

Sweet Chilli Crab with Pink Grapefruit

Preparation time: 20 minutes
Cooking time: 10 minutes

SERVES 6–8 AS A FIRST COURSE, 4 AS A MAIN COURSE

1 pink grapefruit
½ tablespoon soft dark brown sugar
2 × 170 g cans of crabmeat, drained
1 bunch of watercress, broken into sprigs

For the dressing
2 tablespoons olive oil

1 tablespoon sweet chilli sauce
1 tablespoon clear honey
1 × 2.5 cm piece of fresh root ginger, peeled and grated
juice of 1 lime
reserved juice of the grapefruit
finely chopped fresh chives

To prepare ahead: Assemble to the end of stage 3.

1 Preheat the grill to the highest setting.
2 Peel and segment or slice the grapefruit, taking care to reserve the juices for the dressing. If slicing, cut each slice into quarters. Try to remove all the bitter pith from the fruit.
3 Mix all the dressing ingredients together.
4 Place the grapefruit segments on lightly oiled kitchen foil, pat dry and sprinkle with the sugar. Grill until the sugar melts and caramelizes.
5 Toss the crabmeat in half of the dressing and arrange on individual serving plates with the watercress and grapefruit. Drizzle with the remaining salad dressing.

Sweet Herring and Beetroot Salad

Preparation time: 10 minutes

SERVES 6–8 AS A FIRST COURSE, 4 AS A MAIN COURSE

150 g mixed salad leaves or watercress

300 g cooked vacuum-packed beetroot (not preserved in vinegar)

2 × 260 g tubs of sweet marinated herrings, drained and cut into strips

For the dressing

1 × 142 ml pot of soured cream

1 tablespoon horseradish sauce

1 tablespoon chopped fresh dill

salt and freshly ground black pepper

1 Make the dressing: mix together the soured cream, horseradish sauce and dill. Season to taste with salt and pepper.
2 Chop the beetroot into approximately 1 cm chunks.
3 Toss the salad leaves and beetroot together and divide between individual plates.
4 Divide the herrings between the plates and spoon over the dressing.
5 Serve immediately.

VARIATION: Use marinated anchovies in place of the herrings.

Thai Prawn and Avocado Salad

Preparation time: 20 minutes

SERVES 6–8 AS A FIRST COURSE, 4 AS A MAIN COURSE

20 tiger prawns, cooked and peeled

2 ripe avocados, peeled, stoned and sliced

For the dressing

4 tablespoons olive oil

grated zest of ½ lime

juice of 1 lime

1 red chilli, deseeded and chopped

1 tablespoon roughly chopped fresh coriander

salt and freshly ground black pepper

To garnish

sprigs of fresh coriander

To serve

crusty bread

1 Make the dressing: whisk together the oil, lime zest and juice and season with salt and pepper. Stir in the chilli and coriander.
2 Arrange the prawns and sliced avocados on individual plates and drizzle over the dressing. Garnish with the sprigs of coriander.
3 Serve immediately with crusty bread.

Tuna and Cannellini Bean Salad

This salad is also delicious made without the canned tuna, to accompany a fresh tuna steak.

Preparation time: 15 minutes

SERVES 4 AS A MAIN COURSE

1 × 400 g can of cannellini beans, drained and rinsed

170 g French beans, trimmed, blanched and refreshed (see page 9)

1 bunch of spring onions, washed, trimmed and finely sliced on the diagonal

2 × 185 g cans of tuna fish in brine, drained

1 × 200 g bag of rocket

For the dressing

4 tablespoons olive oil

2 teaspoons wholegrain mustard

grated zest and juice of ½ lemon

salt and freshly ground black pepper

1 Make the dressing: mix all the ingredients together and season well with salt and pepper.
2 Add the dressing to the beans and spring onions. Mix well. Toss in the tuna.
3 Add the rocket and stir together gently.
4 Divide between individual plates and serve.

Seared Tuna with Capers and Red Onion

Preparation time: 5 minutes
Cooking time: 5 minutes

SERVES 6 AS A FIRST COURSE, 4 AS A MAIN COURSE

450 g fresh tuna in one piece

5 tablespoons olive oil

1 small red onion, very finely chopped

2 tablespoons capers, drained and rinsed well

1 tablespoon lemon juice

1 × 100 g pack of rocket or Little Gem lettuces, torn into bite-sized pieces

salt and freshly ground black pepper

1 Season the tuna with salt and pepper, then rub with 2 tablespoons of the oil.
2 Heat a heavy frying pan until really hot, add the tuna and sear on each side for 30 seconds to colour rather than cook. Set aside.
3 Mix the onion with the capers. Add the remaining oil and the lemon juice. Season to taste with salt and pepper.
4 Divide the rocket or Little Gem lettuce between individual plates. Slice the tuna very thinly. Arrange on top of the salad and pour over the dressing.

Tuna Niçoise

Preparation time: 15 minutes
Cooking time: 10 minutes

SERVES 8 AS A FIRST COURSE, 4 AS A MAIN COURSE

3 plum tomatoes, peeled (see page 22) and quartered

100 g French beans, blanched and refreshed (see page 9)

½ red onion, finely sliced

1 red pepper, cored, deseeded and sliced

2 Little Gem lettuces, washed and separated, any large leaves torn into bite-sized pieces

6 good-quality anchovy fillets, split in half lengthways

10 good-quality black olives, pitted and cut in half

12 quail's eggs, hardboiled, peeled and cut in half

1 tablespoon oil

4 × 150 g tuna steaks (halved if serving as a first course)

For the dressing

1 tablespoon balsamic vinegar

3 tablespoons olive oil

½ clove of garlic, crushed

salt and freshly ground black pepper

1 Mix together the dressing ingredients and whisk well.

2 Put all the salad ingredients, except the eggs, oil and tuna, into a bowl and gently stir in the dressing. Do not overmix. Divide the salad between individual plates, then scatter over the eggs.

3 Heat the oil in a griddle or frying pan. Season the tuna steaks with salt and pepper. Fry the tuna for about 3 minutes on each side, depending on the thickness of the steak and how you like it cooked.

4 Cut the tuna steaks in half on the diagonal and arrange on the salad. Serve immediately.

VARIATION: Use 4 chicken's eggs, peeled and cut into quarters, in place of the quail's eggs.

Soy-glazed Tuna with Crunchy Hot and Sour Salad

Preparation time: 10 minutes
Marinating time: 1 hour
Cooking time: 15 minutes

SERVES 8 AS A FIRST COURSE, 4 AS A MAIN COURSE

4 × 170 g tuna steaks (halved if serving as a first course)

150 g cashew nuts

1 teaspoon sea salt crystals

1 teaspoon black mustard seeds

250 g beansprouts

100 g mangetout, roughly chopped

1 small can of water chestnuts, sliced

grated zest and juice of ½ lime

1 tablespoon chopped fresh coriander

For the marinade

5 tablespoons light soy sauce

1 tablespoon sesame oil

1 teaspoon clear honey

For the dressing

3 tablespoons rice wine vinegar

1 red chilli, finely chopped

1 tablespoon caster sugar

1 tablespoon sunflower oil

To prepare ahead: Make in advance to the end of stage 3.

1 Combine the marinade ingredients and pour over the tuna steaks. Leave for up to 1 hour.

2 Make the hot and sour dressing: place the vinegar, chilli and sugar in a small saucepan and heat gently without boiling until the sugar has dissolved. Leave to cool, then add the sunflower oil.

3 Gently fry the cashew nuts in a heavy frying pan until lightly browned, then add the salt and mustard seeds and fry for 1 minute, or until the seeds start to pop. Set aside.

4 In a hot pan, fry the tuna steaks for about 3 minutes on each side – no extra oil in the pan should be required. Cook for a little longer if you prefer the tuna to be completely cooked through.

5 Combine the beansprouts, water chestnuts, lime zest and juice and coriander. Toss in the dressing, pile on to individual plates and serve topped with the soy-glazed tuna.

VARIATION: This works well with salmon fillets in place of the tuna steaks.

Tuna with Pineapple and Chilli Salad

Preparation time: 20 minutes
Cooking time: 5–10 minutes

SERVES 8 AS A FIRST COURSE, 4 AS A MAIN COURSE

2 tomatoes

2 spring onions, finely sliced

1 red chilli, deseeded and finely chopped

½ red pepper, diced

½ bag mixed salad leaves, torn into very small pieces

¼ fresh pineapple, peeled, cored and diced

4 tuna steaks, halved if serving as a first course

handful of coriander, roughly chopped

For the dressing

freshly grated zest and juice of 2 limes

4 tablespoons olive oil, plus extra for frying

salt and freshly ground black pepper

1 Make the salad: cut the tomatoes into quarters, remove the seeds and dice finely. Place in a large bowl.
2 Add the spring onions, chilli, red pepper, salad leaves and pineapple.
3 Make the dressing: mix together the lime zest and juice with the olive oil. Season well with salt and pepper. Set aside.
4 Season the tuna steaks. Heat a frying pan with a tablespoon of oil until very hot.
5 Fry the steaks for 3–4 minutes on each side.
6 Meanwhile, add the coriander to the salad. Pour on the dressing and toss well. Divide the salad between the plates.
7 Place the tuna fish on top of the salad leaves and serve.

NOTE: This is also good with grilled chicken. Buy fresh, prepared pineapple to save time.

Smoked Mackerel and Beetroot Salad with Horseradish Dressing

Preparation time: 15 minutes
Cooking time: 15 minutes

SERVES 6–8 AS A FIRST COURSE, 4 AS A MAIN COURSE

250 g new potatoes

4 smoked mackerel fillets

250 g vacuum-packed cooked beetroot (not
   preserved in vinegar)

2 Little Gem lettuces, washed and torn into bite-
   sized pieces

For the dressing

3 tablespoons horseradish sauce

3 tablespoons crème fraîche

salt and freshly ground black pepper

To prepare ahead: Prepare all the ingredients except the potatoes. When ready to serve, cook the potatoes and assemble. Alternatively cook the potatoes in advance and serve the salad cold.

1 Bring a small pan of salted water to the boil, add the new potatoes and cook for about 15 minutes, until tender.

2 Skin the mackerel fillets and break into 2.5 cm pieces. Cut the beetroot into 2 cm cubes.

3 Make the dressing: mix together the horseradish and crème fraîche and season to taste.

4 Cut the new potatoes in half whilst still warm.

5 Toss together the lettuce, dressing, smoked mackerel and potatoes.

6 Divide the salad between individual plates and scatter the beetroot over the top.

VARIATION: Smoked trout can be used in place of mackerel.

Maple and Soy Salmon Salad

Preparation time: 10 minutes
Marinating time: at least 2 hours
Cooking time: 15 minutes

SERVES 8 AS A FIRST COURSE, 4 AS A MAIN COURSE

4 × 170 g salmon fillets, skinned and pinboned

4 tablespoons dark soy sauce

4 tablespoons maple syrup

1 tablespoon sesame oil

1 × 250 g bag of mixed salad leaves

12 cherry tomatoes, halved

1 avocado, peeled, stoned and sliced

6 spring onions, finely sliced on the diagonal

For the dressing

1 tablespoon dark soy sauce

1 tablespoon maple syrup

1 tablespoon sesame oil

1 tablespoon sunflower oil

juice of 1 lime

1 tablespoon white wine vinegar

To garnish

1 tablespoon sesame seeds, toasted

To prepare ahead: Leave the salmon to marinate overnight.

Thai Prawn and Avocado Salad

Tuna and Cannellini Bean Salad

Tuna with Pineapple and Chilli Salad

Seared Tuna with Capers and Red Onion

Warm Duck and Pink Grapefruit Salad with Potato Croûtons

Basil Chicken with Three Tomato Salad

Chicken, Avocado and Almond Salad

Beef and Coconut Chilli Salad

Goat's Cheese and Cherry Salad

Poached Egg Salad

Nectarine, Rocket and Feta Salad

1 If serving as a first course, cut the salmon fillets in half. Lay the salmon in a dish, mix together the soy sauce, maple syrup and sesame oil and pour over the fish. Leave to marinate in the refrigerator for at least 2 hours, turning the fillets halfway through the marinating time.

2 Preheat the oven to 180°C|350°F|gas mark 4.

3 Remove the salmon from the marinade. Heat a large ovenproof frying pan over a high heat, add the salmon and fry on one side for 30 seconds or until well browned. Turn the salmon over, pour over the marinade and put into the oven for 5–10 minutes, or until just cooked through.

4 Place the salad leaves, tomatoes, avocado and spring onions in a bowl. Mix all the dressing ingredients together and toss the salad in the dressing. Pile the salad on to plates and serve topped with the salmon and sprinkled with the sesame seeds.

Salmon, Avocado and Potato Salad

Preparation time: 20 minutes
Marinating time: at least 1 hour
Cooking time: 15 minutes

SERVES 4 AS A FIRST COURSE, 2 AS A MAIN COURSE

4 tablespoons light soy sauce

1 red chilli, diced

350 g salmon fillet, skinned, pinboned and cut into finger-length strips

seasoned plain flour

1 tablespoon sesame oil

sunflower oil

100 g new potatoes, cooked

1 avocado, peeled, stoned and cut into chunks

1 small bag of salad leaves

½ cucumber, cut into thin slices

2 spring onions, finely sliced

a squeeze of lime juice

salt and freshly ground black pepper

To serve

sweet chilli dipping sauce

To prepare ahead: Leave the salmon to marinate overnight.

1 Mix together the soy sauce and chilli. Add the salmon strips and leave to marinate, covered, in the refrigerator for at least 1 hour.

2 Remove the salmon from the marinade, pat dry and toss in the seasoned flour.

3 Heat the oven to a low heat to use as a warming oven.

4 Heat the sesame oil in a frying pan, add the salmon pieces and fry until just cooked. Remove to a plate and keep warm in the oven. Using the same frying pan, heat a little sunflower oil, add the potatoes and fry over a high heat until just crisp.

5 Mix together the avocado, salad leaves, cucumber, spring onions, potatoes and lime juice. Toss together, season with salt and pepper and arrange on individual plates.

6 Place the salmon on top of the salad and drizzle the sweet chilli dipping sauce around the edge of each plate. Serve immediately.

Warm Honey and Soy Salmon Salad

Preparation time: 10 minutes
Marinating time: at least 1 hour
Cooking time: 15 minutes

SERVES 4 AS A FIRST COURSE, 2 AS A MAIN COURSE

350 g salmon fillet, skinned and pinboned

2 tablespoons dark soy sauce

4 tablespoons orange juice

1 tablespoon clear honey

2 tablespoons oil

50 g button or chestnut mushrooms, quartered or sliced

1 bag of herb salad

50 g mangetout, finely sliced on the diagonal

To prepare ahead: The salmon can be marinated overnight.

1 Cut the salmon into 2 or 4 pieces, depending on how many you are serving. Mix together the soy sauce, orange juice and honey in a bowl, add the salmon and coat in the marinade. Cover and leave to marinate in the refrigerator for at least 1 hour.

2 Heat half of the oil in a heavy frying pan, add the mushrooms and cook over a low heat until tender. Remove from the pan and set aside.

3 Heat the remaining oil in the pan. Using a slotted spoon, remove the salmon from the marinade and place in the pan. Cook for 1 minute on each side. Return the mushrooms to the pan with the marinade and continue to cook for 1 minute. Remove the salmon and continue to reduce the marinade until it reaches a syrupy consistency and the mushrooms are coated in the glaze.

4 Meanwhile, divide the salad between individual plates, scatter over the mangetout and place the mushrooms and salmon on the top. Serve immediately.

Warm Sushi Salad

Preparation time: 10 minutes
Cooking time: 35 minutes

SERVES 6–8 AS A FIRST COURSE, 4 AS A MAIN COURSE

250 g sushi rice

3 tablespoons rice wine

2 tablespoons light soy sauce

1 tablespoon caster sugar

wasabi paste

½ cucumber, peeled and diced

6 spring onions, chopped

250 g smoked salmon, sliced

1 avocado, peeled, stoned and chopped

2 sheets of nori seaweed, shredded

To serve

2 teaspoons roughly chopped Japanese pickled ginger

1 Soak the rice, then cook it according to the manufacturer's instructions.
2 While the rice is still warm, mix together the rice wine, soy sauce and sugar and add a little wasabi to taste. Pour the mixture over the rice.
3 Add all the remaining ingredients, reserving some of the shredded nori for the garnish. Pile into a serving dish and scatter over the reserved nori.
4 Serve the warm salad with pickled ginger.

Salmon with Potatoes and Sugarsnap Peas

This salad is designed to feed a large number of people. However, the quantities can be reduced to feed just a few.

Preparation time: 10 minutes
Cooking time: 30 minutes

SERVES 8–10

500 g salmon fillet, skinned and pinboned
670 g new potatoes
220 g sugarsnap peas
1 × 100 g bag of rocket
salt and freshly ground black pepper

For the dressing

6 tablespoons olive oil
2 tablespoons white wine vinegar
2 tablespoons horseradish sauce

To prepare ahead: Complete to the end of stage 6, then toss together when ready to serve.

1 Preheat the oven to 200°C|400°F|gas mark 6.
2 Place the salmon in an ovenproof dish. Season with salt and pepper. Cover with greaseproof paper and bake in the oven for 15 minutes, or until the salmon is just cooked – it should be opaque.
3 Meanwhile, cook the potatoes in boiling salted water until tender (about 15 minutes). Drain well and cut in half.
4 Cook the sugarsnap peas for 2 minutes in boiling salted water. Drain and refresh by plunging into a bowl of ice-cold water. Drain well.
5 Mix the dressing ingredients together and season with salt and pepper.
6 Gently break the salmon into large flakes.
7 When ready to serve, mix the salmon, potatoes, sugarsnap peas and rocket together with the dressing, taking care not to let the salmon break up too much.
8 Pile on to a large serving dish.

Basil Chicken with Three Tomato Salad

Preparation time: 15 minutes
Cooking time: 30 minutes

SERVES 4 AS A MAIN COURSE

4 plum tomatoes, halved lengthways

olive oil

4 chicken breasts, boned, skin left on

1 bunch of fresh basil

8 salad tomatoes, halved, deseeded and cut into
    slivers

225 g cherry tomatoes, quartered

225 g mixed salad leaves

For the dressing

5 tablespoons tomato sauce (see page 504)

2 tablespoons balsamic vinegar

salt and freshly ground black pepper

To prepare ahead: Make in advance to the end of stage 3.

1 Preheat the oven to 200°C|400°F|gas mark 6.

2 Place the plum tomatoes, cut side up, in a shallow roasting pan. Sprinkle with oil, salt and pepper and bake until just browning on the top but still firm. Allow to cool. Keep the oven on.

3 Lift one side of the skin on each chicken breast and place 3 basil leaves under the skin, then pull it back into place. Put the chicken breasts into an ovenproof dish, drizzle with a little oil, season with salt and pepper and sprinkle over some of the remaining basil leaves. Cover and chill until required.

4 Bake the chicken on the top shelf of the oven for 20–25 minutes, or until golden brown and cooked through.

5 Make the dressing: whizz together the tomato sauce and vinegar, using a blender or food processor. Season to taste with salt and pepper.

6 Mix the salad leaves, the remaining basil leaves, tomato slivers, cherry tomatoes, roast plum tomatoes and dressing together in a large bowl. Pile on to individual plates and serve with the chicken.

NOTE: Any soft herbs such as coriander, flat-leaf parsley or oregano can be used in place of the basil. Use a good-quality organic tomato sauce.

Chicken, Avocado and Almond Salad

Preparation time: 10 minutes
Marinating time: 10 minutes
Cooking time: 10 minutes

SERVES 4 AS A MAIN COURSE

4 chicken breasts, skinned and boned

2 tablespoons balsamic vinegar

1 large cos lettuce, washed

2 avocados

3 spring onions, finely sliced on the diagonal

75 g blanched almonds, toasted and roughly chopped
  (see page 17)

1 small punnet cherry tomatoes, halved

For the dressing

¼ teaspoon vegetable stock powder

3 tablespoons mayonnaise (see page 513)

1 tablespoon tarragon vinegar

a pinch of caster sugar

salt and freshly ground black pepper

1 Season the chicken breasts with salt and pepper and coat with the vinegar. Leave to marinate for 10 minutes.

2 Griddle or fry the chicken in a hot pan for 10 minutes on each side, or until cooked through. After the initial browning, the heat should be turned down to prevent the flesh from burning. When the chicken is cool enough to handle, shred roughly and set aside.

3 Tear the lettuce into bite-sized pieces. Peel and stone the avocados and cut the flesh into 1 cm cubes.

4 Make the dressing: add 1 tablespoon boiling water to the vegetable stock and stir until dissolved. Whisk all the dressing ingredients together thoroughly. Season to taste with salt and pepper.

5 Mix the avocado with the lettuce, spring onions, almonds, tomatoes and chicken and toss with the dressing. Serve immediately.

VARIATION: This recipe also works well using leftover roast chicken. Shred the chicken, omit the marinade and continue from stage 3.

Lime Chicken and Chilli Salad

This is a good recipe for using up leftover roast chicken. Mince the chicken in a food processor or shred it finely.

Preparation time: 10 minutes
Marinating time: 30 minutes–2 hours

SERVES 4 AS A MAIN COURSE

250–350 g cooked chicken, minced or finely
   chopped
iceberg lettuce, shredded
1 small bunch of fresh coriander leaves
¼ cucumber, deseeded and diced

For the marinade

4 tablespoons nam pla (Thai fish sauce)
4 tablespoons lime juice
3 tablespoons caster sugar
1–2 red chillies, deseeded and finely sliced
4 spring onions, finely sliced on the diagonal
½ red onion, finely sliced

To prepare ahead: Prepare the chicken to the end of stage 2.

1 Place the chicken in a bowl.
2 Mix together the nam pla, lime juice and sugar. Add the chillies and onions and pour over the chicken. Mix well and leave to marinate for 30 minutes, or up to 2 hours in the refrigerator.
3 Mix together the lettuce and coriander and arrange on individual plates. Scatter over the cucumber.
4 Spoon over the chicken and marinade and serve immediately.

VARIATION: Turkey may be used instead of chicken.

Warm Chicken Salad with Chilli Oil and Coriander

Preparation time: 15 minutes
Cooking time: 10 minutes

SERVES 6–8 AS A FIRST COURSE, 4 AS A MAIN COURSE.

4 plum tomatoes
3 tablespoons chilli oil
4 chicken breasts, skinned and cut into 2.5 cm cubes
2 tablespoons sesame seeds, lightly toasted (see page 17)
4 tablespoons balsamic vinegar
6 tablespoons roughly chopped fresh coriander

1 tablespoon sweet chilli sauce
1 × 300 g bag mixed salad leaves
olive oil, to drizzle
salt and freshly ground black pepper

To garnish
fresh coriander leaves

1 Quarter and deseed the tomatoes. Cut into slivers lengthways.

2 In a wok or sauté pan, heat the chilli oil until hot. Add the chicken and stir-fry for about 5 minutes, or until golden in colour and cooked through. Add the sesame seeds and stir-fry for a further 30 seconds.

3 Add the tomatoes, vinegar and coriander. Stir thoroughly and season to taste with salt and pepper. Add the sweet chilli sauce.

4 Remove from the heat and add the salad leaves, stirring well with a large spoon.

5 Drizzle enough of the olive oil over the salad to coat the leaves. When the leaves start to wilt, serve immediately.

Pesto Chicken Salad

Buy ready-cooked chicken breasts or use up leftover roast chicken in this recipe.

Preparation time: 20 minutes
Cooking time: 20 minutes

SERVES 4 AS A FIRST COURSE, 2 AS A MAIN COURSE

100 g new potatoes

30 g cashew nuts

1 × 100 g bag of rocket or mixed salad leaves

10 cherry tomatoes, halved

2 chicken breasts, cooked and sliced

5 tablespoons ready-made basil pesto (or see page 512)

2 tablespoons olive oil

To garnish

Parmesan cheese shavings

1 Bring a small saucepan of salted water to the boil, add the new potatoes and cook for about 15 minutes, or until tender. Drain well.

2 Meanwhile, heat a frying pan, add the cashew nuts and cook over a low heat until lightly browned, stirring all the time. Remove from the pan.

3 Place the salad leaves, tomatoes and cashew nuts in a large bowl.

4 Add the chicken and potatoes.

5 Whisk the pesto with the oil until well emulsified. Add to the salad and toss lightly.

6 Pile into a serving dish and garnish with Parmesan shavings.

VARIATION: Pinenuts may be used in place of cashew nuts.

Sweet and Sour Chicken Salad

This salad is great for feeding a large number of people. The quantities can also easily be reduced to serve fewer.

Preparation time: 15 minutes
Marinating time: overnight
Cooking time: 20 minutes

SERVES 8 AS A MAIN COURSE

8 chicken breasts, skinned and boned
125 g cornflour
125 g plain flour
½ teaspoon salt
oil, for frying
150 g blanched almonds
1 small iceberg lettuce, torn into bite-sized pieces
1 bunch of spring onions, chopped

For the marinade

150 ml light soy sauce
150 ml dry sherry
1 tablespoon peeled and finely chopped fresh root ginger
1 clove of garlic, crushed

For the dressing

175 ml salad oil
125 ml white wine vinegar
150 g caster sugar
1½ tablespoons light soy sauce
¼ teaspoon dry English mustard

To prepare ahead: Leave to marinate overnight.

1 Mix together the marinade ingredients. Add the chicken, cover and refrigerate for several hours or overnight.
2 Remove the chicken from the marinade and pat dry with kitchen paper.
3 Combine the cornflour, flour and salt on a plate. Coat the chicken in the flour mixture, shaking to remove any excess.
4 Heat the oil in a large frying pan, add the chicken and fry over a low heat for 5 minutes, or until golden brown and cooked through. Remove from the pan and leave to cool.
5 Wipe the pan clean and add the almonds. Cook over a low heat until lightly toasted, stirring all the time. Remove from the pan.
6 Mix together the dressing ingredients. Slice the chicken, place in a large bowl and stir in the dressing.
7 Add the lettuce, spring onions and almonds. Toss together.
8 Divide between individual plates, or pile on to a large platter, and serve immediately.

Oriental Chicken Salad

This recipe is ideal for using up cold roast chicken.

Preparation time: 10 minutes

SERVES 8 AS A FIRST COURSE, 4 AS A MAIN COURSE.

4 boneless chicken breasts, cooked and skinned

200 g beansprouts

1 bunch of fresh coriander, roughly chopped

a pinch of sugar

1 clove of garlic, crushed

1 red chilli

1 × 2.5 cm piece of fresh root ginger

For the dressing

2 tablespoons light soy sauce

juice of 1 lime

1 tablespoon sesame oil

To garnish

50 g dry roasted peanuts, chopped

To prepare ahead: Prepare to the end of stage 3.

Serving suggestions: Crisp green salad leaves, shredded Chinese leaves, green papaya

1 Mix together the soy sauce, lime juice, sesame oil, sugar and garlic. Combine well.

2 Finely chop the chilli and peel and grate the ginger. Add to the dressing.

3 Shred the chicken or cut into bite-sized pieces.

4 Stir the dressing through the chicken and mix in the beansprouts and coriander.

5 Divide between individual plates. Scatter over the peanuts and serve.

NOTE: If you don't have chicken leftovers, grill or fry chicken breasts until cooked through (see page 209), or buy cooked chicken breasts to save time.

Smoked Chicken Salad with Black Pudding

Allow ½ egg and 1 slice of black pudding per person, whether serving as a first or main course.

Preparation time: 10 minutes
Cooking time: 10 minutes

SERVES 6–8 AS A FIRST COURSE, 4 AS A MAIN COURSE

1 × 250 g bag of bistro salad

60 g cherry tomatoes, quartered

2 smoked chicken breasts, cut into slices

2–4 soft-boiled eggs (see page 51), shelled and
  halved

For the dressing

1 tablespoon balsamic vinegar

3 tablespoons good-quality olive oil

1 teaspoon wholegrain mustard

salt and freshly ground black pepper

1 Make the dressing: mix all the ingredients together throughly.
2 Fry the black pudding in a heavy frying pan until crisp on both sides.
3 Mix together the salad leaves and tomatoes and toss in half the dressing.
4 Divide the salad between individual plates and, arrange the smoked chicken slices on top.
5 Place the black pudding on top of the chicken and the soft-boiled egg half on the very top.
6 Drizzle over a little more of the dressing and serve immediately.

VARIATIONS: Ordinary cooked chicken may be used in place of the smoked chicken and slices of chorizo sausage in place of the black pudding.

Warm Smoked Chicken, Avocado and Bacon Salad

Preparation time: 15 minutes
Cooking time: 10 minutes

SERVES 6–8 AS A FIRST COURSE, 4–6 AS A MAIN COURSE

1 × 100 g bag of rocket

1 small smoked chicken

1 large ripe avocado

50 g sunblush tomatoes, halved

8 rashers of smoked streaky bacon

For the dressing

3 tablespoons olive oil (or sunblush tomato oil if
  available)

1 tablespoon balsamic vinegar

1 teaspoon sugar

½ teaspoon Dijon mustard

a squeeze of lemon juice

salt and freshly ground black pepper

1 Wash and dry the rocket and place in a large bowl.
2 Skin the chicken and remove the bones. Tear the chicken into strips as long as possible, and add to the rocket.
3 Peel the avocado, remove the stone and cut the flesh into long strips. Add to the bowl along with the tomatoes.
4 Make the dressing: mix all the ingredients together and season to taste.
5 Cut the bacon rashers in half if serving 8. Fry the bacon over a fairly high heat to colour it well on both sides, and to release the fat into the pan. Remove the bacon and place on kitchen paper to drain.
6 Add the dressing to the pan and allow to bubble for a few seconds, then pour over the salad ingredients in the bowl. Toss immediately and divide between individual plates.
7 Place 2 or 4 bacon pieces on top of each salad and serve immediately.

BLT Salad

Preparation time: 10 minutes
Cooking time: 30 minutes

SERVES 6–8 AS A FIRST COURSE, 4 AS A MAIN COURSE

8 rashers of rindless smoked streaky bacon
100 g cherry tomatoes
oil, for frying
½ focaccia or ciabatta loaf, cut into 2 cm chunks (any remaining bread can be served with the salad)

4 plum or salad tomatoes
4 tablespoons ready-made mayonnaise (or see page 513)
2 tablespoons water
1 tablespoon wholegrain mustard
1 × 200 g pack of mixed continental salad leaves
salt and freshly ground black pepper

1 Preheat the oven to 200°C|400°F|gas mark 6.
2 Stretch the bacon rashers on a chopping board with the back of a knife and place on a baking sheet with the cherry tomatoes. Bake in the oven until the rashers are crisp and brown, removing the tomatoes when they soften and begin to colour. Turn the oven off so it can be used as a warming oven.
3 Heat oil at least 1 cm deep in a heavy frying pan until a cube of bread sizzles and browns in about 20 seconds. Fry the chunks of bread, a handful at a time, until evenly browned. Remove with a slotted metal spoon, then drain on kitchen paper and sprinkle with a little salt. Keep warm in the oven.
4 Slice the plum or salad tomatoes. Whisk the mayonnaise, water and mustard together and season to taste with salt and pepper.
5 Toss the salad leaves, sliced tomatoes, cherry tomatoes and bacon rashers, broken into pieces, together with the dressing. Pile on to plates and garnish with the croûtons.

Poached Egg Salad

Preparation time: 10 minutes

SERVES 2 AS A MAIN COURSE OR 4 AS A FIRST COURSE

1 large head (about 450 g) frisée lettuce

2–4 very fresh eggs (1 per person)

For the dressing

7 tablespoons vegetable oil

175 g smoked bacon lardons

2 garlic cloves, finely sliced

5 tablespoons red wine vinegar

1 teaspoon Dijon mustard

freshly ground black pepper

small handful of croûtons (see page 380)

To prepare ahead: Complete to the end of stage 4. Reheat the dressing, cook the eggs and assemble the salad.

1 Discard the tough outer green leaves from the frisée and pull apart the central leaves and break into bite-sized pieces. Wash, dry well and put in a bowl.

2 Bring a large saucepan of water to the boil for poaching the eggs.

3 Heat 1 tablespoon of the oil in a frying pan, add the bacon and fry, stirring occasionally. When the bacon is well browned and the fat is rendered, lower the heat and discard some of the fat if you have more than 3-4 tablespoons.

4 Add the garlic to the pan and cook until it is soft but not browned, about 30 seconds. Add the vinegar and boil until reduced by half, then whisk in the remaining oil and mustard and season with black pepper. Remove from the heat.

5 Poach the eggs (see page 13).

6 Whisk the dressing together so that it is emulsified then pour it over the salad and toss together. Divide the salad between plates.

7 Place the poached egg on top of the salad and scatter over the croûtons. Serve immediately.

VARIATION: Use soft- or hardboiled eggs in place of the poached eggs. Add cubes of cheese such as Gruyère or Jarlsberg to the salad.

Warm Duck and Pink Grapefruit Salad with Potato Croûtons

Preparation time: 15 minutes
Marinating time: 15 minutes–3 hours
Cooking time: 30 minutes

SERVES 4 AS A MAIN COURSE

4 duck breasts, skinned

grated zest of 1 pink grapefruit

6 tablespoons olive oil

3 large potatoes

135 g watercress, washed, any coarse stalks
   removed

4 spring onions, finely chopped

2 pink grapefruit, segmented or sliced, all pith and
   membrane removed

sea salt flakes and freshly ground black pepper

For the dressing

juice of 1 pink grapefruit (about 290 ml)

1 teaspoon clear honey

4 tablespoons olive oil

To prepare ahead: Prepare to the end of stage 3. Reheat the potatoes when assembling the salad.

1 Preheat the oven to 200°C | 400°F | gas mark 6.
2 Place the duck breasts in a bowl with the grapefruit zest and 2 tablespoons of the oil, making sure the zest coats the breasts. Leave for at least 15 minutes.
3 Peel the potatoes and cut into 2 cm cubes. Place them in a bowl and stir in half the remaining oil and 1 tablespoon sea salt flakes. Spread out on a baking sheet and bake in the oven for 30 minutes, or until brown and crisp, stirring occasionally.
4 Meanwhile, heat the remaining oil in a large, heavy frying pan. Season the duck breasts with salt and pepper. When the pan is hot, fry them for 2 minutes each side, or until lightly browned. Reduce the heat and continue to cook for 3 minutes on each side, or until the duck is still pink inside. Remove from the pan and set aside.
5 Make the dressing: pour the oil out of the frying pan and add the grapefruit juice and honey. Reduce by two-thirds by boiling rapidly. Remove from the heat and whisk in 4 tablespoons olive oil until well combined. Season to taste with salt and pepper.
6 Toss the watercress, spring onions and grapefruit segments with the dressing. Pile on to individual plates.
7 Slice the duck breasts thinly. Arrange in overlapping slices over the salad. Sprinkle with the potato croûtons and serve immediately.

NOTE: To cut down the cooking time, omit the potato croûtons and use bought bread croûtons or cooked new potatoes instead.
VARIATION: Use 2 oranges in place of the grapefruit.

Avocado, Potato and Bacon Salad

Preparation time: 15 minutes
Cooking time: 15 minutes

SERVES 6–8 AS A FIRST COURSE, 4 AS A MAIN COURSE

5 tablespoons olive oil

175 g bacon lardons

3 tablespoons balsamic vinegar

350 g new potatoes, halved horizontally

2 avocados

1 × 250 g bag of mixed salad leaves

1 soft-boiled egg (see page 13) per person, peeled

salt and freshly ground black pepper

To garnish

1 tablespoon chopped fresh chives

To prepare ahead: Prepare to the end of stage 2. Warm the bacon and dressing through before serving the salad.

1 Heat 1 tablespoon of the oil in a heavy frying pan, add the bacon and fry until golden brown. Add the remaining oil and the vinegar to the pan and season with pepper. Remove the pan from the heat and set aside.

2 Boil the new potatoes in salted water for about 10–15 minutes, or until cooked. Drain and add to the frying pan with the bacon and dressing. Stir well, then set aside and allow the potatoes to absorb the dressing while preparing the other ingredients.

3 Peel and stone the avocados and cut the flesh into slices or chunks. Toss together with the salad leaves. Divide between individual plates, then pile the potato and bacon on to the centre of each bed of salad leaves.

4 Cut the soft-boiled eggs in half and place 2 halves on the very top of each serving. Garnish with the chives.

Italian Bread Salad

Preparation time: 20 minutes
Standing time: 1 hour

SERVES 6–8

1 loaf slightly stale Italian bread, crust removed

1 large red onion, finely chopped

1 cucumber, peeled and chopped

1 small bunch of fresh basil leaves, roughly chopped

10 black olives, pitted and chopped

3 large beef tomatoes, roughly chopped

2 tablespoons good-quality capers, drained and rinsed

6 tablespoons olive oil

3 tablespoons red wine vinegar

salt and freshly ground black pepper

1 Break the bread into small pieces and place in a large bowl.
2 Add the onion, cucumber, basil, olives, tomatoes and capers. Make sure that all the juice from the tomatoes is added to the salad.
3 Add the oil and vinegar; mix well and season to taste with salt and pepper. Leave to stand for 1 hour before serving.

Beef and Coconut Chilli Salad

Preparation time: 10 minutes
Cooking time: 10 minutes

SERVES 4–5 AS A MAIN COURSE

450 g sirloin steak, about 5cm thick
1 teaspoon Sichuan peppercorns, crushed
oil, for frying
250 g French beans
250 g Chinese leaves, shredded
1 red chilli, deseeded and finely chopped
a handful of fresh coriander leaves
salt

For the dressing

150 ml coconut milk
2 tablespoons sweet chilli dipping sauce
grated zest and juice of ½ lime
1 tablespoon nam pla (Thai fish sauce)

To garnish

50 g roasted salted peanuts, roughly chopped

To prepare ahead: Assemble to the end of stage 3.

1 Remove any fat or gristle from the steak. Season with salt and Sichuan pepper. Heat a little oil in a frying pan, add the steak and brown well on both sides. Turn the heat down to medium and cook for a further 4 minutes on each side for rare steak; longer for well done. (If your steak is thinner than 5 cm it will require a shorter cooking time.) Remove the steak, transfer to a wire rack and leave to cool completely.
2 Bring a saucepan of water to the boil, add the beans and cook for 5 minutes. Plunge them into a bowl of ice-cold water and leave to cool completely, then drain.
3 Mix together the beans, Chinese leaves, chilli and coriander.
4 Whisk together the dressing ingredients and toss in the bean mixture. Divide the salad between individual plates and sprinkle with the peanuts.
5 Cut the steak into very thin strips and scatter over the salad. Serve immediately.

Sesame Beef Salad

Preparation time: 10 minutes
Marinating time: 2 hours or overnight
Cooking time: 30 minutes

SERVES 6 AS A MAIN COURSE

450 g sirloin steak, about 5 cm thick, fat and gristle
   removed
oil, for frying
250 g button mushrooms, sliced
250 g mangetout

For the marinade

2 onions, finely sliced
5 tablespoons dry sherry
5 tablespoons light soy sauce

3 tablespoons sesame oil
freshly ground black pepper

For the dressing

6 tablespoons grapeseed oil
3 tablespoons white wine vinegar
1 tablespoon Dijon mustard
1 teaspoon clear honey

To prepare ahead: Marinate the steaks overnight. Alternatively prepare to the end of stage 4.

1 Mix together the marinade ingredients, add the steak and leave to marinate for at least 2 hours or overnight. Turn the steak occasionally if not completely submerged in the marinade.

2 Remove the beef and the onions from the marinade. Reserve the marinade. Heat a little oil in a heavy frying pan and brown the steak well on both sides. Turn the heat down to medium and cook for a further 4 minutes on each side for rare steak; longer for well done. Remove the steak, transfer to a wire rack and leave to rest.

3 Add the onions from the marinade to the frying pan with the mushrooms and cook over a medium heat for about 10 minutes or until soft, then increase the heat and brown well. Add the marinade to the pan and boil vigorously until it has reduced to about 2 tablespoons.

4 Place the dressing ingredients in a bowl and whisk until well emulsified. Pour over the mushroom and onion mixture.

5 When you are ready to serve, cut the steak into very thin strips and add to the dressing.

6 Bring a small saucepan of salted water to the boil, add the mangetout and cook for 1 minute, then drain and add to the remaining ingredients. Toss together and pile on to individual plates.

VARIATION: This recipe also works well with tuna steaks instead of sirloin.

Beef and Horseradish Salad

This is a good recipe for using up leftover roast beef.

Preparation time: 20 minutes
Cooking time: 10 minutes

SERVES 8 AS A FIRST COURSE, 4 AS A MAIN COURSE

8 slices of rare roast beef
2 tablespoons olive oil
1 clove of garlic, crushed
3 large beef tomatoes, cut into 1 cm slices
250 g watercress, any coarse stalks removed
olive oil

For the dressing

1 tablespoon horseradish sauce
1 tablespoon ready-made mayonnaise (or see page 513)

1 teaspoon white wine vinegar
1 tablespoon warm water
1 tablespoon shredded fresh basil leaves
a pinch of sugar
salt and freshly ground black pepper

To garnish

a handful of pitted black olives

1 Cut the slices of beef into 2–3 strips, depending on their size.
2 Heat the oil in a frying pan, add the garlic and cook for 30 seconds, until beginning to soften but not brown. Add the tomato slices and warm them through over a very low heat (they must not soften too much). Remove the pan from the heat.
3 Whisk the dressing ingredients together and season well with salt and pepper.
4 Toss the watercress in a little oil and season with salt and pepper. Arrange it over individual serving plates. Lay the tomato slices on top and pour over any juices from the frying pan. Arrange the beef slices over the tomato and sprinkle with a little salt. Drizzle with the dressing and scatter with the olives.

NOTE: Instead of using leftover or bought slices of rare roast beef, cook a piece of beef fillet so that it is extremely rare (see page 240), then slice thinly.

Chinese Beef Salad

Preparation time: 20 minutes
Marinating time: overnight
Cooking time: 15 minutes

SERVES 6–8 AS A FIRST COURSE, 4 AS A MAIN COURSE

300 g sirloin steak, thinly sliced

2 tablespoons oil

1 × 125 g pack of baby sweetcorn, finely sliced on the diagonal

½ × 220 g can of water chestnuts, sliced

1 bunch of spring onions, finely sliced on the diagonal

1 head bok choi, shredded

110 g mangetout, sliced on the diagonal

1 × 200 g bag of beansprouts

For the marinade

100 ml dark soy sauce

50 ml sherry

1 × 2.5 cm piece of fresh root ginger, bruised

2 cloves of garlic, crushed

2 red chillies, sliced

2 tablespoons clear honey

To serve

3–4 sheets of medium or fine egg noodles

To prepare ahead: The steak can be left to marinate overnight.

1 Mix together the marinade ingredients, add the beef and marinate overnight or for as long as possible.
2 Remove the beef from the marinade (strain and reserve the marinade) and pat very lightly with kitchen paper.
3 Meanwhile, cook the noodles according to the manufacturer's instructions, then drain well.
4 Heat the oil in the wok, add the beef and stir-fry quickly for 1 minute. Remove from the frying pan with a slotted spoon and set aside.
5 Add the sweetcorn, water chestnuts, spring onions and bok choi to the wok and stir-fry for 2 minutes. Add the mangetout and beansprouts and cook for a further 2 minutes. Remove the vegetables from the pan.
6 Add the marinade to the pan and reduce by boiling rapidly to half the original quantity. Return the beef and vegetables to the pan, reheat and coat with the reduced marinade. Serve either on top of the noodles or with the noodles stirred through.

Caesar Salad

Preparation time: 10 minutes
Cooking time: 15 minutes

SERVES 4

1 large clove of garlic, peeled and sliced

50 ml olive oil

2 slices of bread, crusts removed and cut into cubes

1 cos or romaine lettuce, washed and torn into bite-sized pieces

For the dressing

3 tablespoons ready-made mayonnaise (or see page 513)

30 g Parmesan cheese, finely grated

1 tablespoon lemon juice

2 tablespoons water

½ teaspoon made English mustard

1 anchovy fillet, finely chopped (optional)

a pinch of sugar

freshly ground black pepper

To garnish

Parmesan cheese shavings

To prepare ahead: Prepare to the end of stage 4.

1 Preheat the oven to 200°C|400°F|gas mark 6.

2 Mix the garlic with the oil in a small pan. Warm slightly, then remove from the heat and leave to stand for 10 minutes. Strain off 1 tablespoon of the oil and reserve to make the dressing.

3 Make the croûtons: place the pieces of bread in a bowl and toss in the remaining garlic oil. Discard the slices of garlic. Spread the bread out on a baking sheet and bake in the oven for 10–15 minutes, or until golden brown.

4 Whizz the reserved tablespoon of garlic oil with the dressing ingredients in a blender or food processor. Alternatively, whisk well with a balloon or sauce whisk. Add a little more water if the dressing is too thick.

5 Toss the lettuce in the dressing. Sprinkle over the croûtons and Parmesan shavings and serve immediately.

VARIATION: Use bought croûtons to save time. Add shredded chicken to the salad and toss with the lettuce in the dressing.

Caramelized Onion, Blue Cheese and Rocket Salad

Preparation time: 15 minutes
Cooking time: 30 minutes

SERVES 6–8 AS A FIRST COURSE, 4 AS A MAIN COURSE

2 tablespoons oil

2 red onions, peeled, root removed, cut into 8 wedges

1 onion, peeled, root removed, cut into 8 wedges

5 tablespoons balsamic vinegar

½ tablespoon soft light brown sugar

60 g walnuts, roughly chopped

1 × 135 g bag of rocket or rocket and spinach salad

60 g Stilton cheese, crumbled

To prepare ahead: Prepare to the end of stage 3.

1 Heat the oil in a frying pan over a low to medium heat. Add the onions and sweat over a low heat until soft but not coloured.

2 Turn up the heat and allow the onions to become caramelized and start to brown. Add the vinegar and the sugar, stir gently and continue to cook over a medium heat, so that the vinegar begins to reduce.

3 When the vinegar has become thick and sticky and coats the onions, add the walnuts and stir through. Remove from the heat.

4 Divide the rocket between individual plates and spoon over the onion and walnut mixture. Scatter over the Stilton.

Goat's Cheese and Cherry Salad

Preparation time: 15 minutes

SERVES 6 AS A FIRST COURSE

1 × 50 g bag of rocket

350 g fresh ripe cherries, stoned (use an olive stoner) and halved

100 g walnuts, roughly chopped

250 g goat's cheese, crumbled

For the dressing

2 tablespoons olive oil

¾ tablespoon balsamic vinegar

salt and freshly ground black pepper

1 Mix the rocket leaves with the cherries and walnuts. Mix together the oil and vinegar and season well with salt and pepper. Toss the salad in the dressing.

2 Divide the salad between individual plates and scatter over the goat's cheese.

VARIATIONS: Other cheeses such as Lancashire, Cheshire or feta can be used in place of the goat's cheese, or a slice of soft goat's cheese log.

Beetroot, Roasted Onion and Goat's Cheese Salad

Preparation time: 10 minutes
Cooking time: 30 minutes

SERVES 6–8 AS A FIRST COURSE, 4 AS A MAIN COURSE

3 red onions, peeled, root removed, cut into 6 wedges

6 tablespoons olive oil

50 g pinenuts

2 tablespoons balsamic vinegar

600 g cooked beetroot (not preserved in vinegar), peeled and cut into large cubes

350 g goat's cheese, cut into cubes

1 × 250 g bag of mixed salad leaves

salt and freshly ground black pepper

1 Preheat the oven to 200°C|400°F|gas mark 6.

2 Toss the onions in 4 tablespoons of the oil and roast in the oven for about 20–25 minutes, or until just tender. Remove and allow to cool slightly.

3 Turn the oven down to 150°C|300°F|gas mark 2 and carefully toast the pinenuts, making sure not to burn them as they cook quickly (see page 17).

4 Mix together the remaining oil and the vinegar. Add the cubed beetroot and season with salt and pepper. Add the warm onion, including the oil, and mix. Stir in the goat's cheese.

5 Divide the salad leaves between individual plates. Spoon over the red onion, beetroot and goat's cheese mixture and sprinkle with the toasted pinenuts.

Nectarine, Rocket and Feta Salad

Preparation time: 10 minutes
Cooking time: 5 minutes

SERVES 6–8 AS A FIRST COURSE, 4 AS A MAIN COURSE,

3 ripe nectarines

175 g pancetta, cubed

8 tablespoons balsamic vinegar

1 oakleaf lettuce

80 g feta cheese, crumbled

6 fresh basil leaves, shredded

1 large bag of rocket

salt and freshly ground black pepper

To prepare ahead: Prepare to the end of stage 3. Gently reheat the dressing before assembling.

1 Wash the nectarines, remove the stones and chop the flesh into bite-sized pieces.

2 Fry the pancetta in a heavy frying pan until golden brown, then drain off the excess fat.

3 Add the vinegar to the pan and reduce by boiling to about 3 tablespoons.

4 Put the lettuce, feta and basil into a large bowl. Add the pancetta, rocket and nectarines. Mix well and season with salt and pepper. Pour over the reduced vinegar and serve immediately.

VARIATION: Watermelon may be used in place of the nectarines.

Red Onion, Feta and Pumpkin Seed Salad

Preparation time: 10 minutes

SERVES 4–6

1 red onion

4 vine-ripened tomatoes

3 tablespoons olive oil

1 tablespoon lemon juice

1 tablespoon fresh oregano, roughly chopped

250 g feta cheese, crumbled

50 g pumpkin seeds

salt and freshly ground black pepper

To prepare ahead: Prepare to the end of stage 3.

1 Slice the onion finely.

2 Quarter and deseed the tomatoes, then cut into slivers lengthways.

3 Mix together the oil and lemon juice. Add the oregano and season with salt and pepper.

4 Mix all the ingredients, including the pumpkin seeds, together, stirring carefully to avoid breaking up the tomatoes too much. Pile on to individual plates and serve.

Honeyed Goat's Cheese Salad

Preparation time: 10 minutes
Cooking time: 10 minutes

SERVES 6–8 AS A FIRST COURSE, 4 AS A MAIN COURSE

2 tablespoons oil

100 g bacon lardons

4 tablespoons balsamic vinegar

4 crottin goat's cheeses

150 g mixed salad leaves

4 teaspoons clear honey

2 tomatoes, deseeded and diced

To prepare ahead: Prepare to the end of stage 3.

1 Preheat the grill to the highest setting.

2 Heat half the oil in a heavy frying pan. Add the lardons and cook until golden brown. Add the vinegar and the remaining oil to the pan and stir well, scraping any sediment off the bottom of the pan. Leave in the pan but remove from the heat.

3 Cut each crottin in half horizontally.

4 Wash and dry the salad leaves and tear into bite-sized pieces.

5 Put the crottins cut side up on a baking sheet and drizzle the honey over the cut sides. Place under the grill until golden brown and beginning to bubble.

6 Reheat the dressing and lardons and add the tomatoes. Pour over the salad leaves and toss.

7 Arrange the salad leaves, bacon, tomatoes and dressing on individual plates and place 1 or 2 crottin halves on top.

Main Courses

We have concentrated on quick-cook cuts in this section and the ingredients our students and friends tell us they like to eat, such as chicken breasts and salmon fillet. There are a large number of recipes using ingredients from all over the world to bring some new ideas to the dinner table.

Vegetarian

Cherry Tomato Tatin

Preparation time: 10 minutes
Cooking time: 30 minutes

SERVES 4–6

2 tablespoons oil

700 g cherry tomatoes, stalks removed

2 tablespoons chopped fresh thyme

2 teaspoons caster sugar

375 g ready-rolled puff pastry

150 ml balsamic vinegar

salt and freshly ground black pepper

To prepare ahead: This can be prepared ahead and then baked at the last minute. Alternatively, cook completely but do not turn out: to serve, warm through in the pan in the preheated oven, then turn out.
Serving suggestions: Mixed green salad (see page 381), grilled courgettes

1 Preheat the oven to 200°C | 400°F | gas mark 6.
2 Pour the oil into a 25 cm metal-handled frying pan and add the tomatoes, thyme, salt, pepper and sugar. Shake to make sure that the tomatoes are covered in the seasonings.
3 On a floured surface, cut out a 25 cm circle from the pastry. Place the pastry over the top of the tomatoes. Bake in the oven for 20 minutes, or until the pastry is golden brown.
4 Remove the frying pan from the oven. Gently tip the pan to one side, drain off any liquid and pour into a small saucepan.
5 Add the vinegar to the reserved juices in the pan and bring to the boil, then reduce to a syrupy consistency.
6 Invert a large plate over the pastry and turn the pan over (be very careful as any remaining hot juices will come out from under the pastry).
7 Drizzle the reduced vinegar mixture over the top and serve immediately.

Cheese Fondue

Preparation time: 10 minutes
Cooking time: 15 minutes

SERVES 4

1 clove of garlic, peeled and halved
juice of ½ lemon
250 ml dry white wine
250 g Gruyère cheese, grated
250 g Emmental cheese, grated
2 tablespoons kirsch
2 teaspoons cornflour
freshly grated nutmeg

salt and freshly ground black pepper

To serve
chunks of French bread
fresh vegetables such as cauliflower, carrots and
    broccoli
boiled new potatoes
green salad (see page 381)

1 Rub the cut side of the garlic over the base and sides of a heavy saucepan.
2 Put the lemon juice and wine into the pan and gradually bring to the boil.
3 Add the cheeses to the pan and allow to melt gently, bringing the mixture up to the boil. If it begins to go lumpy, increase the heat slightly.
4 Mix the kirsch and cornflour together and add to the fondue mix, stirring until thickened and smooth.
5 Season with nutmeg, salt and pepper and keep warm until ready to serve with the bread and vegetables for dunking, accompanied by the salad.

Cheese and Tomato Fondue

Preparation time: 10 minutes
Cooking time: 10 minutes

SERVES 4

150 ml tomato passata
2 teaspoons brandy
250 g Gruyère cheese, grated
250 g Emmental cheese, grated
1 teaspoon Worcestershire sauce (optional)
salt and freshly ground black pepper

To serve
chunks of crusty bread
boiled new potatoes
green salad (see page 381)

1 Place the passata and brandy in a small saucepan. Bring to the boil and gradually stir in the cheeses until melted. Season with Worcestershire sauce, salt and pepper. Keep it warm and serve with the bread and potatoes for dunking, accompanied by the salad.

Halloumi Barbecue Brochettes

Marinating time: 20 minutes–overnight
Preparation time: 20 minutes
Cooking time: 10 minutes

MAKES 4–5

1 × 250 g pack of halloumi cheese, cut into 16
  equal pieces
1 red chilli, finely diced
3 tablespoons chilli oil
1 courgette, sliced

1 yellow pepper, cored, deseeded and cut into
  squares
1 red pepper, cored, deseeded and cut into squares
1 red onion, cut into wedges
wooden skewers, soaked in water

To prepare ahead: Leave to marinate overnight.

1 Place the cheese in a shallow dish and add the chilli and chilli oil. Leave to marinate for at
  least 20 minutes or as long as possible, turning occasionally.
2 When ready to cook, thread the vegetables and cheese on to wooden skewers.
3 When the barbecue is hot, grill, turning regularly until the vegetables are cooked and the
  halloumi has a good golden crust. Baste with the chilli oil.

Gem Squash with Mushrooms

Preparation time: 15 minutes
Cooking time: 20 minutes

SERVES 4

1 tablespoon oil
2 red onions, finely chopped
2 cloves of garlic, crushed
450 g mushrooms, sliced
4 gem squash

2 tablespoons chopped fresh lemon thyme
4 tablespoons crème fraîche
salt and freshly ground black pepper

To serve
Parmesan cheese shavings

To prepare ahead: Assemble the squash and keep refrigerated. Reheat at 190°C|375°F|gas mark 5 for 30
minutes or until hot through.
Serving suggestions: Green salad (see page 381), soda bread (see page 462), avocado couscous salad (see
page 354)

1 Heat the oil in a large saucepan, add the onions and sweat over a low heat until soft, but
  not coloured. Add the garlic and cook for 45 seconds, then add the mushrooms and
  allow to cook until softened and any liquid has evaporated.

2 Meanwhile, cut the tops off the gem squash and scoop out the fibres and seeds. Bring a large pan of salted water to the boil and boil the squash and their tops for 5–8 minutes, or until just tender.

3 Add the thyme and crème fraîche to the mushroom mixture and stir through. Season with salt and pepper and allow to reduce by boiling rapidly until the sauce is creamy.

4 Season the inside of the squash lightly with salt and pepper and pile the mushroom filling into them so that it comes above the tops. Sprinkle over the Parmesan, replace the lids and serve immediately.

Chickpea and Spinach Curry

Preparation time: 10 minutes
Cooking time: 20 minutes

SERVES 4

4 tablespoons olive oil
1 red onion, finely chopped
2 cloves of garlic, crushed
1 red chilli, deseeded and chopped
1 × 5 cm piece of fresh root ginger, peeled and grated
1 tablespoon ground cumin
1 teaspoon ground cinnamon
1 teaspoon ground coriander
½ teaspoon ground turmeric

½ teaspoon ground cardamom
1 × 400 g can of cooked chickpeas, rinsed and drained
1 teaspoon caster sugar
1 × 400 g can of chopped tomatoes
1 × 200 g bag of baby spinach leaves
salt and freshly ground black pepper

To garnish
chopped fresh coriander

To prepare ahead: Make in advance to the end of stage 3, then refrigerate or freeze, but only add the spinach just before serving. If frozen, make sure the curry is thoroughly defrosted before reheating.
Serving suggestions: Basmati rice (see page 374), mango chutney, poppadoms

1 Heat the oil in a heavy saucepan, add the onion and fry until brown. Add the garlic, chilli and ginger and cook for 1 further minute.
2 Add the spices and cook for 1 minute.
3 Add the chickpeas, sugar and tomatoes and simmer for 20 minutes, or until the sauce is fairly thick. If too thin, boil vigorously for a couple of minutes; if too thick, add water.
4 Add the spinach and stir until just wilted. Season to taste with salt and pepper. Pile onto a warmed serving dish and garnish with coriander.

NOTE: You can use 1–2 tablespoons Indian curry paste (see page 35) in place of the dry spices.

Sweet Potato and Lychee Curry

Preparation time: 10 minutes
Cooking time: 30 minutes

SERVES 4

1 tablespoon oil
1 onion, finely chopped
2 cloves of garlic, sliced
1 tablespoon green curry paste
400 ml coconut milk
1 teaspoon sugar

water
300 g sweet potato, peeled and cubed
1 × 400 g can of lychees (in juice, not syrup),
    drained and halved
a small handful of fresh coriander, roughly
    chopped

To prepare ahead: Make the curry, then refrigerate or freeze. Reheat as required. If frozen, make sure it is completely defrosted before reheating.
Serving suggestion: Jasmine rice (see page 375)

1 Heat the oil in a large, heavy saucepan, add the onion and sweat over a low heat until soft but not coloured. Add the garlic and fry until golden brown, then add the curry paste and gradually blend in the coconut milk and sugar. Add enough water to make a thin sauce, the consistency of single cream.

2 Bring the sauce to the boil and add the sweet potato cubes. Simmer for about 10 minutes, or until the sweet potato is beginning to soften. Add the lychees and continue to simmer until the sweet potato is completely cooked.

3 Stir in the coriander and serve immediately.

VARIATION: A small bag of washed baby spinach leaves can be stirred in at the end of cooking.

Spiced Sweet Potato Stew

Preparation time: 15 minutes
Cooking time: 40 minutes

SERVES 4

2 tablespoons oil
2 onions, sliced
1 tablespoon mustard seeds
1 tablespoon garam masala
½ teaspoon ground cinnamon
1 teaspoon ground cumin
2 green chillies, chopped
5 cloves of garlic, crushed
30 g fresh root ginger, peeled and sliced

250 g sweet potatoes, peeled and cubed
250 g parsnips, peeled and cubed
1 × 400 g can of chopped tomatoes
lemon juice to taste
salt and freshly ground black pepper

To garnish
fresh coriander leaves

To prepare ahead: This stew can be prepared in advance, then refrigerated or frozen and reheated as required. If frozen, make sure it is completely defrosted before reheating.

Serving suggestions: Brown rice pilaf and sesame seeds (see page 376), fried rice with pinenuts (see page 375), Indian-style green beans (see page 350), green salad (see page 381), wilted spinach, French beans

1 Heat the oil in a large, heavy saucepan, add the onions and sweat over a low heat until soft but not coloured.
2 Add the mustard seeds, garam masala, cinnamon and cumin and cook until the seeds pop.
3 Add the chillies, garlic and ginger and cook for 1 further minute.
4 Add the sweet potatoes, parsnips and tomatoes. Cover and simmer very gently until the vegetables soften. If necessary add a little water or vegetable stock.
5 Season to taste with lemon juice, salt and pepper. Sprinkle with the coriander leaves and serve.

NOTE: You can use 1–2 tablespoons Indian curry paste (see page 35) in place of the dry spices.

Red Pumpkin and Green Bean Curry

Preparation time: 10 minutes
Cooking time: 25 minutes

SERVES 4

1 tablespoon red Thai curry paste
1 × 400 ml can of coconut milk
400 ml water
350 g pumpkin, peeled and cut into 2.5 cm cubes

170 g potatoes, peeled and cut into 1.25 cm cubes
2 kaffir lime leaves, shredded
225 g French beans, topped, tailed and halved
a handful of sweet basil leaves (horapa), torn

To prepare ahead: Make in advance and reheat as required, but be careful not to overcook the beans.
Serving suggestions: Jasmine rice (see page 375), pineapple rice (see page 376)

1 Place the curry paste in a large, heavy saucepan. Add enough coconut milk to make a smooth paste. Gradually add the remaining coconut milk and then add the water. Stir well. Place the pan over the heat and bring gradually to the boil.
2 Add the pumpkin, potatoes and kaffir lime leaves. Simmer gently for 10 minutes, or until the potatoes are almost tender.
3 Add the beans and continue to simmer until they are tender.
4 Remove from the heat, stir in the sweet basil and serve.

Butternut Squash and Lentil Curry

Preparation time: 15 minutes
Cooking time: 35 minutes

SERVES 4

110 g Puy or beluga lentils
olive oil
1 large red onion, finely chopped
2 cloves of garlic, crushed
1 teaspoon ground cumin
½ teaspoon ground cinnamon
½ teaspoon ground coriander
1 tablespoon chilli powder

1 × 675 g butternut squash, peeled, deseeded and
  chopped into 1.25 cm chunks
1 × 400 g can of chopped tomatoes
1 tablespoon tomato purée
150 ml water
1 teaspoon sugar
5 tablespoons chopped fresh coriander
salt and freshly ground black pepper

1 Cook the lentils in boiling water for 15 minutes, or until just tender. Drain well.

2 Meanwhile, heat 2 tablespoons of the oil in a saucepan, add the onion and sweat over a low heat until soft but not coloured. Add the garlic and the spices and continue to cook for 1 further minute.

3 Add the butternut squash, tomatoes, tomato purée, water and sugar and most of the chopped coriander, reserving some for the garnish.

4 Bring to the boil, then simmer for about 20 minutes, or until the squash is soft. Add a little more water if the curry becomes dry.

5 Add the lentils and simmer for a further 10 minutes, or until they are tender.

6 Season to taste with salt and pepper and sprinkle with the remaining coriander.

VARIATIONS: Pumpkin can be substituted for the butternut squash. You can use 1–2 tablespoons Indian curry paste (see page 35) in place of the dry spices.

Moroccan-style Filo Pie

Preparation time: 20 minutes
Cooking time: 15 minutes

SERVES 4

2 tablespoons olive oil
1 red onion, sliced
1 × 400 g can of chopped tomatoes with chilli
150 ml water or stock
1 × 400 g can of mixed pulses, drained and rinsed
100 g pitted dried dates, chopped

1 tablespoon chopped fresh flat-leaf parsley
5 sheets of filo pastry
60 g butter, melted with a large pinch of ground
  cinnamon
salt and freshly ground black pepper

To prepare ahead: The pie can be assembled and refrigerated or frozen. Defrost and bake when required.

Serving suggestions: Green salad (see page 381), lemon buttered couscous (see page 357)

1 Preheat the oven to 200°C|400°F|gas mark 6.
2 Heat the oil in a large, heavy saucepan, add the onion and sweat over a low heat until soft. Add the tomatoes, water or stock and the pulses. Season with salt and pepper and bring to the boil, then simmer for 6–7 minutes, stirring occasionally. Add the dates and parsley, mix well and turn into a casserole dish.
3 Cover the pie with the layers of filo pastry, brushing each layer with the melted butter and cinnamon. Bake in the oven for 15 minutes, or until the pastry is golden brown.

Baked Butternut Squash with Couscous

Preparation time: 15 minutes
Cooking time: 45 minutes

SERVES 2

1 small butternut squash	30 g pinenuts, toasted (see page 17)
olive oil	grated zest of ½ lemon
60 g couscous	salt and freshly ground black pepper
vegetable stock	
60 g pitted dried dates, chopped	**To garnish**
30 g apricots, chopped	fresh coriander leaves, roughly chopped

To prepare ahead: Make in advance to the end of stage 3. Reheat, covered with kitchen foil, for about 25 minutes in a preheated oven before serving.

Serving suggestions: Green salad (see page 381), ratatouille (see page 347), Italian tomato salad (see page 334), Middle Eastern salad (see page 334)

1 Preheat the oven to 200°C|400°F|gas mark 6.
2 Cut the squash in half lengthways and scoop out the fibres and seeds with a teaspoon. Drizzle with a little oil and season with salt and pepper. Place in a roasting pan and bake in the oven for 35 minutes, or until cooked through and tender.
3 Meanwhile, cook the couscous in the stock according to the manufacturer's instructions. Add the dates, apricots, pinenuts and lemon zest. Season to taste with salt and pepper and fluff up with a fork.
4 Remove the squash from the oven and pile the couscous mixture into the centre.
5 Return to the oven for a further 5 minutes, or until hot through.
6 Scatter the coriander on the top and serve immediately.

NOTE: Butternut squash varies in shape. If it does not have a very big cavity it may be necessary to remove some of the cooked flesh, chop it and add to the couscous stuffing mixture.

Fish

At Leiths we are very aware that various species of fish are at risk. The list of species that are decreasing in waters all around the globe changes from year to year.

The Marine Stewardship Council (MSC) is an independent, global non-profit organization that was set up to find a solution to the problem of overfishing. First established by Unilever, the world's largest buyer of seafood, and the World Wildlife Fund (WWF), the international conservation organization, in 1997, the MSC is now fully independent of both organizations.

MSC spent two years developing an environmental standard for sustainable and well-managed fisheries. This standard was put together following worldwide consultation with scientists, fisheries experts, environmental organizations and other people with a strong interest in preserving fish stocks for the future.

Many supermarkets sell fish that have come from an area which has been certified by the MSC as reaching this environmental standard. These products are distinguished by a blue MSC product label. Further information is available on www.msc.org.

Cooking Fish

Fillets or cutlets of fish can be seasoned and rapidly cooked and accompanied by delicious salads, vegetables and sauces to make a quick and healthy meal.

Frying Fish

Here the fish is fried over a high heat to give instant colour to the flesh, but the cooking is then continued in the oven to give a more gentle, even heat which keeps the flesh moist.

This method is appropriate for all types of fish, although very thin fillets such as sole may not need to be put into the oven at all as they will be cooked by the time both sides are brown. Fish can be dusted with seasoned flour (see page 20) to give extra colour and texture and to protect the delicate flesh.

The time needed to cook a piece of fish will depend on the thickness of the cut and the temperature of the fish. Test the fish is cooked by pressing lightly on the top. If you can feel the flakes of the fish gently giving under your touch, this means the fish is cooked. Salmon and tuna are often served slightly undercooked or even rare.

You will need thick fish fillets such as salmon with the skin on.

1 Preheat the oven to 200°C | 400°F | gas mark 6.
2 Lightly oil and heat a frying pan or griddle pan.

3 Season the fish with salt and pepper and place in the hot pan. Cook for a minute or two on each side, or until nicely browned.

4 Transfer to a roasting pan and bake in the oven for a further 6–8 minutes.

5 Serve immediately.

Grilling Fish

1 Preheat the grill to the highest setting.

2 Place the fish on an oiled baking sheet and brush the surface with oil. Season well with salt and pepper.

3 For thin fillets, just grill until the surface is well browned and serve. For thicker fillets, grill until the first side is brown, then carefully turn with a fish slice or palette knife, brown on the other side and serve.

Poaching Fish

The delicate flesh of fish benefits from being very gently cooked. Where the fish to be poached still has its skin, leave it on until after cooking as it can then be easily peeled off and helps to prevent the fish from drying out. The milk used can be infused with slices of onion, herbs and peppercorns to add extra flavour. Fish can be poached in the oven, or on the hob.

1 To poach in the oven, preheat the oven to 190°C|375°F|gas mark 5.

2 Place the fish in a small roasting pan or ovenproof dish, the skin side up. Pour in enough milk to come nearly to the top of the fish.

3 Cover with a piece of greaseproof paper and a lid or baking sheet. Cook until the flesh is opaque and when you press the fish, you can feel that flakes have formed. The skin should also peel off easily if the fish is cooked.

To poach fish on the hob, place in a saucepan, skin side down. Continue as above.

Serving Suggestions

New potato, dill and caper salad (see page 337); Baked new potatoes en papillote (see page 362); Bean and parsley mash (see page 372); Flavoured mashed potatoes (see page 359); Cooked cucumber with dill (see page 345); Puy lentils and pancetta (see page 374); Orange, fennel and almond salad (see page 333); Potatoes Florentine (see page 139); Rosemary roast vegetables (see page 346); Simmered miso squash (see page 353); Wild rice salad (see page 352); Pea purée (see page 348). See also: Pestos (see page 512); Flavoured butters (see page 242); Hollandaise sauce (see page 514); Mayonnaise (see page 513); Salsas (see page 508)

Quick Sauces

- Melted butter, capers and gherkins
- Garlic and dill mayonnaise
- Warmed olive oil, chopped olives, tomatoes and basil
- Good-quality hollandaise and dill sauce
- Good-quality hollandaise and tarragon sauce
- Good-quality mustard and dill sauce
- Crème fraîche and dill sauce
- Lemon, chive and olive oil dressing

Griddled Salmon with Lemon and Dill Butter

Chilling time: 20 minutes
Preparation time: 5 minutes
Cooking time: 10 minutes

SERVES 4

60 g unsalted butter, softened
grated zest and juice of ½ lemon
1 tablespoon chopped fresh dill
4 × 170 g salmon fillets, skinned and pinboned
salt and freshly ground black pepper

To garnish
4 lemon wedges

To prepare ahead: Make the butter ahead of time.
Serving suggestions: New potatoes, cucumber cooked in dill (see page 345), couscous (see page 356), roast vegetables (see page 249), bean and parsley mash (see page 372), mashed root vegetables

1 Mix together the butter, lemon zest and juice and dill.
2 Roll the butter in clingfilm in the shape of a thin sausage. Place in the refrigerator to chill completely.
3 Heat a griddle pan. When hot, season the salmon well on both sides with salt and freshly ground black pepper. Cut the butter into thin slices.
4 Cook the fish for 3 minutes on each side over a medium heat.
5 Arrange the salmon on individual plates with a slice of the butter on each fillet. Serve immediately, garnished with the lemon wedges.

NOTE: Use any type of fish. For other ideas for flavoured butters, see page 242.

Gravad Lax

Preparation time: 10 minutes
Marinating time: 12 hours

SERVES 20

1 salmon, filleted into 2 sides, pinboned but not
   skinned
vegetable oil
about 3 tablespoons granulated sugar
1½ tablespoons coarse sea salt
1 tablespoon brandy or vodka

1 tablespoon chopped fresh dill
crushed white peppercorns

To serve
mustard and dill sauce
brown bread and butter

1 Smear the salmon sides all over with oil. Put one of them skin side down on a board.
2 Mix together the sugar and salt and press this mixture in a layer on the flesh side of the
fillet. Sprinkle with brandy or vodka to moisten and cover the top with dill – there
should be enough dill to cover the sugar/salt mixture completely. Sprinkle with the
peppercorns.
3 Put the second side on top of the first, skin side up, so that you have a salmon sandwich
with a thick sugar/salt and dill filling.
4 Wrap the salmon very tightly in 2–3 layers of kitchen foil and place it in a tray or dish
with a good lip. Put another tray on top and weight it down – a couple of large cans of
fruit will do. Chill in the refrigerator for about 6 hours.
5 Unwrap the parcel, taking care not to lose any of the juices, turn the whole sandwich
over and rewrap. Weight down again and refrigerate for a further 6 hours.
6 The gravad lax will be ready when it has been marinating for at least 12 hours.
7 Scrape the marinade from the fish, then slice the salmon thinly and serve with the juices
that have run from the fish. Serve the mustard and dill sauce and brown bread and butter
separately.

NOTE: This can also be made with trout, but you will need less of the sugar/salt mix as the fish is much
smaller. Good-quality mustard and dill sauce is available in jars.

Roast Salmon and Hoisin Sauce

Marinating time: 2 hours–overnight
Preparation time: 5 minutes
Cooking time: 20 minutes

SERVES 4

4 × 170 g salmon fillets, skinned and pinboned
1 × 300 g jar of hoisin sauce

To garnish

3 spring onions, finely sliced on the diagonal

To prepare ahead: Leave to marinate overnight.
Serving suggestions: Egg noodles, stir-fried vegetables, steamed bok choi with soy and ginger (see page 350), Thai rice salad (see page 354), steamed cucumber with star anise (see page 351)

1 Put the salmon into a large bowl and pour over enough of the hoisin sauce to coat the fish. Turn the salmon to ensure that it is completely covered. Leave to marinate in the refrigerator for a minimum of 2 hours or overnight if possible.
2 Preheat the oven to 190°C | 375°F | gas mark 5.
3 Place the salmon in a roasting pan. Pour over all the marinade. Cook in the oven for 15 minutes, or until the fish is firm to the touch.
4 Serve the salmon garnished with the spring onions.

Salmon with Sweet Dill and Mustard Crust

Preparation time: 10 minutes
Cooking time: 15 minutes

SERVES 4

oil, for brushing
3 tablespoons mustard and dill sauce
4 × 170 g salmon fillets, skinned and pinboned
4 tablespoons dried breadcrumbs
1 tablespoon chopped fresh dill
½ tablespoon demerara sugar

½ teaspoon dry English mustard
150 ml crème fraîche
2 teaspoons wholegrain mustard
lemon juice
salt and freshly ground black pepper

To prepare ahead: Make in advance to the end of stage 3, then cover and refrigerate.
Serving suggestions: New potatoes, cucumber with dill (see page 345), artichoke dauphinoise (see page 370)

1 Preheat the oven to 190°C | 375°F | gas mark 5. Lightly oil a baking sheet.
2 Spread the mustard and dill sauce over the salmon fillets.

3 Mix together the breadcrumbs, dill, sugar and dry mustard and press over the crust.

4 Place on the prepared baking sheet and bake in the oven for 15 minutes. If the crust isn't brown after cooking, place under a hot grill until golden.

5 Meanwhile, mix together the crème fraîche and wholegrain mustard with enough lemon juice to make it spoonable. Season with salt and pepper.

6 Serve the salmon with a spoonful of the crème fraîche mixture.

NOTE: Good-quality mustard and dill sauce is available in jars.

Maple-glazed Salmon with Sweet and Sour Couscous

Preparation time: 15 minutes
Cooking time: 20 minutes

SERVES 4

4 × 170 g salmon steaks, skinned and pinboned
maple syrup
light soy sauce
2 tablespoons olive oil
1 red onion, sliced
30 g pinenuts
1 bunch of spring onions, finely sliced on the diagonal
1 clove of garlic, crushed

85 g dried apricots, soaked in hot water for 15 minutes, then drained and roughly chopped
425 ml vegetable stock
½ glass of dry white wine
225 g couscous
1 small bunch of fresh parsley or mixed herbs, chopped
1 tablespoon balsamic vinegar

To prepare ahead: Make in advance to the end of stage 4. Reheat the stock before adding the couscous and cooking the salmon.
Serving suggestions: Green salad (see page 381), courgettes, runner beans, French beans

1 Preheat the grill to the highest setting.

2 Brush the salmon steaks all over with the maple syrup and soy sauce. Chill until required.

3 Heat the oil in a heavy saucepan. Add the onion and sweat over a low heat until soft but not coloured, then add the pinenuts and fry until they are starting to brown. Add the spring onions, garlic and apricots and cook for a further 30 seconds.

4 Add the stock and wine and bring to the boil, then simmer for 2 minutes.

5 Stir in the couscous and turn off the heat. Cover the saucepan with a lid and leave to stand for 10 minutes.

6 Meanwhile, grill the salmon until the flesh is firm and opaque.

7 Stir the herbs and vinegar into the couscous and season with salt and pepper. Serve with the salmon.

Salmon with Spiced Coconut and Spinach Lentils

Marinating time: 15 minutes
Preparation time: 10 minutes
Cooking time: 30 minutes

SERVES 4

2 tablespoons sesame oil

2 tablespoons light soy sauce

4 × 170 g salmon fillets, pinboned

2 tablespoons olive oil

1 onion, chopped

85 g button mushrooms, quartered or sliced

1 tablespoon Thai yellow curry paste

170 g Puy lentils, rinsed

1 × 400 ml can of reduced-fat coconut milk

400 ml chicken stock or water

1 × 250 g bag of baby spinach leaves

To prepare ahead: Cook the lentils, reheat with a little extra liquid and stir in the spinach while the salmon is cooking.

1 Mix the sesame oil and soy sauce together in a shallow dish. Place the salmon in the dish and leave to marinate, turning occasionally.
2 Heat half the olive oil in a large, heavy saucepan, add the onion and sweat over a low heat until beginning to soften. Add the mushrooms and cook for 5 minutes. Add the curry paste and lentils to the pan.
3 Pour over the coconut milk and stock or water and stir well. Bring to the boil, then simmer for about 20 minutes, or until the lentils are cooked. You may need to add more water to the pan. There needs to be enough liquid to make a light sauce, but not so much that it is like a soup.
4 Meanwhile, heat the remaining olive oil in a frying pan over a medium heat. Remove the salmon from the marinade and pat dry. Fry the salmon skin side down for 3–4 minutes, or until the skin is crisp. Turn the fish over and allow to cook through.
5 Stir the spinach into the lentils, cover the pan with a lid and allow the spinach to wilt.
6 To serve: place a large spoonful of the spinach and lentil mixture in warmed bowls and place the salmon, skin side up, on the top.

NOTE: If yellow curry paste is not available, use green curry paste. Alter the amount to taste.

Salmon and Dill Frittata

This is a good recipe for using up leftover cooked salmon.

Preparation time: 5 minutes
Cooking time: 25 minutes

SERVES 4

oil, for frying
1 red onion, sliced
225 g salmon fillet, cooked, skinned and pinboned
4 eggs, beaten
1 tablespoon finely chopped fresh dill
30 g Parmesan cheese, freshly grated

20 g butter
2 tablespoons crème fraîche
salt and freshly ground black pepper

To serve
Green salad (see page 381)

1 Preheat the oven to 190°C|375°F|gas mark 5.
2 Heat some oil in a small saucepan, add the onion and fry until completely soft and golden brown. Set aside.
3 Flake the salmon into large pieces.
4 Mix together the eggs, dill and two-thirds of the Parmesan. Season well with salt and pepper.
5 Heat the butter in a non-stick frying pan with an ovenproof handle. When it is foaming, spread the onion and salmon flakes over the base. Pour over the egg mixture and cook over a medium heat until the base begins to set and starts to brown lightly. Gently shake the pan and use a palette knife to prevent the frittata from sticking.
6 Remove the pan from the heat, place the pan in the oven and continue to cook for 10 minutes, or until it is set.
7 Meanwhile, mix the crème fraîche with the remaining Parmesan cheese and season with salt and pepper. Spread over the frittata, and return to the oven until the Parmesan has melted. Serve wedges of the frittata with green salad.

Salmon with Mustard and Brandy Sauce

Preparation time: 15 minutes
Cooking time: 15 minutes

SERVES 4

30 g unsalted butter

4 × 170 g salmon fillet, skinned, pinboned and cut
   into 2 cm cubes

2 tablespoons plain flour

1 shallot, finely chopped

1 clove of garlic, crushed

450 g button mushrooms, trimmed, wiped and halved

2 tablespoons brandy

1 tablespoon Dijon mustard

225 ml double cream

4 tablespoons water

1 tablespoon finely chopped fresh parsley

salt and freshly ground black pepper

Serving suggestions: Baked new potatoes en papillote (see page 367), flavoured mash (see page 359), basmati rice (see page 374), tagliatelle, broccoli, sugarsnap peas

1 Heat half the butter in a large, heavy frying pan with a lid. Toss the cubes of salmon in the flour and shake off any excess, then fry over a low heat until light golden but not cooked through. Remove from the pan with a slotted spoon.

2 Add the shallot to the pan with the remaining butter and cook over a low heat for 2 minutes. Add the garlic and cook for 30 seconds. Add the mushrooms, cover the pan and cook for 5 minutes, or until soft. Remove the lid, turn up the heat and cook, stirring, until the mushrooms start to sizzle.

3 Add the brandy, mustard, cream and water to the pan. Bring to the boil, stirring constantly and scraping any sediment from the bottom of the pan. Stir in the salmon and parsley and season with salt and pepper. Serve immediately.

Salmon en Croûte

Preparation time: 20 minutes plus chilling time
Cooking time: 35 minutes

SERVES 6–8

500 g puff pastry

900 g salmon fillet, skinned and pinboned

300 g soft garlic and herb cheese

1 egg, beaten

extra pastry, for decoration

To prepare ahead: Make in advance to the end of stage 7.
Serving suggestions: Green salad (see page 381), green vegetables, herb couscous (see page 356), wild rice salad (see page 352)

1 Preheat the oven to 200°C|400°F|gas mark 6.
2 On a floured work surface, roll out the pastry to the thickness of a £1 coin so that it is large enough to wrap around the salmon.
3 Season the salmon well with salt and pepper and spread a generous layer of the soft garlic and herb cheese over the fillet, on the skinned side.
4 Lay the salmon fillet, cheese side down, in the centre of the pastry.
5 Wrap the pastry around the salmon, allowing a little overlap. Cut off any excess pastry. Brush with the beaten egg, to seal.
6 Place on a baking sheet, sealed side down, and make 2 diagonal slashes through the top of the pastry. Brush with more beaten egg.
7 Chill for 15 minutes or overnight.
8 Bake in the oven for 30–35 minutes, or until the pastry is golden brown.

Salmon Baked with a Rocket Pesto Crust

Preparation time: 10 minutes
Cooking time: 15 minutes

SERVES 4

4 × 170 g salmon fillets, skinned and pinboned

4 teaspoons crème fraîche
salt and freshly ground black pepper

For the rocket pesto

60 g rocket
70 ml olive oil
40 g Parmesan cheese, freshly grated
60 g blanched almonds, roughly chopped

For the crust

4 tablespoons fresh white breadcrumbs
1 tablespoon grated Parmesan cheese
salt and freshly ground black pepper

To prepare ahead: Make in advance to the end of stage 5, then refrigerate.
Serving suggestions: Baked new potatoes en papillote (see page 367), mashed potatoes with dill (see page 361), brown rice, special roast potatoes (see page 365)

1 Preheat the oven to 190°C|375°F|gas mark 5. Lightly oil a baking sheet.
2 Place the salmon fillets on the prepared baking sheet.
3 Put the rocket, oil and Parmesan cheese into a blender and whizz until smooth. Season to taste with salt and pepper. Stir in the almonds and the crème fraîche.
4 Make the crust: mix together the breadcrumbs and Parmesan and season.
5 Press the rocket paste over the salmon. Then spread over the breadcrumb mix.
6 Bake in the oven for 15 minutes, or until cooked through.

VARIATION: Use bought pesto if you don't have time to make the rocket pesto.

Honey and Soy Salmon

Marinating time: 30 minutes–overnight
Preparation time: 5 minutes
Cooking time: 15 minutes

SERVES 4

4 × 170 g salmon fillets, skinned and pinboned
3 tablespoons sesame seeds
4 lime wedges

For the marinade

3 tablespoons sesame oil
5 tablespoons clear honey
3 tablespoons light soy sauce

To prepare ahead: Leave the salmon to marinate overnight.
Serving suggestions: Basmati rice (see page 374), pineapple rice (see page 376), seasame noodles (see page 378), egg-fried rice with bok choi (see page 377), chilli and coriander noodles (see page 378), steamed cucumber with star anise (see page 345), stir-fry of green vegetables (see page 352)

1 Preheat the oven to 190°C|375°F|gas mark 5.
2 Mix the marinade ingredients together. Place the salmon in a shallow dish and pour over the marinade.
3 Leave to marinate for at least 30 minutes, turning occasionally.
4 Remove the salmon from the marinade and place on a lightly oiled piece of kitchen foil in a roasting pan. Bake in the oven for 5 minutes.
5 Meanwhile, tip the marinade into a small saucepan and bring to the boil, then simmer for 4–5 minutes. Add the sesame seeds.
6 Spoon the marinade over the salmon and return to the oven for 5–10 minutes.
7 Lift on to a warmed serving dish and garnish with the lime wedges.

Fish Fingers

Preparation time: 5 minutes
Cooking time: 10–15 minutes

SERVES 2

225 g cod fillet, skinned and pinboned
1 egg, beaten
1 tablespoon oil

100 g dried breadcrumbs
salt and freshly ground black pepper

To prepare ahead: Make the fish fingers, then refrigerate or freeze.
Serving suggestions: Sweet potato wedges, petits pois

1 Cut the cod into thick finger-length strips. Season with salt and pepper.

2 Mix the egg and oil together and season with a little salt and pepper. Brush the fish with this mixture.

3 Place the breadcrumbs in a shallow dish and roll the fish strips in them until they are well coated.

4 Place the fish fingers on a plate in a single layer. Do not stack them or they will become soggy. Cover and chill until required.

5 Preheat the oven to 190°C|375°F|gas mark 5.

6 Arrange the fish fingers on a baking sheet. Bake on the top shelf of the oven for 10–15 minutes, or until firm to the touch and the crumb coating is browned.

NOTE: You can use any type of firm white fish.

Smoked Haddock with Mustard Cream Sauce

Preparation time: 5 minutes
Cooking time: 30 minutes

SERVES 4

4 × 170 g smoked haddock fillets, pinboned
about 425 ml milk
900 g potatoes, peeled and cut into even chunks
30 g butter
150 ml crème fraîche

2 tablespoons wholegrain mustard
salt and freshly ground black pepper

To garnish
sprigs of fresh flat-leaf parsley

Serving suggestion: Sautéed spinach

1 Lay the fish fillets in a frying pan, skin side down. Pour over enough milk to come just to the top of the fish. Cover with a lid or baking sheet. Set over a low to medium heat. Poach the fish until the flesh is firm and opaque. Do not allow the milk to boil. Carefully transfer the cooked fish fillets to a plate, peel away the skin and keep warm in a warming oven, covering them with a damp piece of greaseproof paper to prevent them from drying out. Reserve the milk.

2 Meanwhile, boil the potatoes in lightly salted water for 15–20 minutes, or until tender.

3 Drain the potatoes thoroughly. Mash them, adding the butter and 100–150 ml of the reserved milk. Season to taste with salt and pepper.

4 Heat the crème fraîche with the mustard in a small pan. Add water to bring the mixture to a sauce-like consistency. Season with salt and pepper.

5 To serve: place a spoonful of mash on individual plates and lay one of the haddock fillets on top. Spoon over the mustard sauce and garnish with the parsley.

Salmon and Prawn Pie with Chive Mash

Preparation and cooking time: 1 hour

SERVES 6

300 ml milk

150 ml double cream, plus 4 tablespoons

½ onion, sliced

6 black peppercorns

1 bay leaf

500 g salmon fillet, pinboned

180 g tiger prawns, cooked and peeled

5 hardboiled eggs, peeled and quartered (see page 13)

30 g butter

30 g plain flour

6 tablespoons finely chopped fresh chives

125 g smoked salmon, chopped

700 g potatoes, mashed (see page 358)

salt and freshly ground black pepper

To prepare ahead: Make the pie, then refrigerate or freeze. If frozen, defrost thoroughly before reheating.

Serving suggestions: Green vegetables, such as peas, or green salad (see page 381)

1 Preheat the oven to 180°C|350°F|gas mark 4.

2 In a roasting pan heat the milk and 150 ml cream with the onion, peppercorns, bay leaf and a pinch of salt. Add the salmon fillet. Cover with kitchen foil and poach for about 15 minutes or until the salmon is just cooked.

3 Strain off the cooking liquor and reserve. Remove the skin from the salmon. Break the salmon into large pieces and place in the bottom of a pie dish with the prawns and hardboiled eggs.

4 Melt the butter in a heavy saucepan, stir in the flour and cook for 45 seconds. Remove from the heat, then gradually add the reserved cooking liquor. Return to the heat and bring slowly to the boil, stirring all the time. When the sauce has thickened, add 2 tablespoons double cream, 2 tablespoons of the chives and the smoked salmon. Season to taste with salt and pepper. Pour over the fish and mix very gently.

5 Mix the remaining cream and chives into the mashed potato, then spread or pipe the potato over the fish mixture in a criss-cross pattern. Place the pie dish on a baking sheet and cook in the oven for about 30 minutes, or until hot right through.

Lightly Smoked Salmon, Leek and Horseradish Gratin

Preparation time: 10 minutes
Cooking time: 35 minutes

SERVES 4

50 g butter

3 medium leeks, washed and cut into 2 cm chunks

50 g plain flour

600 ml milk

2 tablespoons freshly grated Parmesan cheese

1 tablespoon horseradish sauce

550 g lightly smoked salmon pieces, skinned,
   pinboned and cut into large chunks

1 tablespoon finely chopped fresh parsley

salt and freshly ground black pepper

For the topping

2 tablespoons dried white breadcrumbs

3 tablespoons freshly grated Parmesan cheese

To prepare ahead: Make in advance to the end of stage 6, then refrigerate or freeze. If frozen, defrost thoroughly before cooking.

Serving suggestions: Baked new potatoes en papillote (see page 367), green salad (see page 381), broccoli, runner beans, broad beans, peas

1 Preheat the oven to 180°C|350°F|gas mark 4.

2 Melt the butter in a heavy saucepan. Add the leeks and cook over a low heat for about 10 minutes, or until they begin to soften.

3 Sprinkle the flour over the leeks, stir well and cook for 1 minute.

4 Slowly add the milk, stirring continuously. Bring the mixture to the boil, then simmer for 2 minutes. Remove from the heat.

5 Stir in the Parmesan, horseradish, salmon pieces and parsley. Season to taste with salt and pepper and spoon into an ovenproof dish.

6 Mix the breadcrumbs with the Parmesan. Sprinkle over the salmon mixture.

7 Bake in the oven for 15–20 minutes, or until the topping begins to bubble and is lightly browned. Serve immediately.

Tuna with Black Olive and Red Pepper Dressing

Preparation time: 5 minutes
Cooking time: 10 minutes

SERVES 4

80 ml olive oil, plus extra for frying

80 ml balsamic vinegar

60 g black olives, pitted and roughly chopped

3 large strips of marinated red pepper from a good-
   quality jar, chopped

2 tablespoons chopped fresh basil

4 × 170 g tuna steaks

salt and freshly ground black pepper

To prepare ahead: Make the sauce in advance, then reheat and whisk before pouring over the tuna.
Serving suggestions: Italian tomato salad (see page 334), green salad (see page 381), new potatoes, grilled Mediterranean vegetables (see page 346)

1 Whisk the oil and vinegar together. Add the olives and red pepper. Place in a small saucepan over a low heat.
2 Meanwhile, heat a griddle pan to a medium heat. Brush the tuna steaks with a little oil and season. Griddle for 2 minutes on each side.
3 Place the steaks on a warmed serving plate. Stir the basil into the dressing and pour over the tuna. Serve immediately.

Grilled Tuna Steaks with Pesto

Preparation time: 2 minutes
Marinating time: 30 minutes–2 hours
Cooking time: 6 minutes

SERVES 4

4 × 170 g tuna steaks

freshly ground black pepper

For the marinade

6 tablespoons olive oil

2 tablespoons balsamic vinegar

To garnish

4 tablespoons ready-made pesto (or see page 512)

sprigs of fresh herbs

To prepare ahead: Marinate the tuna for up to 2 hours.
Serving suggestions: Avocado and spring onion salad with soy dressing (see page 332), grilled Mediterranean vegetables (see page 346), linguini, new potatoes

1 Combine the marinade ingredients. Place the tuna steaks in a shallow dish and pour over the marinade. Cover and chill for at least 30 minutes.

2 Preheat the grill to the highest setting.

3 Lift the tuna steaks from the marinade, place on the grill rack and grill for about 3 minutes on each side, or until cooked (they should be lightly browned and firm but still moist). Alternatively, cook for 2–3 minutes per side in a hot griddle pan.

4 To serve: place the tuna steaks on a warmed serving dish, spoon the pesto on top and garnish with the herbs.

NOTE: Chilli and coriander pesto also works particularly well (see page 512).

Barbecued Cod Skewers

Marinating time: 30 minutes–2 hours
Preparation time: 15 minutes
Cooking time: 20 minutes

SERVES 4

4 × 150 g cod steaks, skinned and pinboned

6 tablespoons extra virgin olive oil

grated zest of 3 lemons

12 new potatoes

4 slices of Parma ham

12 cherry tomatoes, halved

salt and freshly ground black pepper

8 wooden skewers, soaked in water

To prepare ahead: Make in advance to the end of stage 4 and refrigerate.
Serving suggestions: Italian tomato salad (see page 334), lemon buttered couscous (see page 357), artichoke and pinenut salad (see page 331)

1 Cut the cod into 4 cm cubes. Put into a bowl, add the oil and lemon zest and season generously with salt and pepper. Leave to marinate for up to 2 hours.

2 Bring a small saucepan of salted water to the boil and cook the new potatoes for about 15 minutes, or until tender. Drain well. Light the barbecue.

3 Cut each Parma ham slice into 3 strips lengthways and wrap each strip around a potato.

4 Thread the cod cubes on to 8 skewers, alternating with the potatoes and tomatoes.

5 Grill on the barbecue (or cook in a very hot griddle or frying pan), turning frequently and basting with the marinade.

Cod with Lemon and Caper Vinaigrette

Preparation time: 5 minutes
Cooking time: 10 minutes

SERVES 4

oil, for frying
4 × 170 g cod fillets, skinned and pinboned
seasoned plain flour (see page 20)

For the dressing

4 tablespoons olive oil
juice of ½ lemon
2 tablespoons capers, drained and rinsed
salt and freshly ground black pepper

Serving suggestions: Crushed new potatoes, green salad (see page 381), pea purée (see page 348), chilli potato wedges (see page 368), steamed green vegetables, dauphinoise potatoes (see page 370)

1 Whisk the dressing ingredients together. Season to taste with salt and pepper.
2 Heat a little oil in a heavy frying pan. Lightly dust the cod fillets in the seasoned flour, then fry in the pan for 3 minutes on each side, or until just cooked through.
3 Place the fish skinned side down on warmed individual plates.
4 Add the dressing to the pan and heat through. Pour over the fish and serve immediately.

NOTE: If the capers are large, chop them up carefully, ensuring not to mash them.

Chunky Cod with Lemon and Coriander Dressing and Sweet Potato Mash

Preparation time: 10 minutes
Cooking time: 25 minutes

SERVES 4

3 large sweet potatoes, peeled and cut into small
   cubes
4 chunky cod fillets, pinboned
2 tablespoons olive oil
30 g butter
a little milk
salt and freshly ground black pepper

For the dressing

a large handful of coriander leaves, roughly chopped
grated zest and juice of 1 lemon
grated zest and juice of 1 lime
6 tablespoons olive oil
2 teaspoons wholegrain mustard
salt and freshly ground black pepper

To garnish

fresh coriander leaves, roughly chopped

To prepare ahead: Make the mash in advance and reheat while cooking the cod.
Serving suggestions: Peas, courgettes, roast tomatoes

1 Preheat the oven to 200°C|400°F|gas mark 6.

2 Combine all the dressing ingredients.

3 Cook the sweet potatoes in a saucepan of boiling salted water for about 15–20 minutes, or until tender. Drain well.

4 Meanwhile, place the cod fillets in an ovenproof dish and brush the skins with oil. Bake in the oven, skin side uppermost, for 10–15 minutes.

5 Mash the potatoes with the butter and a little milk and season well.

6 Serve the cod on top of the mash. Spoon over the dressing and scatter with the coriander.

Cod with Caramelized Puy Lentils

Preparation time: 10 minutes
Cooking time: 30 minutes

SERVES 4

170 g Puy or beluga lentils

a few sprigs of fresh thyme

2 bay leaves

2 tablespoons oil

12 baby onions, peeled and quartered

120 g bacon lardons

5 tablespoons balsamic vinegar

1 tablespoon soft dark brown sugar

4 × 170 g cod fillets, pinboned

seasoned plain flour (see page 20)

salt and freshly ground black pepper

To garnish

sprigs of fresh thyme

To prepare ahead: Make the lentils in advance, then reheat while the cod is cooking.
Serving suggestion: Haricot beans with cream and thyme (see page 342)

1 Preheat the oven to 200°C|400°F|gas mark 6.

2 Cook the lentils in a saucepan of boiling water with the thyme and bay leaves for about 15–20 minutes, or until tender.

3 Heat half the oil in another pan, add the onions and cook for 5 minutes. Add the bacon and continue to fry until both the onions and bacon are golden brown. Remove from the heat and allow to cool slightly, then add the vinegar and sugar. Return to a low heat and allow the onions to caramelize.

4 Season the cod fillets with salt and pepper and dip them, skin side down, in the seasoned flour. Shake off the excess. Heat the remaining oil in a griddle and when smoking hot, fry the fillets skin side down until well browned.

5 Transfer the fillets to a roasting pan, skin side up, and roast in the oven for 5–8 minutes, or until cooked (the flesh should be opaque and firm).

6 Drain the lentils well and remove the thyme and bay leaves. Stir in the caramelized onions and bacon and season to taste with salt and pepper.

7 Place a large spoonful of lentils on each plate and place a cod fillet on top. Serve garnished with sprigs of thyme.

Cod with a Pea and Mint Crust

Preparation time: 5 minutes
Cooking time: 25 minutes

SERVES 4

170 g frozen or fresh peas

10 large fresh mint leaves

4 × 170 g cod fillets, skinned and pinboned

salt and freshly ground black pepper

To prepare ahead: Make in advance to the end of stage 3, then refrigerate.
Serving suggestions: Crushed new potatoes, sweet potato wedges, green salad (see page 381), Vichy carrots (see page 344)

1 Preheat the oven to 190°C|375°F|gas mark 5.
2 Cook the peas in boiling salted water with the mint leaves. When cooked, drain and whizz in a blender or food processor to make a rough purée. Season to taste.
3 Place the cod fillets in a roasting pan and spread with the pea purée.
4 Bake in the oven for 15 minutes. Serve immediately.

Halibut Fillets with a Thai Crust

Preparation time: 10 minutes
Cooking time: 25 minutes

SERVES 4

oil, for greasing

1 tablespoon oil, for frying

4 spring onions, finely sliced on the diagonal

1 red pepper, cored, deseeded and diced

1 yellow pepper, cored, deseeded and diced

2 teaspoons Thai green curry paste

6 tablespoons dry breadcrumbs

4 × 170 g halibut fillets, skinned and pinboned

To garnish

fresh coriander leaves

To prepare ahead: Make in advance to the end of stage 3.
Serving suggestions: Pineapple rice (see page 376), chilli and coriander noodles (see page 378)

1 Preheat the oven to 190°C|375°F|gas mark 5. Lightly grease a baking sheet.
2 Heat the oil in a frying pan, add the spring onions and sweat over a low heat until soft but not coloured. Add the peppers and fry until soft, then add the green curry paste and cook for 1 further minute. Remove the pan from the heat and allow to cool.
3 Add the breadcrumbs to the cooled vegetable mixture and divide the crust between the halibut fillets, pressing down well.
4 Place on the prepared baking sheet and bake in the oven for 15 minutes.
5 Serve immediately, garnished with the coriander.

Fish with Hot Sweet and Sour Sauce

Preparation time: 15 minutes
Cooking time: 25 minutes

SERVES 4

oil, for greasing

2 tablespoons clear honey

300 ml water

5 cloves of garlic, peeled and finely chopped

2 red chillies, crushed or finely chopped

½ onion, sliced

4 tablespoons lemon juice

1 teaspoon salt

8 baby plum tomatoes, quartered

3 shallots, finely sliced

1 tablespoon sunflower oil

4 × 170 g thick white fish fillets, skinned and
pinboned

4 spring onions, finely sliced on the diagonal

fresh coriander leaves, roughly chopped

To prepare ahead: Make the sauce in advance and reheat before pouring over the fish.

Serving suggestions: Thai jasmine rice (see page 375), broccoli with sesame dressing (see page 342), chilli and coriander noodles (see page 378), steamed bok choi with soy and ginger (see page 350), egg-fried frice (see page 377), pineapple rice (see page 376)

1 Preheat the grill to the highest setting. Lightly oil a baking sheet.
2 Place the honey and water in a saucepan over a low heat and bring to the boil.
3 Add the garlic, chillies, onion, lemon juice and salt. Cook for 2 minutes.
4 Add the tomatoes and cook, covered, for about 5 minutes, or until the tomatoes are soft but still hold their shape. Remove from the heat and add more lemon juice, salt or honey as required.
5 Meanwhile, fry the shallots in the sunflower oil until brown and crisp. Set aside.
6 Place the fish on the prepared baking sheet and grill for 10–15 minutes, or until cooked.
7 To serve: arrange the fish on warmed individual plates, spoon over the sauce and scatter over the shallots, spring onions and coriander. Serve immediately.

NOTE: The fish is grilled in this recipe, but it works equally well if it is steamed.

Smoked Haddock with Rarebit Crust

Preparation time: 5 minutes
Chilling time: 30 minutes
Cooking time: 20 minutes

SERVES 4

100 g Gruyère cheese, finely grated
100 g Cheddar cheese, finely grated
4 teaspoons French mustard
cayenne pepper
2 eggs, beaten

2 tablespoons beer
4 × 170 g smoked haddock fillets, skinned and
    pinboned
salt and freshly ground black pepper

To prepare ahead: Make in advance to the end of stage 2, then refrigerate.
Serving suggestions: Roast tomatoes, roast beetroot (see page 341), green vegetables, green salad (see page 381), baked new potatoes en papillote (see page 367)

1 Mix the cheeses together with the mustard, salt and pepper, cayenne, egg and beer.
2 Spread the mixture neatly over the haddock fillets to the edge and chill for 30 minutes.
3 Preheat the oven to 190°C|375°F|gas mark 5.
4 Place the haddock on a baking sheet and bake for 15 minutes.
5 Meanwhile, preheat the grill to the highest setting. Remove the fish from the oven.
6 If the top is not browned, place under the grill. Serve immediately.

Sole with Lime and Cucumber Salsa

Preparation time: 10 minutes
Cooking time: 10 minutes

SERVES 4

12 sole fillets, skinned
seasoned plain flour (see page 20)
oil, for frying

For the salsa
½ cucumber

2 tablespoons oil
1 tablespoon chopped fresh dill
1 tablespoon lime juice
grated zest of ½ lime
½ teaspoon caster sugar
salt and freshly ground black pepper

1 Heat the oven to the lowest setting.
2 Make the salsa: peel the cucumber, or if preferred leave the skin on for the colour. Cut it in half lengthways and scoop out the seeds (see page 12).
3 Cut the cucumber into the smallest dice possible.

4 Mix the cucumber with the remaining salsa ingredients and season with salt and pepper. Set aside.

5 Dip the sole fillets in the seasoned flour and shake off any excess.

6 Heat the oil in a heavy frying pan, add some of the fish fillets and cook over a medium heat until lightly browned, then turn over and brown on the other side (about 2 minutes on each side). Keep the fish warm in the oven and fry the remaining fish in batches.

7 Place 3 fillets of sole on each warmed individual plate with a spoonful of the salsa.

NOTE: This salsa also works well with grilled chicken.

Mackerel with Fennel and Tomato Salsa

Preparation time: 15 minutes
Cooking time: 25 minutes

SERVES 4

4 mackerel, gutted and cleaned, and head and tail removed if desired

7 tablespoons olive oil

1 small bulb of fennel, very finely chopped

½ red onion, very finely chopped

2 tomatoes, deseeded and finely chopped

juice of 2 lemons

3 tablespoons chopped fresh coriander

salt and freshly ground black pepper

To garnish

1 small bunch of watercress

lemon wedges

Serving suggestions: Rocket salad (see page 381), herb couscous (see page 356), potato and beetroot salad (see page 336)

1 Preheat the oven to 190°C|375°F|gas mark 5.

2 Line a large sheet of kitchen foil with an oiled sheet of greaseproof paper (this helps to keep the fish moist). Place on a baking sheet and lay the fish on top, trying to leave gaps between the fish. Slash the sides of the fish.

3 Pour over 4 tablespoons of the oil, season each fish with salt and pepper and cover with another sheet of kitchen foil, scrunching the edges to seal tightly.

4 Bake in the oven for 20–25 minutes, depending on the size of the fish.

5 Mix together the remaining oil, the fennel, onion, tomato, lemon juice and coriander. Season with salt and pepper and set aside to allow the flavours to infuse.

6 Remove the fish from the foil parcel and serve with its juices and a generous spoonful of the salsa. Garnish with sprigs of watercress and lemon wedges.

Monkfish Parcels

Preparation time: 15 minutes
Marinating time: 2 hours
Cooking time: 20 minutes

SERVES 4

4 × 150 g monkfish tail fillets
200 ml ginger wine
1 red chilli, sliced
2 cloves of garlic, peeled and halved
1 stick of lemon grass, bruised and quartered
2 kaffir lime leaves, broken in half (optional)

juice of 1 lime
4 tablespoons double cream or coconut cream
salt and freshly ground black pepper

To garnish
1 tablespoon roughly chopped fresh coriander

To prepare ahead: Leave to marinate for 2 hours.
Serving suggestions: Basmati or Thai jasmine rice (see pages 374,375), Thai rice salad (see page 354), sesame noodles (see page 378), stir-fried vegetables (see page 351), egg-fried rice with bok choi (see page 377)

1 Trim the monkfish fillets if necessary and remove any membrane.
2 Put the monkfish into a bowl with the ginger wine, chilli, garlic, lemon grass, and the kaffir lime leaves, if using. Stir and leave to marinate, covered, in the refrigerator for 2 hours, turning occasionally.
3 Preheat the oven to 200°C|400°F|gas mark 6.
4 Add the lime juice to the marinade and stir thoroughly.
5 Take 4 large squares of tin foil and place a piece of monkfish in the centre of each square. Season with a little salt and pepper and divide the marinade ingredients between the parcels, so that each parcel has a piece of lemon grass and chilli.
6 Put a spoonful of cream into each parcel, then seal tightly, but allow room for the steam to circulate inside.
7 Place the parcels on a baking sheet and cook in the oven for 15 minutes.
8 Remove from the oven, open the parcels, sprinkle over the coriander and reseal.
9 Serve immediately in the sealed parcels, so that diners can open them at the table.

NOTE: If kaffir lime leaves are not available, either use a potato peeler to pare the green rind from a lime, or look for a jar of preserved lime leaves, available in many supermarkets.

Prawn and Monkfish Thai Red Curry

Preparation time: 15 minutes
Cooking time: 25 minutes

SERVES 3–4

2 tablespoons oil

2 shallots, finely diced

1 clove of garlic, crushed

1 teaspoon peeled and grated fresh root ginger

1 stick of lemon grass, very finely diced

½ – 1 tablespoon good-quality Thai red curry paste

1 × 400 ml can of coconut milk

150 ml chicken, fish or vegetable stock

2 kaffir lime leaves, stalks removed and finely chopped

1 tablespoon soft light brown sugar

1 tablespoon nam pla (Thai fish sauce)

1 aubergine, cut into cubes

12 raw tiger prawns, peeled and deveined (see page 00)

225 g monkfish, skinned and sliced

150 g water chestnuts, drained and sliced

salt and freshly ground black pepper

To prepare ahead: Make in advance to the end of stage 3.
Serving suggestions: Thai jasmine rice (see page 375), egg-fried rice with bok choi (see page 377), green salad (see page 381)

1 Heat the oil in a large frying pan, add the shallots and sweat over a low heat until soft but not coloured.
2 Add the garlic, ginger, lemon grass and curry paste and cook for 30 seconds.
3 Add the coconut milk, stock, lime leaves, sugar and nam pla and stir well. Bring to simmering point, then add the aubergines. Simmer gently for 10 minutes, or until the aubergines are cooked.
4 Add the prawns, monkfish and water chestnuts to the simmering sauce and cook for 5 minutes. Check the seasoning and serve immediately.

Prawn Curry

Preparation time: 5 minutes
Cooking time: 20 minutes

SERVES 4

1 tablespoon sunflower oil

1 onion, chopped

1 clove of garlic, crushed

2–3 tablespoons Madras curry paste, or to taste

1 × 400 g can of chopped tomatoes

400 g raw prawns, peeled and deveined (see page 20)

150 g plain or Greek yoghurt

chopped fresh coriander leaves

To garnish

mangetout, finely sliced on the diagonal

To prepare ahead: Make in advance to the end of stage 2, then refrigerate.
Serving suggestion: Nanjing black rice or basmati rice (see page 374)

1 Heat the oil in a large saucepan, add the onion and sweat over a low heat for about 10 minutes, or until soft.

2 Add the garlic and curry paste and cook for a further 30 seconds. Add the tomatoes, bring to the boil, then simmer for 10 minutes, or until the sauce is reduced and becoming thick.

3 Add the prawns and simmer for a further 3 minutes, or until cooked.

4 Stir in the yoghurt and the coriander. Do not allow to boil. Serve on a bed of rice with the mangetout sprinkled on top.

Masala Prawn Stir-fry

Marinating time: 30 minutes–overnight
Preparation time: 5 minutes
Cooking time: 10 minutes

SERVES 4

300 g large prawns, peeled and cooked

2 heaped tablespoons tikka masala or korma paste

250 g medium rice noodles

1 tablespoon oil

1 red onion, sliced

2 red peppers, cored, deseeded and cut into 1 cm strips

2 courgettes, sliced

3 tablespoons water or stock

a handful of roughly chopped fresh coriander

To garnish

peanuts, finely chopped or crushed

4 lime wedges

To prepare ahead: Leave the prawns to marinate overnight in the refrigerator.
Serving suggestion: Green salad including beansprouts (see page 381)

1 Mix the prawns with the curry paste and leave to marinate for at least 30 minutes.
2 Soak the rice noodles in water according to the manufacturer's instructions.
3 Heat the oil in a wok, add the onion and stir-fry for 2 minutes, then add the red peppers and stir-fry for 1 further minute.
4 Add the courgettes and prawns to the wok and cook for 1 further minute, or until heated through.
5 Drain the rice noodles and add to the wok with the water or stock, stirring so that the curry paste coats the noodles. Stir in the coriander.
6 Divide between 4 warmed bowls. Scatter with the peanuts and serve with the lime wedges.

Tiger Prawn Brochettes

Marinating time: 2½ hours
Preparation time: 10 minutes
Cooking time: 10 minutes

SERVES 4

12 raw tiger prawns, peeled and deveined (see page 20)
4 tablespoons olive oil
grated zest of 2 limes
juice of 1 lime
freshly ground black pepper
4 wooden skewers, soaked in water

For the sauce
grated zest of 1 lime
1 red chilli, finely chopped
4 tablespoons mayonnaise (see page 513)
salt and freshly ground black pepper

To garnish
sprigs of fresh coriander

Serving suggestions: Avocado couscous salad (see page 354), artichoke and red pepper salad (see page 331), chilli potato wedges (see page 368), pineapple and chilli salad (see page 147)

1 Place the prawns in a shallow dish and add the oil and half the lime zest. Cover and leave to marinate in the refrigerator for 2 hours.
2 Thread 3 prawns on to each skewer, arranging them so that they lie flat on the skewers. Do not push them too closely together.
3 Whisk the lime juice into the marinade and return the prawn skewers to the dish. Chill for at least 20 minutes.
4 Meanwhile, preheat the grill or light the barbecue.
5 Make the sauce: mix the remaining lime zest and chilli into the mayonnaise and season to taste with salt and pepper.
6 Grill the prawns, basting them with the marinade until they are pink and cooked.
7 Serve the brochettes garnished with the coriander and hand the sauce separately.

Prawn Pilaf

Preparation time: 15 minutes
Cooking time: 40 minutes

SERVES 4

800 g cooked shell-on prawns
550 ml water
100 ml dry white wine
1 slice of lemon
a small handful of fresh parsley stalks
60 g butter
1 medium onion, finely chopped
225 g long-grain rice, washed

2 hardboiled eggs, chopped
lemon juice
salt and freshly ground black pepper

To garnish
1 tablespoon chopped fresh parsley

Serving suggestion: Green salad (see page 381)

1 Peel the prawns. Reserve the prawns and put the shells into a saucepan with the water, wine, salt, pepper, lemon slice and parsley stalks. Bring to the boil, then simmer for 15 minutes. Strain and reserve the liquor.
2 Meanwhile, melt half the butter in a saucepan, add the onion and sweat over a low heat until soft but not coloured.
3 Add the rice and fry slowly until it looks shiny. Add the reserved cooking liquor. Bring to the boil, stirring once or twice, then cover and simmer gently for 25 minutes, or until the rice is tender and the liquid absorbed. Remove from the heat and allow to stand for 10 minutes.
4 Meanwhile, melt the remaining butter in a saucepan, add the peeled prawns and eggs and heat through. Season with salt, pepper and lemon juice. Fork the prawns and eggs into the pilaf rice. Pile into a warmed serving dish and sprinkle with the parsley.

Prawn Skewers with Couscous

Marinating time: 2 hours–overnight
Preparation time: 10 minutes
Cooking time: 15 minutes

SERVES 4

20 raw tiger prawns, peeled and deveined (see page 20)
2 tablespoons harissa paste
170 g couscous
1 tablespoon oil
2 spring onions, finely sliced on the diagonal

1 red chilli, deseeded and diced
½ tablespoon chopped fresh parsley
½ tablespoon chopped fresh coriander
salt and freshly ground black pepper
4 wooden skewers, soaked in water

To prepare ahead: The couscous can be made in advance and heated through in a microwave or saucepan to serve. Add the herbs at the last minute to avoid losing their colour.

Serving suggestions: Green salad (see page 381), chilli corn on the cob (see page 141)

1 Thread the prawns on to the skewers. Place in a shallow dish. Spread the harissa paste over the prawns and leave for at least 2 hours or overnight.
2 Preheat the grill to the highest setting.
3 Cook the couscous according to the manufacturer's instructions and season to taste with salt and pepper.
4 Meanwhile, heat the oil in a large sauté pan, add the spring onions and chilli and sweat over a low heat until soft. Stir into the cooked couscous with the parsley and coriander.
5 Place the prawn skewers under the grill and cook for 2 minutes. Turn and continue to cook for a further 2 minutes, or until pink and cooked through.
6 Place a large spoonful of couscous on each warmed individual plate and place a prawn skewer on top.

Stir-fried Prawns with Orange and Ginger

Preparation time: 15 minutes
Cooking time: 5 minutes

SERVES 4

2 cloves of garlic	2 tablespoons syrup from the stem ginger jar
2 tablespoons oil	3 tablespoons vermouth
500 g raw tiger prawns, peeled and deveined (see page 20)	3 tablespoons orange juice
	2 tablespoons chopped fresh chives
2 pieces of stem ginger, chopped	salt and freshly ground black pepper

Serving suggestions: Steamed bok choi with soy and ginger (see page 350), steamed cucumber with star anise (see page 351), simmered miso squash (see page 353), chilli and coriander noodles (see page 378)

1 Bruise the garlic with a rolling pin, remove the skin and leave the cloves flattened but whole.
2 Heat the oil in a wok or a heavy sauté pan. Add the garlic and fry for 1 minute. Remove and discard the garlic.
3 Add the prawns and stir-fry for about 2 minutes. Add the ginger, syrup, vermouth, orange juice and half the chives. Season to taste with salt and pepper. Continue to stir-fry until the prawns have turned pink and the sauce has become a little syrupy.
4 Pile on to a warmed serving dish and garnish with the remaining chives.

Fried Scallops with Garlic

Preparation time: 10 minutes
Cooking time: 3 minutes

SERVES 4

16 scallops, shells removed

50 g butter

1 small clove of garlic, crushed

juice of ½ lemon

a little chopped fresh parsley

salt and freshly ground black pepper

Serving suggestions: Rocket salad (see page 381), Italian tomato salad (see page 334), pea purée (see page 348), fresh crusty bread

1 Remove the hard muscle from the scallops, opposite the coral or roe (see page 20).
2 Melt the butter in a heavy frying pan. Add the scallops when the butter starts foaming. Fry over a high heat for 30 seconds on each side. Remove the scallops from the pan and set aside.
3 Add the garlic to the butter in the pan and cook for 30 seconds. Remove the pan from the heat, add the lemon juice and parsley and season with salt and pepper. Serve immediately, poured over the scallops.

Poultry and Game

Cooking Chicken

Chicken breasts are quick and easy to cook and complement a whole range of flavours and cooking styles. They do not have as much flavour as the thigh or leg meat, but many people prefer not to have a bone on their plate, and they cook through faster.

Chicken can be marinated before cooking in order to impart extra flavour. When marinating with something sweet, the meat will brown very quickly, so as soon as it has browned, reduce the heat. Chicken pieces are available in a variety of sizes, so cooking time will vary accordingly.

Cooking time: 10–15 minutes

SERVES 4

oil
4 chicken breasts, boned
salt and freshly ground black pepper

Fried Chicken

1 Heat the oil in a large, heavy frying pan.
2 Season the chicken breasts with salt and pepper.
3 Fry the chicken breasts, top side first until brown, then brown the underside.
4 Reduce the heat and cook for a further 5 minutes or so on each side until completely cooked through.
5 Serve immediately, or leave to rest for a few minutes before serving.

Baked Chicken

1 Preheat the oven to 190°C|375°F|gas mark 5.
2 Brown the outside of the chicken in a frying pan (preferably one with an ovenproof handle), as above.
3 Once the outside has browned, transfer to a roasting pan if the frying pan cannot be put into the oven, and cook in the oven for 20–25 minutes for chicken breasts or 30–35 minutes for thighs or until cooked through.

Grilled Chicken

1 Preheat the grill to the highest setting.
2 Place the chicken on a baking sheet, brush or drizzle with a little oil and season well.
3 Cook for 5 minutes on each side, with the grill pan close to the flame or element.
4 Move the pan a little further away from the heat to prevent the outside from burning. Continue to cook for up to 5 minutes on each side, or until cooked through.

Serving suggestions: Dauphinoise potatoes (see page 370), celeriac gratin (see page 373), sauté potatoes (see page 364), simmered miso squash (see page 353), rosemary roast vegetables (see page 346)

Marinades for Chicken

- Soy sauce and maple syrup
- Olive oil, grated lemon zest and black pepper
- Olive oil, fresh sprigs of rosemary and garlic
- Teriyaki sauce
- Stem ginger syrup and soy sauce
- Soy sauce and grated lime zest and juice
- Hoisin sauce
- Black bean sauce
- Grated orange zest, oil and peeled and grated fresh root ginger
- Chilli oil and fresh coriander
- Yoghurt, chilli and fresh mint
- Oil, harissa paste and garlic

It is easy to add extra flavour to chicken breasts either by pushing a stuffing under the skin, or by making a small pocket on the underside of the breast and pushing the stuffing inside. Alternatively, wrap a skinned chicken breast in pancetta or good-quality streaky bacon.

Ideas for Stuffings

- Sundried tomatoes and basil
- Blue cheese and chopped fresh parsley
- Fresh sage leaves and grated lemon zest
- Black olive tapenade (see page 513)
- Pestos (see page 512)
- Grated Cheddar cheese and chopped chives mixed with a little crème fraiche
- Wholegrain mustard
- Mozzarella cheese and chopped fresh basil
- Garlic and chopped fresh herbs
- Ham and Gruyère cheese

Chinese-style Roast Chicken with Spicy Potatoes and Stir-fried Vegetables

Preparation time: 20 minutes
Cooking time: 1½ hours

SERVES 4

1 × 1.35 kg roasting chicken, giblets removed

2 tablespoons dark soy sauce

2 tablespoons olive oil, plus extra for the potatoes

1 stick of cinnamon

1 star anise

900 g old potatoes, cut into 1½ cm cubes, or new potatoes, halved

½ teaspoon ground Chinese five-spice

¼ teaspoon cayenne pepper

1 teaspoon salt

2 tablespoons clear honey, plus extra for stir-frying (optional)

½ glass of sherry mixed with ½ glass of water

2 teaspoons cornflour

450 g mixed vegetables, such as mangetout, broccoli florets, sliced red pepper, baby sweetcorn, prepared ready to stir-fry

salt and freshly ground black pepper

1 Preheat the oven to 200°C|400°F| gas mark 6. Weigh the chicken and calculate the cooking time at 20 minutes per 450 g plus 20 minutes.

2 Smear the chicken all over with the soy sauce, then drizzle with 2 tablespoons oil. Put the cinnamon and star anise inside the cavity of the chicken. Place in a roasting pan and roast at the top of the oven for the calculated time.

3 Meanwhile, toss the potatoes in a little olive oil, the Chinese five-spice, cayenne and 1 teaspoon salt. Roast in the oven for about 30 minutes until golden brown and crisp.

4 After the chicken has been roasting for 1 hour, remove it from the oven and brush it with the honey. Pour the sherry and water mixture into the bottom of the roasting pan and return to the oven until the chicken is cooked.

5 When cooked, remove the chicken from the roasting pan and keep warm. Heat the roasting pan on the hob, scraping any sediment from the bottom of the pan to dissolve it. Taste, and if the flavour is too strong, add more water, if too weak, boil vigorously to reduce. Slake the cornflour into the sauce (see page 21). Bring to the boil, the cook for a further 2 minutes, adding more water if the sauce becomes too thick. Season with salt and pepper.

6 Just before serving, stir-fry the vegetables in a large wok or frying pan with a little soy sauce and 1 teaspoon of honey if desired.

7 Carve the chicken and serve with the vegetables, potatoes and sauce.

Chicken with Basil Dressing

Marinating time: 30 minutes–overnight
Preparation time: 10 minutes
Cooking time: 15–20 minutes

SERVES 4

a large handful of fresh basil leaves

4 chicken breasts, skinned and boned

150 ml olive oil, plus 4 tablespoons for marinating

3 tablespoons red wine vinegar

1 tablespoon Dijon mustard

3 tablespoons hot chicken stock

salt and freshly ground black pepper

To prepare ahead: Leave to marinate overnight.

Serving suggestions: Green salad (see page 381), crusty bread, new potato salad, fried polenta (see page 379)

1 Roughly chop half the basil. Place in a bowl with the chicken breasts and 4 tablespoons of the oil and leave to marinate for 30 minutes or overnight.

2 Heat a non-stick frying pan over a medium heat. Fry the chicken breasts for 5–10 minutes on each side, or until golden brown on both sides and cooked through.

3 Meanwhile, make the dressing: place the remaining basil with the vinegar and mustard in a blender or small food processor attachment. Whizz until smooth. It may be necessary to add some of the oil to help purée the mixture.

4 With the motor still running, trickle the remaining oil on to the blades. Finally, add the stock and season well. Serve the chicken immediately, with the dressing poured over.

Chicken Breasts with Pesto

Preparation time: 10 minutes
Cooking time: 20 minutes

SERVES 4

4 chicken breasts, boned and skin left on

4 tablespoons ready-made pesto (or see page 512)

30 g butter, softened

salt and freshly ground black pepper

To prepare ahead: The chicken breasts can be prepared in advance to the end of stage 2, then refrigerated or frozen. If frozen, defrost completely before cooking.

Serving suggestions: Ratatouille (see page 347), olive oil mash (see page 360), butterbean mash (see page 371), grilled Mediterranean vegetables (see page 346), courgettes with sultanas and pinenuts (see page 345), rosemary roast vegetables (see page 346), garlic bread (see page 379)

1 Preheat the oven to 190°C|375°F|gas mark 5.

2 Loosen the skin of the chicken breasts with a finger or the handle of a teaspoon and push a tablespoon of the pesto under the skin of each breast.

Baked Butternut Squash with Couscous

Mackerel with Fennel and Tomato Salsa

Smoked Haddock with Rarebit Crust

Masala Prawn Stir-fry

Prawn Curry and Nanjing Rice

Salmon Baked with a Rocket Pesto Crust and Pea Purée

Sole with Lime and Cucumber Salsa

Turkey and Apricot Pie

Hoisin Chicken Noodles

3 Transfer the chicken breasts to a roasting pan.

4 Spread the butter over the skin and season with salt and pepper.

5 Bake in the oven for 20–25 minutes.

6 Serve immediately.

NOTE: The chicken can be cooked through and then cooled completely, sliced and served with salads.

Chicken with Chive Butter

Preparation time: 20 minutes
Chilling time: 30–40 minutes
Cooking time: 20 minutes

SERVES 2

2 tablespoons very finely chopped fresh chives

½ clove of garlic, crushed

lemon juice

60 g butter, softened

2 chicken breasts, skinned and boned

plain seasoned flour (see page 20)

1 egg, beaten

dried white breadcrumbs

oil, for deep-frying (see page 12)

salt and freshly ground black pepper

To prepare ahead: Make in advance to the end of stage 4, then refrigerate.

Serving suggestions: Petits pois à la Française (see page 348), cheese and chive mash (see page 360), baked new potatoes en papillote (see page 367), green salad (see page 381)

1 Make the chive butter: mix the chives, garlic, lemon juice and salt and pepper with the butter. Divide into 2 equal pieces, shape into rectangles and chill well.

2 Remove the false fillets from the chicken breasts, cover with clingfilm and flatten gently, using a rolling pin.

3 Using a sharp knife, make a cut about 4 cm long in the thickest part of the breast, then, using the tip of the knife, make a pocket on either side by cutting along the length of the slit within the flesh.

4 Place a piece of the chive butter into the pocket of each breast and cover with the false fillet. Dust lightly with the seasoned flour. Dip into the beaten egg, then roll carefully in the breadcrumbs. Chill for 30–40 minutes.

5 Heat the oil in a deep fryer or large saucepan until a small piece of bread turns golden brown in 30 seconds. Fry the chicken in the oil for 15 minutes, reducing the heat if they brown too quickly. Drain well on kitchen paper and serve.

NOTE: A false fillet is a smaller fillet underneath the breast.

Chicken in Hoegaarden with Prunes

Preparation time: 20 minutes
Cooking time: 1 hour 20 minutes

SERVES 4

4 chicken breasts, skinned and boned

3 tablespoons sunflower oil

2 onions, finely sliced

1 teaspoon tomato purée

2 tablespoons plain flour

300 ml Hoegaarden beer (or pale, blonde beer)

300 ml chicken stock

1 heaped tablespoon soft dark brown sugar

1 tablespoon wholegrain mustard

2 bay leaves

½ tablespoon white wine vinegar

12 ready-to-eat prunes, pitted

salt and freshly ground black pepper

To prepare ahead: Make in advance, then refrigerate or freeze. If frozen, defrost completely before reheating.
Serving suggestions: Mustard mash (see page 359), steamed green vegetables

1 Preheat the oven to 180°C|350°F|gas mark 4.
2 Trim any fat off the chicken breasts.
3 Heat a little of the oil in a frying pan and brown the breasts on both sides. Transfer to a casserole.
4 Add the onions to the pan and sweat over a low heat for 10 minutes. Add the tomato purée and flour and cook for 1 further minute, stirring well.
5 Slowly stir in the beer. Bring to the boil and simmer for 2 minutes. Pour into the casserole with the stock, sugar, mustard, bay leaves and vinegar.
6 Cover the casserole and bake in the oven for 45 minutes. Add the prunes, then return to the oven for a further 20 minutes. Add a little more liquid if too thick, or remove the lid for the final cooking if too thin.
7 Season to taste with salt and pepper.

Honey, Lemon and Rosemary Chicken

Marinating time: 30 minutes–overnight
Preparation time: 5 minutes
Cooking time: 25 minutes

SERVES 4

4 chicken breasts, skinned and boned

4 tablespoons clear honey

grated zest and juice of 1 lemon

4 sprigs of fresh rosemary

salt and freshly ground black pepper

To garnish

sprigs of fresh rosemary

Serving suggestion: Mashed potatoes (see page 358), mashed root vegetables, sweet and sour cabbage (see page 343), green salad (see page 381), rosemary roast vegetables (see page 346)

1 Preheat the oven to 200°C|400°F|gas mark 6.
2 Place the chicken breasts in a shallow dish.
3 Mix together the honey, lemon zest and juice. Pour over the chicken and leave to marinate for at least 30 minutes.
4 Place a large sheet of kitchen foil on a baking sheet and arrange the breasts on it. Pour over the marinade, season with salt and pepper and lay over the sprigs of rosemary. Seal the chicken in the foil leaving enough room for the steam to circulate, and seal tightly at the edges.
5 Bake in the oven for 20–25 minutes.
6 Remove from the oven, discard the rosemary and arrange on a warmed serving plate, garnished with sprigs of rosemary.

Herb Chicken on Baked Tomatoes

Preparation time: 10 minutes
Cooking time: 40 minutes

SERVES 6

3 red onions, thickly sliced
6 cloves of garlic, lightly crushed but not peeled
olive oil
6 chicken breasts, boned, skin left on

150 g cream cheese with garlic and herbs
2 × 250 g punnets of cherry tomatoes
salt and freshly ground black pepper

To prepare ahead: Make in advance to the end of stage 4, then refrigerate.
Serving suggestions: Grilled Mediterranean vegetables (see page 346), hot raw beetroot (see page 339), dauphinoise potatoes (see page 370), baked new potatoes en papillote (see page 367), celeriac and blue cheese gratin (see page 373)

1 Preheat the oven to 190°C|375°F|gas mark 5.
2 Place the onions and garlic in a large roasting pan, drizzle over a little oil, and season with salt and pepper. Stir through so everything is coated.
3 Cook in the oven for 10 minutes.
4 Meanwhile, loosen the skin of the chicken breasts with a finger or the handle of a teaspoon and place a spoonful of the cheese underneath each one, spreading it under the length of the skin.
5 Remove the roasting pan from the oven and scatter the tomatoes and 2 tablespoons of water over the onions. Place the chicken breasts on top. Return to the oven and cook for a further 20–25 minutes.
6 Serve immediately.

Italian Chicken with Pesto Potatoes

Preparation time: 15 minutes
Cooking time: 20–25 minutes

SERVES 4

12 tablespoons balsamic vinegar

4 chicken breasts, skinned and boned

125 g mozzarella cheese, sliced

4 slices of Parma ham

4 small bunches of baby tomatoes on the vine

olive oil

450 g new potatoes

2 tablespoons ready-made pesto (or see page 512)

salt and freshly ground black pepper

To prepare ahead: Make in advance to the end of stage 4, then refrigerate.
Serving suggestions: Carrot and courgette 'pappardelle' (see page 344), French beans, broccoli

1 Preheat the oven to 200°C | 400°F | gas mark 6.
2 Put the vinegar into a small pan and reduce by simmering over a medium heat until syrupy. Set aside.
3 Make a small pocket in each of the chicken breasts. Using a sharp knife, make a cut about 4 cm long in the thickest part of the breast, then, using the tip of the knife, make a pocket in either side by cutting along the length of the slit within the flesh.
4 Season the mozzarella with salt and pepper and push some into each pocket. Wrap a slice of Parma ham around each chicken breast, then place on a baking sheet.
5 Add the bunches of vine tomatoes to the baking sheet, drizzle with a little oil and season everything with salt and pepper. Bake in the oven for 20–25 minutes, or until the chicken is cooked through.
6 Meanwhile, cook the new potatoes in a large pan of boiling salt water for about 15 minutes, or until tender. Drain the potatoes and return to the pan then stir through the pesto.
7 To serve: place the chicken breasts on warmed individual plates with a spoonful of the potatoes. Arrange a bunch of tomatoes on each plate and drizzle over the vinegar.

Thai Crusted Chicken with Satay Stuffing

Preparation time: 15 minutes
Chilling time: 30 minutes
Cooking time: 20–25 minutes

SERVES 4

4 large chicken breasts, skinned and boned

4 tablespoons crunchy peanut butter

1 tablespoon sweet chilli sauce

For the crust

4 tablespoons chopped fresh coriander

2 tablespoons softened butter

2 tablespoon dried white breadcrumbs

1 teaspoon peeled and grated fresh root ginger

1 clove of garlic, crushed

To prepare ahead: Make in advance to the end of stage 3, then refrigerate.
Serving suggestions: Thai rice salad (see page 354), stir-fried vegetables (see page 351), simmered miso squash (see page 353), jasmine rice (see page 375)

1 Preheat the oven to 200°C|400°F|gas mark 6.

2 Make a pocket in each chicken breast. Move the small loose false fillet to one side. Using a sharp knife, make a cut about 4 cm long in the thickest part of the breast, then, using the tip of the knife, make a pocket in either side by cutting along the length of the slit within the flesh.

3 Mix together the peanut butter and chilli sauce and stuff into the pockets in the chicken breasts. Fold the false fillet back over the cut. Place the chicken breasts on a baking sheet, cut side down.

4 Mix together all the crust ingredients and divide between the chicken. Press down firmly and chill for at least 30 minutes.

5 Bake the chicken in the oven for 20–25 minutes, then serve immediately.

NOTE: A false fillet is a smaller fillet underneath the breast.

Lemon and Thyme Chicken with Tomato and Borlotti Beans

Preparation time: 10 minutes
Cooking time: 35 minutes

SERVES 4

4 large chicken thighs (8 if small), skin left on
olive oil
grated zest of 2 lemons
4 tablespoons chopped fresh thyme
caster sugar
1 small onion, chopped
1 clove of garlic, crushed

½ glass of dry white wine
1 × 400 g can of chopped tomatoes
1 × 400 g can of borlotti beans, drained and rinsed
salt and freshly ground pepper

To garnish
sprigs of fresh thyme

To prepare ahead: The tomato and bean mixture can be prepared in advance then refrigerated or frozen until required. Defrost thoroughly before reheating.
Serving suggestions: Green salad (see page 381), herb couscous (see page 356) individual rösti potatoes (see page 366), boulangère potatoes (see page 368), rosemary roast vegetables (see page 346), courgettes with sultanas and pinenuts (see page 345)

1 Preheat the oven to 200°C | 400°F | gas mark 6.
2 Put the chicken thighs into an ovenproof dish and sprinkle with oil, half the lemon zest and half the thyme.
3 Season the chicken with salt, pepper and a pinch of sugar. Bake in the top of the oven for about 30–35 minutes, or until golden brown and cooked through.
4 Meanwhile, heat a little oil in a saucepan, add the onion and sweat over a low heat until soft but not coloured. Add the garlic and cook for a further 30 seconds. Add the wine, tomatoes and beans. Season to taste with salt, pepper and a pinch of sugar, then bring to the boil and simmer for 15–20 minutes.
5 Add the remaining thyme and lemon zest to the tomatoes and beans, and pour over the chicken. Garnish with sprigs of thyme and serve immediately.

VARIATION: Different types of canned beans, such as flageolet beans, can be used.

Chicken Thighs Stuffed with Apricots, Dates and Hazelnuts

Preparation time: 15 minutes
Cooking time: 30–35 minutes

SERVES 4

1 tablespoon oil

2 shallots, finely diced

30 g dried apricots, chopped

30 g pitted dried dates, chopped

150 ml apple juice, plus 2 tablespoons

30 g hazelnuts, roasted and roughly chopped (see page 17)

½ tablespoon chopped fresh parsley

4 large chicken thighs (8 if small), boned, skin left on

salt and freshly ground black pepper

To prepare ahead: This dish can be made in advance, then refrigerated or frozen. Defrost thoroughly before reheating.

Serving suggestions: Rosemary roast vegetables (see page 346), boulangère potatoes (see page 368), parsnip and dauphinoise potatoes (see page 370), Jerusalem artichoke dauphinoise (see page 371)

1 Preheat the oven to 200°C|400°F|gas mark 6.

2 Heat the oil in a small, heavy saucepan. Add the shallots and sweat over a low heat until soft but not coloured. Add the apricots, dates and the 2 tablespoons of apple juice. Allow to reduce until nearly all the apple juice has evaporated, then leave to stand for 10–15 minutes to allow the fruits to swell.

3 Add the hazelnuts and parsley to the pan and season with salt and pepper.

4 Stuff the chicken thighs with the mixture and place seam side down in a roasting pan. Season with salt and pepper, then roast in the oven for 30–35 minutes, or until cooked through.

5 Meanwhile, reduce the 150 ml apple juice by boiling rapidly until reduced by half. Season with salt and pepper.

6 Pour the reduced apple juice over the chicken thighs in the roasting pan. Scrape the bottom of the pan so that any caramelized juices are dissolved into the apple juice.

7 Serve the chicken thighs with the sauce poured over them.

NOTE: Cocktail sticks can be used to secure the thighs once stuffed. Remove before serving.

Peanut Chicken

Preparation time: 15 minutes
Marinating time: overnight
Cooking time: 30–35 minutes

SERVES 4

4 large chicken thighs (8 if small), boned, skin
    left on

For the stuffing

1 tablespoon oil
2 spring onions, finely chopped
1 red chilli, finely chopped
4 tablespoons crunchy peanut butter
½ tablespoon chopped fresh coriander
1 tablespoon dark soy sauce
1 tablespoon lemon juice

For the marinade

100 ml hoisin sauce
1 clove of garlic, crushed
1 × 2 cm piece of fresh root ginger, peeled and
    grated
4 tablespoons dark soy sauce
2 tablespoons clear honey

To garnish

30 g dry-roasted peanuts, chopped
fresh coriander leaves

To prepare ahead: Leave to marinate overnight.
Serving suggestions: Bean and parsley mash (see page 372), lemon buttered couscous (see page 357), sesame noodles (see page 378), chilli and coriander noodles (see page 378), stir-fry of green vegetables (see page 352), steamed cucumber with star anise (see page 351), basmati rice (see page 374), steamed bok choi with soy and ginger (see page 350)

1 Make the stuffing: heat the oil in a heavy wok or frying pan, add the spring onions and chilli and stir-fry for 1 minute. Remove from the pan and mix together with the other stuffing ingredients. Allow to cool completely.
2 Divide the stuffing between the chicken thighs, securing with cocktail sticks.
3 Place the chicken thighs in a shallow dish. Mix together the marinade ingredients and pour over the chicken. Leave overnight or for as long as possible.
4 Preheat the oven to 200°C|400°F|gas mark 6.
5 Remove the chicken from the marinade and place skin side up in a shallow roasting pan. Bake in the oven for 30–35 minutes, or until the skin is golden brown and the chicken is cooked through.
6 Remove the cocktail sticks and serve immediately, sprinkled with the peanuts and coriander.

Flambéed Chicken with Vermouth and Mushroom Sauce

Preparation time: 10 minutes
Cooking time: 40 minutes

SERVES 4

20 g butter

1 tablespoon oil

4 large chicken thighs (8 if small), skin left on

1 tablespoon dry vermouth

1 shallot, chopped

150 g field mushrooms, sliced

2 teaspoons plain flour

150 ml chicken stock

75 ml dry white wine

2 tablespoons double cream

salt and freshly ground black pepper

To garnish

1 tablespoon chopped fresh parsley

To prepare ahead: Make in advance to the end of stage 4, then refrigerate.

Serving suggestions: Brown rice, potato and apple boulangère (see page 369), dauphinoise potatoes (see page 370), individual rösti potatoes (see page 366), steamed green vegetables, couscous

1 Heat the butter and oil in a large frying pan with a lid and brown the chicken pieces all over, skin side first.

2 Add the vermouth and, making sure your arm is not directly over the pan, light it with a match and shake the pan until the flames subside (see page 14). Remove the chicken pieces.

3 Add the shallot and mushrooms to the pan and cook over a low heat until soft. Stir in the flour and cook for 1 minute. Remove from the heat and add the stock and wine. Mix well. Return to the heat and bring slowly to the boil, stirring all the time. Season with salt and pepper.

4 Return the chicken to the pan, cover and simmer gently for 30 minutes, or until the chicken is tender.

5 Remove the chicken pieces and keep warm. Reduce the sauce by boiling rapidly to a syrupy consistency. Add the cream and parsley and season to taste with salt and pepper.

6 Pour the sauce over the chicken, garnish with the parsley and serve immediately.

Couscous Stuffed Chicken Thighs

Preparation time: 20 minutes
Cooking time: 25 minutes

SERVES 2

4 large chicken thighs (8 if small), boned, skin
    left on
1 tablespoon oil
15 g butter
2 tablespoons clear honey

4–6 dried apricots, chopped
4 prunes, stoned and chopped
1 tablespoon chopped fresh parsley
2 teaspoons pinenuts, toasted (see page 17)
salt and freshly ground black pepper

For the stuffing

4 tablespoons couscous
hot chicken stock or water

To garnish

fresh flat-leaf parsley

To prepare ahead: Make in advance to the end of stage 3, then refrigerate.
Serving suggestions: Middle Eastern salad (see page 334), green salad, white bean salad (see page 338)

1 Preheat the oven to 200°C│400°F│gas mark 6.
2 Make the stuffing: place the couscous in a bowl, just cover with hot stock or water and leave for 10 minutes to allow it to swell. Add the apricots, prunes, parsley and pinenuts. Season with salt and pepper and mix well.
3 Stuff the chicken thighs with the stuffing and secure with cocktail sticks.
4 Heat the oil in a frying pan, add the butter and when sizzling, add the chicken thighs. Brown well on the skin side. Place the chicken thighs in a roasting pan and drizzle over the honey. Bake in the oven for 25–30 minutes, or until cooked through.
5 Remove the cocktail sticks and serve garnished with the parsley. Any surplus stuffing can be reheated in the microwave and served on the side, but make sure it has not been in contact with any raw chicken.

Chicken Breasts with Ginger

Preparation time: 5 minutes
Marinating time: 2–24 hours
Cooking time: 20–25 minutes

SERVES 4

4 chicken breasts, skinned and boned
1 large onion, very finely chopped
2 cloves of garlic, crushed
1 × 5 cm piece of fresh root ginger, peeled and
    sliced

5 cardamom pods, cracked
1 teaspoon ground turmeric
4 tablespoons light soy sauce
4 tablespoons dry sherry

To prepare ahead: Marinate overnight.

Serving suggestions: Basmati rice (see page 374), stir-fried vegetables (see page 351), steamed cucumber with star anise (see page 351), steamed bok choi with soy and ginger (see page 350)

1 Place the chicken breasts in a bowl with the onion, garlic, ginger, cardamom, turmeric, soy sauce and sherry. Cover and chill for 2–24 hours, turning the chicken once or twice.
2 Preheat the oven to 200°C|400°F|gas mark 6.
3 Line a shallow baking dish with kitchen foil and arrange the breasts on it. Pour over the marinade and seal the chicken tightly in the foil so that none of the juice can escape, but allow space for air to circulate.
4 Bake in the oven for 20–25 minutes, or until cooked through. Serve immediately.

Chicken with Balsamic Potatoes

Preparation time: 5 minutes
Cooking time: 50 minutes

SERVES 4

2 red onions, sliced
450 g small new potatoes
1 tablespoon balsamic vinegar
3 tablespoons olive oil
grated zest and juice of 1 lime
1 teaspoon roughly chopped fresh thyme

4 large chicken thighs (8 if small), skin left on
3 tablespoons ginger syrup
2 plum tomatoes, halved, deseeded and cut into strips
1 teaspoon rock salt and freshly ground black pepper

Serving suggestions: Green salad (see page 381), green vegetables

1 Preheat the oven to 200°C|400°F|gas mark 6.
2 Place the onions, potatoes, vinegar, oil, lime zest and thyme in a roasting pan. Season with salt and pepper and stir well, making sure all the ingredients are well mixed. Bake in the oven for 10 minutes.
3 Place the chicken, skin side up, on top of the vegetables, then bake in the oven for a further 25 minutes, stirring the vegetables occasionally.
4 Add the lime juice and ginger syrup to the roasting pan, and return to the oven for 5–10 minutes, or until the chicken is cooked.
5 Remove the chicken from the pan and bubble the remaining mixture on the hob until syrupy and strong-flavoured. Add the tomatoes and stir until hot. Pile the mixture on to individual warmed plates, and top each with a piece of chicken.

Chicken, Pea and Mushroom Pie

Preparation time: 25 minutes
Cooking time: 25 minutes

SERVES 4

oil

30 g butter

1 onion, finely chopped

60 g mushrooms, chopped

30 g plain flour

1 teaspoon dry English mustard

200 ml chicken stock

1 glass of white wine

100 ml milk

100 g frozen peas

350 g cooked chicken or turkey

100 g cooked ham, cubed

375 g ready-rolled puff pastry

1 egg, beaten

salt and freshly ground black pepper

To prepare ahead: The pie can be assembled in advance, then refrigerated or frozen. If you freeze it, make sure the filling is cold before putting on the pastry lid, and defrost thoroughly before baking.

1 Preheat the oven to 200°C|400°F|gas mark 6.
2 Heat a little oil with the butter in a large saucepan. Add the onion and sweat over a low heat until soft and golden brown. Add the mushrooms to the pan and cook until they are soft and the liquid has evaporated. Add the flour and mustard to the mixture and stir well, then cook for 1 minute.
3 Remove from the heat and gradually add the stock and the wine. Return to the heat and bring slowly to the boil. Add enough milk to obtain a good coating-consistency sauce. Simmer for 2 minutes, then season well with salt and pepper. Add the peas and return to the boil.
4 Add the chicken or turkey and the ham and pile into a pie dish.
5 Cut the pastry to fit the dish. Place it on top of the pie filling and brush with beaten egg. Mark the edges with the prongs of a fork.
6 Bake in the oven for 25 minutes, or until the pastry is golden and the filling hot through.

Hoisin Chicken Noodles

Preparation time: 10 minutes
Marinating time: 20 minutes–overnight
Cooking time: 15 minutes

SERVES 6

6 chicken breasts, skinned, boned and cut into strips

200 ml hoisin sauce

5 tablespoons dark soy sauce

2 tablespoons sesame oil

1 packet of medium egg noodles

oil, for frying

1 × 300 g pack of prepared stir-fry vegetables

To garnish

5 spring onions, finely shredded

To prepare ahead: Leave the chicken to marinate overnight.

Serving suggestions: Steamed bok choi with soy and ginger (see page 350), stir-fried vegetables (see page 351)

1 Place the chicken in a bowl. Add the hoisin sauce, soy sauce and sesame oil. Stir well and cover. Leave in the refrigerator to marinate for as long as possible, ideally overnight.
2 Place the chicken into a sieve over a bowl. Reserve the strained marinade.
3 Cook the noodles according to the manufacturer's instructions. Drain well.
4 Heat a little oil in a wok or large frying pan until hot. Add the chicken pieces and stir-fry until almost cooked. Add the vegetables and continue to stir-fry until the chicken is cooked.
5 Add the reserved marinade with 2 tablespoons water and boil the sauce vigorously.
6 Add the noodles and toss thoroughly to ensure that they are well coated in the sauce.
7 Pile into a warmed serving dish and serve garnished with the spring onions.

Stir-fried Chicken with Cashew Nuts

Preparation time: 20 minutes
Cooking time: 15 minutes

SERVES 4

4 chicken breasts, skinned and boned	300 ml chicken stock
2 tablespoons oil	½ red pepper, cored, deseeded and cut into thick strips
1 × 2.5 cm piece fresh root ginger, peeled and grated	90 g button mushrooms, quartered
3 cloves of garlic, finely chopped	1 red chilli, sliced (optional)
1 teaspoon black pepper	2 tablespoons oyster sauce
1 teaspoon caster sugar	90 g cashew nuts, toasted (see page 17)
1 tablespoon light soy sauce	2–3 spring onions, cut on the diagonal into
½ onion, cut into thick slices and rings separated	2.5 cm pieces

Serving suggestions: Rice, chilli and coriander noodles (see page 378), sesame noodles (see page 378), stir-fried vegetables (see page 351), steamed bok choi with soy and ginger (see page 350)

1 Place the chicken breasts between 2 sheets of damp greaseproof paper or clingfilm and bat out until they are about 1 cm thick. Cut into strips.
2 Heat the oil in a wok or large frying pan with a lid. Add the ginger and garlic and stir-fry for 1 minute. Add the chicken and cook for 1 further minute, then add the pepper and sugar.
3 Add the soy sauce and the onions and stir-fry for 30 seconds.
4 Add half the stock, cover the pan and cook for 3 minutes.
5 Remove the lid and add the remaining stock, red pepper, mushrooms and the chilli, if using. Cover and cook for a further 3 minutes.
6 Add the oyster sauce, cashew nuts and spring onions and stir-fry until the sauce has reduced and is coating the vegetables. Serve immediately.

Stir-fried Chicken with Lemon Grass

Preparation time: 15 minutes
Chilling time: 1 hour
Cooking time: 15 minutes

SERVES 4–6

2 heaped tablespoons cornflour

5 tablespoons water

3 chicken breasts, skinned, boned and cut into strips

2 sticks of lemon grass

3 tablespoons oil

1 clove of garlic, sliced

2 slices of peeled fresh root ginger

1 small red onion, finely sliced

1 red pepper, cored, deseeded and sliced

2 tablespoons sesame seeds, toasted (see page 17)

1 × 220 g can of water chestnuts, drained and sliced

100 g baby sweetcorn, cut in half lengthways

90 g sugarsnap peas

120 g beansprouts

2 tablespoons sherry

2 tablespoons soy sauce

1 tablespoon sweet chilli dipping sauce

grated zest of 1 lemon

2 tablespoons chopped fresh coriander

To prepare ahead: Assemble all the vegetables in advance and prepare to the end of stage 1.
Serving suggestions: Rice, sesame noodles (see page 378), chilli and coriander noodles (see page 378), stir-fried vegetables (see page 351)

1 Mix together the cornflour and 4 tablespoons of the water. Add the chicken pieces, stir and chill for 1 hour.
2 Pull off the coarse outer leaves of the lemon grass and cut the leaves into 2.5 cm pieces. Add to the oil in a frying pan with the garlic and ginger. Heat until the oil starts to sizzle, then remove from the heat and leave to infuse for 10 minutes. Finely chop the remaining lemon grass, discarding the coarser ends.
3 Strain the chicken pieces in a sieve placed over a bowl. Strain the oil from the pan into a wok or large frying pan. Heat, then add the chicken and stir-fry until golden and just cooked through. Remove from the pan with a slotted spoon and set aside.
4 Add the onion and red pepper to the pan and stir-fry until beginning to soften. Add the sesame seeds, chestnuts, sweetcorn, peas and beansprouts and stir-fry for 1 minute. Increase the heat and add the chopped lemon grass, sherry, soy sauce, chilli sauce, lemon zest and the remaining tablespoon water. Allow to bubble for 30 seconds, then add the chicken and coriander.
5 Serve immediately.

NOTE: To save time, use 1–2 bags ready-prepared stir-fried vegetables.

Chicken Tagine with Lemon and Lime

A tagine is a classic Moroccan cooking pot with a conical lid. The dish takes its name from the pot it is cooked in, like a casserole or a terrine.

Preparation time: 15 minutes
Cooking time: 1¼ hours

SERVES 4

3 tablespoons olive oil

1 large onion, finely sliced

2 cloves of garlic, crushed

4 chicken breasts, skinned, boned and and cut into bite-sized pieces

2 teaspoons ground cinnamon

1 teaspoon ground ginger

½ teaspoon ground coriander

grated zest and juice of ½ lemon

grated zest and juice of ½ lime

2 tablespoons clear honey

1 tablespoon white wine vinegar

300 ml chicken stock

60 g raisins

60 g whole blanched almonds, lightly toasted (see page 17)

salt and freshly ground black pepper

To garnish

1 tablespoon roughly chopped fresh flat-leaf parsley

To prepare ahead: The dish can be made in advance, then refrigerated or frozen and reheated. If frozen, defrost thoroughly before reheating.

Serving suggestions: Couscous, Middle Eastern salad (see page 334), green salad (see page 381)

1 Heat half the oil in a tagine or a heavy saucepan. Add the onion and sweat over a low heat until soft, then increase the heat and cook until golden brown. Add the garlic and cook for 1 minute. Remove from the pan and wipe out the pan with kitchen paper.

2 Add the remaining oil to the pan, add the chicken pieces and fry until lightly browned all over. Add the dry spices and cook, stirring, for 1 minute.

3 Mix together the lemon and lime zest and juice, honey, vinegar and stock and pour over the chicken. Return the onion and garlic to the pan, stir well and cover with a lid. Cook over the lowest heat for 1 hour.

4 Remove the lid, add the raisins and increase the heat. Reduce the sauce by boiling rapidly until it has a syrupy consistency. Stir in the almonds and season to taste with salt and freshly ground black pepper.

5 Garnish with the parsley and serve.

Chicken Dhal

Preparation time: 10 minutes
Cooking time: 40 minutes

SERVES 4

5 tablespoons oil
1 red onion, finely sliced
1 leek, sliced and washed
1 clove of garlic, crushed
1 teaspoon nigella or mustard seeds
1 teaspoon ground cumin
1 teaspoon garam masala
½ teaspoon ground chilli

½ glass of dry white wine
600 ml chicken stock
225 g yellow mung dhal lentils or yellow split peas
3 chicken breasts, skinned, boned and cut into bite-sized pieces

To garnish
2 tablespoons roughly chopped fresh coriander

To prepare ahead: The dish can be completely prepared in advance, then refrigerated or frozen. If frozen, defrost thoroughly before reheating.
Serving suggestions: Indian-style green beans (see page 350)

1 Heat 3 tablespoons of the oil in a large saucepan, add the onion and leek and fry until beginning to brown. Add the garlic and dry spices and cook for 1 further minute.
2 Add the wine and stock and bring to the boil. Add the lentils and simmer for 20 minutes.
3 Heat the remaining oil in a frying pan, add the chicken and fry until golden brown on the outside. Add the chicken to the lentil mixture and cook for a further 10 minutes, or until the chicken is tender, the lentils are cooked and the liquid has reduced.
4 Serve in warmed bowls, garnished with the coriander.

VARIATION: Use 1–2 tablespoons Indian curry paste (see page 35) in place of the dry spices.

Baked Curried Chicken

Marinating time: 2 hours–overnight
Preparation time: 5 minutes
Cooking time: 30 minutes

SERVES 4

1½ tablespoons curry paste, mild to hot depending on taste
2 cloves of garlic, crushed
400–425 ml soured cream or coconut milk

4 chicken breasts, skinned and boned
80 g fresh white breadcrumbs

To garnish
chopped fresh parsley

To prepare ahead: Make in advance to the end of stage 2.
Serving suggestions: Basmati rice (see page 374), peas, green salad (see page 381)

1 Mix together the curry paste, garlic and soured cream or coconut milk.
2 Put the chicken breasts into an ovenproof dish and pour over the curry and cream mixture. Cover and leave to marinate in the refrigerator for 2 hours or overnight if possible.
3 Preheat the oven to 190°C│375°F│gas mark 5.
4 Sprinkle the breadcrumbs over the top of the chicken and bake in the oven for 30 minutes.
5 Sprinkle the parsley over the top and serve immediately.

Green Chicken Curry

Preparation time: 5 minutes
Cooking time: 15 minutes

SERVES 4

1 tablespoon oil	3 small green Thai aubergines, quartered if large, or
2 cloves of garlic, sliced	1 medium purple aubergine, chopped
2 tablespoons green curry paste	4 chicken breasts, skinned, boned and cut into strips
400 ml coconut milk	20 sweet basil leaves (horapa)
2 tablespoons nam pla (Thai fish sauce)	3 kaffir lime leaves, shredded
1 teaspoon caster sugar	

Serving suggestions: Jasmine rice, pineapple rice (see page 376), stir-fried vegetables (see page 351), salad with spinach and beansprouts (see page 381)

1 Heat the oil in a large frying pan, add the garlic and fry until golden brown. Add the green curry paste, then gradually blend in the coconut milk, nam pla and sugar.
2 Add the aubergines and cook for 7 minutes, then add the chicken and cook for a further 5 minutes. You may need to add extra water to the pan if it becomes too dry.
3 Stir in the basil leaves and lime leaves and serve immediately.

NOTE: This recipe makes quite a hot curry, so if you prefer a milder flavour, start with 1 tablespoon green curry paste and add more to taste. If fresh lime leaves are not available, they are available preserved in a jar from some supermarkets, or use grated lime zest instead. If you can get hold of fresh lime leaves, they freeze well.

Turkey Curry

This curry works well when using up leftover meat. Chicken could also be used.

Preparation time: 10 minutes
Cooking time: 20 minutes

SERVES 4

3 tablespoons oil

1 large onion, finely sliced

about 2 tablespoons curry paste, depending on type and strength

3 tablespoons water

1 × 200 g can of chopped tomatoes

sugar to taste

450 g cooked turkey, cut into pieces

300 g full-fat natural yoghurt

salt and freshly ground black pepper

To garnish

chopped fresh coriander

1 Heat the oil in a heavy frying pan, add the onion and sweat over a low heat until soft but not coloured. Add the curry paste and cook for 1 minute.
2 Add the water and simmer the sauce for 2 minutes. Add the tomatoes, season to taste with sugar, salt and pepper and heat through.
3 Add more water if necessary and allow to simmer for 2 minutes.
4 Add the turkey and heat the curry through completely. Gradually stir in the yoghurt, taking care not to let the mixture boil after it has been added.
5 Serve garnished with the coriander.

Crisp Turkey Escalopes

Preparation time: 10 minutes
Chilling time: 30 minutes
Cooking time: 10 minutes

SERVES 4

4 small turkey breast escalopes

4 tablespoons seasoned flour

¼ teaspoon ground chilli

2 eggs, beaten

60 g dried white breadcrumbs

To prepare ahead: Prepare the escalopes to the end of stage 1, then refrigerate.
Serving suggestions: Pineapple rice (see page 376), tomato salsa (see page 510), green salad (see page 381), new potatoes, garlic bread (see page 379)

1 Place the turkey escalopes between 2 sheets of damp greaseproof paper or clingfilm and flatten with a rolling pin until approximately 1½ cm thick. Dip into the flour with the chilli added and pat off the excess. Dip carefully into the beaten egg and finally cover in

breadcrumbs. Make sure that the escalopes are completely covered, then lay in a single layer on a large plate and chill for 30 minutes.

2 Heat enough oil to cover the bottom of a heavy frying pan to a depth of about 1 cm. Check it is hot enough before frying the turkey by dropping in a crumb, which should sizzle at once. Do not leave the oil unattended when it is on the heat.

3 Fry the escalopes until cooked and golden brown. Drain well on kitchen paper and sprinkle with salt. Serve immediately.

Turkey and Ham Pie

This recipe is very good for using up leftover roast turkey or chicken. If you have leftover mashed potato this can be used on the top instead of cooking and slicing potatoes.

Preparation time: 10 minutes
Cooking time: 1 hour

SERVES 4–6

450 g potatoes	300 ml milk
2 tablespoons oil	300 ml chicken or turkey stock
1 large onion, finely chopped	450 g cooked boneless turkey, shredded
225 g mushrooms, sliced	250 g cooked ham, cut into cubes
60 g butter	2 tablespoons chopped fresh parsley
60 g plain flour	salt and freshly ground black pepper

1 Preheat the oven to 200°C|400°F|gas mark 6.

2 Peel the potatoes and cook for 10 minutes in boiling salted water. Drain and allow to cool. The potatoes should not be fully cooked through at this stage.

3 Heat the oil in a large, heavy saucepan, add the onion and sweat over a low heat until soft but not coloured. Add the mushrooms and cook until soft and any liquid has evaporated. Remove from the pan and set aside.

4 Melt the butter in the saucepan, add the flour and stir over a low heat for 1 minute. Remove from the heat and gradually add the milk, a little at a time, stirring well. Return to the heat and bring to the boil, then add the stock and stir. Simmer for 2–3 minutes, then season to taste with salt and pepper.

5 Stir the mushroom mixture into the sauce and add the turkey, ham and parsley. Stir well, check the seasoning and spoon into a pie dish.

6 Slice the potatoes thinly and arrange them in overlapping rows or circles on the top of the pie. Brush with a little oil and season with salt and pepper.

7 Bake on the top shelf of the oven for 20–30 minutes, or until the potatoes are golden brown and the filling is piping hot.

Turkey and Apricot Pie

Preparation time: 10 minutes
Cooking time: 1 hour

SERVES 6–8

375 g ready-rolled puff pastry

2 tablespoons oil

1 large onion, finely chopped

225 g mushrooms, sliced

1 tablespoon finely chopped fresh lemon thyme

85 g butter

85 g plain flour

450 ml milk

450 ml chicken or turkey stock

700 g cooked boneless turkey, cut into bite-sized
 pieces

170 g dried apricots, sliced

1 egg, beaten

salt and freshly ground black pepper

To prepare ahead: Make sure that the sauce is completely cold before adding the other ingredients, then chill or freeze. Cook as required. If frozen, defrost thoroughly before baking.

Serving suggestion: Peas and baby sweetcorn

1 Preheat the oven to 200°C│400°F│gas mark 6.

2 Heat the oil in a large, heavy saucepan, add the onion and sweat over a low heat until soft but not coloured. Add the mushrooms and cook until soft and any liquid has evaporated, then add the thyme and set aside.

3 Melt the butter in another pan, then add the flour and stir over a low heat heat for 1 minute. Remove from the heat and gradually add the milk a little at a time, stirring well. Return to the heat and bring to the boil, then add the stock and stir. Simmer for 2–3 minutes and season with salt and pepper.

4 Add the turkey, apricots and mushroom mixture to the sauce. Stir well and season to taste with salt and pepper, then spoon into a large pie dish.

5 Cut out a pastry lid to fit the pie dish. From the trimmings cut a band of pastry the width of the lip of the dish and press on to the rim. Cut out leaves or other decorations. Brush the pastry band with beaten egg and lay the pastry lid over the top. Press to join the edges, and trim off the excess. Make a hole or a couple of slits in the top of the pie and arrange the leaves or other decoration on top. Brush the pastry with the beaten egg.

6 Bake on the top shelf of the oven for 30–40 minutes, or until the pastry is golden brown and the filling piping hot.

NOTE: Leftover chicken or ham from the bone can be used instead of turkey.

Duck Breasts with Blackberry and Apple Sauce

Preparation time: 10 minutes
Cooking time: 20 minutes

SERVES 4

4 large duck breasts, skin left on	1½ tablespoons water
110 g blackberries	grated zest of ½ lemon
1 small dessert apple, peeled, cored and cut into 2 cm chunks	sugar to taste
	oil, for frying
1 tablespoon port	salt and freshly ground black pepper

To prepare ahead: Brown the duck breasts and make the sauce in advance then chill. Reheat the sauce while cooking the duck, which will take a little longer to cook from cold.

Serving suggestions: Mashed potatoes (see page 358), crushed new potatoes, dauphinoise potatoes (see page 370), wilted spinach

1 Score a lattice pattern on the duck skin with a sharp knife and sprinkle with salt.
2 Preheat the oven to 220°C|425°F|gas mark 7.
3 Wash the blackberries and put into a small saucepan with the apple. Add the port, water, lemon zest and about 20 g caster sugar (less if the blackberries are very ripe). Heat very gently until the fruit begins to soften and the juices are thick and syrupy. Taste and season with black pepper, adding more sugar if the sauce is very tart, but not too much as the finished sauce should be a little sharp.
4 Heat a small amount of oil in a heavy frying pan. When hot, add the duck breasts, skin side down, and fry until the skin becomes a good even brown colour (it should take about 5 minutes). Drain the fat from the frying pan 2 or 3 times during this process. Remove the duck from the frying pan and place, skin side up, in a roasting pan.
5 Roast in the oven for 8–10 minutes, or until the duck is cooked but still pink inside.
6 Remove from the oven and allow to rest for 5 minutes, then cut the duck breasts into slices on the diagonal and serve with the warm blackberry and apple sauce.

Duck Breasts with Calvados and Apple

Preparation time: 5 minutes
Cooking time: 25 minutes

SERVES 4

4 large duck breasts, skin left on
2 tablespoons oil
salt and freshly ground black pepper

For the sauce
100 ml Calvados
1 × 142 ml pot of double cream

To garnish
30 g unsalted butter
2 firm dessert apples, peeled, cored and cut into eighths
a little caster sugar
sprigs of watercress

To prepare ahead: The duck breasts can be browned and the sauce made in advance, and then refrigerated. Cook the duck through when reheating the sauce, remembering that they will take a little longer to cook from cold.

Serving suggestions: Potato and apple boulangère (see page 369), new potatoes, French beans and almonds (see page 341), Vichy carrots (see page 344), steamed vegetables

1 Preheat the oven to 220°C|425°F|gas mark 7.

2 Score a lattice pattern on the duck skin with a sharp knife and season with salt. Heat the oil in a sauté pan. Add the duck breasts and brown the skin until golden brown (this should take about 5 minutes). Drain off any excess fat. Add the Calvados to the pan and allow it to bubble. Stand well back as it may flame, in which case gently shake the pan until the flames subside. Remove the duck breasts from the pan and place in a roasting pan.

3 Roast in the oven for 8–10 minutes, or until the duck breasts are firm but still pink in the middle. Leave to rest for 5 minutes.

4 Meanwhile, add the cream to the Calvados in the sauté pan and season well with salt and pepper. Set aside.

5 Make the garnish: melt the butter in a second frying pan, add the apples and fry over a medium heat with a little sugar until golden brown.

6 To serve: reheat the sauce and slice the duck breasts on the diagonal. Garnish with the apples and watercress and pour the sauce around the sliced duck. Serve immediately.

Caramelized Duck Breasts with Honey, Lime and Ginger Sauce

Preparation time: 10 minutes
Cooking time: 15 minutes

SERVES 4

4 large duck breasts, skin left on	grated zest of 1 lime
caster sugar	juice of ½ lime
2 tablespoons olive oil	225 ml strong chicken stock
3 tablespoons clear honey	15 g fresh root ginger, peeled and grated
175 ml dry white wine	salt and freshly ground black pepper

To prepare ahead: Pan-fry the duck until golden brown, leave on the racks to cool then refrigerate and finish the dish when ready to serve. The duck breasts will take a little longer to cook from cold.

Serving suggestions: Chilli noodles (see page 378), stir-fried vegetables (see page 351), egg-fried rice with bok choi (see page 377)

1 Preheat the oven to 220°C | 425°F | gas mark 7.
2 Using a sharp knife, score the duck skin in a lattice pattern. Rub salt, pepper and sugar into the skin.
3 Heat the oil in a large, heavy frying pan and when sizzling, add the duck breasts, skin side down, and fry for 4–5 minutes, or until golden brown. Turn the breasts over and place them, skin side up, on a wire rack over a roasting pan. Brush with half the honey.
4 Roast in the oven for 8–10 minutes.
5 Meanwhile, drain off the fat from the frying pan. Add the wine, lime zest and juice and the remaining honey and boil until the liquid has reduced by half.
6 Add the stock and ginger and bring back to the boil. Allow to simmer until the sauce starts to thicken.
7 Remove the duck breasts from the oven and leave to rest for 5 minutes. Slice and arrange on warmed individual plates. Add any meat juices from the pan to the sauce and simmer for a further minute or two. Pour over the duck and serve immediately.

Duck with Stir-fried Vegetables and Noodles

Marinating time: 2 hours–overnight
Preparation time: 15 minutes
Cooking time: 20 minutes

SERVES 4

8 tablespoons light soy sauce
2 tablespoons clear honey (or stem ginger syrup)
2 red chillies, finely chopped
4 duck breasts, skinned
1 pack of medium egg noodles
1 tablespoon sesame oil
1 bunch of spring onions, finely chopped
1 red pepper, cored, deseeded and sliced

1 yellow pepper, cored, deseeded and sliced
1 small pack of baby sweetcorn, halved on the diagonal
1 small pack of mangetout
30 g sesame seeds, toasted
freshly ground black pepper

To garnish
fresh coriander leaves

To prepare ahead: Marinate the duck overnight.

1 In a shallow dish, mix together the soy sauce, honey, black pepper and half the chilli. Add the duck breasts and turn in the marinade. Cover and refrigerate overnight or for as long as possible, turning occasionally.
2 Preheat the oven to 200°C|400°F|gas mark 6.
3 Place the duck breasts in a roasting pan and roast in the oven for 15–20 minutes, basting with half the marinade. Reserve the remaining marinade.
4 Cook the noodles according to the manufacturer's instructions. Meanwhile, heat the sesame oil in a wok, add the remaining chilli and stir-fry for 1 minute. Add the remaining vegetables and stir-fry until cooked, then stir in the remaining marinade and cook for a further 30 seconds. Add the noodles to the vegetables, together with half the sesame seeds. Toss together.
5 Remove the duck breasts from the oven, leave to rest for 5 minutes and cut into slices on the diagonal.
6 To serve: arrange the vegetables and noodles on warmed individual plates, arrange the sliced duck breast over the top and garnish with the remaining sesame seeds and the coriander. Serve immediately.

Confit of Duck

Preparation time: 2 days
Cooking time: 4 hours, plus 20 minutes

SERVES 4

4 duck or goose legs, or 1 duck, jointed

2 bay leaves, crushed

For the marinade

30 g sea salt

1 tablespoon black peppercorns, cracked

2 cloves, crushed

4 sprigs of fresh rosemary, chopped

For the confit

olive oil

675 g duck or goose fat

5 cloves of garlic, unpeeled

5 sprigs of fresh thyme

To prepare ahead: As long as it is completely sealed, the confit may be stored for up to 1 month in the refrigerator.

Serving suggestions: Parsnip and crème fraîche purée (see page 363), green vegetables. Or use for duck pancakes (see page 490)

1 Mix together the salt, peppercorns, cloves, rosemary and bay leaves. Rub into the duck.
2 Place the duck in a dish in a single layer. Cover with clingfilm and weigh down. Chill in the refrigerator for 24 hours.
3 Preheat the oven to 150°C|300°F|gas mark 2.
4 Pour off any liquid from the duck and scrape off the marinade.
5 Heat the oil in a flameproof casserole, just large enough to hold all the ingredients.
6 Brown the duck all over in the oil, then add the fat and the garlic and thyme. The duck should be entirely submerged in the fat.
7 Bake in the oven for 2½–3 hours, or until the meat is very tender when pierced with a skewer.
8 Remove from the oven, then remove the lid and allow to cool.
9 Remove the duck from the fat and use kitchen scissors to trim off any exposed bone. Place the duck in a dish, jar or bowl. Strain the fat over the duck, making sure that the duck is covered and there are no pockets of air. Allow to set, then refrigerate until required.

To reheat the confit:
1 Preheat the oven to 220°C|425°F|gas mark 7.
2 Remove the duck from the container and scrape the fat from the joints. Place on a wire rack over a roasting tin.
3 Bake for 15–20 minutes or until heated through.

Pheasant Breasts with Pancetta and Rosemary

Preparation time: 5 minutes
Cooking time: 15–20 minutes

SERVES 4

oil, for greasing
4 pheasant breasts, skinned and boned
4 sprigs of fresh rosemary, finely chopped
salt and freshly ground black pepper

125 g pancetta, cut into thin slices, or dry-cure
  streaky bacon

To garnish
1 small bunch of watercress

Serving suggestions: Cumberland sauce (see page 506), cabbage and caraway (see page 343), petits pois à la Française (see page 348), herb potato mash (see page 361), artichoke dauphinoise (see page 370) potato and apple boulangère (see page 369)

1 Preheat the oven to 200°C|400°F|gas mark 6. Oil a baking sheet.
2 Season the pheasant breasts lightly with salt and pepper.
3 Sprinkle the rosemary on each breast and cover them with the pancetta slices or bacon rashers, folding the overlap underneath.
4 Place the pheasant breasts in a single layer on the prepared baking sheet. Cover the baking sheet tightly with kitchen foil and bake in the oven for 5 minutes. Remove the foil and cook for a further 10 minutes, or until the pheasant is cooked and the pancetta or bacon lightly browned.
5 Transfer to a warmed serving dish. Garnish with the watercress, and serve immediately.

Whiskied Pheasant

Preparation time: 10 minutes
Cooking time: 50 minutes

SERVES 2–4

60 g butter
1 onion, finely chopped
1 plump ovenready pheasant, jointed
100 ml whisky
100 ml stock or water
1 × 284 ml pot of double cream

1–2 tablespoons Dijon mustard
juice of 1 lemon
salt and freshly ground black pepper

To garnish
1 bunch of watercress

Serving suggestions: Parsnip and crème fraîche purée (see page 363), green vegetables

1 Preheat the oven to 190°C|375°F|gas mark 5.
2 Melt the butter in a large, heavy pan, add the onion and fry over a low heat until golden, then remove from the pan and set aside. Add the pheasant pieces and brown on all sides.

3 Pour over the whisky and set alight (see page 14), shaking the pan until the flames subside. Return the onions to the pan with the stock or water and season with salt and pepper. Transfer the contents of the pan to a flameproof casserole and cover closely. Cook in the oven for 40 minutes, or until the pheasant is tender.

4 Remove the pheasant from the casserole and keep warm.

5 Place the casserole over a high heat and boil the juices to reduce to 5 tablespoons, stirring all the time. Then gradually add the cream, boiling down until you have a coating sauce.

6 Remove from the heat, add the mustard and season to taste with salt and pepper. Add the lemon juice, pour over the pheasant and serve garnished with the watercress.

Peppered Venison Steaks

Preparation time: 5 minutes
Chilling time: 2 hours–overnight
Cooking time: 5–10 minutes

SERVES 4

4 × 150 g venison steaks, cut from the fillet

2 tablespoons black peppercorns

1 tablespoon oil

30 g unsalted butter

2 tablespoons brandy

1 × 142 ml pot of double cream

salt

To garnish

chopped fresh parsley

To prepare ahead: Leave the steaks to chill overnight.

Serving suggestions: Cabbage, dauphinoise potatoes (see page 370), parsnip and potato dauphinoise (see page 370), blue cheese and celeriac gratin (see page 373), spicy potato wedges with chilli (see page 368), caramelized onion mash (see page 360), bubble and squeak (see page 366)

1 Wipe the steaks and trim off any gristle and fat.

2 Crush the peppercorns coarsely in a mortar or under a rolling pin and press them into the surface of the meat on both sides.

3 Cover the steaks and chill for at least 2 hours or overnight to allow the flavour to penetrate the meat.

4 Heat the oil in a heavy frying pan, add the butter and when foaming add the steaks and fry until done to your liking (about 2 minutes per side for blue, 3 minutes for rare, 3½ minutes for medium and 4 minutes for well done). Drain any excess fat from the pan.

5 Flame the brandy and pour over the steaks (see page 14). When the flames have subsided, add the cream and a pinch of salt. Stir the contents of the pan thoroughly, scraping up any sediment stuck to the bottom. Add a little water if necessary.

6 Transfer the steaks to a warmed serving platter.

7 Boil up the sauce again, then simmer to a syrupy consistency, or add water if too thick, and pour over the meat. Serve immediately, sprinkled with the parsley.

Meat

Fried Steak

The length of cooking time varies according to the type of steak, the degree of heat, the weight of the frying pan, etc. With experience it is possible to tell from the feel of the steak how well cooked it is: it feels very soft when blue; just firm when medium. But if you want to be certain, cut a tiny slit in the thickest part of the meat and take a look. Do not do this until you are fairly sure that the steak is ready – too many cuts will mean loss of juices.

Standing time: 30 minutes
Preparation time: 2 minutes
Cooking time: 4–10 minutes

SERVES 4

4 sirloin steaks, cut 2 cm thick, or 4 fillet steaks, cut 2.5 cm thick

salt and freshly ground black pepper
oil, for frying

1 Season the steaks with pepper. Trim off any gristle or excess fat. Leave to come to room temperature if they have been chilled. Sprinkle lightly with salt just before cooking.
2 Brush a frying pan with a little oil and place over a medium-high heat until it is beginning to smoke.
3 Brown the steaks quickly on both sides. For a blue or rare steak, keep the heat fierce for the whole cooking time. For better-done steaks, lower the temperature to medium after an initial good browning. Cooking times, assuming a good hot pan, would be very approximately as below:

SIRLOIN

Blue	1 minute per side
Rare	$1\frac{1}{2}$ minutes per side
Medium-rare	2 minutes per side
Medium	$2\frac{1}{4}$ minutes per side

FILLET

Blue	$1\frac{1}{2}$ minutes per side
Rare	$2\frac{1}{4}$ minutes per side
Medium-rare	$3\frac{1}{4}$ minutes per side
Medium	$4\frac{1}{2}$ minutes per side

Sauces to Serve with Steak

SERVES 4

Wild Mushroom Sauce

30 g butter

2 shallots, chopped

100 g wild mushrooms, such as horn of plenty, chanterelles, etc.

60 g flat mushrooms, sliced

450 ml beef stock

100 ml dry white wine

170 g unsalted butter, chilled and cut into small pieces

1 Melt the 30 g butter in a frying pan, add the shallots and sweat over a low heat until soft. Increase the heat and cook until golden brown.

2 Add the mushrooms to the pan and cook for 2 minutes. Remove the mushrooms with a slotted spoon and reserve.

3 Add the stock and wine to the pan. Boil until reduced to about 150 ml. Lower the heat under the pan.

4 Using a small wire whisk, gradually add the 170 g butter, piece by piece. Whisk vigorously after each addition. This process should take about 5 minutes and the sauce should become thick and creamy.

5 Return the mushrooms to the sauce, check the seasoning and serve.

Green Peppercorn Sauce

2 teaspoons canned green peppercorns in brine

2 tablespoons brandy

4 tablespoons double cream

2 tablespoons water

salt

1 Drain and rinse the peppercorns.

2 Cook the steaks as on page 240, until done to your liking.

3 Flame the brandy and pour over the steaks (see page 14).

4 When the flames subside, remove the steaks from the pan and place on warmed individual plates.

5 Add the peppercorns, cream, water and a pinch or two of salt to the pan. Mix well, scraping up any sediment from the bottom of the pan. Bring to the boil and pour over the steaks.

Easy Béarnaise Sauce

Heat 1 jar good-quality hollandaise sauce and add 1 teaspoon finely chopped fresh tarragon and 1 teaspoon finely chopped fresh chervil.

Savoury Butters to Serve with Steaks

Flavoured butters are good served not only with grilled or fried fish or with plainly grilled chicken but also with meat dishes. After preparation the butter should be shaped into a cylinder, rolled up in foil or damp greaseproof paper and chilled. It can then be sliced and used as required. If it is to be kept for more than 2 days it should be frozen.

Maître d'Hôtel Butter

60 g butter

2 teaspoons lemon juice

1 teaspoon finely chopped fresh parsley

salt and freshly ground black pepper

Cream the butter until very soft, stir in the lemon juice and parsley and season to taste with salt and pepper. Mix well, shape and chill.

Garlic Butter

60 g butter

1 large clove of roasted garlic, crushed

2 tablespoons lemon juice

freshly ground black pepper

large pinch of salt

Cream the butter until soft, add the remaining ingredients and beat well. Shape and chill.

Mint and Mustard Butter

60 g butter

1 teaspoon Dijon mustard

1 tablespoon finely chopped fresh mint

Cream the butter until very soft and beat in the mustard and mint. Season with salt and pepper. Shape and chill.

Thai Chilli Butter

60 g butter
½–1 red chilli, finely chopped
grated zest of 1 lime
juice of ½ lime

2 tablespoons finely chopped fresh coriander
1 × 1.5 cm piece of fresh root ginger, peeled and
  grated (optional)
salt and freshly ground black pepper

Cream the butter until very soft, add the remaining ingredients and beat well. Shape and chill.

Beef Medallions with Mustard Mushrooms

Preparation time: 5 minutes
Cooking time: 30 minutes

SERVES 4

60 g salted butter, softened
½ tablespoon wholegrain mustard
½ tablespoon made English mustard
4 large field mushrooms

4 beef medallions
oil, for frying
freshly ground black pepper

To prepare ahead: Complete to the end of stage 2, then refrigerate until required.
Serving suggestions: Green salad (see page 381); spicy potato wedges (see page 368), crusty bread

1 Preheat the oven to 190°C|375°F|gas mark 5.
2 Mix together the butter and the mustards. Spread over the gill side of the mushrooms.
3 Place the mushrooms in a shallow dish, butter side up. Bake in the oven for 25–30 minutes, or until the mushrooms are cooked.
4 Meanwhile, season the beef medallions with pepper. Heat a little oil in a heavy frying pan, add the medallions and cook for 2 minutes on each side (see page 240).
5 Place a beef medallion on each of the mushrooms and serve immediately.

Quick Beef Stew

Preparation time: 12 minutes
Cooking time: 20 minutes

SERVES 4

700 g sirloin steak

30 g butter

oil, for frying

2 large red onions, sliced

110 g button mushrooms, sliced

1 tablespoon tomato purée

1 teaspoon dry English mustard

300 ml beef stock

1 × 142 ml pot of soured cream

salt and freshly ground black pepper

To garnish

chopped fresh parsley

Serving suggestions: Basmati rice (see page 374), dauphinoise potatoes (see page 370)

1 Trim the steak and cut into strips the size of your little finger. Season with salt and pepper.
2 Melt the butter in a large, heavy frying pan, add the onions and sweat over a low heat until soft but not coloured. Increase the heat and allow the onions to brown slightly. Add the mushrooms and cook for a further 2 minutes.
3 Heat a little oil in a second frying pan and fry the meat in 2 or 3 batches, until lightly browned all over. Add to the onions and the mushrooms.
4 When all the meat has been fried, add the tomato purée, mustard and stock to the pan. Season to taste with salt and pepper, bring slowly to the boil and simmer gently for 5–10 minutes, or until the meat is tender.
5 Remove from the heat and allow to cool slightly, then add the soured cream.
6 Serve immediately, garnished with parsley.

Sweet Chilli Beef

Preparation time: 5 minutes
Cooking time: 10 minutes

SERVES 4

oil, for frying

4 spring onions, finely sliced on the diagonal

450 g rump steak, sliced

100 ml sweet chilli dipping sauce

juice of 2 limes

2 sheets of thin rice noodles

3 tablespoons coriander leaves, washed

60 g roasted salted peanuts, chopped

1 Heat a little oil in a wok or large, heavy frying pan. Stir-fry the spring onions until just softening, then remove from the pan. Add a little more oil to the pan and when hot, add the beef and stir-fry until just cooked. Remove from the pan. Add the chilli sauce and lime juice to the wok and allow to reduce by simmering until syrupy in consistency.

2 Cook the rice noodles according to the manufacturer's instructions. Drain well and toss together with the spring onions, coriander and peanuts.

3 Meanwhile, return the beef to the pan and coat in the sauce.

4 Pile the noodles into a warmed bowls, and serve the beef on top.

Teriyaki Beef with Mushrooms and Noodles

Marinating time: 30 minutes
Preparation time: 5 minutes
Cooking time: 20 minutes

SERVES 4–6

4 × 170 g sirloin steaks, trimmed of fat

150 ml teriyaki sauce

3 tablespoons medium-dry sherry

3 tablespoons dark soy sauce

3 tablespoons oil

2 onions, finely sliced

450 g oyster mushrooms, torn into pieces

450 g chestnut mushrooms, sliced

4 sheets of thick egg noodles

200 g frozen petits pois

salt

To prepare ahead: Make in advance to the end of stage 3.

Serving suggestion: Steamed bok choi with soy and ginger (see page 350)

1 Marinate the steaks in the teriyaki sauce, sherry and soy sauce for 30 minutes.

2 Meanwhile, heat 2 tablespoons of the oil in a frying pan with a lid, add the onions and sweat over a low heat until soft but not coloured.

3 Add the mushrooms to the pan. Stir well and cover the pan, stirring occasionally until the mushrooms have released some liquid. Remove the lid and increase the heat, stirring, until the onions and mushrooms are nicely browned. Remove the mixture from the pan and set aside.

4 Remove the steaks from the marinade. Scrape off any marinade clinging to the meat. Reserve the marinade. Wipe out the frying pan and heat the remaining oil.

5 When the pan is very hot, fry the steaks until brown on both sides (about 1 minute per side). Reduce the heat and continue to fry the steaks for about 2 minutes each side, or until rare. Leave the steaks to rest on a chopping board, then cut into thin slices, about 5 mm thick.

6 Place the noodles and the peas in a pan of vigorously boiling salted water. Cook according to the noodle manufacturer's instructions. Drain.

7 Return the mushroom mixture to the heat and when sizzling, add the marinade and 5 tablespoons water. Bring to the boil, then stir in the noodles and peas. Remove from the heat and stir in the steak.

8 Pile on to warmed individual plates and serve.

VARIATIONS: Use any type of mushroom. Mangetout or sugarsnap peas can be substituted for the petits pois. Sliced bok choi or a handful or beansprouts could also be added to the mushrooms in stage 7.

Steak Wellington

Preparation time: 25 minutes
Chilling time: 10 minutes
Cooking time: 15 minutes

SERVES 4

4 × 170 g fillet steaks or tournedos
Worcestershire sauce
1 tablespoon oil
60 g flat mushrooms, chopped
90 g chicken liver pâté
500 g puff pastry

1 egg, beaten
salt and freshly ground black pepper

To garnish
watercress

To prepare ahead: The parcels can be made to the end of stage 5 a day in advance and kept refrigerated.
Serving suggestions: Special roast potatoes (see page 365), new potatoes, Vichy carrots (see page 344), ratatouille (see page 347), green vegetables

1 Trim any fat or membrane from the steaks. Season with pepper and a few drops of Worcestershire sauce.
2 Heat the oil in a frying pan and brown the steaks quickly on both sides. The outside should be brown, the middle absolutely raw. Reserve the frying pan, unwashed. Leave the meat to cool on a wire rack. Preheat the oven to 230°C|450°F|gas mark 8.
3 Heat a little more oil in the pan and cook the mushrooms. Tip them into a bowl.
4 Beat the pâté into the mushrooms. Check the seasoning. Spread one side of each steak with the mixture. On a floured surface, roll out the pastry to the thickness of a £1 coin. Cut into 4 × 18 cm squares.
5 Place each steak, pâté side down, on a piece of pastry. Brush the pastry edges with water and draw them together over the steak, making a neat and well-sealed parcel. Trim off any excess pastry. Place the parcels on a damp baking sheet, pâté side up, and brush with the beaten egg. Make a small slit in the top of each parcel so that the steam can escape. Decorate with leaves made from the pastry trimmings. Brush these with egg too. Chill for 10 minutes to allow the pastry to relax.
6 Brush the steak parcels with a little more beaten egg. Bake in the oven for 15 minutes, or until the pastry is golden brown and the meat pink.
7 Arrange the steak parcels on a warmed serving plate. Garnish with watercress.

Barbecued Garlic and Rosemary Lamb

Marinating time: 2 hours–overnight
Preparation time: 10 minutes
Cooking time: 1 hour

SERVES 8–10

1 shoulder or leg of lamb, boned

6 cloves of garlic, cut into slivers

2 large sprigs of fresh rosemary, broken into smaller
  sprigs

4 tablespoons olive oil

salt and freshly ground black pepper

To prepare ahead: Leave to marinate overnight.

Serving suggestions: New potato salad, avocado couscous salad (see page 354), haricot beans with cream and thyme (see page 342), grilled Mediterranean vegetables (see page 346), French bread

1 Make small slits in the lamb with a sharp knife and insert the garlic slivers and rosemary sprigs. Place in a shallow dish or plastic bag, pour over the oil and season with pepper. Cover and leave to marinate for a couple of hours or overnight.

2 When the barbecue is hot, season the lamb with a little salt and place on the grill. Cook, turning occasionally and basting as necessary with any remaining marinade, for 20–50 minutes, depending on the thickness of the meat.

3 Cut into thick slices and serve.

NOTE: This will work well with any size of boned leg or shoulder of lamb, but the cooking time will need to be adapted accordingly. Cut into the meat at the thickest point to check it is cooked to your taste. Most butchers will bone a shoulder or leg of lamb so that it opens out to a flat piece of meat, rather than having a hole or 'tunnel' where the bone once was. If they have not done so, it is simple to do by cutting through the underside with a knife.

Rack of Lamb with a Mustard Crust

Preparation time: 10 minutes
Chilling time: 30 minutes
Cooking time: 15 minutes

SERVES 2

1 rack (best end) of lamb, trimmed

1½ tablespoons Dijon mustard

2 tablespoons fresh white breadcrumbs

1½ tablespoons chopped mixed fresh herbs, such as
  mint, chives, parsley, thyme

50 g unsalted butter

salt and freshly ground black pepper

To prepare ahead: Put the crust on the lamb and refrigerate overnight.
Serving suggestions: Crushed new potatoes, herbed potato mash (see page 361), special roast potatoes (see page 365), French beans with almonds (see page 341), onion sauce (see page 503), grilled Mediterranean vegetables (see page 346), rosemary roast vegetables (see page 346)

1 Preheat the oven to 220°C│425°F│gas mark 7.
2 Trim off as much fat as possible from the meat.
3 Mix together the mustard, breadcrumbs, herbs and butter and season. Press a thin layer of this mixture over the rounded, skinned side of the lamb. Chill for 30 minutes.
4 Place, crumbed side up, in a roasting pan and roast in the oven for 15 minutes for a 7-cutlet best end, less for a smaller one. This will give pink, slightly underdone lamb. Serve with the butter and juices from the pan poured over the top.

VARIATION: Omit the mustard and use horseradish cream or wasabi paste.

Lamb Cutlets Grilled with Herbs

Preparation time: 5 minutes
Cooking time: 8 minutes

SERVES 4

30 g butter, melted

1 tablespoon oil

12 lamb cutlets

a selection of chopped fresh herbs, such as thyme,
  basil, mint, parsley, marjoram, rosemary

salt and freshly ground black pepper

Serving suggestions: Dauphinoise potatoes (see page 370), parsnip and potato dauphinoise (see page 370), French beans with almonds (see page 365), herbed potato mash (see page 361), ratatouille (see page 347), petits pois à la Française (see page 348)

1 Preheat the grill to the highest setting.
2 Mix the butter and oil and brush the cutlets with the mixture. Sprinkle over half the herbs and season with salt and pepper.
3 Place the cutlets under the grill, about 8 cm away from the heat. Cook for 3–4 minutes (alternatively, use a griddle pan on the hob for 2 minutes each side).
4 Turn the cutlets over, baste with the fat from the bottom of the pan and sprinkle over the remaining herbs.
5 Grill for 3–4 minutes (3 minutes on each side for pink meat, 4 minutes for well-done lamb).
6 Arrange the cutlets on warmed individual plates and pour over the pan juices. Serve immediately.

Lamb Steaks with Balsamic Sauce and Roast Vegetables

Preparation time: 10 minutes
Cooking time: 35 minutes

SERVES 4

4 salad tomatoes, halved horizontally	a little plain flour
2 red peppers, cut into eighths lengthways	150 ml vegetable or chicken stock
2 courgettes, cut into 5 mm slices	4 tablespoons balsamic vinegar
1 large red onion, cut into eighths	1 bunch of fresh basil
olive oil	salt and freshly ground black pepper
4 lamb leg steaks	

1 Preheat the oven to 200°C|400°F|gas mark 6.
2 Place the vegetables, cut side up, on a large baking sheet or in a roasting pan. Sprinkle with salt and pepper and drizzle with oil. Roast in the oven until beginning to brown, then remove the tomatoes and turn the other vegetables over. When the second side begins to colour, remove from the oven.
3 Meanwhile, season the lamb all over with salt and pepper and dust with the flour. Heat 2 tablespoons oil in a heavy frying pan and fry the lamb until brown on all sides (this may need to be done in 2 batches). Remove the lamb from the pan and place in a roasting pan. Cook in the oven for about 5 minutes, or until the lamb is pink in the middle.
4 Add the stock and vinegar to the frying pan, scraping the brown sediment from the bottom, then reduce the sauce by boiling rapidly until it coats the back of a spoon lightly.
5 Tear the basil into pieces, reserving 4 sprigs for the garnish. Stir the basil into the roast vegetables.
6 Serve the lamb on a bed of the roast vegetables, garnished with the basil sprigs.

NOTE: Use lamb cutlets or chops if lamb steaks are not available.

Barbecued Lamb with Potato Skewers

Preparation time: 10 minutes
Marinating time: 20 minutes–overnight
Cooking time: 20 minutes

SERVES 4

4 lamb leg steaks	8–12 new potatoes
6 tablespoons olive oil	olive oil
1 tablespoon balsamic vinegar	rock salt and freshly ground black pepper
4 cloves of garlic, bruised	4 rosemary skewers (long woody sprigs of rosemary,
3 sprigs of fresh rosemary, chopped	leaves removed)

To prepare ahead: The skewers can be assembled in advance, and the lamb may be left to marinate overnight.
Serving suggestions: Green salad (see page 381), fennel and tomato salad (see page 335), chilli potato wedges (see page 368), corn on the cob, garlic bread (see page 379)

1 Put the lamb steaks into a shallow dish. Mix together the oil and vinegar, add the garlic, rosemary and pepper and pour over the lamb. Allow to marinate for as long as possible, turning occasionally.
2 Bring a small saucepan of salted water to the boil. Cook the new potatoes for about 15 minutes, or until soft, then cut them in half and thread them on to the skewers.
3 When the barbecue is hot, season the steaks with a little salt and place on the grill. Brush the potatoes with a little oil and place on the grill. Cook the steaks for about 3 minutes on each side, brushing with the marinade to prevent them drying out. Keep turning the potatoes.
4 When cooked, sprinkle a little salt over the potatoes and serve immediately with the lamb steaks.

VARIATIONS: Use beef instead of lamb. Use metal skewers or wooden skewers soaked in water instead of rosemary, and sprinkle chopped rosemary over the potato skewers before cooking.

Lamb Koftas

Preparation time: 10 minutes
Cooking time: 10 minutes

SERVES 4

500 g finely minced lamb	1 red chilli, finely diced
1 small red onion, finely chopped	oil, for brushing
1 small bunch of fresh coriander, stems finely	salt and freshly ground black pepper
chopped, leaves roughly chopped	8 wooden skewers, soaked in water

To prepare ahead: The koftas can be shaped in advance and cooked or frozen as required. Defrost thoroughly before cooking.

Serving suggestions: Couscous, Middle Eastern salad (see page 334), pitta bread, tzatziki (see page 495)

1 In a large bowl mix together the lamb, onion, coriander and chilli. Season with salt and pepper.
2 Divide the mixture into 8 equal portions and wrap in a sausage shape around the skewers.
3 Heat the barbecue or grill. Brush the koftas with a little oil and cook for 8–10 minutes, turning regularly until browned all over. Serve immediately.

VARIATION: Use mint in place of coriander. Add ¼ teaspoon each of ground cinnamon and cumin to the mixture.

Marmalade and Mustard-glazed Gammon

Preparation time: 5 minutes
Cooking time: 1 hour

SERVES 4

1 × 675 g piece of gammon	2 fresh parsley stalks
½ onion, sliced	6 black peppercorns
1 small carrot, cut into chunks	1 tablespoon thick-cut marmalade
1 bay leaf	1 tablespoon wholegrain mustard

Serving suggestions: Mashed sweet potato, broad beans in parsley sauce, peas

1 Place the gammon in a saucepan, cover with cold water and add the onion, carrot, bay leaf, parsley stalks and peppercorns. Bring slowly to the boil, then simmer for 40 minutes.
2 Preheat the oven to 220°C|425°F|gas mark 7.
3 Leave the gammon to cool slightly in the stock. Then lift out and carefully pull off the skin and a little of the fat.
4 Mix the marmalade and mustard together and spread it evenly over the fat.
5 Bake in the oven for 15 minutes, or until dark and sticky.

NOTE: If cooking a larger joint, allow 25 minutes per 450 g for the simmering time.

Moroccan Spiced Lamb with Couscous

Preparation time: 15 minutes
Cooking time: 30 minutes

SERVES 4

olive oil

1 red onion, sliced

1 red pepper, halved, cored, deseeded and cut into strips

1 small aubergine, cut into small cubes

1 clove of garlic, crushed

85 g pitted dried dates, roughly chopped

2 tablespoons ras el hanout spice blend

500 ml vegetable stock

½ glass of dry white wine

4 lamb chops, trimmed of fat

1 tablespoon ground ginger

1 tablespoon ground cinnamon

1 teaspoon ground cumin

2 teaspoons plain flour

225 g couscous

1 small bunch of fresh parsley or mixed herbs, chopped

45 g whole almonds, skinned and toasted until pale brown (see page 17)

salt and freshly ground black pepper

To prepare ahead: Make in advance to the end of stage 3. Reheat the stock and add the couscous when cooking the lamb.
Serving suggestions: Middle Eastern salad (see page 334), green salad (see page 381)

1 Preheat the oven to 200°C|400°F|gas mark 6.
2 Heat some oil in a heavy saucepan. Add the onion and pepper and sweat over a low heat until beginning to soften. Add the aubergine and cook for a further 5 minutes or until brown. Add the garlic, dates and ras el hanout spice and cook for a further 30 seconds.
3 Add the stock and wine to the browned vegetables. Bring to the boil, then simmer for 2 minutes.
4 Meanwhile, place the lamb chops, the remaining spices and the flour in a plastic bag, then shake well to coat lightly. Brush a baking sheet with oil, transfer the chops to the baking sheet, brush with more oil and bake in the oven for 15 minutes, or until cooked. Turn the chops after the first 10 minutes of cooking.
5 Meanwhile, stir the couscous into the vegetable mixture and turn off the heat. Cover the saucepan with a lid and leave to stand for 10 minutes.
6 Stir the herbs and almonds into the couscous and season with salt and pepper. Serve with the lamb chops.

Chinese-style Pork with Noodles

Marinating time: 2 hours–overnight
Preparation time: 10 minutes
Cooking time: 30 minutes

SERVES 4

2 pork tenderloins (fillets), trimmed

For the marinade

3 tablespoons hoisin sauce

1½ tablespoons light soy sauce

1½ tablespoons rice wine

1 tablespoon soft light brown sugar

1 clove of garlic, crushed

1 teaspoon peeled and grated fresh root ginger

For the noodles

1 packet of thick rice noodles

soy sauce

sesame oil

4 small bok choi, quartered lengthways

To prepare ahead: Leave the pork to marinate overnight.
Serving suggestions: Stir-fried vegetables (see page 351)

1 Mix together all the ingredients for the marinade. Place the pork tenderloins in the marinade and leave for at least 2 hours or overnight.

2 Preheat the oven to 190°C│375°F│gas mark 5. Place the pork tenderloins in a roasting pan and roast in the oven for about 30 minutes, or until just cooked through. Baste regularly with the remaining marinade.

3 Meanwhile, bring a saucepan of salted water to the boil and cook the noodles according to the manufacturer's instructions. Drain, reserving the cooking water. Drizzle a little soy sauce and sesame oil over the noodles and toss together until well coated.

4 Bring the cooking water back to the boil and add the bok choi. Boil for 30 seconds, then drain and stir the bok choi into the noodles.

5 Remove the pork from the pan and cut into slices on the diagonal.

6 Pile the noodles into warmed individual bowls and arrange the pork on top.

Pork Meatballs

Preparation time: 10 minutes
Cooling time: 15 minutes
Cooking time: 30 minutes

SERVES 4

2 tablespoons oil

1 onion, finely chopped

2 cloves of garlic, crushed

1 red chilli, chopped

1 tablespoon chopped fresh parsley

450 g minced pork

1 × 400 g can of chopped tomatoes with chilli

150 ml good-quality chicken stock

1 teaspoon tomato purée

350 g tagliatelle or pappardelle

salt and freshly ground black pepper

To prepare in advance: Cook the meatballs in the tomato sauce, then refrigerate or freeze. If frozen, defrost thoroughly before reheating.
Serving suggestion: Green salad (see page 381)

1 Heat half the oil in a heavy frying pan, add the onion and sweat over a low heat until soft but not coloured. Add the garlic, chilli and parsley and cook for 1 further minute. Remove from the heat and allow to cool.
2 Stir the onion mixture into the minced pork. Season with salt and pepper.
3 With floured hands, shape the mixture into equal-sized meatballs.
4 Heat a little more oil in a frying pan and fry the meatballs until golden brown all over. It may be necessary to do this in several batches.
5 Heat the tomatoes, stock and tomato purée in a large saucepan. Add the meatballs and allow to simmer for 15 minutes until they are hot through and the sauce has reduced.
6 Cook the pasta and drain well. Mix with the meatballs and sauce and serve immediately.

Roast Fillet of Pork with Garlic and Rosemary Mash

Preparation time: 5 minutes
Infusing time: 2 hours–overnight
Cooking time: 25 minutes

SERVES 4

150 ml olive oil

4 large cloves of garlic, crushed

3 sprigs of fresh rosemary, torn in half

800 g potatoes

2 pork tenderloins (fillets) trimmed

30 g unsalted butter

salt and freshly ground black pepper

To prepare ahead: Make the mash and reheat as required.
Serving suggestions: Green vegetables, roast Mediterranean vegetables (see page 346)

1 Preheat the oven to 180°C|350°F|gas mark 4.

2 Put the oil, garlic and rosemary into a shallow dish and heat in the oven for 10 minutes.

3 Remove from the oven and allow to cool slightly, then pour into a pot or jam jar so that the oil covers the garlic and most of the rosemary. Leave for at least 2 hours or overnight.

4 Peel the potatoes and cook in boiling salted water until soft.

5 Season the pork tenderloins with a little pepper. Melt the butter in a heavy frying pan and when foaming, brown the pork tenderloins on all sides (this should take about 5 minutes). Transfer to the oven and cook through for a further 15–20 minutes.

6 Meanwhile, mash the potatoes with the infused olive oil and keep warm.

7 Remove the pork from the oven and cut into slices on the diagonal.

8 Transfer the pork slices on to individual warmed plates, pour over any juices from the pan and serve with the mashed potato.

Pork Medallions with Mustard Sauce

Preparation time: 5 minutes
Cooking time: 10 minutes

SERVES 2

1 pork tenderloin (fillet)

30 g butter

150 ml crème fraîche

2 tablespoons Dijon mustard

salt and freshly ground black pepper

To garnish

chopped fresh parsley

To prepared ahead: Flatten the medallions and keep covered in the refrigerator until ready to cook.
Serving suggestions: Tagliatelle, mashed potato (see page 358), cabbage with caraway (see page 343), green vegetables

1 Trim the pork of any fat and membrane. Cut into slices 2 cm thick. Place the pork medallions between 2 sheets of damp greaseproof paper or clingfilm and flatten with a rolling pin until 1–1½ cm thick.

2 Season the pork with salt and pepper. Melt the butter in a large, heavy frying pan and when foaming, add the pork slices to the pan and cook for 2 minutes on each side, or until they are browned and cooked through (you may need to do this in batches). Remove from the pan and keep warm.

3 Add 3 tablespoons water to the pan and scrape the bottom of the pan to loosen any sediment. Add the crème fraîche and mustard and heat through. Check the seasoning and add salt and pepper if necessary.

4 Arrange the pork slices on warmed individual plates and pour over the sauce. Garnish with the parsley and serve immediately.

Maple and Mustard Pork Loin Steaks

Preparation time: 5 minutes
Marinating time: 20 minutes–overnight
Cooking time: 10 minutes

SERVES 4

3 tablespoons maple syrup

2 tablespoons made English mustard

4 pork loin steaks

To prepare ahead: Leave to marinate overnight.
Serving suggestions: Mashed potato (see page 358), mashed root vegetables, apple and potato boulangère (see page 368), green vegetables

1 Mix together the maple syrup and the mustard. Coat the loin steaks well on each side with the mixture and place, covered, in the refrigerator to allow the flavours to penetrate the meat. Leave to marinate for at least 20 minutes or overnight.
2 Preheat the grill to the highest setting well in advance of cooking the steaks.
3 Place the pork steaks on a baking sheet and spoon over any marinade. Grill for 6–8 minutes, or until the first side is beginning to brown. Turn over and baste with any juices and continue to grill for a further 6–8 minutes, or until cooked through and browning. You may need to move the grill pan further away from the heat if the pork browns quickly, to avoid burning.
4 Serve with any juices poured over the top.

Pork Medallions with Prunes and Cranberries

Preparation time: 5 minutes
Cooking time: 10 minutes

SERVES 4

8 pork medallions

30 g unsalted butter

8 ready-to-eat prunes, chopped

2 tablespoons cranberry sauce

200 ml dry red wine

salt and freshly ground black pepper

To garnish
chopped fresh parsley

To prepare ahead: Flatten the medallions and keep covered in the refrigerator until ready to cook.
Serving suggestions: Dauphinoise potatoes (see page 370), French beans with almonds (see page 341), buttered lemon couscous (see page 357), special roast potatoes (see page 365), roast beetroot (see page 341)

1 Place the pork medallions between 2 sheets of damp greaseproof paper or clingfilm and flatten with a rolling pin until 1–1½ cm thick.
2 Melt half of the butter in a large frying pan and when foaming, add the pork medallions. Fry for 2 minutes on each side, then remove to a warmed serving plate and keep warm.
3 Add the prunes, cranberry sauce and wine to the pan. Bring up to the boil, then simmer for 2 minutes. Season with salt and pepper.
4 Whisk in the remaining butter so that the sauce thickens very slightly.
5 Pour the sauce over the pork medallions and garnish with the chopped parsley. Serve immediately.

Pork Fillets in Cider

Preparation time: 10 minutes
Cooking time: 30–40 minutes

SERVES 4

1 tablespoon oil
15 g butter
2 pork tenderloins (fillets), trimmed
1 medium onion, finely chopped
150 ml chicken or vegetable stock
300 ml cider

1 bay leaf
1 tablespoon single cream
salt and freshly ground black pepper

To garnish
chopped fresh parsley

Serving suggestions: Apple and potato boulangère (see page 368), mustard potato mash (see page 359), steamed green vegetables, artichoke dauphinoise (see page 370), French beans with almonds (see page 341)

1 Preheat the oven to 180°C|350°F|gas mark 4.
2 Heat the oil in a heavy frying pan. Add the butter and when hot, add the pork and brown quickly all over. Remove to a plate. Reduce the heat, add the onion to the pan and sweat over a low heat until soft. Return the pork to the pan. Add the stock, cider and bay leaf. Bring to the boil, then tip into a flameproof casserole. Season with salt and pepper, cover and cook in the oven for 15–20 minutes.
3 Take the pork out of the casserole and keep warm.
4 Remove the bay leaf from the cooking liquor.
5 Boil the cooking liquor rapidly until reduced to a syrupy consistency. Add the cream. Taste and adjust the seasoning if necessary.
6 Slice the pork thickly. To serve: pour over the sauce and sprinkle with parsley, or serve the sauce separately.

Pork Chops with Roast Autumn Vegetables

Preparation time: 15 minutes
Cooking time: 35 minutes

SERVES 4

1 sweet potato, peeled and cut into 5 cm chunks

1 parsnip, peeled and cut into 5 cm chunks

250 g new potatoes, halved

oil

2 tablespoons clear honey

1 teaspoon Dijon mustard

2 small Cox's apples, peeled, cored and cut into 5 cm chunks

4 pork chops, trimmed

salt and freshly ground black pepper

To prepare ahead: Make in advance to the end of stage 2 and refrigerate until required.
Serving suggestions: Steamed green vegetables

1 Preheat the oven to 220°C|425°F|gas mark 7. Preheat the grill to the highest setting.
2 Place the sweet potato, parsnip and new potatoes in a roasting pan. Sprinkle with oil and season well with salt and pepper. Roast in the oven for 15 minutes.
3 Mix the honey and mustard together. Add the apples to the roasting pan and stir in the honey and mustard. Roast for a further 20 minutes.
4 Meanwhile, grill the pork chops for 6–8 minutes on each side, or until tender and cooked right through. Serve the pork chops with the roast vegetables.

Pork Marsala

Preparation time: 10 minutes
Cooking time: 10 minutes

SERVES 4

4 × 150 g pork escalopes

30 g butter

2 tablespoons Marsala wine

4 tablespoons double cream

lemon juice

salt and freshly ground black pepper

To prepare ahead: Prepare the pork to the end of stage 2. Keep covered in the refrigerator until required.
Serving suggestions: French beans with almonds (see page 341), Vichy carrots (see page 344), boulangère potatoes (see page 368), rice

1 Preheat the oven to the lowest setting to use as a warming oven.
2 Put the escalopes between 2 sheets of damp greaseproof paper or clingfilm and beat lightly with a mallet or rolling pin until about 1 cm thick. Season with salt and pepper.

3 Melt the butter in a frying pan and when it is foaming, fry the escalopes briskly to brown them lightly on both sides (1–2 minutes per side). Remove them to a warmed plate and keep warm.

4 Tip off any fat in the pan. Add 4 tablespoons water and the Marsala, swill it about and bring to the boil. Add the cream and season well with salt, pepper and a squeeze of lemon juice. Add a little water to the sauce if it becomes too thick. Return the pork to the pan and heat gently until cooked through. Serve.

Pork with Pumpkin and Pecans

Preparation time: 20 minutes
Cooking time: 30 minutes

SERVES 4

2 tablespoons oil

1 Spanish onion, finely chopped

½ teaspoon ground cinnamon

½ teaspoon ground cumin

½ teaspoon ground coriander

1 tablespoon soft light brown sugar

500 g pumpkin or butternut squash, peeled, deseeded and cut into 2.5 cm chunks

100 ml medium sherry

150 ml chicken stock

500 g lean pork, cut into 2.5 cm cubes

50 g pecan nuts, roughly chopped

30 g fresh thyme, chopped

salt and freshly ground black pepper

To prepare ahead: The complete dish can be made in advance, then refrigerated or frozen. If frozen, defrost thoroughly before reheating.

Serving suggestions: Basmati rice (see page 374), herb couscous (see page 356), herb potato mash (see page 361), Indian-style French beans (see page 350)

1 Heat half the oil in a large non-stick saucepan, add the onion and sweat over a low heat until soft but not coloured.

2 Add the spices and sugar, turn up the heat and stir until the onion caramelizes. Add the pumpkin and cook for 2 minutes, stirring continuously and adding a little water if necessary to prevent the onion from burning. Add the sherry and stock.

3 Heat the remaining oil in a large, heavy frying pan. Add the pork and fry until lightly browned.

4 Add the browned pork to the pumpkin mixture. Bring to the boil, then simmer for about 15 minutes, or until the pork and pumpkin are tender. Add more water if the mixture becomes too dry.

5 Add the chopped nuts and thyme and season to taste with salt and pepper. Serve immediately.

Sweet and Sour Pork

Preparation time: 10 minutes
Cooking time: 20 minutes

SERVES 4

700 g lean boneless pork, cut into 2 cm cubes
½ teaspoon salt
1 tablespoon cornflour
4 tablespoons oil
1 red onion, sliced
1 red pepper, cored, deseeded and cut into squares
2 slices of pineapple, chopped
1 × 220 g can of water chestnuts, drained and sliced

For the sweet and sour sauce

1 teaspoon cornflour, plus extra for dusting
4 tablespoons cold water
2 tablespoons caster sugar
2 tablespoons wine vinegar
2 tablespoons tomato purée
2 tablespoons orange or apple juice
2 tablespoons soy sauce

To prepare ahead: Cut all the vegetables in advance.
Serving suggestions: Basmati rice (see page 374), steamed bok choi with soy and ginger (see page 350)

1 Make the sauce: blend the cornflour with the water, then mix in the sugar, vinegar, tomato purée, fruit juice and soy sauce.
2 Sprinkle the pork with the salt and toss in the cornflour.
3 Heat half the oil in a wok or wide frying pan. Add the pork and fry until golden brown and cooked through. Remove from the pan. This may need to be done in batches.
4 Wipe out the wok or frying pan and heat the remaining oil. Add the onion and red pepper and fry until just beginning to brown. Add the pineapple and water chestnuts and cook for 1 further minute. Reduce the heat, add the sauce to the pan and cook for 1 further minute. Stir in the pork and heat through for 2–3 minutes. If the sauce seems too thick, add a little water before serving.

Mustard Toad in the Hole

Preparation time: 10 minutes
Chilling time: 30 minutes
Cooking time: 45 minutes

SERVES 4

1 tablespoon oil
8 good-quality pork sausages

For the batter
110 g plain flour
a good pinch of salt
2 eggs

150 ml water, mixed with 150 ml milk
1½ tablespoons wholegrain mustard
2 tablespoons Dijon mustard
1 teaspoon made English mustard

To prepare ahead: Make the batter the day before, but you will need to add a little more milk to it before cooking as it will thicken up. Add the mustards just before cooking.

Serving suggestions: Green salad (see page 381), green vegetables, onion gravy (see page 502)

1 Make the batter: sift the flour with the salt into a bowl and make a well in the centre, exposing the bottom of the bowl. Break the eggs into this well.

2 Using a wooden spoon or whisk, mix the eggs. then gradually draw in the flour from the sides as you mix, adding just enough of the milk and water mixture to the eggs to make a fairly thin paste. When all the flour has been incorporated, stir in the remaining liquid. (The batter can also be made by placing all the ingredients together in a blender or food processor and whizzing for a few seconds.)

3 Cover the bowl and chill for about 30 minutes. This is done so that the starch cells will swell, giving a lighter result.

4 Preheat the oven to 220°C|425°F|gas mark 7.

5 Heat the oil in a large flameproof dish or casserole. When it is really hot, add the sausages, turn in the fat and put into the oven for 3 minutes. Turn the sausages and return to the oven.

6 When the sausages are beginning to brown and the fat is smoking hot, add the mustards to the batter, stir well and pour over the sausages.

7 Bake in the oven for 40 minutes, or until the toad in the hole is risen and brown.

NOTE: The basic batter without mustard works well with a number of combinations. Try Merguez sausages cooked in chilli oil for a spicy version.

Sausages and Parsnips with Honey and Mustard

Preparation time: 20 minutes
Cooking time: 1 hour

SERVES 4

8–12 good-quality pork sausages

450 g parsnips, peeled and cut into small wedges

3 onions, peeled and cut into eighths

oil (optional)

1½ tablespoons clear honey

1½ tablespoons wholegrain mustard

2 teaspoons made English mustard

salt and freshly ground black pepper

To prepare ahead: Make in advance to the end of stage 4. To reheat, return to the oven for about 25 minutes, or until piping hot.

Serving suggestions: Chive potato mash (see page 192), crisp green vegetables

1 Preheat the oven to 190°C|375°F|gas mark 5.
2 Place the sausages in a large roasting pan. Roast in the oven for 10 minutes, or until the fat is beginning to run from them. Add the parsnips and onions to the pan and toss together in the fat. If the sausages are very lean and no fat has been released, then add a little bit of oil.
3 Continue to roast the sausages and vegetables for further 40 minutes, turning them every so often so that they begin to brown on all sides.
4 Mix together the honey and mustards. Pour over the sausages and vegetables and stir through.
5 Return to the oven for a further 10 minutes. Serve immediately.

Marmalade-glazed Sausages with Onion and Marmalade Gravy

Preparation time: 5 minutes
Cooking time: 25 minutes

SERVES 4

8–12 good-quality pork sausages

1 tablespoon oil

1 large onion, sliced

½ tablespoon soft light brown sugar

½ tablespoon plain flour

300 ml chicken stock

2 tablespoons thick-cut Seville orange marmalade

salt and freshly ground black pepper

To prepare ahead: The marmalade gravy can be made in advance and reheated whilst cooking the sausages.

Serving suggestions: Mustard potato mash (see page 359), petits pois à la Française (see page 348), Vichy carrots (see page 344)

1 Preheat the oven to 200°C|400°F|gas mark 6.
2 Place the sausages in a roasting pan and cook in the oven for 15–20 minutes, or until beginning to brown, shaking the pan occasionally.
3 Meanwhile, heat the oil in a heavy saucepan, add the onion and sweat over a low heat until soft. Increase the heat and allow to brown. Add the sugar and let it caramelize, then add the flour and cook for 30 seconds.
4 Gradually add the stock and half the marmalade to the pan. Bring to the boil, then reduce by simmering for about 10 minutes. Season with salt and pepper.
5 Add the remaining marmalade to the sausages, shake and continue to cook for 5–10 minutes, or until cooked and nicely glazed.
6 Serve with the marmalade gravy.

Sausages with Red Onion and Port Sauce

Preparation time: 5 minutes
Cooking time: 35 minutes

SERVES 4

1 tablespoon oil	150 ml chicken stock
8–12 good-quality sausages	½ teaspoon redcurrant jelly
2 red onions, finely sliced	1 teaspoon finely chopped fresh thyme
1 heaped teaspoon plain flour	salt and freshly ground black pepper
75 ml port	

To prepare ahead: The sauce can be made in advance and reheated whilst cooking the sausages.
Serving suggestions: Mashed potatoes (see page 358), crisp green vegetables

1 Preheat the oven to 180°C|350°F|gas mark 4.
2 Heat the oil in a large, heavy frying pan, add the sausages and fry over a medium heat until lightly browned. Remove the pan from the heat and transfer the sausages to a roasting tin. Finish cooking them in the oven for 20–30 minutes.
3 Remove the excess oil from the frying pan, add the onions and cook until soft and golden brown.
4 Add the flour to the pan and cook, stirring, for 1 minute.
5 Slowly add the port, stock and redcurrant jelly to the pan. Bring to the boil, then simmer for 3 minutes. Add the thyme, season to taste with salt and pepper and serve with the sausages.

Sausage Hotpot

Preparation time: 15 minutes
Cooking time: 1¼ hours

SERVES 4

6–8 good-quality pork and leek sausages or similar

1 tablespoon olive oil

1 large onion, sliced

2 medium sticks of celery, cut into 2.5 cm chunks

2 medium carrots, cut into 2.5 cm chunks

2 large Portobello mushrooms, roughly chopped

1 tablespoon plain flour

600 ml chicken stock

a splash of Worcestershire sauce

½ glass of red wine

2 large white potatoes, parboiled and cut into 1 cm slices

30 g butter, melted

salt and freshly ground black pepper

To prepare ahead: Cook completely, then refrigerate or freeze. Reheat in a 190°C│375°F│gas mark 5 oven for about 30 minutes, ensuring the hotpot is piping hot throughout before serving. If frozen, ensure the hotpot is fully defrosted before reheating.

Serving suggestions: Green vegetables, crusty bread

1 Preheat the grill to the highest setting and grill the sausages until evenly brown all over. Cut in half. Preheat the oven to 190°C│375°F│gas mark 5.

2 Meanwhile, put the oil into a large flameproof casserole or dish with a lid. Add the onion, celery and carrots and fry, uncovered, over a low heat until lightly browned.

3 Add the mushrooms, increase the heat and cook until the mushrooms have softened and any moisture has evaporated.

4 Add the flour and cook for 1 minute, then remove from the heat and gradually add the stock. Return the pan to the heat and bring to the boil. Add the Worcestershire sauce and red wine and season with salt and pepper. Simmer for 2 minutes. Add the sausages and stir well.

5 Arrange the potatoes in concentric circles on top of the sausages and drizzle over the butter.

6 Cover and bake in the oven for 40 minutes. Remove the lid and cook uncovered for a further 10–15 minutes, or until the potato topping is golden brown. Alternatively, brown the potato under a hot grill.

Spicy Sausage and Lentil 'Cassoulet'

Preparation time: 5 minutes
Cooking time: 1 hour

SERVES 6–8

1 tablespoon oil

500 g chorizo-style spicy sausages, cut into 1 cm
    slices or dice

1 large onion, finely sliced

1 clove of garlic, crushed

500 g green or brown lentils

1 × 400 g can of chopped tomatoes

100 ml red wine

1 tablespoon herbes de Provence

salt and freshly ground black pepper

To prepare ahead: Cook the complete dish, then refrigerate and reheat when required.
Serving suggestions: Green salad (see page 381), Italian tomato salad (see page 334)

1 Heat the oil in a large, heavy saucepan, add the pieces of sausage and fry until well browned.

2 Reduce the heat, add the onion to the pan and cook until beginning to soften, then add the garlic and cook for a further 2 minutes.

3 Add the lentils, tomatoes and enough water to cover. Bring to the boil and add the wine and herbs.

4 Cover and simmer very slowly for about 35–45 minutes, or until the lentils are soft but not mushy. Check every so often to make sure that the mixture is not getting too dry. If it is, add extra water. Season to taste with salt and pepper.

VARIATIONS: If preferred, use ordinary sausages and brown well before adding the other ingredients. Use Puy or beluga lentils, but reduce the cooking time accordingly.

Mince

Minced meat can be used in a wide variety of recipes. It is worth having a basic recipe as a guide which can be adapted to suit your purpose. Minced meat takes at least 45 minutes' simmering to cook – any less and it can be tough. With gentle simmering and topping up with water as necessary, you can cook it for up to 2 hours, and this will give a very tender finished dish.

SERVES 4

oil for frying

1 onion, finely chopped

450 g minced beef

1 clove of garlic, crushed

2 teaspoons plain flour

liquid (for quantities see below)

salt and freshly ground black pepper

1 Heat 1 tablespoon of the oil in a saucepan and add the onion and mince. Brown the mince, breaking up the clumps with the back of a fork and stirring through the onions. There should be no large lumps of mince left.

2 Add the garlic and cook for 45 seconds. Add the flour and cook for a further 30 seconds.

3 Add the liquid to the pan, stirring well to mix in the flour.

4 Add water to the pan so that the mixture is nearly submerged. Cover with a lid and simmer for at least 45 minutes or up to 2 hours, topping up with more water as necessary.

5 Reduce until the required consistency is reached and season to taste with salt and pepper.

EASY VARIATIONS ON THE BASIC RECIPE

Bolognese	Chili Con Carne	Cottage or Shepherd's Pie

Add 100 g chopped bacon to the mince and onion.
    Add sliced or quartered button mushrooms before the flour.
    Add herbes de Provence.
	Add chilli powder with the garlic and 1 × 400 g cans of kidney beans towards the end of simmering time.	Use minced beef or lamb. Add 1 carrot, peeled and diced, and 1 stick of celery, diced, to the mince and onion when browning.
		    Add 1 bouquet garni.

Liquid
100 ml red wine
2 × 400 g cans of chopped
    tomatoes
200 ml chicken or beef stock
1½ tablespoons tomato purée
	Liquid
	200 ml chicken or beef stock
	2 × 400 g cans of chopped
	    tomatoes
	1 tablespoon tomato purée
		Liquid
		750 ml chicken or beef stock
		a dash of Worcestershire sauce
		1 teaspoon tomato purée
		    or 1 tablespoon tomato
		ketchup

In the basic form the bolognese should be served with spaghetti, the chilli con carne with rice and the shepherd's pie topped with mashed potato or cooked sliced potatoes before being baked at 200°C|400°F|gas mark 6 for 30 minutes. Further adaptations to the recipes include:

Moussaka: Omit the carrot and add oregano to the basic shepherd's pie mixture, then layer it up with cooked aubergine slices and top with a white sauce (see page 502), then a layer of cooked sliced potatoes, before baking.

Lasagne: Make the bolognese mixture and layer with lasagne sheets. Top with a béchamel sauce (see page 503), then with grated Parmesan and shredded mozzarella, and bake at 200°C|400°F|gas mark 6 for 30 minutes. (If you have time, make a large quantity of béchamel sauce and layer it through the dish on top of each pasta layer.)

Tacos: Use the chilli con carne mixture and serve with tacos, salsas (see page 508), guacamole (see page 494) and grated cheese.

Enchiladas: Use the chilli con carne or bolognese mixture and wrap in tortillas. Place them seam side down in an ovenproof dish, top with tomato sauce (or see page 504) and grated cheese and bake at 200°C|400°F|gas mark 6 for 20 minutes or until hot through.

Savoury pancakes: Use any of the basic recipes and wrap in pancakes. Place them seam side down in an ovenproof dish, top with cheese sauce (see page 503) and grated cheese and bake at 200°C|400°F|gas mark 6 for 20 minutes or until hot through.

Stuffed vegetables: Cut peppers in half, stuff with any of the reheated mince mixtures and bake at 200°C|400°F|gas mark 6 for 20 minutes.

Halve courgettes or marrows lengthways, remove the seeds with a teaspoon and bake at 200°C|400°F|gas mark 6 for 10 minutes or until beginning to soften. Add any of the reheated mince mixtures, top with cheese sauce or grated cheese and return to the oven for a further 10–20 minutes.

Jacket potatoes: Chilli con carne is a good filling for jacket potatoes. Cook the potatoes, split them open and spoon over hot chilli con carne. Sprinkle over grated cheese and a spoonful of soured cream.

Quesadillas: Warm flour tortillas, spread a layer of bolognese or chilli con carne mixture on one and top with a second tortilla. Cook in a frying pan for 2–3 minutes on each side. Slice into quarters or eighths and serve with refried beans and salad.

Cannelloni: Use the bolognese mixture to stuff cannelloni tubes, or roll up the bolognese in fresh or cooked dried lasagne sheets. Place in an ovenproof dish, cover with tomato sauce (see page 504), sprinkle with grated cheese and bake at 200°C|400°F|gas mark 6 for 20 minutes.

Chilli Con Carne

Preparation time: 5 minutes
Cooking time: 2 hours

SERVES 6

oil, for frying

1 onion, finely chopped

450 g minced beef

1 clove of garlic, crushed

2 teaspoons chilli powder, or to taste

2 teaspoons plain flour

200 ml beef stock

2 × 400 g cans of chopped tomatoes

2 teaspoons tomato purée

1 × 400 g can of kidney beans, drained and rinsed

salt and freshly ground black pepper

To garnish

soured cream

To prepare ahead: The chilli can be made in advance, then refrigerated or frozen. If frozen, defrost thoroughly before reheating.

Serving suggestions: Boiled rice, green salad (see page 381), guacamole

1 Heat 1 tablespoon of the oil in a small saucepan and add the onion and mince. Brown the mince and cook the onion, breaking up the clumps of mince with the back of a fork while stirring through the onion. There should be no large lumps of mince left.

2 Add the garlic and the chilli and cook for 30 seconds. Add the flour and cook for a further 30 seconds.

3 Add the stock, tomatoes and tomato purée, stirring well to mix in the flour.

4 Add water to the pan so that the mixture is nearly submerged. Cover with a lid and simmer for at least 45 minutes, topping up with more liquid as necessary.

5 Add the kidney beans, remove the lid and simmer gently for about 30 minutes, or until the liquid has reduced down to a syrupy sauce and the mince is tender. Season to taste with salt and pepper.

6 Serve with the soured cream.

Cottage or Shepherd's Pie

Preparation time: 15 minutes
Cooking time: 2 hours

SERVES 4–6

oil, for frying
1 onion, finely chopped
1 carrot, finely chopped
1 stick of celery, finely chopped
675 g minced beef or lamb
2 teaspoons plain flour
600 ml beef stock

1 bay leaf or 1 bouquet garni
1 teaspoon Worcestershire sauce (optional)
1 teaspoon tomato purée or 1 tablespoon tomato
   ketchup
salt and freshly ground black pepper

For the topping
900 g mashed potato (see page 358)

1 Heat 1 tablespoon of the oil in a heavy saucepan and add the onions, carrots, celery and mince. Brown the mince and cook the vegetables, breaking up the clumps of mince with the back of a fork, and stirring through the vegetables. There should be no large lumps of mince left, the mince should be brown and the vegetables beginning to soften.

2 Add the flour and cook for 1 minute. Then add the stock, bay leaf or bouquet garni, Worcestershire sauce, tomato purée, salt and pepper and bring slowly to the boil, stirring constantly.

3 Reduce the heat to a simmer, cover and leave to cook for 1–2 hours. Check every so often and add extra water if the pan becomes too dry.

4 Preheat the oven to 200°C|400°F|gas mark 6.

5 Remove the bay leaf or bouqet garni from the mince and transfer the meat to a pie dish, using a slotted spoon.

6 Skim any fat from the liquid and reduce by boiling until syrupy. Add to the pie dish.

7 When slightly cooled, spread the potato over the top.

8 Fork it up to leave the surface rough, or draw the fork over the surface to mark with a pattern.

9 Bake in the oven for 30 minutes, or until the potato topping is brown and crusty.

NOTE: Shepherd's Pie is classically made with lamb and Cottage Pie with beef. However, nowadays they are frequently interchangeable. For full bolognese recipe see page 306.

Roasts, Casseroles and Stews

Roasts are simple to cook, but need a certain amount of planning and organization. This section will explain how to have all elements of the meal ready at the same time.

Casseroles and stews are easy to prepare, but due to the particular ingredients, can take some time to cook. They can therefore be prepared when there is time to cook, and served when there is not. You can also set aside a day to cook lots of dishes, which you can then freeze and eat over the following weeks; these recipes are ideal for this.

How to Organize Cooking a Roast

Cooking a roast lunch presents its own difficulties as everything must emerge from the oven perfectly cooked, at exactly the same time. Below are some tips to help relieve some of the stress involved in this, and an example of a timeplan which can be adapted to whatever roast is being cooked. The key is to do as much as possible of the preparation and cooking in advance.

- The meat can rest, covered in kitchen foil, for 30 minutes before serving, so that potatoes or Yorkshire puddings can be given a blast of high heat to crisp them up before serving.
- Calculated cooking times for joints of meat are always approximate. A long, thin joint will take less time than a compact one. Meat on the bone cooks faster than meat off the bone.
- Check the meat 30 minutes before you intend to serve it. If it is not fully cooked, but you want to start the gravy, put the meat into a new roasting pan and return it to the oven. Make the gravy using the juices from the original pan.
- If the gravy looks too pale, season with a little soy sauce and Worcestershire sauce rather than just salt and pepper. A little Marmite or miso paste can also be added.
- Vegetables can be prepared the day before.
- Potatoes for roasting can be parboiled the evening before.
- Never underestimate the time roast potatoes can take to brown in a crowded oven. It is often better to put them into the oven too early, remove when nearly done and then put them back in at a high temperature when nearly ready to serve.
- Sauces such as bread sauce, apple sauce and horseradish sauce can be made in advance, as can stuffing.

Example of a Timeplan for Roast Chicken

Roast chicken (see page 272)
Cocktail sausages
Bacon rolls
Gravy
Roast potatoes (see page 364)
Boiled carrots
Boiled French beans
Bread sauce (see page 507)
Stuffing (see page 273)

This plan assumes a dining time of 1 p.m.

- Advance preparation: potatoes peeled, bread sauce made and refrigerated. Carrots and beans prepared and refrigerated. Chicken prepared for roasting. Bacon rashers, sausages and stuffing prepared.
- Preheat the oven to 200°C|400°F|gas mark 6. Calculate the cooking time for the chicken (see page 272).
- *10.30 a.m.* Put the potatoes into a saucepan and cover with cold water. Add a little salt but not too much or the water will not be usable for the gravy. Partially cook the potatoes (about 10 minutes). Drain well.
- Meanwhile, heat the fat for the potatoes.
- *10.50 a.m.* Put the potatoes into the oven on the middle shelf.
- *11.00 a.m. (about)* Put the chicken into the oven.
- *11.30 a.m.* Baste the chicken and put the bacon rolls and sausages alongside it. Turn the potatoes over. Place the stuffing in a dish and put into the oven.
- *12.00 p.m.* Check the potatoes. If they are nearly brown enough, remove from the oven and set aside; if not, turn again and continue to cook.
- *12.30 p.m.* Check the chicken. If cooked, remove from the oven and place on a chopping board covered with kitchen foil. If not cooked, transfer to another roasting pan and return to the oven.
- *12.30 p.m.* Make the gravy, using stock and potato water. Put on 2 saucepans of lightly salted water for the carrots and beans.
- *12.50 p.m.* Warm through the bread sauce. Cook the carrots and beans.
- *12.55 p.m.* Carve the chicken.
- *1.00 p.m.* Strain the gravy and serve.

Roast Chicken

Calculate the cooking time for roast chicken at 20 minutes per 450 g plus 20 minutes.

Preparation time: 30 minutes
Cooking time: 1½–2 hours

SERVES 4

30 g butter
1 × 1.35 kg roasting chicken
½ onion, quartered
cloves of garlic
wedge of orange or lemon (optional)
4 rashers of rindless streaky bacon
8 cocktail sausages
salt and freshly ground black pepper

For the gravy

1 scant tablespoon plain flour
300 ml chicken stock or a mixture of stock and
    vegetable cooking liquid. Be sure that the cooking
    water is not too salty

To serve

bread sauce (see page 507)
stuffing (see page 273)

1 Preheat the oven to 200°C|400°C|gas mark 6.

2 Smear a little butter all over the chicken and season with salt and pepper. Place the onion, garlic and orange or lemon wedge, if using, inside the chicken. Roast in the oven for about 1½ hours, or until the juices run clear when the thigh is pierced with a skewer.

3 Cut each bacon rasher into short lengths and roll each cocktail sausage up in a piece of bacon. Secure with a cocktail stick if necessary.

4 After the chicken has been roasting for 30 minutes, put the sausage and bacon rolls into the pan alongside the chicken.

5 Baste occasionally and check that the sausage and bacon rolls are not sticking to the side of the pan and getting burnt.

6 When the chicken is cooked, lift it out on to a warmed serving dish. Surround with the bacon rolls and sausages and keep warm while you make the gravy.

7 Slowly pour off all but 1 tablespoon of the fat from the roasting pan, taking care to keep any juices. Add the flour and stir over a low heat for 1 minute. Add the stock, increase the heat and stir until the sauce boils. Simmer for 3 minutes. (If the gravy is a bit insipid, add a little Marmite and redcurrant jelly and stir in until melted.) Check the seasoning. Strain into a warmed gravy boat.

8 Serve the chicken with bread sauce, stuffing and the gravy.

NOTE: Good quality-packet stuffing can be bought that only requires the addition of water before baking. However, packet stuffing is often improved if you add your own sweated onion or bacon.

Stuffing for Chicken

Preparation time: 10 minutes
Cooking time: 15 minutes

30 g butter
1 onion, finely chopped
50 g fresh white breadcrumbs
1 small cooking apple, grated

2 teaspoons chopped mixed fresh herbs
grated zest of ½ lemon
½ egg, beaten
salt and freshly ground black pepper

1 Melt the butter in a saucepan, add the onion and sweat over a low heat until soft but not coloured.
2 Mix the breadcrumbs, apple, herbs and lemon zest together in a mixing bowl.
3 Add the softened onion and enough beaten egg to bind the mixture together. Do not make it too wet. Season to taste with salt and pepper, then cool.
4 Use to stuff under the skin of a chicken. Alternatively, shape into balls and bake in a greased shallow dish in the oven preheated to 200°C|400°F|gas mark 6 for 20–30 minutes.

English Roast Beef

If allowed to rest for 20 minutes before serving, the meat will be easy to carve, and juicy.

Preparation time: 5 minutes
Cooking time: Approximately 1½–2 hours depending on exact weight (see stage 2)

SERVES 10

2.3 kg sirloin or rib of beef
a little dry English mustard
salt and freshly ground black pepper

To serve
horseradish cream (see page 506)

1 Preheat the oven to 220°C|425°F|gas mark 7.
2 Weigh the beef to calculate the cooking time. The beef will need 20 minutes in the oven, then allow 10–15 minutes per 450 g for very rare meat, and 20 minutes per 450 g for medium meat at the lower temperature (see below).
3 Place the beef in a roasting pan and sprinkle with salt, a little mustard and plenty of pepper.
4 Roast in the oven for 20 minutes.
5 Turn the oven down to 170°C|325°F| gas mark 3 and roast until done to your liking (as calculated in stage 2). Leave to rest, then serve the beef with the horseradish cream in a separate dish.

Yorkshire Pudding

Preparation time: 10 minutes
Resting time: 30 minutes
Cooking time: 40 minutes

SERVES 4

100 g plain flour
a good pinch of salt
2 eggs, beaten

300 ml milk, or milk (200 ml) and water (100 ml)
    mixed
4 tablespoons beef dripping or 2 tablespoons oil

1 Sift the flour and salt into a bowl. Make a well in the centre and add the eggs.
2 Beat the eggs with a wooden spoon, gradually drawing in more flour to the centre.
3 Add the milk little by little until the batter is smooth. The batter can also be made by whizzing the ingredients together in a blender. Chill for at least 30 minutes before use.
4 Preheat the oven to 200°C|400°F|gas mark 6.
5 Heat the dripping or oil in a roasting pan, flameproof dish or Yorkshire pudding tin until very hot.
6 Pour in the batter. Bake in the oven for 40 minutes, or until the pudding is risen and golden. Yorkshire puddings baked in individual patty moulds take about 15 minutes and 25 minutes in muffin tins. You will need a little more fat or oil to make individual Yorkshire puddings.

Gravy

Cooking time: 15 minutes

2 tablespoons plain flour
600 ml stock or a mixture of stock and vegetable
    cooking water; potato water is particularly good

– it should not be too salty; avoid vegetable
cooking water with too strong a flavour, such
as cabbage

1 Pour off the fat and juices from the roasting pan. Return 2 tablespoons of the fat to the pan. Add the flour to the fat and stir over a low heat until the flour has browned and any sediment from the bottom of the pan is loosened.
2 Add up to 600 ml stock or water and stir or whisk until boiling. Reduce by boiling to achieve the desired consistency and strength of flavour. Season to taste with salt and pepper. Strain into a warmed sauce boat.

Roast Pork

1.35 kg pork on the bone will serve 4 people. 1.35 kg boneless pork will serve 6 people.

Preparation time: 10 minutes
Cooking time: about 1½ hours (see stage 2)

1.35 kg loin of pork, rind intact
oil
salt

300 ml chicken stock
a splash of wine
salt

For the gravy
2 teaspoons plain flour

To serve
apple sauce (see page 507)

1 Preheat the oven to 220°C|425°F|gas mark 7.
2 Weigh the pork to establish the cooking time, allowing 25 minutes at the higher temperature, then 25 minutes per 450 g at the lower temperature (see below).
3 Make sure the rind is dry, then score it with a sharp knife in cuts about 1–2 cm apart, cutting through the rind but not right through the fat.
4 Brush the rind with oil and sprinkle with salt to help give crisp crackling.
5 Place the pork in a roasting pan and roast in the oven for 25 minutes. Reduce the temperature to 190°C|375°F|gas mark 5. Cook for the calculated time (see stage 2).
6 Once the pork is cooked, turn off the oven, transfer the pork to a serving dish and return it to the oven, leaving the door ajar if it is still very hot.
7 Tip all but 2 tablespoons of the fat from the roasting pan, reserving as much of the meat juices as possible.
8 Add the flour and stir over a low heat until well browned.
9 Remove from the heat, add the stock and wine and mix well with a whisk or a wooden spoon. Return to the heat and bring slowly to the boil, whisking all the time. Simmer for a few minutes until the gravy has thickened. Season to taste with salt and pepper. Strain into a warmed gravy boat.
10 Serve with the gravy and apple sauce.

NOTE: If the crackling is not crisp by the time you come to make the gravy, remove it from the joint with a large knife and put it into the top of a hot oven on a baking sheet until crisp and golden brown.

Garlic and Thyme Baked Chicken

Preparation time: 5 minutes
Cooking time: 50 minutes

SERVES 4

2 tablespoons olive oil

4 large chicken thighs (8 if small), skin on

2 bulbs of garlic, separated but not peeled

2 teaspoons chopped fresh thyme

150 ml chicken stock

2 tablespoons Calvados or brandy

4 tablespoons double cream

salt and freshly ground black pepper

To garnish

chopped fresh parsley

1 Preheat the oven to 170°C | 325°F | gas mark 3.

2 Heat the oil in a flameproof casserole, add the chicken thighs and fry, turning the chicken pieces over, to brown the skin well. Reduce the heat, add the garlic and thyme and season with salt and pepper. Cover and bake in the oven for 30 minutes.

3 Remove the lid and continue to cook for a further 15–20 minutes, or until the chicken is cooked and golden brown.

4 Remove the chicken from the casserole and keep warm. Place the casserole dish over a medium heat.

5 Add the stock and Calvados or brandy to the casserole and bring to the boil, scraping the sediment from the bottom of the pan and squashing the garlic cloves.

6 Boil to reduce the sauce to a syrupy consistency. Stir in the cream and check the seasoning. Push the sauce through a sieve over the chicken and serve garnished with the parsley.

Pheasant Breasts with Pancetta and Rosemary

Sweet Chilli Beef

Teriyaki Beef with Mushrooms and Noodles

Lamb and Butterbean Casserole

Barbecued Lamb with Potato Skewers

Lamb Shanks Braised in Red Wine and Root Vegetable Mash

Herb Chicken on Baked Tomatoes

Roast Chicken

Pork with Pumpkin and Pecans

Sausages and Parsnips with Honey and Mustard

New Potato, Red Onion, Parsley and Pepper
Salad

Stir-fry of Green Vegetables

Broccoli with Sesame Dressing

Grilled Mediterranean Vegetables

Chicken Gratin with Hazelnuts

This recipe works well with leftover roast chicken or turkey.

Preparation time: 20 minutes
Cooking time: 45 minutes

SERVES 6

about 1 kg boneless cooked chicken or turkey
30 g butter
100 g hazelnuts, skinned

For the sauce
55 g butter
2 heaped tablespoons plain flour
750 ml milk
½ small glass of white port

175 g Cheddar cheese grated
2 large cloves of garlic, crushed
2 tablespoons freshly grated Parmesan cheese
2 tablespoons dried breadcrumbs
salt and freshly ground black pepper

To garnish
chopped fresh parsley

To prepare ahead: The gratin can be made in advance, then refrigerated or frozen. If frozen, defrost thoroughly before reheating.

Serving suggestion: Green salad (see page 381)

1 Heat the oven to 170°C│325°F│gas mark 3.

2 Cut the chicken into pieces and arrange in a large, fairly shallow ovenproof dish. Melt the butter in a frying pan and add the hazelnuts. Cook over a low heat until golden brown, stirring all the time. Remove from the pan and allow to cool slightly. Chop roughly, then sprinkle them over the chicken.

3 To make the sauce: melt the butter in a fairly large, heavy saucepan. Remove from the heat and stir in the flour with a wooden spoon. Gradually stir in the milk and then the port. Bring to the boil, stirring all the time, to make a thick and smooth white sauce. Let it simmer, still stirring, for 2–3 minutes. Then remove from the heat and add the Cheddar cheese, garlic, salt and pepper. Stir until the cheese has melted.

4 Pour the sauce over the chicken and hazelnuts. Mix together the Parmesan and breadcrumbs and sprinkle over the top. Bake in the centre of the oven for 30–45 minutes, or until the topping is golden brown. Sprinkle with the chopped parsley to serve.

NOTE: If white port is not available, use dry sherry, dry white wine or vermouth.

Chicken and Tomato Casserole

Preparation time: 30 minutes
Cooking time: 1 hour

SERVES 4

2 tablespoons oil
8 chicken joints, skin on
1 onion, roughly chopped
100 g streaky bacon, cut into lardons
100 g field mushrooms

1 tablespoon tomato purée
300 ml chicken stock
2 bay leaves
salt and freshly ground black pepper

To prepare ahead: This can be made in advance, then refrigerated or frozen. If frozen, defrost thoroughly before reheating.

Serving suggestion: Rice or mashed potatoes (see page 358) and green beans

1 Preheat the oven to 180°C│350°F│gas mark 5.
2 Heat half the oil in a frying pan and brown the chicken pieces. Transfer the chicken to a casserole dish.
3 Heat the rest of the oil in the frying pan and fry the onions, until beginning to brown. Add the bacon and fry until golden brown, then add the mushrooms and cook until any water they produce is driven off. Add the tomato purée and stock and bring to the boil. Pour over the chicken and add the bay leaves.
4 Cover the casserole and place in the preheated oven for 45 minutes–1 hour, or until the chicken is cooked through.
5 Remove the chicken from the casserole and keep warm. Remove the bay leaves from the sauce and reduce it by boiling rapidly until it is the consistency of double cream. Taste and season if necessary.
6 Return the chicken to the casserole with the sauce. Serve immediately.

Pork and Apricot Casserole

Preparation time: 15 minutes
Cooking time: 1½ hours

2 pork tenderloins (fillets), trimmed
seasoned plain flour (see page 20)
20 g unsalted butter
1 onion, finely chopped
2 carrots, peeled and chopped

150 ml apple juice
350 ml chicken stock
100 g dried apricots
salt and freshly ground black pepper

To prepare ahead: Make the casserole, then refrigerate or freeze. If frozen, defrost thoroughly before reheating.

Serving suggestion: Boiled rice and mangetout

1 Preheat the oven to 150°C|300°F|gas mark 2.
2 Cut the pork fillet into 2.5 cm cubes and dust in the seasoned flour. Shake off any excess.
3 Melt the butter in a heavy frying pan, add the onion and sweat over a low heat for 10 minutes or until soft. Add the carrots and cook until beginning to soften. Remove to a plate.
4 Increase the heat and add the pork, a few pieces at a time, until lightly browned. Remove the browned pieces to the plate while you continue to brown the remainder.
5 Return the pork to the pan with the onions and carrots, add the apple juice, stock and apricots and season to taste with salt and pepper. Bring slowly to the boil, then cover and bake in the oven for 1 hour, or until the meat is meltingly tender.

NOTE: Any leftovers can be placed in a pie dish, covered with puff pastry and reheated for 20–30 minutes, to make a quick pie.

Chinese Pork Stew

Preparation time: 15 minutes
Cooking time: 1½–2 hours

SERVES 4–6

1 kg pork shoulder, boned and cubed
3 tablespoons sunflower oil
1 tablespoon sesame oil
1 bunch of spring onions, sliced on the diagonal
2 bird's-eye chillies, chopped
1 teaspoon Sichuan peppercorns, finely ground with a pestle and mortar or the end of a rolling pin
1 litre cold water
85 g palm sugar or soft light brown sugar

200 ml Chinese cooking wine
150 ml light soy sauce
3 cloves of garlic, crushed
1 × 2 cm piece of fresh root ginger, peeled and finely grated
2 star anise
1 cinnamon stick
2 strips of orange zest
225 g shiitake mushrooms, quartered

To prepare ahead: The stew can be made completely, then refrigerated or frozen. If frozen, defrost thoroughly before reheating.

Serving suggestions: Basmati rice (see page 374), stir-fry of green vegetables (see page 352)

1 Preheat the oven to 170°C|325°F|gas mark 3.
2 Trim the pork. Heat the oils in a large, heavy frying pan and brown the pork. Lift out with a slotted spoon and transfer to a casserole.
3 Add the spring onions, chillies and Sichuan peppercorns to the frying pan. Cook for 1 minute, then add to the pork in the casserole.
4 Add some of the water to the frying pan and bring to the boil, scraping the bottom of the pan to loosen any sediment. Add the sugar and allow to dissolve. Pour it over the meat.
5 Add the remaining ingredients, except for the mushrooms, and cook for 1 hour.
6 Add the mushrooms and stir. Cook for a further 30 minutes, or until the pork is completely tender.
7 Remove and discard the star anise, cinnamon stick and strips of zest.

Roast Loin of Pork with Fruit Chutney

Preparation time: 15 minutes
Cooking time: about 1½ hours

SERVES 6–8

1.25 kg loin of pork, rind on

Bramley apple, peeled, cored and diced

150 ml apple juice

grated zest of ½ lemon

60 g dried ready-to-eat apricots, chopped

60 g dried ready-to-eat peaches, chopped

60 g dried ready-to-eat prunes, chopped

1 tablespoon chopped fresh lemon thyme

salt and freshly ground black pepper

To prepare ahead: The chutney can be made in advance and reheated as required.
Serving suggestion: Sautéed spinach and crushed new potatoes

1 Preheat the oven to 200°C|400°F|gas mark 6.
2 Weigh the joint to calculate the cooking time, allowing 25 minutes per 450 g, plus 25 minutes. Using a very sharp knife, score the pork rind at regular intervals, making the cuts 1–2 cm apart. Rub with the oil and press the salt into the skin.
3 Place the pork in a roasting pan, rind side uppermost, and roast in the oven for the calculated cooking time. Leave to stand for 10 minutes before carving.
4 Meanwhile, make the chutney; in a small saucepan, cook the apple with the apple juice and lemon zest until soft. Add the dried fruit and lemon thyme and season to taste with salt and pepper. Cook until the liquid has reduced by half.
5 To serve: slice the pork and arrange in overlapping slices on warmed individual plates. Serve with a spoonful of the chutney.

Spare Ribs

Preparation time: 15 minutes
Marinating time: 2 hours–overnight
Cooking time: 1¾–2¾ hours

SERVES 4

1.25 kg rindless pork belly pieces (American spare ribs)

For the marinade
4 tablespoons clear honey

2 tablespoons light soy sauce
4 cloves of garlic, crushed
juice of 1 lemon
salt and freshly ground black pepper

To prepare ahead: The ribs can be left to marinate overnight.
Serving suggestion: Corn on the cob with chilli butter (see page 141)

1 Cut the pork into individual ribs with a large knife. Place in a large, shallow dish.
2 Mix together the ingredients for the marinade and pour over the spare ribs. Leave to marinate in the refrigerator for at least 2 hours or overnight. The longer the ribs marinate, the better.
3 Preheat the oven to 180°C | 350°F | gas mark 4.
4 Put the ribs with the marinade into a roasting pan and roast, covered with tinfoil, for 1–2 hours. Increase the temperature to 200°C | 400°F | gas mark 6. Remove the cover and roast, basting occasionally, for a further 45 minutes, or until glazed and sticky.

Slow Roast Pork

Preparation time: 20 minutes
Cooking time: 2 hours 40 minutes

SERVES 6

2 kg pork loin, chine bones removed
4 onions, peeled and quartered, or cut into eighths if large
3 sprigs of fresh rosemary

300 ml chicken stock or water
150 ml dry white wine
1 tablespoon oil
salt and freshly ground black pepper

Serving suggestions: Mustard potato mash (see page 359), courgettes

1 Preheat the oven to 200°C | 400°F | gas mark 6.
2 Remove the rind from the pork loin. Score the rind with a sharp knife and rub salt into it. Place the rind in a small roasting pan and place in the oven while you prepare the pork.
3 Place the onions in a roasting pan with the chine bones, if you have them. Scatter over the rosemary and add the stock or water and the wine.
4 Heat the oil in a frying pan. When hot, add the pork and sear it lightly on all sides. Place it on top of the onions.

5 Reduce the oven temperature to 170°C|325°F|gas mark 3.

6 Roast the pork in the oven for 2½ hours.

7 Remove the pork from the oven and allow to rest.

8 Increase the oven temperature to 200°C|400°F|gas mark 6 and continue to cook the crackling while making the gravy.

9 Using a slotted spoon, lift the onions on to a warmed serving plate, discarding the bones, if using, and the rosemary.

10 Skim any fat from the meat juices and reduce, by boiling rapidly, until syrupy. Season to taste with salt and pepper. Slice the pork and place on top of the onions. Pour over some of the sauce.

11 Remove the crackling from the oven and serve, sliced, on top of the pork. Serve with the remaining sauce.

Slow-roast Duck with Thai Marinade

Preparation time: 10 minutes
Marinating time: 8 hours–overnight
Cooking time: 2¼ hours

SERVES 4

1 × 1.5 kg ovenready duck

For the marinade
3 tablespoons chopped galangal
2 green chillies, deseeded and finely chopped
2 sticks of lemon grass, finely chopped
5 tablespoons light soy sauce

1 tablespoon nam pla (Thai fish sauce)
2 tablespoons chopped fresh coriander
freshly ground black pepper

To garnish
sprigs of fresh coriander

Serving suggestions: Steamed bok choi with soy and ginger (see page 350), roast butternut squash (see page 179)

1 Prick the duck all over with a fork. Place the duck on a wire rack over a roasting tin.

2 Mix together all the marinade ingredients and rub over the duck skin and inside the body cavity. Cover and refrigerate for at least 8 hours or overnight.

3 Preheat the oven to 200°C|400°F|gas mark 6.

4 Roast the duck in the oven for 30 minutes, then reduce the oven temperature to 170°C|325°F| gas mark 3. Cover with kitchen foil and roast for a further 1–1½ hours, or until the duck is cooked, basting frequently.

5 Remove the duck from the oven and allow to stand for 10 minutes. Joint and garnish with the coriander.

NOTE: If galangal is unavailable, use peeled grated ginger. Any leftovers can be used to make duck pancakes (see page 490).

Glazed Ham with Leek and Cider Sauce

Preparation time: 10 minutes
Cooking time: 1½ hours

SERVES 4

1 × 1.4 kg ham or gammon joint
1 onion, sliced
1 carrot, sliced
2 sprigs of fresh thyme
5 black peppercorns
1 can of dry cider
55 g butter
4 small leeks, finely sliced and rinsed

55 g plain flour
300 ml milk
2 tablespoons clear honey
2 tablespoons made English mustard
1 heaped tablespoon wholegrain mustard
1 tablespoon finely chopped fresh parsley
freshly ground black pepper

Serving suggestion: New potatoes and broad beans

1 Weigh the ham or gammon and calculate the cooking time at 25 minutes per 450 g.
2 Place the joint in a large saucepan with the onion, carrot, thyme, peppercorns and cider. Cover it with cold water and bring to the boil, then simmer for the calculated cooking time. Make sure the water level is topped up to cover the ham during cooking.
3 Melt the butter in a small saucepan, add the leeks and cook over a very low heat until completely soft but not brown.
4 Stir in the flour, and cook over a low heat, stirring, for 1 minute. Remove the pan from the heat and gradually add all the milk, stirring continuously. Set aside until the ham or gammon is cooked. Preheat the oven to 220°C│425°F│gas mark 7.
5 Remove the joint from the pan and leave to cool slightly. Turn the heat up under the pan and reduce the liquid by boiling rapidly until the flavour is strong, but not too salty.
6 Wearing rubber gloves, remove the skin from the ham or gammon but leave the fat underneath. Mix together the honey and English mustard and spread over the joint. Place on a baking sheet and bake in the oven for 20 minutes, or until brown and caramelized.
7 Strain the reduced cooking liquor and slowly add 600 ml of it to the leek sauce, stirring. Bring the sauce to the boil, then simmer for 2–3 minutes. Stir in the wholegrain mustard and parsley and season with pepper. Serve with the glazed ham or gammon.

NOTES: The ham can be soaked in cold water overnight to prevent it being too salty. Any leftover ham can be served cold, or made into Turkey and Ham Pie (see page 231), using any leftover cooking liquid from making this dish in place of the chicken or turkey stock.

Belly of Pork with Garlic, Lemon and Thyme

Preparation time: 10 minutes
Marinating time: overnight
Cooking time: 2 hours

SERVES 4

1 × 1.5 kg piece of pork belly, rind on
12 cloves of garlic, peeled and roughly chopped
grated zest of 3 lemons
2 tablespoons chopped fresh thyme
2 tablespoon olive oil
salt and freshly ground black pepper

For the salsa verde

1 bunch of fresh flat-leaf parsley
1 bunch of fresh basil
1 bunch of fresh coriander
2 cloves of roasted garlic (see page 14), peeled
150 ml olive oil
lemon juice to taste
salt and freshly ground black pepper

Serving suggestion: Mashed potatoes (see page 358) and roast beetroot (see page 341)

1 Pierce the pork rind all over with a skewer or the point of a small, sharp knife, going through the fat but not into the flesh. Boil a kettle of water and pour over the rind. Leave to drain, then dry well.

2 Mix together the garlic, lemon zest, thyme, oil and salt and pepper. Rub this mixture well into the flesh side of the pork and leave to marinate overnight in the refrigerator.

3 Preheat the oven to 200°C|400°F|gas mark 6. Place the pork on a wire rack, rind side up, and place the wire rack over a roasting pan half filled with water. Sprinkle the rind with salt and roast for 15 minutes to start the crackling forming. Then reduce the oven temperature to 180°C|350°F|gas mark 4 and continue to cook for 1½ hours. Top up the water in the roasting pan as necessary.

4 Meanwhile, make the salsa verde: in a food processor mix the herbs and garlic to a paste, then gradually pour in the oil to make an emulsion. Season to taste with salt, pepper and lemon juice.

5 Increase the oven temperature to 230°C|450°F|gas mark 8 and roast the pork for a further 15 minutes.

6 Remove the pork from the oven and slice. Serve with the salsa verde.

Beef Casserole with Horseradish Dumplings

Preparation time: 25 minutes
Cooking time: 1¾ hours

SERVES 4

oil

900 g chuck steak (trimmed weight), cut into 2.5 cm
  cubes

1 onion, finely sliced

1 clove of garlic, crushed

2 teaspoons plain flour

1 × 340 ml can of consommé or beef stock

300 ml water

1 tablespoon redcurrant jelly

2 teaspoons Worcestershire sauce

salt and freshly ground black pepper

For the dumplings

110 g self-raising flour

½ teaspoon salt

55 g shredded suet

1 tablespoon chopped fresh parsley

3 tablespoons creamed horseradish

To prepare ahead: Make the casserole, then refrigerate or freeze. If frozen, defrost the casserole thoroughly, make the dumplings and cook them while reheating the casserole.

Serving suggestions: Leeks in cheese sauce (see page 503) and Vichy carrots (see page 344)

1 Preheat the oven to 170°C│325°F│gas mark 3.

2 Heat a little oil in a large, heavy frying pan. Add the beef, a few pieces at a time, and fry until evenly browned on all sides. Remove to a plate as each batch is browned.

3 Add the onion to the pan and sweat over a low heat until soft, then add the garlic and cook for 1 further minute. Add the flour and cook for 1 further minute.

4 Remove the pan from the heat and add the consommé or stock and water. Mix well, return to the heat and bring gradually up to the boil, stirring continuously. Simmer for 2 minutes, then add the redcurrant jelly and Worcestershire sauce. Stir well and season with salt and pepper.

5 Return the meat to the pan and tip everything into a casserole. Cover and cook in the oven for 1¼ hours, or until the meat is very tender.

6 Meanwhile, prepare the dumplings: sift the flour into a bowl with the salt, stir the suet into the flour, add the parsley and horseradish and enough water to make a soft dough. Take care not to overwork the dough.

7 Shape the dumplings into small balls and place on top of the stew.

8 Cover the casserole and cook for a further 20 minutes. Increase the oven temperature to 175°C│350°F│gas mark 5. Remove the casserole lid and continue to cook for about 20 minutes to dry the surface of the dumplings.

Soy-braised Beef with Orange

Preparation time: 30 minutes
Cooking time: 3 hours

SERVES 4

4 tablespoons oil

900 g chuck steak, trimmed and cut into 3 cm cubes

2 red onions, sliced

1 × 2 cm piece of fresh root ginger, peeled and
  grated

2 cloves of garlic, crushed

2 oranges

2 tablespoons cornflour

5 tablespoons light soy sauce

2 tablespoons balsamic vinegar

2 tablespoons soft light brown sugar

425 ml beef stock

salt and freshly ground black pepper

To prepare ahead: Complete to the end of stage 7, then refrigerate or freeze and reheat as required, adding the orange segments just before serving. If frozen, defrost thoroughly before reheating.

Serving suggestions: Basmati rice (see page 374), stir-fried vegetables (see page 351)

1 Preheat the oven to 150°C|300°F|gas mark 2.

2 Heat 2 tablespoons of the oil in a large, heavy frying pan. Brown the beef on all sides, a few pieces at a time, and transfer to a flameproof casserole. If the bottom of the pan becomes too brown and sticky, pour in a little stock and scrape the sediment from the bottom. Pour this into the casserole with the meat, then add a little more oil and continue browning the meat until all is transferred to the casserole.

3 Use the remaining oil to fry the onions in the pan until golden brown. Add the ginger and garlic and cook for 1 further minute. Transfer to the casserole.

4 Finely grate the zest from both oranges and add to the casserole. Place the cornflour in a bowl and stir in the soy sauce and vinegar. Stir well until smooth. Stir into the casserole with the sugar and the stock.

5 Bring to the boil, then simmer for 2 minutes. Cover the casserole and cook in the oven for 3 hours, or until the meat is tender. Meanwhile, peel one of the oranges with a knife, as you would an apple, making sure all the pith is removed. Remove the segments (see page 11). Squeeze the juice from the other orange.

6 Approximately 30 minutes before the meat is cooked, add the orange juice to the casserole and remove the lid.

7 Add the orange segments just before serving and stir through until hot.

8 If the sauce is too strong-tasting or too thick, add some water. If the sauce is too thin or insipid once the beef has cooked, strain off the liquid and reduce by boiling rapidly.

Quick Irish Stew

Preparation time: 25 minutes
Cooking time: 2½ hours

SERVES 6–8

1.5 kg leg of lamb

450 g onions, finely sliced

450 g carrots, peeled and diced

1 bouquet garni

60 g pearl barley

800 ml good-quality lamb or chicken stock

salt and freshly ground black pepper

To garnish

chopped fresh parsley

To prepare ahead: The dish can be made in advance, then refrigerated or frozen. If frozen, defrost thoroughly before reheating.

Serving suggestions: Irish champ (see page 365), mash and green vegetables, carrots

1 Preheat the oven to 150°C | 300°F | gas mark 2.
2 Trim the lamb of any excess fat, and cut into 2.5 cm cubes.
3 Layer the lamb, onions and carrots in a deep flameproof casserole with the bouquet garni in the middle, seasoning each layer with salt and pepper as you go. Add the barley and the stock.
4 Bring the contents of the casserole to the boil. Skim off any fat.
5 Cook in the oven, covered, for about 2½ hours, or until tender.
6 Remove the bouquet garni, sprinkle with parsley and serve.

Slow-cooked Roast Lamb

Preparation time: 15 minutes
Cooking time: 9 hours

SERVES 6–8

1 large leg of lamb	2 sprigs of fresh thyme
4 cloves of garlic	olive oil
2 tablespoons chopped fresh thyme	a generous ½ bottle of red wine
1 tablespoon sea salt	1 tablespoon redcurrant jelly
4 red onions, peeled and quartered	salt and freshly ground black pepper

Serving suggestions: Parsnip and crème fraîche purée (see page 363), carrots, green beans

1 Preheat the oven to 200°C | 400°F | gas mark 6.
2 Trim the lamb of any excess fat. Peel the cloves of garlic and cut them into slivers. Cut some small slashes into the flesh of the lamb and stud with the slices of garlic.
3 Mix together the chopped thyme and salt. Rub the lamb with some oil and press half of the thyme and salt mixture over the top of the lamb.
4 Put the onions and thyme sprigs into the bottom of a roasting tray. Place the lamb on top and season with pepper. Cook the lamb in the oven for 45 minutes, then reduce the oven temperature to 150°C | 300°F | gas mark 2.
5 Turn the lamb over and press the remaining thyme and salt mixture over the lamb. Cook for a further 30 minutes. Pour over the wine and cook for a further 7–8 hours, basting regularly. Cover with kitchen foil when the meat begins to get dark – this will probably be after 3½ hours. Turn the lamb over again for the last half hour of the cooking time and spread the redcurrant jelly over the top.
6 Place the lamb on a warmed serving dish with the onions. Skim off any fat from the meat juices. Taste, and add water if the juices are too strong or thick, or reduce by boiling if they are too thin or insipid. Season with salt and pepper if necessary and add more redcurrant jelly, if desired. Serve with the meat.

Lamb and Flageolet Bean Stew

Preparation time: 25 minutes
Cooking time: 1½ hours

SERVES 6–8

1.5 kg shoulder of lamb
2 tablespoons oil
150 ml red wine
2 medium onions, sliced
100 g button mushrooms
1 tablespoon chopped fresh thyme
1 large red pepper, cored, deseeded and sliced
1 clove of garlic, crushed
1 teaspoon soft light brown sugar

30 g plain flour
1 × 200 g can of chopped tomatoes
225 g can of flageolet beans, drained and rinsed
300 ml lamb or chicken stock
1 bay leaf
salt and freshly ground black pepper

To garnish

chopped fresh parsley

To prepare ahead: The stew can be made in advance completely, then refrigerated or frozen. If frozen, defrost thoroughly before reheating.

Serving suggestion: Sweet potato mash (see page 196) and green vegetables

1 Trim the lamb of any excess fat, and cut into 2.5 cm cubes.
2 Heat half the oil in a large heavy pan or flameproof casserole and brown the lamb, a few pieces at a time. Remove to a dish or bowl.
3 Pour a little water into the pan and bring to the boil, scraping the bottom of the pan to loosen any sediment. Pour over the meat. Add the wine to the pan and bring to the boil. Simmer for 30 seconds. Pour over the meat.
4 Heat the remaining oil in the pan, add the onions, mushrooms, thyme and red pepper and cook over a low heat for 5 minutes. Increase the heat until the vegetables begin to brown. Add the garlic, soft brown sugar and flour and cook for 1 further minute.
5 Add the tomatoes, beans, stock and bay leaf. Bring slowly to the boil, stirring all the time. Season with salt and pepper. Return the lamb and juices to the pan.
6 Simmer slowly for 45–60 minutes, adding more stock or water if the pan begins to dry out. Pile into a warmed serving dish and sprinkle with the parsley.

Lamb Tagine

Preparation time: 15 minutes
Cooking time: 1¼ hours

SERVES 6

1.5 kg shoulder of lamb

1 teaspoon smoked paprika

1 teaspoon ground coriander

1 teaspoon ground cumin

1 teaspoon cayenne pepper

1 teaspoon ground turmeric

1 teaspoon ground ginger

1 teaspoon salt

1 teaspoon freshly ground black pepper

2 tablespoons oil

2 large Spanish onions, chopped

3 cloves of garlic, peeled and finely chopped,
or crushed

1 heaped teaspoon plain flour

225 g fresh ripe tomatoes, peeled, deseeded and
chopped (see page 22)

750 ml chicken stock

100 g raisins, soaked in water

100 g dried apricots, chopped and soaked in water

To garnish

1 tablespoon mixed fresh coriander and flat-leaf
parsley, chopped

toasted flaked almonds

To prepare ahead: Make to the end of stage 5, then refrigerate or freeze and reheat as required, stirring in the herbs just before serving. If frozen, defrost thoroughly before reheating.

Serving suggestions: Herb or fruit couscous (pages 356 and 355), green salad (see page 381)

1 Trim the lamb of most of the membrane and fat. Cut into 2.5 cm cubes and toss them in the ground spices, salt and pepper.

2 Heat the oil in a large heavy pan or flameproof casserole, add the onions and cook until soft but not coloured. Add the garlic and continue to cook for 30 seconds.

3 Add the lamb to the pan and cook over a medium heat for a further 5 minutes. Add the flour to the pan and cook for 1 further minute.

4 Add the tomatoes and enough stock to cover everything. Bring slowly up to the boil and season with salt and pepper. Reduce the heat, cover the pan and simmer for 40 minutes.

5 Add the raisins and the apricots and simmer for a further 20 minutes. Season to taste, with salt and pepper.

6 Stir through the coriander and flat-leaf parsley, scatter over the toasted flaked almonds and serve immediately.

Lamb Shanks Braised in Red Wine

Preparation time: 20 minutes
Marinating time: overnight
Cooking time: 2½ hours

SERVES 4

4 lamb shanks

2 cloves of garlic, peeled and sliced

150 g streaky bacon, diced

1 onion, sliced

1 bottle of Cabernet Sauvignon or other full-bodied
   red wine

1 tablespoon oil

4 tablespoons plain flour

1 bouquet garni

850 ml lamb or chicken stock

3 tablespoons port

salt and freshly ground black pepper

To prepare ahead: This dish can be made in advance, then refrigerated or frozen. If frozen, defrost thoroughly before reheating.

Serving suggestions: Parsnip and crème fraîche purée (see page 363), green beans or broccoli

1 Trim the lamb shanks of any excess fat, then put them into a large non-metallic bowl with the garlic, bacon and onion, and pour over the wine. Leave to marinate overnight.

2 Preheat the oven to 170°C│325°F│gas mark 3.

3 Remove the lamb shanks from the wine and lift out the bacon and onion, using a slotted spoon.

4 Heat the oil in a heavy pan and brown the bacon and onion. Lift out, using a slotted spoon, and place in a deep casserole dish.

5 Brown the lamb shanks on all sides in the pan and place on top of the bacon and onion. Add the flour to the pan and stir well. Pour the wine into the pan and scrape the base to loosen any sediment. Add the stock and bring to the boil for 2 minutes.

6 Pour over the lamb shanks and add the bouquet garni to the casserole.

7 Cook, covered, in the oven for 2½ hours, or until the meat will come away from the bone easily.

8 Lift out the lamb shanks and place on a warmed serving dish. Keep warm.

9 Pour the sauce into a bowl and carefully skim off as much of the fat as you can.

10 Return the sauce to the pan. Add the port and boil to reduce to a syrupy consistency. This could take 5–10 minutes. Season to taste with salt and pepper and pour over the lamb shanks.

Lamb Shanks with Red Peppers and Chickpeas

Preparation time: 15 minutes
Cooking time: 2½ hours

SERVES 4

4 tablespoons oil

4 lamb shanks

1 red onion, roughly diced

2 cloves of garlic, finely chopped

¼ teaspoon crushed chillies

1 red pepper, deseeded and roughly diced

1 small aubergine, roughly diced

1 tablespoon plain flour

2 × 400 g cans of plum tomatoes

1 × 400 g can of chickpeas, drained and rinsed

1 glass of red wine

2 bay leaves

300 ml lamb or beef stock

salt and freshly ground black pepper

To prepare ahead: This dish can be made in advance, then refrigerated or frozen. If frozen, defrost thoroughly before reheating.

Serving suggestion: Green vegetables and crusty bread

1 Preheat the oven to 180°C|350°F|gas mark 4.
2 Heat half the oil in a large, heavy pan, add the lamb shanks and brown, then set aside.
3 Heat the remaining oil in a flameproof casserole, add the red onion and garlic and cook over a low heat until soft.
4 Add the chillies and cook for 1 further minute.
5 Add the red pepper and aubergine and fry for 1 further minute. Add the flour and cook for 1 further minute.
6 Finally add the tomatoes, chickpeas, wine, bay leaves, salt, pepper and stock. Bring up to the boil, stirring well to break down the tomatoes a little, then add the lamb shanks to the casserole, cover and cook in the oven for 2½ hours.
7 Taste the sauce and check the consistency. If the sauce tastes too strong or is too thick, add some water. If the sauce is too thin or insipid, strain off the liquid once the lamb has cooked, and reduce by boiling rapidly.

Baked Spiced Lamb

Preparation time: 15 minutes
Cooking time: 1 hour 15 minutes

SERVES 4–6

4 tablespoons oil

2 red onions, chopped

2 cloves of garlic, crushed

1 medium aubergine, diced into 1 cm pieces

2 teaspoons ground cinnamon

1 teaspoon ground ginger

1 teaspoon ground coriander

1 teaspoon ground cumin

1 teaspoon cayenne pepper

1 tablespoon tomato purée

700 g minced lamb

1 × 225 g can of chopped tomatoes

85 g pitted dried dates, soaked in boiling water to
  cover

3 tablespoons brandy

For the sauce

60 g butter

60g plain flour

600 ml milk

60 g ground almonds

salt and freshly ground black pepper

To prepare ahead: Complete the dish, then refrigerate or freeze. If frozen, defrost throughly before reheating.

Serving suggestions: Green vegetables or green salad (see page 381), couscous with chickpeas (see page 355), saffron potato mash (see page 362), brown rice pilaf with sesame seeds (see page 376)

1 Preheat the oven to 200°C|400°F|gas mark 6.

2 Heat the oil in a large saucepan, add the onions, garlic and aubergine and cook over a low heat until soft. Increase the heat and cook until beginning to brown.

3 Stir in the spices and cook for 1 minute. Stir in the tomato purée.

4 Break the minced lamb up with a fork and stir it into the pan. Cook until the mince is brown. Add the tomatoes, cover with a lid and continue to cook.

5 Meanwhile, whizz the dates with their soaking liquid and the brandy in a food processor until smooth.

6 Stir into the lamb. When the lamb has been cooking for 45 minutes, remove the lid and increase the heat slightly. Skim off as much fat as possible. Continue to cook for 10 minutes, or until the liquid has nearly all evaporated. Season the lamb well with salt and pepper and pour into an ovenproof serving dish.

7 Make the sauce: melt the butter in a heavy saucepan. Stir in the flour. Gradually add the milk, stirring well all the time. Bring up to the boil. Add the ground almonds and simmer for 2 minutes. Season with salt and pepper and pour over the lamb.

8 Bake in the oven for 15 minutes or until piping hot and golden brown.

Lamb and Butterbean Casserole

Preparation time: 15 minutes
Cooking time: 1 hour 45 minutes

SERVES 6–8

1.5 kg shoulder of lamb

4 tablespoons oil

1 onion, finely chopped

2 carrots, chopped

seasoned plain flour (see page 20)

150 ml lamb or chicken stock

2 × 400 g cans of chopped tomatoes

2 × 400 g cans of butterbeans, drained and rinsed

1 bouquet garni

salt and freshly ground black pepper

To garnish

chopped fresh parsley

To prepare ahead: Complete the dish, then refrigerate or freeze. If frozen, defrost thoroughly before reheating.

Serving suggestion: Green beans and garlic bread (see page 379)

1 Preheat the oven to 170°C|325°F|gas mark 3.

2 Trim the lamb of any excess fat, and cut into 2.5 cm chunks.

3 Heat 2 tablespoons of the oil in a frying pan. Add the onion and sweat for 10 minutes or until soft, then add the carrots and cook until beginning to soften. Transfer to a casserole.

4 Toss the lamb cubes in the seasoned flour and then heat the remaining oil in the frying pan. In batches, brown the cubes on all sides in the pan and transfer to the casserole. Add a little water to the pan, scrape to loosen any sediment and add this to the casserole with the stock.

5 Add the tomatoes and butterbeans to the casserole, stir and season with a little salt and pepper. Add the bouquet garni.

6 Cook in the oven for 1½ hours. Remove the bouquet garni.

7 Sprinkle with the parsley and serve.

Pasta Dishes

Pasta is an after-work staple for many. Do not feel constrained to match one type of sauce with one particular shape of pasta. The general rule is that chunky sauces work best with pasta shapes which have lots of nooks and crannies, such as fusilli or penne, to trap the chunks in the sauce. Plain oil or smooth tomato sauces work best with smooth shapes such as tagliatelle or spaghetti.

Pasta dishes are best served with a green salad made of complementary ingredients. Serving quantities are for main courses, but as a general guide, they will serve twice as many for a starter. Grana Padano can be used instead of Parmesan.

Rich Tomato Pasta Sauce

Preparation time: 5 minutes
Cooking time: 20 minutes

oil

1 large onion, finely chopped

2 cloves of garlic, crushed

2 × 400 g cans of chopped tomatoes

2 tablespoons ready-made pesto (or see page 512)

2 tablespoons tomato ketchup

200 g mascarpone

salt and freshly ground black pepper

To prepare ahead: This sauce can be prepared in advance, then refrigerated or frozen.

1 Heat the oil in a large sauté pan, add the onion and sweat over a low heat until soft. Add the garlic and cook for a further 45 seconds.
2 Add the tomatoes, pesto, ketchup and salt and pepper. Stir well and bring to the boil, then simmer for 10–15 minutes, or until the sauce has reduced.
3 Remove from the heat and allow to cool slightly before placing in a blender or liquidizer. Blend until smooth.
4 Return to the saucepan, reheat gently and stir in the mascarpone. Adjust the seasoning as necessary with salt and pepper and more pesto if desired.

VARIATIONS
- 1 red chilli, finely chopped, cooked with the onion
- Omit the mascarpone and stir in a shredded ball of mozzarella cheese
- Make with a punnet of fresh tomatoes or chopped salad tomatoes in place of the canned variety; you may want to put the sauce through a sieve.
- Use dried herbs if you do not have pesto
- Add some chopped peeled peppers

Uncooked Pasta Sauce

This sauce should be served on the day after it has been made in order to allow the flavours to develop. It can be served with hot or cold pasta.

Preparation time: 5 minutes
Draining time: 30 minutes

6 large tomatoes, peeled and finely chopped
1 red onion, finely chopped
2 cloves of garlic, finely chopped
4 tablespoons chopped fresh basil

1 tablespoon chopped fresh parsley
6 tablespoons extra virgin olive oil
juice of ½ lemon
salt and freshly ground black pepper

1 Put the tomatoes into a sieve and leave to drain for 30 minutes.
2 Mix the tomatoes with the onion, garlic and herbs. Add the oil and lemon juice. Season to taste with salt and pepper.

Spaghetti with Garlic and Chilli

Preparation time: 10 minutes
Cooking time: 8 minutes

SERVES 4

4 tablespoons olive oil
5 cloves of garlic, crushed
a pinch of dried chilli flakes
350 g spaghetti

1–2 tablespoons chopped fresh parsley
salt and freshly ground black pepper

To serve
freshly grated Parmesan cheese

1 Heat a little of the oil in a sauté pan, add the garlic and cook over a low heat until soft but not coloured. Add the chilli flakes.
2 Cook the spaghetti in plenty of boiling salted water according to the manufacturer's instructions. Drain well.
3 Add the cooked garlic and chilli mixture to the spaghetti, then add the remaining oil with the parsley, salt and pepper. Toss well together and pile into a warmed serving dish. Scatter over the Parmesan and serve immediately.

NOTE: This can be served on its own but also goes well with griddled chicken.

Lemon and Parsley Pasta

Preparation time: 10 minutes
Cooking time: 10 minutes

SERVES 2–4

350 g pappardelle
4 tablespoons olive oil
grated zest of 1 lemon
3 tablespoons lemon juice
large handful of fresh parsley, finely chopped

60 g freshly grated Parmesan cheese
salt and freshly ground black pepper

To garnish
Parmesan cheese shavings

1 Cook the pasta in plenty of boiling salted water according to the manufacturer's instructions.
2 Meanwhile, whisk together the oil, lemon zest and juice. Season with a little salt and pepper. Drain the pasta well and pour over the dressing and the parsley. Toss together well with the grated Parmesan.
3 Pile into a warmed serving dish, sprinkle with the Parmesan shavings and serve immediately.

VARIATIONS: Use rocket in place of the parsley. This pasta can also be served as an accompaniment for griddled chicken, fish or prawns.

Simple Mushroom Pasta

Preparation time: 10 minutes
Cooking time: 20 minutes

SERVES 4

2 tablespoons oil
1 large onion, finely chopped
2 cloves of garlic, crushed
225 g Portobello mushrooms, thickly sliced and halved
225 g button mushrooms, wiped clean and halved or quartered

350 g pasta
200 ml crème fraîche
1 heaped tablespoon finely chopped fresh parsley
salt and freshly ground black pepper

To garnish
Parmesan cheese shavings

To prepare ahead: Make the sauce in advance and reheat as you cook the pasta.

1 Heat the oil in a large, heavy pan, add the onion and sweat over a low heat until soft but not coloured, then add the garlic and cook for 1 further minute. Add the mushrooms and cook until soft and any liquid has evaporated.

2 Meanwhile, cook the pasta in plenty of boiling salted water according to the manufacturer's instructions.

3 Add the crème fraîche and parsley to the mushroom mixture and season with a little salt and pepper.

4 Drain the pasta thoroughly and divide between 4 warmed pasta bowls. Spoon over the mushroom mixture and garnish with the Parmesan shavings. Serve immediately.

Courgette and Chilli Pasta

Preparation time: 15 minutes
Cooking time: 5 minutes

SERVES 2

200 g linguine

1 tablespoon oil

1 red chilli, finely chopped

1 clove of garlic, crushed

2 courgettes, grated

2 tablespoons crème fraîche

salt and freshly ground black pepper

To serve

Parmesan shavings

To prepare ahead: Infuse the chilli and garlic in the oil and reheat as required.

1 Cook the pasta in plenty of boiling salted water according to the manufacturer's instructions.

2 Meanwhile, heat the oil in a heavy, medium-sized pan, add the chilli and garlic and cook over a low heat to infuse the oil, without allowing the chilli or garlic to burn.

3 Add the courgettes to the pan and turn up the heat. Cook the courgette through – this will only take a few minutes – and allow as much excess water as possible to evaporate. Stir through the crème fraîche and season with salt and pepper.

4 Drain the pasta very thoroughly. Add the courgette mixture to the pasta and toss through.

5 Pile into a warmed serving dish, scatter with the Parmesan shavings and serve immediately.

Pasta with Goat's Cheese, Courgettes and Beans

Preparation time: 10 minutes
Cooking time: 10 minutes

SERVES 4

350 g cellentani pasta

2 tablespoons oil

200 g bacon, or pancetta if available, cubed

3 courgettes, cut into ½ cm cubes

1 tablespoon balsamic vinegar

100 g cooked broad beans, blanched, refreshed and
  skinned (see page 9)

100 g hard goat's cheese, crumbled

60 g sunblush tomatoes, roughly chopped

salt and freshly ground black pepper

1 Cook the pasta in plenty of boiling salted water according the manufacturer's instructions.

2 Meanwhile, heat half the oil in a small frying pan, add the bacon and cook over a medium heat until the fat has rendered and the bacon is golden brown. Add the courgettes and continue to cook for a couple of minutes until the courgette is cooked. Remove the bacon and courgette from the pan with a slotted spoon and drain on kitchen paper.

3 Add the remaining oil and the vinegar to the pan and heat gently for about 30 seconds, scraping any sediment from the bottom of the pan. Remove from the heat.

4 Drain the pasta and place in a large warmed serving bowl with the courgettes, bacon, and broad beans. Pour over the dressing, season with salt and pepper, and toss well together. Stir through the goat's cheese and tomatoes.

VARIATION: Use peas or frozen soya beans in place of the broad beans. For a milder flavour, use crème fraîche instead of the goat's cheese.

Pea and Asparagus Pasta

Preparation time: 10 minutes
Cooking time: 10 minutes

SERVES 4

350 g pasta

100 g frozen peas

100 g mangetout

70 g asparagus tips

3 tablespoons olive oil

2 tablespoons crème fraîche or mascarpone

½ tablespoon chopped fresh mint

salt and freshly ground black pepper

To garnish

Parmesan cheese shavings

1 Cook the pasta in plenty of boiling salted water according to the manufacturer's instructions. Add the vegetables 3 minutes before the end of the cooking time.

2 Drain the pasta and vegetables and return to the pan.

3 Stir through the oil, crème fraîche or mascarpone and the mint. Season well with salt and pepper. Pile into a warmed serving dish, scatter with the Parmesan shavings and serve immediately.

Linguine with Peas

Preparation and cooking time: 15 minutes

SERVES 4

400 g linguine
200 g frozen peas
150 ml crème fraîche
2 tablespoons roughly chopped fresh basil
salt and freshly ground black pepper

To garnish

Parmesan cheese shavings
a few fresh basil leaves

1 Cook the linguine in plenty of boiling salted water according to the manufacturer's instructions. Add the peas to the pan 2 minutes before the end of the cooking time.
2 Drain well and return to the pan with the crème fraîche, basil and salt and pepper. Mix together well.
4 Pile into a warmed serving dish, scatter with the Parmesan shavings and basil leaves and serve immediately.

VARIATION: Shredded ham or crisp bacon makes a good addition to this recipe.

Linguine with Roquefort and Olives

Preparation time: 5 minutes
Cooking time: 10 minutes

SERVES 4

60 g Roquefort cheese, crumbled
4 tablespoons half-fat crème fraîche
60 g black or green olives, pitted and sliced

1 small bunch of fresh basil, chopped
350 g linguine
salt and freshly ground black pepper

1 Mix together the Roquefort and crème fraîche, then add the olives and half of the basil.
2 Cook the pasta in plenty of boiling salted water according to the manufacturer's instructions. Drain well.
3 Mix the Roquefort mixture with the pasta and season with salt and pepper. Pile into a warmed serving dish, sprinkle with the remaining basil and serve immediately.

Spring Vegetable Open Ravioli

Preparation time: 15 minutes
Cooking time: 20 minutes

SERVES 4

225 g podded broad beans

100 g frozen peas

1 tablespoon oil

1 bunch of spring onions, sliced

4 baby courgettes, sliced on the diagonal

4 sheets of fresh lasagne

finely grated zest of 1 lemon

1 tablespoon lemon juice

1 tablespoon crème fraîche

2 tablespoons chopped fresh basil

salt and freshly ground black pepper

To garnish

Parmesan cheese shavings

olive oil

fresh basil leaves

1 Blanch and refresh the beans and peas. Remove the skins from the beans if desired (see page 10).

2 Heat the oil in a heavy frying pan, add the spring onions and cook over a low heat until soft. Add the courgettes and cook until just softened. Remove the pan from the heat.

3 Add the beans and peas to the pan, season well with salt and pepper and keep warm.

4 Meanwhile, cut the lasagne sheets in half to make 2 squares and cook in plenty of boiling salted water according to the manufacturer's instructions. Drain thoroughly.

5 Add the lemon zest and juice, crème fraîche and basil to the vegetables.

6 Place 1 piece of lasagne on each of 4 warmed plates. Divide the vegetables over the pasta and cover with a second piece of lasagne. Sprinkle with the Parmesan shavings, drizzle over the oil and garnish with whole basil leaves.

VARIATION: Fill the ravioli with roast vegetables.

Spinach and Cambozola Pasta

Preparation time: 15 minutes
Cooking time: 10 minutes

SERVES 4–6

350 g pasta, such as farfalle

1 large bag of fresh spinach, washed and any large
  stalks removed

170 g Cambozola cheese, chopped

90 g pine nuts, toasted (see page 17)

200 ml crème fraîche

salt and freshly ground black pepper

1 Cook the pasta in plenty of boiling salted water according to the manufacturer's instructions.
2 Drain the pasta very thoroughly. Stir in the remaining ingredients and season lightly.
3 Mix well – the heat of the pasta will melt the cheese and wilt the spinach. If necessary, put a lid on the pan and leave for 2 minutes.
4 Pile into a warmed serving dish and serve immediately.

Pasta with Blue Cheese and Walnuts

Preparation time: 5 minutes
Cooking time: 10 minutes

SERVES 4

350 g pasta, such as penne

salt

200 ml crème fraîche

120 g Stilton or Gorgonzola cheese, crumbled or
  chopped into small pieces

50 g walnuts, roughly chopped

60 g cherry tomatoes, quartered

10 sundried tomatoes, roughly chopped

salt and freshly ground black pepper

To garnish

2 tablespoons roughly chopped fresh basil

1 Cook the pasta in plenty of boiling salted water according to the manufacturer's instructions.
2 Meanwhile, mix together the crème fraîche and cheese, add the walnuts and season.
3 Drain the pasta well and return to the pan. Pour the cheese and nut mixture over the top and stir to coat the pasta completely. Add the fresh and dried tomatoes and heat until the fresh tomatoes are just beginning to soften.
4 Pile into a warmed serving dish and garnish with the basil. Serve immediately.

Hot-smoked Salmon Pasta

Preparation time: 5 minutes
Cooking time: 10 minutes

SERVES 4–6

450 g hot-smoked salmon, cut into thick slices
350 g pasta, such as tagliatelle
4 tablespoons crème fraîche
8 tablespoons ready-made mustard and dill sauce
freshly ground black pepper

To garnish
lemon juice
1 tablespoon chopped fresh dill

1 Preheat the oven to 180°C|350°F|gas mark 4. Put the salmon slices on to a baking sheet and place in the oven for 10 minutes or until warmed through.
2 Cook the pasta in plenty of boiling salted water according to the manufacturer's instructions.
3 Drain the pasta well. Return to the pan and stir through the crème fraîche, mustard and dill sauce and black pepper.
4 Divide between warmed pasta bowls and place the warmed salmon slices on top. Drizzle with the lemon juice and sprinkle over the chopped dill. Serve immediately.

VARIATION: Break up the salmon and stir through the pasta and sauce.

Smoked Salmon Pasta

Preparation time: 5 minutes
Cooking time: 10 minutes

SERVES 4

350 g pasta
225 g mangetout, cut in half on the diagonal
200 ml crème fraîche
juice of ½ lemon

225 g smoked salmon, cut into strips
salt and freshly ground black pepper

To garnish
chopped fresh chives

1 Cook the pasta in plenty of boiling salted water according to the manufacturer's instructions. Add the mangetout 2 minutes before the end of the cooking time.
2 Meanwhile, heat the crème fraîche in a small saucepan and add the lemon juice and plenty of salt and pepper. Drain the pasta and mangetout well and return to the pan. Pour over the warm crème fraîche, add the smoked salmon and stir through gently. Pile into a warmed serving dish, scatter over the chives and serve.

Grilled Gravad Lax with Tagliatelle Verde

Preparation time: 10 minutes
Cooking time: 10 minutes

SERVES 4

400 g gravad lax (see page 183)
350 g tagliatelle verde (spinach tagliatelle)
50 g butter, melted
a large handful of baby spinach leaves

200 ml crème fraîche
3 tablespoons chopped fresh chives
salt and freshly ground black pepper

1 Slice the gravad lax on the diagonal into pieces 5 mm thick.
2 Preheat the grill to the highest setting and place a sheet of well-buttered kitchen foil on the top of the grill pan. Place the gravad lax slices on the foil and grill very quickly on one side so that the salmon is barely cooked.
3 Meanwhile, boil the tagliatelle in plenty of boiling salted water according to the manufacturer's instructions, until al dente. Drain well and toss with the melted butter. Season with salt and pepper, then stir through the spinach and half of the crème fraiche.
4 Place a pile of tagliatelle on each of 4 warmed individual plates and arrange the slices of grilled gravad lax on top of each. Spoon over the remaining crème fraîche and sprinkle with the chives. Serve immediately.

Spaghetti Bolognese

Preparation time: 20 minutes
Cooking time: 1¼–2 hours

SERVES 6

500 g spaghetti

For the sauce

100 g unsmoked bacon rashers, diced
2 tablespoons olive oil
450 g lean minced beef
1 onion, finely chopped
1 clove of garlic, crushed
150 g mushrooms, sliced
2 teaspoons flour
150 ml red wine (optional)

300 ml beef stock
2 × 400 g cans of tomatoes
1½ tablespoons tomato purée
1 teaspoon Worcestershire sauce
1 teaspoon dried mixed herbs
1 bouquet garni (optional)
salt and freshly ground black pepper

To serve

6 tablespoons freshly grated Parmesan cheese

To prepare ahead: The bolognese sauce can be refrigerated or frozen, then reheated when required, and in fact benefits from being eaten the day after it is made. If frozen, defrost thoroughly before reheating.

1 Fry the bacon slowly in its own fat in a large saucepan, until lightly browned. Add a little of the oil to the pan, add the mince and onion and allow to brown while continually forking through to break up the mince. There should be no large lumps left. Add the garlic and cook for 30 seconds.
2 Add the mushrooms and cook for 5 minutes, then add the flour and cook for a further 30 seconds.
3 Add the wine to the pan and bring to the boil, scraping the bottom of the pan with a wooden spoon to loosen all the sediment. (If you are not using wine, use extra stock or water at this point.) Stir in the stock, tomatoes, tomato purée and Worcestershire sauce. Add the mixed herbs and the bouquet garni, if using, and season to taste with salt and pepper. Cover and simmer for 1–1½ hours, or until the meat is tender. If greasy, skim off as much of the fat as possible.
4 When the sauce has nearly finished cooking, cook the spaghetti in a large saucepan of boiling salted water according to the manufacturer's instructions. Drain well.
5 Place the spaghetti on warmed individual plates and pour over the bolognese sauce. Serve with Parmesan cheese sprinkled on top.

Spaghetti con Vongole
(Spaghetti with Clams)

Preparation time: 20 minutes
Cooking time: 35 minutes

SERVES 4

900 g baby clams in their shells

6 tablespoons olive oil

2 cloves of garlic, peeled and bruised

4 large tomatoes, peeled and chopped (see page 22)

1 tablespoon chopped fresh parsley

400 g spaghetti

salt and freshly ground black pepper

1 Wash and scrub the clams thoroughly.

2 Heat 1 tablespoon of the oil in a large saucepan, add the clams, cover and shake until they have opened. Discard any that have remained closed. Remove the clams from the pan and strain the juice. Reserve both.

3 Heat 4 tablespoons of the remaining oil in the pan, add the garlic and cook until golden brown, then remove and discard. Add the tomatoes, reserved clam juice, salt and pepper and cook for about 15 minutes, or until the juice has reduced to a strong-tasting sauce. Return the clams to the pan and cook over a low heat for 1–2 minutes. Stir in the parsley.

4 Meanwhile, cook the spaghetti in plenty of boiling salted water with the remaining oil until al dente. Drain well and mix with the tomato and clam sauce. Serve immediately and provide finger bowls.

Linguine with Mussels

It is possible to buy ready-cleaned mussels, which saves time, but you should still check over each one before cooking and discard any that are cracked or that remain open when tapped.

Preparation time: 10 minutes
Cooking time: 15 minutes

SERVES 4

100 ml dry white wine

100 ml fish stock

2 shallots, finely chopped

1 red chilli, finely chopped

1 × 2.5 cm piece of fresh root ginger, peeled and finely chopped

4 sticks of lemon grass, finely chopped

900 g mussels, prepared

350 g linguine

30 g unsalted butter

fresh lime juice

salt and freshly ground black pepper

To prepare ahead: Make the broth in advance and bring to a simmer before adding the mussels.

1 Put the wine, stock, shallots, chilli, ginger and lemon grass into a large saucepan. Bring to the boil, then reduce the heat and simmer for 3–4 minutes or until the liquid is reduced by half.

2 Add the mussels to the pan, cover with a lid and cook over a high heat until all, or nearly all, the mussel shells have opened fully (see stage 4). Meanwhile, cook the linguine in plenty of boiling salted water according to the manufacturer's instructions.

3 Strain the mussels in a colander and return the liquid to the pan. Reduce the mussel cooking liquid in the pan to about 6 tablespoons by boiling rapidly. Remove the pan from the heat and whisk in the butter, a small piece at a time. Season to taste with salt, pepper and lime juice.

4 Discard any mussels that have remained closed. Reserve 12 of the mussels in their shells and then remove the rest of the mussels from their shells. Return the mussel meat to the sauce.

5 Drain the linguine. Add to the pan with the mussels and the sauce and toss together.

6 Divide between warmed pasta bowls and garnish with the mussels in their shells.

Spicy Prawn and Coconut Spaghetti

Preparation time: 5 minutes
Cooking time: 10 minutes

SERVES 4

350 g spaghetti

oil

2 shallots, finely chopped

½ teaspoon Thai red curry paste

200 ml coconut cream

450 g large peeled, cooked prawns

a large handful of roughly chopped fresh coriander leaves

salt

To garnish

1 large spring onion, finely sliced on the diagonal

Courgette and Chilli Pasta

Grilled Gravad Lax with Tagliatelle Verde

Gnocchi Bake

Noodles with Sweet Chilli Crab

Red Pepper and Pepperoni Pasta

Bacon and Cambozola Risotto

Smoked Haddock Risotto with Roast Tomatoes

Dill-crusted Salmon with Spinach Risotto

Risotto Cakes

Butternut Squash and Goat's Cheese Gratin

Chilli Potato Wedges with Spicy Salsa

1 Cook the spaghetti in plenty of boiling salted water according to the manufacturer's instructions.
2 Meanwhile, heat a little oil in a heavy saucepan, add the shallots and sweat over a low heat until softened. Add the curry paste and stir for 15 seconds, then gradually add the coconut cream.
3 Heat the mixture to simmering point, add the prawns and keep the pan over the heat until they are heated through. Stir in the coriander.
4 Drain the pasta well and toss with the sauce. Divide between warmed pasta bowls and scatter the spring onion on top. Serve immediately.

Crab and Tomato Pasta

Preparation time: 10 minutes
Cooking time: 10 minutes

SERVES 2

60 ml olive oil
2 cloves of garlic, flattened but not crushed
225 g ripe cherry tomatoes, roughly chopped
180 g spaghetti
8 large fresh basil leaves, roughly torn

1 × 170 g can of crabmeat, drained and flaked
salt and freshly ground black pepper

To garnish
fresh basil leaves

1 Place the oil and garlic in a heavy saucepan and set over a low heat to infuse for a few minutes.
2 Remove and discard the garlic and add the tomatoes. Heat gently until they are soft but not pulpy.
3 Meanwhile, cook the spaghetti in plenty of boiling salted water according to the manufacturer's instructions.
4 Stir the crab meat into the tomato mixture and stir in the basil leaves. Season with a little salt and pepper.
5 Drain the pasta well and toss with the sauce. Pile the pasta into a warmed serving dish, garnish with basil leaves and serve immediately.

Noodles with Sweet Chilli Crab

Preparation time: 20 minutes
Cooking time: 12 minutes

SERVES 2

1 × 170 g can of white crabmeat in brine

2 sheets of rice noodles

2 tomatoes, deseeded and chopped

2 spring onions, finely sliced

2 tablespoons sesame oil

juice of ½ lime

2–3 tablespoons sweet chilli dipping sauce

1 teaspoon nam pla (Thai fish sauce)

2 tablespoons roughly chopped fresh coriander

To serve

lime wedges

crushed salted peanuts (optional)

1 Drain the crabmeat.
2 Cook the noodles according to the manufacturer's instructions.
3 Drain the noodles and return to the pan. Mix together all the remaining ingredients except the coriander and add to the pan. Stir over a low heat until piping hot.
4 Pile on to warmed individual plates and serve sprinkled with the coriander and the peanuts, if using, with lime wedges on the side.

VARIATION: This can be made using tagliatelle or spaghetti instead of noodles.

Salmon 'Lasagne' with Coriander Dressing, Baked Pumpkin and Conchiglie Pasta

Preparation time: 25 minutes
Cooking time: 20 minutes

SERVES 4

900 g pumpkin or butternut squash, peeled, deseeded
  and cut into large chunks

175 ml olive oil

4 × 170 g thick salmon fillets, skinned and pinboned

4 tablespoons sundried tomato paste

1 bunch of coriander leaves

2 teaspoons Dijon mustard

2 tablespoons red wine vinegar

225 g dried conchiglie

salt and freshly ground black pepper

1 Preheat the oven to 200°C|400°F|gas mark 6.
2 Toss the pumpkin chunks in a little of the oil, season with salt and pepper and place on a baking sheet. Roast in the oven until soft and golden brown.
3 Cut each salmon steak into 3 horizontally. Spread the bottom layer with the sundried tomato paste, then cover with the next layer. Sprinkle this layer with a few coriander

leaves and cover with the top layer. Place in an ovenproof dish and refrigerate until required.

4 Make the dressing: roughly chop the remaining coriander (including the stalks). Place in a liquidizer or blender with the mustard and vinegar and blend until smooth, dribbling in the remaining oil in a slow, steady stream until it is all incorporated. Season to taste with salt and pepper.

5 Season the salmon with salt and pepper and place on a baking sheet. Bake in the oven for about 15 minutes until firm and opaque.

6 Cook the pasta in plenty of boiling salted water, according to the manufacturer's instructions, until al dente. Drain and mix with half of the coriander dressing and the cooked pumpkin.

7 Serve each salmon 'lasagne' with a pool of the remaining dressing and a pile of the pumpkin and conchiglie.

Penne with Chicken and Green Olives

Preparation time: 15 minutes
Cooking time: 20 minutes

SERVES 4

40 g butter

3 tablespoons plain flour

500 ml milk

5 tablespoons vermouth

100 g pitted green olives, roughly chopped

450 g skinless, boneless chicken breasts, cut into
    2 cm chunks

200 g baby spinach leaves, washed and dried

1 teaspoon Dijon mustard

3 tablespoons freshly grated Parmesan cheese

300 g penne

salt and freshly ground black pepper

To prepare ahead: Make the sauce to the end of stage 3, then reheat while cooking the pasta.

1 Melt the butter in a large, heavy saucepan. Add the flour and stir over the heat for 1 minute. Remove the pan from the heat. Gradually pour in the milk and vermouth, mixing well and beating out any lumps.

2 Return the pan to the heat and stir continuously until boiling. Simmer for 2–3 minutes.

3 Add the olives, chicken, spinach, mustard and Parmesan to the sauce. Simmer gently for about 10 minutes until the chicken is cooked. Season with salt and pepper. Add a little more milk if necessary.

4 Meanwhile, cook the penne in plenty of boiling salted water until al dente. Drain and stir into the sauce. Pile into a warmed serving dish and serve immediately.

Turkey and Mushroom Pappardelle

This is ideal for using leftover cooked turkey.

Preparation time: 15 minutes
Cooking time: 25 minutes

SERVES 4

10 g dried porcini mushrooms

1 tablespoon oil

1 onion, finely chopped

1 clove of garlic, crushed

120 g chestnut mushrooms, sliced

120 g oyster mushrooms, torn

300 g pappardelle

1 small glass of white wine

1 × 284 ml pot of double cream

220 g cooked turkey meat, shredded

salt and freshly ground black pepper

To garnish

½ tablespoon chooped fresh parsley

To prepare ahead: Make the sauce in advance. Add the turkey and reheat thoroughly while cooking the pasta.

1 Soak the porcini mushrooms in 150 ml boiling water.
2 Heat the oil in a heavy pan. Add the onion and sweat over a low heat until soft but not coloured, then add the garlic and continue to cook for 1 further minute. Add the chestnut and oyster mushrooms and cook until soft and any liquid has evaporated.
3 Remove the porcini mushrooms from the water and add to the pan. Strain the mushroom water through kitchen paper to remove any grit and reserve.
4 Cook the pasta in plenty of boiling salted water according to the manufacturer's instructions. Drain well.
5 Meanwhile, add the wine to the pan and allow to boil until reduced by half. Add the mushroom water and the cream, bring to the boil and reduce by boiling gently to a sauce consistency. Stir from time to time to prevent the sauce from sticking. Add the turkey and allow to heat through. Season to taste with salt and pepper.
6 Mix the sauce and pasta together, pile into a warmed serving dish and garnish with the parsley. Serve immediately.

NOTES: To use chicken from raw, cut into bite-sized pieces, brown and cook through, remove from the pan and then continue to follow the recipe from stage 2.
    To save time, omit the porcini mushrooms and only use the fresh ones.

Ragout of Duck with Pappardelle

Preparation time: 30 minutes
Cooking time: 3 hours

SERVES 4

oil, for frying	2 glasses of red wine
4 duck legs, skin removed	900 ml hot chicken stock
4 tablespoons plain flour	a sprig of fresh thyme
½ onion, thickly sliced	75 ml double cream
1 carrot, peeled and cut into chunks	2 teaspoons finely chopped fresh thyme
1 stick of celery, cut into chunks	350 g pappardelle
1 field mushroom, cut into thick slices	salt and freshly ground black pepper

To prepare ahead: The ragout can be refrigerated or frozen. If frozen, defrost thoroughly before reheating.

1 Preheat the oven to 170°C|325°F|gas mark 3.
2 Heat a thin layer of oil in a large, heavy frying pan. Put the duck legs with the flour and a pinch of salt into a large plastic bag, and shake until the legs are evenly dusted.
3 Over a medium heat, fry the duck legs until lightly browned all over, then transfer to a casserole. Add the vegetables to the frying pan, with a little more oil if necessary, and fry until brown. Add them to the casserole.
4 Discard the oil left in the frying pan and add the wine. Boil for 1 minute, then pour over the duck and vegetables. Add the stock to the casserole with the sprig of thyme.
5 Cook in the oven for 2½ hours, or until the meat is falling off the bones.
6 Remove the duck legs from the casserole, cool and then pull all the meat from the bones and shred. Set aside.
7 Skim all the fat off the cooking liquid, then strain, pressing as much of the softened vegetables as possible through the sieve. Reduce by boiling until a syrupy consistency is reached. Add the cream and simmer for 2 minutes. Add the duck and chopped thyme and heat through. Season to taste with salt and pepper.
8 Meanwhile, cook the pasta in plenty of boiling salted water, according to the manufacturer's instructions, until al dente. Drain well. Mix well with the sauce, pile into a warmed serving dish and serve immediately.

Red Pepper and Pepperoni Pasta

Preparation time: 15 minutes
Cooking time: 25 minutes

SERVES 4

3 tablespoons olive oil

1 large red onion, cut into wedges

225 g good-quality pepperoni sausage, diced

1 clove of garlic, crushed

½ red chilli, finely chopped

75 ml red wine

3 large red peppers, deseeded, skinned and cut into strips (see page 19) or bought in jars

450 g tomatoes, roughly chopped

1 tablespoon chopped fresh thyme

350 g penne, or any other similar pasta

2 tablespoons crème fraîche

salt and freshly ground black pepper

To garnish

fresh basil leaves, roughly chopped

1 Heat the oil in a heavy saucepan, add the onion and sweat over a low heat until soft but not coloured. Add the pepperoni and continue cooking for 2 minutes, or until both the onion and pepperoni are golden brown.

2 Add the garlic and chilli and cook for a further 30 seconds, then add the wine, red peppers, tomatoes and thyme. Simmer for 10 minutes, then season to taste with salt and pepper.

3 Meanwhile cook the pasta in plenty of boiling salted water, according to the manufacturer's instructions, until al dente. Drain well.

4 Toss the pasta with the crème fraîche. Pile on to a warmed serving dish, spoon the pepperoni mixture on top and sprinkle with the chopped basil.

Rigatoni with Chorizo and Sage

Preparation time: 15 minutes
Cooking time: 20 minutes

SERVES 4

3 tablespoons olive oil

170 g best-quality chorizo sausages, skin removed and cut into thick slices on the diagonal

2 shallots, finely chopped

2 red peppers, halved, deseeded and cut into 1 cm slices

2 cloves of garlic, crushed

1 red chilli, deseeded and finely chopped

150 ml red wine

2 teaspoons Worcestershire sauce

½ teaspoon caster sugar

6 plum tomatoes, peeled, deseeded and roughly chopped (see page 22)

350 g dried rigatoni

6 fresh sage leaves, finely shredded

freshly grated Parmesan cheese

salt and freshly ground black pepper

To prepare ahead: Make the sauce in advance and reheat while cooking the pasta.

1 Heat the oil in a heavy pan, add the slices of chorizo and fry until lightly browned. Reduce the heat, remove the chorizo with a slotted spoon and set aside.

2 Add the shallots to the oil in the pan and sweat over a low heat until beginning to soften. Add the peppers and cook until the shallots begin to brown.

3 Add the garlic and chilli and cook for a further 2 minutes.

4 Increase the heat and add the wine, Worcestershire sauce and sugar. Bring to the boil, then simmer for 2 minutes.

5 Add the browned chorizo and chopped tomatoes to the pan and simmer for a further 10 minutes.

6 Meanwhile, cook the pasta in plenty of boiling salted water according to the manufacturer's instructions.

7 Add the sage to the sauce and season with salt and pepper to taste.

8 Drain the pasta well and toss thoroughly with the sauce. Pile on to a warmed serving dish and sprinkle with the Parmesan. Serve immediately.

Spaghetti Carbonara

Preparation time: 5 minutes
Cooking time: 15 minutes

SERVES 4

350 g spaghetti
1 tablespoon oil
100 g streaky bacon, cut into small strips
4 egg yolks
100 ml double cream
60 g Parmesan cheese, freshly grated
salt and freshly ground black pepper

1 Cook the spaghetti in plenty of boiling salted water, according to the manufacturer's instructions, until al dente.

2 Meanwhile, heat the oil in a fairly large frying pan, add the bacon and fry over a medium heat until the fat has melted and the bacon is cooked. Remove the pan from the heat and set aside. Keep warm.

3 Whisk the egg yolks in a bowl, then whisk in the cream and half the Parmesan and season generously with pepper.

4 Drain the spaghetti. Transfer it to the frying pan with the bacon and place over a medium heat. When the pan has warmed up, turn off the heat and pour in the egg mixture. Stir quickly until just thickening, pile into a warmed serving dish and serve immediately, with the remaining Parmesan sprinkled over the top.

Sausage and Bean Pasta

Preparation time: 25 minutes
Cooking time: 20 minutes

SERVES 4

20 g butter

1 onion, finely chopped

2 cloves of garlic, crushed

200 g sausagemeat

½ teaspoon paprika

plain flour

1 tablespoon oil

1 × 400 g can of chopped tomatoes

1 × 400 g can of borlotti beans, drained and rinsed

2 tablespoons chopped fresh basil

300 g pasta, such as penne or fusilli

salt and freshly ground black pepper

To garnish

chopped fresh basil

1 Melt the butter in a saucepan, add the onion and sweat over a low heat until soft. Add the garlic and cook for 1 further minute. Remove from the heat and leave to cool.

2 Mix the sausagemeat, onion, garlic and paprika together. Season with salt and pepper and, with floured hands, shape into 2.5 cm balls.

3 Heat the oil in a sauté pan and brown the sausagemeat balls evenly all over. Add the tomatoes and season with salt and pepper, then simmer for 15 minutes. Add the borlotti beans and basil and simmer for a further 5 minutes. Add a little water if the sauce becomes very thick.

4 Meanwhile, cook the pasta in plenty of boiling salted water according to the manufacturer's instructions.

5 Drain the pasta well and mix with the sausagemeat balls and bean sauce. Pile into a warmed serving dish and sprinkle with the basil. Serve immediately.

NOTE: Instead of the sausagemeat balls, good-quality sausages, cooked and then cut into thick slices, can be added to the tomatoes with the onions and garlic to save time.

Macaroni Cheese with Bacon and Stilton

Preparation time: 15 minutes
Cooking time: 35 minutes

SERVES 4

350 g macaroni
110 g smoked streaky bacon, chopped
oil, for frying
40 g butter
40 g plain flour
a pinch of cayenne pepper
a pinch of dry English mustard

400 ml milk
110 g strong Cheddar cheese, grated
85 g Stilton cheese, crumbled
1 tablespoon finely chopped fresh chives
½ tablespoon fresh white breadcrumbs
salt and freshly ground black pepper

To prepare ahead: Complete the dish and refrigerate or freeze, defrosting thoroughly before cooking. Cook when required in an oven preheated to 190°C|375°F|gas mark 5 for 30 minutes or until heated through.

1 Cook the macaroni in plenty of boiling salted water, according to the manufacturer's instructions, until just tender. Drain well and rinse under boiling water.

2 In a small pan, gently fry the bacon in a little oil until golden brown. Remove the bacon from the pan and set aside. Discard the oil.

3 Melt the butter in a saucepan and add the flour, cayenne pepper and mustard. Cook, stirring, for 1 minute. Remove from the heat. Pour in the milk and mix well. Return to the heat and stir until boiling. Simmer, stirring continuously, for 2 minutes or until it thickens. Add a little more milk if necessary.

4 Stir the macaroni into the sauce and reheat if necessary. Stir in all but 1 tablespoon of the Cheddar cheese, all the Stilton, the bacon and the chives. Season to taste with salt and pepper. Turn the mixture into an ovenproof dish.

5 Preheat the grill to the highest setting.

6 Mix the remaining Cheddar cheese with the breadcrumbs and sprinkle evenly over the top: make sure that all the sauce is covered or it will form brown blisters under the grill.

7 Grill fairly quickly until the top is browned and crisp.

VARIATIONS: Replace the Stilton with more Cheddar or Gruyère. For speed, use a bought white sauce – you will need about 450 ml. Add quartered cherry tomatoes before turning into an ovenproof dish.

Gnocchi Bake

Preparation time: 10 minutes
Cooking time: 15 minutes

SERVES 4

500 g gnocchi

1 × 350 g jar of ready-made tomato sauce with
  garlic and chilli

60 g Parmesan cheese, freshly grated

2 large mozzarella cheeses, shredded

300 ml white sauce (see page 502)

salt and freshly ground black pepper

To prepare ahead: Prepare to the end of stage 4, then refrigerate.

1 Preheat the oven to 200°C|400°F|gas mark 6.
2 Cook the gnocchi in plenty of boiling salted water according to the manufacturer's instructions. Drain well.
3 Mix the gnocchi with the tomato sauce and half of the cheeses, then season with salt and pepper. Pile into a pie dish.
4 Spoon the white sauce over the gnocchi and sprinkle with the remaining cheeses.
5 Bake in the oven for 25 minutes, or until hot and golden brown.

NOTE: Try to use an organic tomato sauce.

Gnocchi with Garlic Mushrooms

Preparation time: 5 minutes
Cooking time: 10 minutes

SERVES 4

500 g gnocchi

3 tablespoons olive oil

350 g mixed mushrooms (such as closed cup,
  chestnut, Portobello), sliced

1 clove of garlic, crushed

150 g soft garlic and herb cheese

2 tablespoons single cream

salt and freshly ground black pepper

1 Cook the gnocchi in plenty of boiling salted water according to the manufacturer's instructions.
2 Heat the oil in a heavy frying pan, add the mushrooms and garlic in batches and fry over a low heat until soft.
3 Drain the gnocchi well, and stir through the mushrooms. Add the soft garlic and herb cheese and set over a low heat if necessary until all the cheese has melted.
4 Add the cream and season well with salt and pepper. Serve immediately.

Gnocchi with Blue Cheese, Mushrooms and Rocket

Preparation time: 15 minutes
Cooking time: 10 minutes

SERVES 4

1 tablespoon oil

100 g chestnut mushrooms, thickly sliced

500 g gnocchi

150 g blue cheese, such as Gorgonzola, roughly chopped

2 tablespoons crème fraîche

110 g rocket

30 g pinenuts, toasted (see page 17)

salt and freshly ground black pepper

1 Heat the oil in a sauté pan over a medium heat, add the mushrooms and cook until softened and any liquid has evaporated.

2 Meanwhile, cook the gnocchi in plenty of boiling salted water according to the manufacturer's instructions.

3 Add the cheese and crème fraîche to the mushrooms, stirring until the cheese begins to melt, then season to taste with salt and pepper.

4 Drain the gnocchi well. Stir the rocket, together with the mushroom and cheese mixture, into the gnocchi so that the rocket begins to wilt.

5 Scatter over the pinenuts and serve immediately in warmed pasta bowls.

Risottos

Risotto must be one of the most versatile of dishes. Once you have grasped the basic technique, there are very few limits to the ingredients you can use, including leftovers. This means that you can make a risotto for almost any occasion, from a light summer first course to a robust autumn supper.

You can also cook risotto to your favoured consistency. Some like drier risottos; others prefer a more soupy consistency. On this basis the amount of liquid stated in the recipe is only a guideline.

There are many types of risotto rice. The most readily available in this country are arborio, carnaroli and vialone nano. You will need quite a wide and deep pan with a lid, to allow for the continual stirring and the volume of the final risotto.

The stock should be hot before it is added gradually to the risotto, so that the risotto keeps cooking at an even temperature. Most risottos call for white stock, so that the finished dish is pale in colour. The stock could be chicken, fish or vegetable, depending on the other ingredients and who you are cooking for. Make sure you use vegetable instead of chicken stock if you are cooking for vegetarians.

Risottos do need quite a lot of care and attention as they require stirring throughout the cooking process. However, you can **prepare ahead** by par-cooking the risotto, so that about half the stock has been absorbed, and then allowing it to cool completely. When you want to serve, you can warm it through and add the remaining stock and it will only take a few minutes to reach the al dente stage. Cheese and other ingredients can then be added without a stodgy result.

We would suggest allowing the finished risotto to rest, covered, for 3–5 minutes once the final ingredients have been added as this makes it more creamy.

Risottos can also be cooked in the oven for convenience and ease, although this doesn't necessarily give the very creamy risottos which are the result of stirring: stirring sloughs off the outer edges of the rice grains. To oven-cook risotto, follow the recipe as if cooking on the hob, and once the rice grains have been coated in the butter or oil and any wine has been added and absorbed, add all the remaining liquid at once. Stir well, then transfer to the oven preheated to 170°C | 350°F | gas mark 3 for 35–40 minutes, stirring once after 20 minutes. Leave the risotto to rest as described above before serving.

The best accompaniment to a risotto is a crisp green salad. As in the pasta section, we frequently refer to Parmesan, but you can use Grana Padano or any other hard cheese instead.

Chicken and Leek Risotto

This can be made with leftover cooked chicken.

Preparation time: 10 minutes
Cooking time: 30 minutes

SERVES 4

50 g butter
3 leeks, washed and finely sliced
1 clove of garlic, crushed
300 g risotto rice
150 ml dry white wine
1 litre hot chicken stock

225 g cooked chicken, shredded
2 tablespoons chopped fresh parsley
salt and freshly ground black pepper

To garnish
Parmesan cheese shavings

To prepare ahead: See page 320

1 Melt 30 g of the butter in a large, heavy saucepan, add the leeks and cook, covered, until beginning to soften. Remove the lid, add the garlic and cook for 1 further minute.
2 Add the rice and cook, stirring, for 1 minute. Add the wine and bring to the boil. Cook until the wine is absorbed (about 3 minutes), then reduce the heat and stir gently and continuously.
3 Start adding the stock to the rice a little at time, stirring gently. Allow the stock to become absorbed after each addition, stirring constantly. Keep adding the stock until the rice is cooked but still al dente (about 20 minutes) and season with salt and pepper.
4 Add the chicken to the rice and continue to cook until the chicken is heated through (about 3 minutes).
5 Stir in the remaining butter and half of the parsley. Cover the pan and leave to rest for 3 minutes.
6 Pile on to a warmed serving dish and garnish with the Parmesan shavings and the remaining parsley.

VARIATION: Fry 300 g chopped smoked bacon, then add the leeks and continue the recipe, omitting the chicken.

Turkey Risotto

This is ideal for using up leftover roast turkey or chicken.

Preparation time: 10 minutes
Cooking time: 35 minutes

SERVES 6

80 g unsalted butter

1 large onion, chopped

100 g mushrooms, sliced

350 g risotto rice

150 ml dry white wine

1.2 litres hot turkey or chicken stock

350 g cooked turkey, shredded or cut into bite-sized
  pieces

110 g frozen peas (optional)

3 tablespoons crème fraîche or double cream

60 g Parmesan cheese, freshly grated

salt and freshly ground black pepper

To garnish

chopped fresh chives

To prepare ahead: See page 320.

1 Melt 50 g of the butter in a large saucepan, add the onion and sweat over a low heat until soft and lightly coloured. Add the mushrooms and allow to soften. Add the rice, stir to coat in the butter, then add the wine and bring to the boil, stirring until the wine is absorbed.
2 Gradually start to add the stock, a ladleful at a time. Keep the pan at a simmer and allow each ladleful of stock to be almost fully absorbed before you add the next, stirring gently and continuously. After about 17 minutes, when the rice will be almost cooked, add the turkey and the peas, if using. Bring back to a simmer, continue to add the stock, and allow to simmer until the rice is cooked but still al dente. Season to taste with salt and pepper.
3 Remove the pan from the heat and add the remaining butter, the crème fraîche or cream and the Parmesan. Stir, then cover and allow the risotto to rest for 3 minutes.
4 Serve garnished with the chives.

Thai Green Chicken Risotto

This is another good recipe for using up leftover chicken or turkey.

Preparation time: 20 minutes
Cooking time: 35 minutes

SERVES 6

3 tablespoons oil

1 bunch of spring onions, sliced

1 red chilli, finely chopped

170 g shiitake mushrooms, sliced

2–3 tablespoons Thai green curry paste

350 g risotto rice

1.2 litres hot chicken stock

200 ml coconut cream

125 g baby sweetcorn, halved on the diagonal

250 g cooked chicken, shredded into large pieces

90 g mangetout, finely shredded

3 tablespoons roughly chopped fresh coriander

salt and freshly ground black pepper

To prepare ahead: See page 320.

1 Heat 2 tablespoons of the oil in a large, heavy saucepan, add the spring onions and sweat over a low heat for 5 minutes. Add the chilli and cook for 1 further minute, then add the mushrooms and cook until beginning to soften. Add another tablespoon of the oil and the curry paste and cook for a further 45 seconds.

2 Add the rice and cook, stirring, for 1 minute. Add about 150 ml of the stock to the pan and cook until it is absorbed. Add half of the coconut cream, then reduce the heat and stir gently and continuously.

3 Continue to add the stock to the rice a little at time, stirring gently. Allow the stock to become absorbed after each addition, stirring gently and continuously.

4 After about 10 minutes add the baby sweetcorn and after a further 5 minutes add the chicken and the remaining coconut cream. Cook for a further 5 minutes, adding the stock as necessary, until the rice is cooked but still al dente and most of the liquid has been absorbed and the chicken is hot through. Season to taste.

5 Remove the pan from the heat and stir in the mangetout. Cover the pan and leave for 3 minutes.

6 Stir in 2 tablespoons of the coriander and serve immediately, sprinkled with the remaining coriander.

VARIATION: Prawns or crabmeat can be used instead of the chicken, and like the chicken, they need to be added about 5 minutes before the end of cooking and heated through thoroughly.

Pea and Lemon Risotto

Preparation time: 10 minutes
Cooking time: 30 minutes

SERVES 4

1 tablespoon oil

1 medium onion, chopped

1 clove of garlic, crushed

300 g risotto rice

1 glass of dry white wine

1 litre hot chicken stock

250 g frozen garden peas or petits pois

grated zest of 2 lemons

60 g Parmesan cheese, freshly grated

juice of 1 lemon

salt and freshly ground black pepper

To garnish

3 spring onions, finely chopped

To prepare ahead: See page 320.

1 Heat the oil in a large pan, add the onion and sweat over a low heat for 15 minutes. Add the garlic and cook for 30 seconds, then add the rice, and stir.

2 Add the wine (the mixture may sizzle at this point).

3 Stir in the stock, a little at a time, stirring gently and continuously until absorbed. Continue to add more stock, stirring, until the risotto has a creamy texture but the rice is still al dente – this will take about 20 minutes.

4 Add the peas and lemon zest. Stir and leave for 1 minute, then stir in the Parmesan and salt and pepper to taste. Cover and leave to rest for 3 minutes to allow the cheese to melt. Stir in the lemon juice and serve immediately.

NOTE: This risotto can be served as a main course or as an accompaniment to griddled chicken or fish.
VARIATION: Stir prawns in towards the end of cooking so that they have time to cook and heat through.

Bacon and Cambozola Risotto

Preparation time: 30 minutes
Cooking time: 25–30 minutes

SERVES 4

2 tablespoons olive oil

1 medium onion, chopped

200 g bacon, chopped

200 g button mushrooms, finely sliced

1 clove of garlic, crushed

300 g risotto rice

1 glass of dry white wine

1 litre hot chicken stock

250 g frozen garden peas or petits pois

170 g Cambozola cheese, cubed

salt and freshly ground black pepper

To prepare ahead: See page 320.

1 Heat the oil in a large pan, add the onion and sweat over a low heat for 15 minutes. Add the bacon and fry until the fat has rendered down and the bacon is cooked. Add the mushrooms and cook until any liquid has evaporated. Add the garlic and cook for 30 seconds, then add the rice, and stir.

2 Add the wine (the mixture may sizzle at this point).

3 Stir in the stock, a little at a time, stirring until absorbed. Continue to add more stock, stirring gently and continuously, until the risotto has a creamy texture but the rice is still al dente – this will take about 20 minutes.

4 Add the peas, stir and leave for 1 minute, then stir in the cheese and salt and pepper to taste. Cover and leave to rest for 3 minutes to allow the cheese to melt before serving.

Smoked Salmon and Asparagus Risotto

Preparation time: 20 minutes
Cooking time: 30 minutes

SERVES 4

2 tablespoons olive oil

1 onion, chopped

300 g risotto rice

75 ml dry white wine

1 litre hot chicken stock

100 g asparagus, cut into 5 cm pieces and blanched

1 tablespoon chopped fresh chives

finely grated zest of 1 lime

85 g smoked salmon, cut into strips

3 tablespoons crème fraîche

salt and freshly ground black pepper

To serve

lime wedges

To prepare ahead: See page 320.

1 Heat the oil in a large, heavy saucepan, add the onion and sweat over a low heat for 15 minutes, or until soft but not coloured. Add the rice and stir.

2 Add the wine (the mixture may sizzle at this point).

3 Add the stock, a little at a time, stirring gently and continuously until the liquid is absorbed. Continue to stir in more stock until the risotto has a creamy texture but the rice is still al dente – this will take about 20 minutes.

4 Add the asparagus, chives, lime zest and smoked salmon, stir and leave for 1 minute. Stir in the crème fraîche, and salt and pepper to taste. Cover and leave to rest for 3 minutes, to allow the risotto to become creamy.

5 Serve with lime wedges.

Smoked Haddock and Spinach Risotto

Preparation time: 5 minutes
Cooking time: 12 minutes

SERVES 2

1 × 250 g packet of saffron risotto rice
170 g smoked haddock
170 g baby spinach, washed and destalked
salt and freshly ground black pepper

To serve

Parmesan cheese, freshly grated

1 Place the rice in a large pan and add water according to the manufacturer's instructions.
2 Bring to the boil and allow to cook for 10 minutes, stirring occasionally.
3 Cut the smoked haddock into bite-sized pieces and add to the rice. Stir gently and allow to cook for 2 minutes.
4 Gently stir in the spinach, taking care not to break up the fish. Cook until the spinach just wilts.
5 Season to taste with salt and pepper. Serve immediately with the Parmesan cheese.

Smoked Haddock Risotto with Roast Tomatoes

Preparation time: 10 minutes
Cooking time: 25 minutes

SERVES 4–6

2 bunches of cherry tomatoes on the vine, broken in
   half, or 4 small bunches
olive oil
50 g unsalted butter
1 onion, finely chopped
300 g risotto rice
1 large glass of dry white wine or vermouth

1 litre hot fish or chicken stock
225 g smoked haddock, skinned and cut into bite-
   sized pieces
2 tablespoons chopped fresh chives
30 g Parmesan cheese, freshly grated
salt and freshly ground black pepper

To prepare ahead: See page 320.

1 Preheat the oven to 190°C|375°F|gas mark 5.
2 Place the bunches of vine tomatoes on a baking sheet, drizzle over a little oil and season with salt and pepper. Cook in the oven for 20 minutes.
3 Meanwhile, melt 30 g of the butter in a large, heavy pan, add the onion and sweat over a low heat until soft but not coloured.
4 Add the rice and cook, stirring, for 1 minute. Add the wine and bring to the boil, then cook until the wine is absorbed (about 2 minutes). Reduce the heat.

5 Start adding the stock to the rice a little at time, stirring gently and continuously. Allow the stock to become absorbed after each addition, stirring constantly. Continue to add the stock until the rice is al dente – this will take about 20 minutes.

6 Add the haddock and half the chives to the rice with the remaining butter, and season with pepper. Stir gently and allow to cook for 2 minutes. Remove from the heat, add the Parmesan cheese and allow to stand, covered, for 3 minutes.

7 Ladle into large warmed risotto bowls, place a bunch of the roast tomatoes on the top of each and scatter over the remaining chives.

Lemon and Rocket Risotto with Honey Salmon

Preparation time: 10 minutes
Cooking time: 30 minutes

SERVES 4

450 g salmon fillet, skinned, pinboned and cut into 2 cm wide strips	1 glass of dry white wine
2 tablespoons clear honey	1 litre hot fish or chicken stock
2 tablespoons oil	grated zest of 2 lemons
1 medium onion, chopped	60 g Parmesan, freshly grated
1 clove of garlic, crushed	60 g rocket
300 g risotto rice	juice of 1 lemon
	salt and freshly ground black pepper

To prepare ahead: See page 320.

1 Toss the salmon in the honey and a little pepper.

2 Heat half the oil in a large pan, add the onion and sweat for 15 minutes. Add the garlic and cook for 30 seconds, then add the rice, and stir.

3 Add the wine (the mixture may sizzle at this point).

4 Stir in the stock, a little at a time, stirring until absorbed. Continue to add more stock, stirring gently and continuously, until the risotto has a creamy texture, but the rice is still al dente – this will take about 20 minutes.

5 Add the lemon zest, stir and leave for 1 minute. Then stir in the Parmesan, salt and pepper to taste and add the rocket, reserving a few leaves for the garnish. Cover and leave to rest for 3 minutes.

6 Meanwhile, heat the remaining oil in a frying pan, add the pieces of salmon and cook for about 1 minute on each side.

7 Stir the lemon juice into the risotto, divide between 4 warmed bowls and place the salmon on top. Garnish with the reserved rocket leaves. Serve immediately.

Dill-crusted Salmon with Spinach Risotto

Preparation time: 5 minutes
Cooking time: 30 minutes

SERVES 4

30 g butter

1 onion, finely chopped

250 g spinach-flavoured risotto rice

½ glass of dry white wine

about 450 ml hot water

4 × 170 g salmon steaks, skinned and pinboned

1 bunch of dill, finely chopped

½ egg, beaten

55 g dried breadcrumbs

1 tablespoon sesame seeds

100 g fresh spinach leaves, washed and roughly torn into strips

salt and freshly ground black pepper

To prepare ahead: Put the crust on the salmon and cook when finishing the risotto (see page 320).
Serving suggestions: Green salad (see page 381), spinach salad, asparagus

1 Preheat the grill to the highest setting. Preheat the oven to 190°C|375°F|gas mark 5.

2 Melt the butter in a heavy saucepan, add the onion and sweat over a low heat until soft but not coloured. Stir in the rice and cook for 1 further minute, then add the wine (the mixture may sizzle at this point) and allow it to become almost fully absorbed by the rice. Add the water, a ladleful at a time, stirring gently and continuously and allowing the water to become absorbed after each addition. Cook until the rice is cooked but still al dente – this will take about 20 minutes.

3 Meanwhile, roll the salmon in half the dill. Mix the remaining dill with the egg, breadcrumbs, sesame seeds, salt and pepper. Press on to the top of the salmon steaks.

4 Place the steaks under the grill until the topping is beginning to brown, then bake in the oven until firm, about 5–7 minutes, or until cooked to your liking.

5 Stir the spinach into the risotto 5 minutes before serving. Season to taste with salt and pepper. Serve with the salmon on top of the risotto.

Crab Risotto

Preparation time: 10 minutes
Cooking time: 30 minutes

SERVES 4

50 g unsalted butter

1 large onion, finely chopped

300 g risotto rice

150 ml dry white wine

800 ml water or fish stock

1 × 425 g can of good-quality crab bisque

225 g cooked crabmeat

4 tomatoes, quartered, deseeded and diced

30 g unsalted butter

a large handful of fresh basil, torn into shreds

salt and freshly ground black pepper

To prepare ahead: See page 320.

1 Melt the butter in a large, heavy saucepan, add the onion and sweat over a low heat for 15 minutes, or until soft but not coloured. Add the rice and stir until all the grains are coated with butter. Add the wine and bring to the boil (the mixture may sizzle at this point), then cook until the wine is absorbed (about 3 minutes). Reduce the heat and stir gently and continuously.

2 Meanwhile, heat the water or stock and the bisque together in a second pan. Allow to simmer gently.

3 Start adding the hot liquid to the rice, a ladleful at a time, stirring gently. Allow the liquid to become absorbed after each addition, stirring gently and continuously. Keep adding the liquid until the rice is cooked but still al dente – this will take about 20 minutes.

4 Stir in the crabmeat and tomatoes, and allow them to heat through. Remove the pan from the heat, stir in the butter and season to taste with salt and pepper. Cover and leave to rest for 3 minutes, then stir in the basil and serve immediately.

Risotto-stuffed Peppers

Use leftover risotto for this dish, or make up a risotto using a pack of flavoured quick-cook risotto. If using leftover risotto, place it in the peppers at stage 4 and cook in the oven until the peppers are hot through and beginning to soften.

Preparation time: 10 minutes
Cooking time: 25–30 minutes

SERVES 4

250 g quick-cook risotto rice or leftover risotto
4 red peppers
olive oil

4 teaspoons freshly grated Parmesan cheese
salt and freshly ground black pepper

1 Preheat the oven to 200°C|400°F|gas mark 6.
2 If using quick-cook risotto, make according to the manufacturer's instructions.
3 Meanwhile, cut the peppers in half lengthways, keeping the stalks intact. Remove all the seeds and membrane.
4 Drizzle oil over the peppers, season with salt and pepper and bake in the oven for 30 minutes.
5 Stuff the peppers with the risotto and sprinkle with the Parmesan.
6 Serve warm.

VARIATION: Additional ingredients such as chorizo can be added to the risotto before filling the peppers. This dish can also be made with couscous rather than risotto.

Risotto Cakes

This is a leftover risotto dish. However, if you want to make it and don't have any leftover risotto, use a packet of quick-cook flavoured risotto.

Preparation time: 10 minutes
Cooking time: 10 minutes

mozzarella cheese, diced
leftover risotto or cooked quick-cook risotto
seasoned plain flour
beaten egg

dried white breadcrumbs
oil, for frying

To serve
sweet chilli dipping sauce or salsas (see page 508)

To prepare ahead: Complete to the end of stage 3, up to a day in advance. Alternatively, cook to the end of stage 5 and reheat completely in the oven before serving.
Serving suggestion: Green salad (see page 381)

1 Stir the mozzarella through the risotto and spread over a tray or baking tin so that it is about 2.5 cm deep. Cover and refrigerate to cool completely.
2 Cut the risotto into approximately 5 cm rounds with a pastry cutter. Dip the rounds in seasoned flour and pat to remove any excess.
3 Dip the risotto cakes into the beaten egg, then into the breadcrumbs.
4 Heat the oil in a heavy frying pan to a depth of about 1.5 cm, add the risotto cakes and fry until crisp and golden brown on all sides.
5 Serve immediately with sweet chilli dipping sauce or salsa.

NOTE: The quantity of cheese depends on the amount of risotto you have.

Accompaniments

Some of these dishes are very quick, ideal for midweek suppers or for when the main dish will take some time to prepare and something is needed that will not add too much to the preparation time. Some of the accompaniments take longer to cook. A gratin, for example, may take an hour, but can be made in advance and in many cases frozen in portions. Many of the recipes that take longer to cook are extremely quick to prepare, so can be cooking while the preparation for the main dish is done.

Some of these recipes are almost too full of flavours to accompany a main course which already has lots of ingredients and will best accompany plain meat or fish. However, they can also be turned into a main courses by the addition of a few ingredients such as shredded cooked chicken, flakes of poached salmon, smoked turkey or grilled halloumi cheese. Most of the dishes can be added to, making them an ideal way to use up leftovers. They can be served on individual plates or a large serving dish.

Artichoke Heart, Pinenut and Red Pepper Salad

Preparation time: 15 minutes
Cooking time: 15 minutes

SERVES 6–8

2 red peppers, grilled and peeled (see page 19)
1 × 400 g can of artichoke hearts in brine
1 large bunch of basil, leaves torn into rough pieces
140 g bag of mixed salad, including rocket

4 teaspoons lemon juice
1 tablespoon balsamic vinegar
3 tablespoons extra virgin olive oil
salt and freshly ground black pepper

For the dressing
1 clove of garlic, crushed

To garnish
60 g pinenuts, toasted (see page 17)

1 Slice the peppers into thick strips.
2 Drain the artichoke hearts well, then cut each one into quarters. Mix with the peppers, basil and salad leaves.
3 Mix the dressing ingredients together thoroughly and season with salt and pepper, then use to toss the salad. Sprinkle with the pinenuts and serve.

NOTE: Use a jar of peeled peppers to save time.

Avocado and Spring Onion Salad with Lemon Soy Dressing

Preparation time: 5 minutes

SERVES 4

2 avocados, peeled, stones removed, and cut into
   1 cm chunks
2 spring onions, finely sliced on the diagonal
¼ iceberg lettuce, broken into small pieces

For the dressing

2 tablespoons light soy sauce
grated zest of ½ lemon
1 tablespoon lemon juice
1 teaspoon clear honey
a pinch of Chinese five-spice powder

1 Mix together the avocados, spring onions and lettuce.
2 Mix the dressing ingredients together thoroughly and use to toss the salad.

NOTE: Add cold roast chicken or flaked salmon to make this a delicious main course.

Radish, Apple and Cucumber Salad

Preparation time: 15 minutes

SERVES 6

¼ cucumber
1 bunch of radishes
1 Bramley apple
1 round lettuce, washed and dried and torn into bite-
   sized pieces

For the dressing

1 tablespoon sunflower oil
1 tablespoon white wine vinegar
2 teaspoons caster sugar
1 tablespoon poppy seeds
salt and freshly ground black pepper

1 Slice the cucumber and radishes finely.
2 Mix the dressing ingredients together thoroughly and season to taste with salt and pepper.
3 Just before serving, core and slice the apple finely and toss in the dressing, together with the other ingredients.

Spring Onion, Radish and Pepper Salad

Preparation time: 15 minutes

SERVES 2

1 bunch of spring onions (approximately 12)

2 red peppers

1 bunch of radishes or 15 cm mooli radish

30 g sesame seeds, toasted (see page 17)

2 red chillies, deseeded and finely chopped (see page 10)

For the dressing

4 tablespoons rice wine vinegar or white wine vinegar

finely grated zest and juice of 1 lime

1 tablespoon light soy sauce

1 tablespoon ginger syrup

1 tablespoon sesame oil

To garnish

chopped fresh coriander

To prepare ahead: The ingredients can be prepared in advance, then tossed in the dressing when ready to serve.

1 Slice the spring onions finely on the diagonal. Place in a bowl. Cut the peppers into quarters and remove the seeds and membrane, then slice finely. Add to the bowl. Thinly slice the radishes or, if using mooli radish, peel and shred. Add to the bowl with the sesame seeds and the chillies.

2 Mix the dressing ingredients together thoroughly and use to toss the salad. Sprinkle with the coriander to serve.

Orange, Fennel and Almond Salad

Preparation time: 10 minutes

SERVES 4

4 oranges

2 bulbs of fennel

30 g flaked almonds, toasted (see page 17)

3 tablespoons olive oil

1 tablespoon lemon juice

salt and freshly ground black pepper

To prepare ahead: The dish can be assembled a few hours in advance.

1 Peel the oranges, taking care to remove all the pith, and cut into segments or slices which should then be cut again into quarters (see page 11).

2 Slice the fennel finely, reserving any fronds.

3 Mix together the oil and lemon juice. Season well with salt and pepper.

4 Toss all the ingredients together with the dressing. Garnish with any reserved fennel fronds.

Italian Tomato Salad

Preparation: 10 minutes
Cooking: 40 minutes

SERVES 8

4 small plum tomatoes, halved lengthways
olive oil
a small handful of basil leaves, torn into pieces
16 salad tomatoes, halved
250 g cherry tomatoes, cut into quarters

1 × 200 g bag of mixed salad leaves, torn into small, bite-sized pieces
salt and freshly ground black pepper

For the dressing

75 ml plain organic tomato pasta sauce
2 tablespoons balsamic vinegar

1 Preheat the oven to 200°C|400°F|gas mark 6.
2 Place the plum tomatoes, cut side up, in a shallow roasting tin. Sprinkle with oil, a little of the basil and salt and pepper. Bake in the oven for 30–40 minutes until just browning on the top but still firm. Allow to cool.
3 Deseed the salad tomatoes (see page 22), reserve half the seeds and cut the tomato halves into slivers.
4 Make the dressing: whizz together the tomato sauce, balsamic vinegar, 2 tablespoons olive oil and the reserved tomato seeds in a food processor until smooth. Season to taste with salt and pepper.
5 Mix the salad leaves, the remaining basil leaves, cherry tomatoes, tomato slivers, roast plum tomatoes and dressing together in a large bowl.

Middle Eastern Salad

Preparation time: 15 minutes

SERVES 4

baby spinach leaves
rocket
fresh coriander leaves
110 g feta cheese
1 bunch of radishes, cleaned and diced or sliced
1 bunch of spring onions, finely sliced on the diagonal
½ cucumber, deseeded and diced

For the dressing

1½ tablespoons olive oil
4 tablespoons lemon juice
salt and freshly ground black pepper.

1 Make the dressing: whisk together the oil and lemon juice. Season to taste.
2 Spread the spinach, rocket and coriander over a large platter.
3 Scatter over the remaining ingredients and drizzle with the dressing.

Borlotti Bean, Fennel and Tomato Salad with a Horseradish Dressing

Preparation time: 10 minutes

SERVES 4–6

1 bulb of fennel

1 × 400 g can of borlotti beans

1 punnet of baby plum tomatoes or cherry tomatoes

1 bunch of fresh chervil

For the dressing

3 tablespoons olive oil

1 tablespoon lemon juice

2 teaspoons horseradish sauce

salt and freshly ground black pepper

1 Trim the fennel bulb and cut it in half, then slice it as thinly as you can, discarding any tough stalks.

2 Drain the beans and rinse well under cold water.

3 Cut the tomatoes in half.

4 Mix the dressing ingredients together thoroughly. Season to taste.

5 Chop the chervil and combine with the other ingredients and the dressing.

NOTE: If preferred, the fennel can be sliced and then blanched or steamed (see page 9). This goes well with roast beef.

New Potato, Red Onion, Parsley and Pepper Salad

Preparation time: 5 minutes

Cooking time: 10 minutes, plus standing time

SERVES 4–6

600 g new potatoes, scrubbed and halved

5 tablespoons olive oil

3 tablespoons balsamic vinegar

1 small red onion, very finely diced

1 × 250 g jar of cooked, sliced red peppers, drained

3 tablespoons roughly chopped flat-leaf parsley

salt and freshly ground black pepper

1 Cook the new potatoes in boiling salted water until tender (about 10–15 minutes). Drain well and return to the saucepan.

2 Make the dressing: in a small saucepan, mix together the oil and vinegar, season with salt and pepper and add the onion and peppers.

3 When the potatoes are cooked, heat the dressing and pour it over the potatoes. Add the parsley and toss together gently.

4 Cover the saucepan with a lid and leave to stand for 10 minutes before serving.

Beetroot and Potato Salad

Preparation time: 5 minutes
Cooking time: 15 minutes, plus cooling time

SERVES 4

200 g new potatoes, scrubbed

2 eggs

200 g beetroot, cooked and peeled (vacuum-packed
  but not preserved in vinegar)

2 tablespoons capers, drained and rinsed

12 small gherkins

3 tablespoons mayonnaise

salt and freshly ground black pepper

To garnish

chopped fresh parsley

To prepare ahead: Make in advance and store, covered, in the refrigerator.

1 Cook the potatoes in a large pan of boiling salted water until tender (about 10–15 minutes). Drain and allow to cool. Cut in half.
2 Bring another small pan of water to the boil. Add the eggs and simmer for 12 minutes. Remove from the pan and cool in a bowl of cold water. Peel the eggs, then chop roughly. Set aside.
3 Cut the beetroot into chunks.
4 Stir together the potatoes, capers and gherkins and season with salt and pepper.
5 Gently stir in the hardboiled eggs and mayonnaise. Finally stir through the beetroot, which will colour the rest of the salad.
6 Sprinkle liberally with parsley before serving.

NOTE: Potato salad is a good way of using up leftover boiled potatoes. This salad goes well with smoked fish and cold roast beef.

New Potato, Dill and Caper Salad

Preparation time: 5 minutes
Cooking time: 10 minutes

SERVES 4–6

600 g new potatoes (Anya or Pink Fir Apple are
   good), scrubbed
200 ml crème fraîche
2 tablespoons balsamic vinegar
3 tablespoons capers

2 tablespoons chopped fresh dill
salt and freshly ground black pepper

To garnish
60 g rocket, dressed with 1 tablespoon olive oil and
   1 tablespoon balsamic vinegar

1 Cook the new potatoes in boiling salted water until tender (about 10–15 minutes).
2 Drain and allow to cool. Cut the potatoes in half if large, then toss them in the crème
fraîche and balsamic vinegar. Place in the refrigerator to chill.
3 Stir in the capers and dill. Season to taste with salt and pepper.
4 Serve garnished with the dressed rocket leaves.

NOTE: Potato salad is a good way of using up leftover boiled potatoes

---

Potato Salad with Radishes and Spring Onions

Preparation time: 5 minutes
Cooking time: 15 minutes, plus cooling time

SERVES 4

450 g new potatoes, scrubbed
1 × 250 g bunch of radishes, trimmed
4 spring onions, sliced on the diagonal

For the dressing
3 tablespoons olive oil
2 tablespoons good-quality balsamic vinegar
½ teaspoon sugar
1 teaspoon wholegrain mustard
salt and freshly ground black pepper

1 Cook the potatoes in boiling salted water until tender (about 10–15 minutes). Drain
well. Cut any large potatoes in half.
2 Mix together the dressing ingredients thoroughly. Season to taste with salt and pepper.
3 Mix the dressing with the potatoes. Allow to cool, then stir in the radishes and spring
onions.

Spicy New Potato Salad

Preparation time: 20 minutes
Cooking time: 15 minutes

SERVES 6

750 g new potatoes, scrubbed and halved
250 g chorizo sausage, skinned and cut into chunks
2 tablespoons chopped fresh parsley

1 bunch of spring onions, sliced on the diagonal
3 tablespoons lemon juice
salt and freshly ground black pepper

1 Cook the potatoes in boiling salted water until just tender (about 10–15 minutes). Drain well.
2 Heat a frying pan, add the chorizo and fry until becoming brown and crisp. The chorizo will release quite a lot of oil: do not discard this as it will form the base of the dressing. Remove the chorizo from the pan and add to the potatoes while they are still warm. Season to taste with salt and pepper.
3 Add the parsley, spring onions and lemon juice to the pan, whisk together and season. Add the dressing to the potatoes and chorizo.

NOTE: This recipe can also be made using leftover roast potatoes or baked potatoes. Cut them up, add them to the pan and reheat with the chorizo.

White Bean Salad

Preparation time: 10 minutes

SERVES 4

1 × 400 g can of cannellini beans
1 × 400 g can of butterbeans
2 tomatoes, cut into quarters
a small bunch of parsley, coarsely chopped

For the dressing
2 tablespoons olive oil
finely grated zest and juice of ½ lemon
salt and freshly ground black pepper

1 Drain and rinse the beans.
2 Deseed the tomatoes and cut into dice.
3 Make the dressing: whisk all the ingredients together thoroughly and season with salt and pepper. Add more lemon juice if necessary.
4 Combine the beans, tomatoes and parsley in a bowl. Toss with the dressing.

NOTE: Cherry tomatoes, halved or quartered, can be used instead of chopped tomato. Crumbled feta cheese is a delicious addition.

Puy Lentil Salad

Preparation time: 10 minutes
Cooking time: 20 minutes

SERVES 4–6

250 g Puy lentils
85 g Parma ham
200 g sunblush tomatoes
½ tablespoon wholegrain mustard

2 tablespoons balsamic vinegar
100 g feta cheese, crumbled
a small bunch of flat-leaf parsley, coarsely chopped
salt and freshly ground black pepper

To prepare ahead: Prepare a few hours in advance, but add the Parma ham just before serving.

1 Preheat the grill to the highest setting.
2 Cook the lentils according to the manufacturer's instructions.
3 Meanwhile, grill the Parma ham until crisp.
4 Remove the lentils from the heat, drain and run under cold water.
5 Remove the tomatoes from their oil, reserving the oil, and chop roughly.
6 Whisk together the mustard and balsamic vinegar and add some tomato oil to make the dressing. Season to taste with salt and pepper.
7 Mix the lentils into the dressing. Break the Parma ham into pieces and add it to the lentils with the cheese and parsley.

NOTE: This can also be made with Beluga lentils or green lentils.

Hot Raw Beetroot

Preparation time: 10 minutes
Cooking time: 3 minutes

SERVES 4

500 g raw beetroot
50 g butter

a squeeze of lemon juice
salt and freshly ground black pepper

1 Peel the beetroot and put it through the julienne blade of a food processor, or grate it on the coarsest side of the grater. (If using a grater wear rubber gloves.)
2 Heat the butter in a frying pan until starting to foam. Toss the beetroot in it for 2 minutes until hot but still crunchy. Season with salt, pepper and lemon juice. Serve immediately.

NOTE: Chopped dill, grated horseradish or a teaspoon of grainy mustard can be added to the beetroot.

Red Cabbage

Preparation time: 15 minutes
Cooking time: 1½ hours

SERVES 4

450 g red cabbage, finely sliced

225 g dessert apples, peeled, cored and grated

140 g red onion, sliced

80 ml red wine

60 ml red wine vinegar or sherry vinegar

150 ml water

2 tablespoons soft dark brown sugar

ground nutmeg, cinnamon and cloves, to taste

salt and freshly ground black pepper

1 Place all the ingredients in a heavy saucepan or flameproof casserole.
2 Stir well and cook over a low to medium heat for 1½ hours, or until the cabbage is cooked through and soft. Stir frequently to ensure the mixture does not catch. Top the pan up with more water if it gets too dry.
3 When the cabbage is cooked, season with salt and pepper.

Cauliflower Cheese

Preparation time: 5 minutes
Cooking time: 20 minutes

SERVES 4–6

1 large cauliflower

300 ml white sauce or 1 sachet (or see page 502)

60 g Cheddar cheese, grated

1 teaspoon made English mustard

1 teaspoon dried white breadcrumbs

1 tablespoon freshly grated Parmesan cheese

salt and freshly ground black pepper

1 Preheat the grill to the highest setting.
2 Break the cauliflower into florets and cook in boiling salted water until just tender (about 5 minutes). Drain well.
3 Reheat the sauce or make up the sachet according to the manufacturer's instructions. Remove from the heat and stir in the Cheddar cheese and mustard and season.
4 Put the cauliflower into an ovenproof dish and coat with the sauce.
5 Sprinkle with the breadcrumbs and Parmesan and place under the grill until brown.

VARIATION: Use leeks cut into 5 cm lengths, cooked, in place of the cauliflowers to make leek cheese.

Roast Beetroot

Preparation time: 5 minutes
Cooking time: 30 minutes–1½ hours

900 g beetroot
6 tablespoons olive oil

4 tablespoons water
sea salt flakes and freshly ground black pepper

1 Preheat the oven to 220°C|425°F|gas mark 7. Trim the stalks and roots from the beetroot, then peel and cut in half or into quarters if large. Scrub very well and leave unpeeled and whole if small.
2 Put the beetroot into a small roasting tin. Drizzle over some oil, season with salt and pepper, and toss together.
3 Roast the beetroot in the oven for 40 minutes. Remove, turn the beetroot over a few times and then sprinkle over the water. Roast for a further 30–40 minutes until tender. Serve hot.

NOTE: Beetroot cooking times can vary enormously, so check for tenderness every so often – baby beetroot may take only a total of 30 minutes to cook.

French Beans with Almonds

Preparation time: 5 minutes
Cooking time: 10 minutes

SERVES 4

500 g whole French beans, topped and tailed
20 g butter
30 g flaked almonds

a squeeze of lemon juice
salt and freshly ground black pepper

1 Cook the beans in a saucepan of boiling salted water until just tender (about 7 minutes).
2 Meanwhile, melt the butter and, when foaming, add the almonds. Fry until golden brown, cool for 30 seconds, then add the lemon juice.
3 Drain the beans well and mix with the buttery almonds. Season with pepper and serve immediately.

Haricot Beans with Cream and Thyme

Preparation time: 5 minutes
Cooking time: 10 minutes

SERVES 4

1 × 400 g can of haricot beans

2 rashers of smoked streaky bacon

1 small glass of dry white wine

1 teaspoon very finely chopped fresh thyme

5 tablespoons double cream

salt and freshly ground black pepper

To prepare ahead: This dish can be made in advance. Some water may need to be added when reheating.

1 Drain the beans and rinse well.
2 Chop the bacon into thin slices. Fry in a saucepan over a medium heat until golden brown.
3 Add the wine and boil until nearly evaporated.
4 Tip in the beans and thyme. Stir until warm.
5 Add the cream and simmer until the beans are just glazed. Season well with salt and pepper.

Broccoli with Sesame Dressing

Preparation time: 5 minutes
Cooking time: 2 minutes

SERVES 4

1 head of broccoli, broken into florets

2 tablespoons sesame seeds, toasted (see page 17)

salt and freshly ground black pepper

For the dressing

1 tablespoon rice wine vinegar

1 tablespoon dark soy sauce

½ tablespoon sesame oil

½ teaspoon clear honey

1 Bring a saucepan of salted water to the boil. Add the broccoli and cook for 2 minutes. Drain well.
2 Mix all the dressing ingredients together thoroughly and use to toss with the florets. Sprinkle with the sesame seeds and serve immediately.

NOTE: This recipe uses hot broccoli but it can equally well be made with blanched and refreshed broccoli (see page 9) and served as a salad.

Sweet and Sour Cabbage

Preparation time: 10 minutes
Cooking time: 5 minutes

SERVES 4

3 tablespoons sunflower oil
1 tablespoon sesame oil
450 g white cabbage, finely shredded
1 red chilli, deseeded and chopped

1½ tablespoons clear honey
3½ tablespoons rice wine vinegar
1 teaspoon salt

1 Heat the oils in a large frying pan or wok. Add the cabbage and stir-fry for 2 minutes, making sure that the cabbage is well coated in oil.

2 Add the chilli and cook for a further 30 seconds. Add the honey and continue to stir-fry until the cabbage is coated in the honey.

3 Add the vinegar and stir it in quickly as it will evaporate very fast. Add the salt and mix well. Serve immediately.

Cabbage with Caraway

Preparation time: 10 minutes
Cooking time: 10 minutes

SERVES 4

30 g butter
2 onions, sliced
450 g white cabbage, finely shredded

1 teaspoon caraway seeds
1 teaspoon vinegar or lemon juice
salt and freshly ground black pepper

1 Melt the butter in a frying pan and add the onions. Cook over a low heat until soft.

2 Meanwhile, put the cabbage into a saucepan of boiling salted water. Simmer for about 5 minutes until tender, then drain well.

3 Add the caraway seeds and vinegar to the onion and cook gently for 1 further minute, then stir into the drained cabbage and season well with salt and pepper.

Vichy Carrots

Preparation time: 10 minutes
Cooking time: 10–15 minutes

SERVES 4

500 g baby carrots
2 teaspoons butter
½ teaspoon salt
1 teaspoon caster sugar

1 teaspoon chopped fresh mint
1 teaspoon chopped fresh parsley
freshly ground black pepper

1 Wash the carrots well, using a new scouring pad to remove the skin and any mud. Cut off any carrot tops, leaving ½ cm of green stalk.
2 Put the carrots into a saucepan with the butter, salt and sugar. Half-cover them with water and boil until the water has almost evaporated and the carrots are tender. Then turn down the heat and allow the carrots to glaze in the remaining butter and sugar, watching to make sure they do not burn.
3 Season with pepper and mix in the herbs.

NOTE: It is important not to oversalt the water. When the water has evaporated the entire quantity of salt will remain with the carrots.

Courgette and Carrot 'Pappardelle'

Preparation time: 5 minutes
Cooking time: 3 minutes

SERVES 2

2 medium courgettes
2 medium carrots

butter
salt and freshly ground black pepper

1 Wash and trim the courgettes. Peel the carrots.
2 Using a potato peeler, peel strips off the vegetables to make long thin slices or 'pappardelle'.
3 Steam or stir-fry the vegetables for about 2 minutes, or until just cooked. Toss in a little butter and season with salt and pepper before serving.

Courgettes with Sultanas and Pinenuts

Preparation time: 10 minutes
Cooking time: 15 minutes

SERVES 4

30 g sultanas
450 g courgettes
3 tablespoons olive oil
1 clove of garlic, crushed
1 teaspoon caster sugar
grated zest of ½ lemon

30 g pinenuts, toasted (see page 17)
2 tablespoons lemon juice
salt and freshly ground black pepper

To garnish
roughly chopped flat-leaf parsley

1 Cover the sultanas in boiling water and leave to soak.
2 Cut the courgettes into slices on the diagonal.
3 Heat the oil and fry the courgettes until golden brown.
4 Add the garlic and cook for 1 further minute.
5 Drain the sultanas and stir them into the courgettes with the sugar, lemon zest, and pinenuts.
6 Turn off the heat and add the lemon juice. Season well with salt and pepper, sprinkle with the parsley and serve immediately.

Cooked Cucumber with Dill

Preparation time: 10 minutes
Cooking time: 5 minutes

SERVES 4

2 cucumbers
30 g butter
a squeeze of lemon juice

2 teaspoons chopped fresh dill
salt and freshly ground black pepper

1 Put a saucepan of salted water on to boil.
2 Peel the cucumbers and cut in half lengthways. Scoop out the seeds with a teaspoon, then cut the flesh into even slices, about 1–2 cm thick.
3 Drop them into the boiling salted water and cook for 30 seconds.
4 Rinse under cold running water and drain well.
5 Melt the butter in a frying pan over a high heat and when foaming add the cucumber.
6 When the cucumber is beginning to turn pale brown, reduce the heat and season with pepper and lemon juice. Shake the pan briefly to coat the cucumber. Add the dill and serve immediately.

Grilled Mediterranean Vegetables

Preparation time: 10 minutes
Cooking time: 30 minutes

SERVES 4

olive oil

2 onions, sliced

3 large red peppers, halved and deseeded

1 aubergine, cut into slices lengthways

6 medium courgettes, finely sliced on the diagonal

3 tomatoes, quartered and deseeded

balsamic vinegar

finely chopped fresh basil

salt and freshly ground black pepper

To prepare ahead: The flavours develop well if this is made in advance, even the day before it is needed. Bring to room temperature before serving.

1 Preheat the grill to the highest setting.
2 Heat a little of the oil in a frying pan, add the onions and cook over a low heat until soft. Increase the heat and continue to fry until they are golden brown.
3 Grill the peppers skin side up until they are charred and blistered. Place in a plastic bag and tie shut to allow the skins to steam.
4 Paint each side of the aubergine slices lightly with oil and grill until dark brown but not burnt.
5 Remove the skin from the peppers and cut the flesh into strips.
6 Lightly oil the courgettes and grill until just cooked.
7 Place all the vegetables in a bowl and sprinkle with balsamic vinegar and basil. Season with salt and pepper. Stir well.

NOTE: Use jarred peeled peppers to save time.

Rosemary Roast Vegetables

Preparation time: 5 minutes
Cooking time: 50 minutes

SERVES 6–8

2 medium red onions, cut into wedges

2 courgettes, trimmed and cut into 6–8 pieces

2 red peppers, halved and deseeded

1 aubergine, trimmed and cut into pieces the same
   size as the courgettes

2 sprigs of fresh rosemary

1 bulb of garlic, cut in half horizontally

olive oil

salt and freshly ground black pepper

1 Preheat the oven to 200°C|400°F|gas mark 6.

2 Place the prepared vegetables in a roasting pan. Add the rosemary and garlic.

3 Drizzle with oil and season well with salt and pepper.

4 Bake in the oven for 40–50 minutes, basting and turning occasionally.

NOTE: The vegetables used can be changed according to availability and seasonality.

Ratatouille

Preparation time: 15 minutes
Cooking time: 45 minutes

SERVES 6–8

olive oil

1 large onion, sliced

2 small aubergines

1 medium green pepper, cored, deseeded and cut into bite-sized chunks

1 small red pepper, cored, deseeded and cut into bite-sized chunks

2 courgettes

1 clove of garlic, crushed

1 × 400 g can of chopped tomatoes

a pinch of caster sugar

a handful of fresh basil leaves, roughly torn

salt and freshly ground black pepper

To prepare ahead: The ratatouille can be prepared in advance, then refrigerated or frozen. The flavours develop when it is made in advance.

1 Heat a little oil in a large, heavy saucepan and add the onion. Cook over a low heat until soft but not coloured, then add the aubergines and fry until pale brown, adding more oil if necessary.

2 Add the peppers, courgettes and garlic to the pan. Cover and cook for 2 minutes.

3 Add the tomatoes and season to taste with the sugar, salt and pepper. Cook for about 20 minutes, adding a little water if the mixture becomes too dry.

4 Stir in half the basil and serve with the remaining basil sprinkled on top.

Petits Pois à la Française

Preparation time: 10 minutes
Cooking time: 30 minutes

SERVES 4

300 g peas, shelled (use frozen peas if fresh are not available)
1 large onion, finely sliced
1 small lettuce, shredded
150 ml water
30 g butter

a few sprigs of fresh mint
a few sprigs of fresh parsley
1 small clove of garlic, bruised
1 teaspoon caster sugar
salt and freshly ground black pepper

To prepare ahead: Keep in a warming oven for up to 1 hour. Or make in advance and reheat to serve.

1 Mix the peas, onion and lettuce together in a saucepan. Add the water, butter, herbs, garlic and sugar. Season with a little salt and pepper.
2 Cover with a tight-fitting lid.
3 Cook for about 30 minutes over the lowest possible heat until the peas are completely soft. Check the seasoning and add extra salt and pepper if required before serving.

NOTE: This dish benefits from being cooked very slowly, so alternatively cook in a casserole in the oven preheated to 170°C|325°F|gas mark 3 for 1–2 hours.

Pea Purée

Preparation time: 5 minutes
Cooking time: 2 minutes

SERVES 4

450 g frozen petits pois
a little milk or cream (optional)
60 g butter

grated zest of 1 lemon
juice of ½ lemon
salt and freshly ground black pepper

To prepare ahead: This can be made 24 hours in advance but may need a little more liquid when reheating. Add the lemon zest and juice before serving.

1 Cook the peas in a saucepan of boiling salted water for 2 minutes.
2 Drain well and refresh under very cold water.

3 Place in a food processor and whizz briefly. Add a little water, milk or cream if the purée becomes too stiff.

4 Return the purée to the rinsed-out pan and add the butter, lemon zest and juice. Season well with salt and pepper.

VARIATION: Fresh mint can be added whilst the peas are cooking and removed before whizzing. Alternatively, stir through a little chopped fresh mint after whizzing.

Parmesan Baked Tomatoes

Preparation time: 20 minutes
Cooking time: 30 minutes

SERVES 4

60 g butter

1 red onion, cut into 1 cm wedges

450 g tomatoes, peeled (see page 22)

1 teaspoon finely chopped fresh thyme

1 × 142 ml pot of double cream

85 g Parmesan cheese, freshly grated

2 tablespoons dry white breadcrumbs

salt and freshly ground black pepper

To prepare ahead: Assemble the dish, refrigerate and bake when required.

1 Preheat the oven to 180°C|350°F|gas mark 4.

2 Melt the butter in a frying pan, add the onion wedges and fry over a low heat until well softened.

3 Cut the tomatoes horizontally into slices 1 cm thick.

4 Place the tomato slices with the onions in a flat, shallow dish, so that they are no more than 3–4 slices deep.

5 Stir the thyme into the cream with half the Parmesan cheese and season well with salt and pepper. Pour over the tomatoes and sprinkle with the remaining Parmesan mixed with the breadcrumbs.

6 Bake for 25–30 minutes or until the tomatoes have softened but not turned to pulp and the top has browned. If the top has not browned sufficiently, place under a hot grill for a few minutes before serving.

Indian-style Green Beans

Preparation time: 5 minutes
Cooking time: 10 minutes

SERVES 4

250 g green beans, trimmed
2 tablespoons olive oil
1 teaspoon mustard seeds
½ teaspoon cayenne pepper

½ teaspoon ground cumin
½ teaspoon salt

To garnish
1 tablespoon chopped fresh coriander

To prepare ahead: Make the spiced oil in advance, then toss with the hot beans to serve.

1 Cook the beans in boiling salted water for about 5 minutes or until just tender.
2 Meanwhile, heat the oil in a small saucepan and add the mustard seeds. When they begin to pop, add the spices and salt. Stir well and remove from the heat.
3 Drain the beans. Toss in the spiced oil and serve sprinkled with the coriander.

Steamed Bok Choi with Soy and Ginger

Preparation time: 5 minutes
Cooking time: 5 minutes

SERVES 4

2 tablespoons oil
2 cloves of garlic, crushed
1 × 2.5 cm piece of fresh root ginger, peeled and grated

6 tablespoons light soy sauce
4 heads of bok choi, cut in half

1 Heat the oil in a small pan, add the garlic and fry over a low heat until beginning to turn a golden brown.
2 Add the ginger and cook for a further 30 seconds.
3 Add the soy sauce and bring to the boil, then remove from the heat.
4 Meanwhile, steam the bok choi for 1–2 minutes (see page 21). Arrange on a warmed serving dish and pour over the soy sauce mixture. Serve immediately.

Steamed Cucumber with Star Anise

Preparation time: 2 minutes
Infusing time: 10–30 minutes
Cooking time: 2 minutes

SERVES 4

2 large cucumbers

2 star anise

½ tablespoon sesame oil

1 tablespoon light soy sauce

½ tablespoon clear honey

1 tablespoon rice wine vinegar

1 Peel the cucumbers and remove the seeds. Cut into slices 1 cm thick on a slight diagonal.

2 Put all the remaining ingredients into a small pan and bring to simmering point, then turn off the heat. Leave for up to 30 minutes.

3 Using a steamer, steam the cucumber for 2 minutes (see page 21), toss it in the dressing and serve immediately.

Stir-fried Vegetables

Preparation time: 15 minutes
Cooking time: 5 minutes

SERVES 4–6

2 tablespoons oil

1 × 2.5 cm piece of fresh root ginger, peeled and finely grated

1 clove of garlic, crushed

100 g baby sweetcorn, cut in half lengthways

100 g mangetout, topped and tailed

3 sticks of celery, cut into fine strips

2 carrots, peeled and cut into strips

1 red pepper, cut into strips

3 spring onions, finely sliced

80 g Chinese leaves, finely shredded

2 tablespoons light soy sauce

2 teaspoons sesame oil

1 Heat the oil in a heavy frying pan or wok. Add the ginger and garlic and fry over a low heat for 1 minute.

2 Add the baby sweetcorn, mangetout, celery and carrots. Stir-fry for 2 minutes.

3 Add the red pepper, spring onions and Chinese leaves. Stir-fry until the Chinese leaves begin to wilt. Add the soy sauce and sesame oil, stir and serve immediately.

NOTE: The ingredients can be varied according to availability and preference. Canned water chestnuts or bamboo shoots and beansprouts make very good additions.

Stir-fry of Green Vegetables

Preparation time: 10 minutes
Cooking time: 5 minutes

SERVES 4

1 teaspoon sesame oil
1 teaspoon vegetable oil
2 cloves of garlic, crushed
2 teaspoons peeled and grated fresh root ginger
140 g green beans

4 small bok choi, halved lengthways
120 g sugarsnap peas, topped and tailed
120 g asparagus, woody ends removed
2 tablespoons hoisin sauce
2 tablespoons Chinese cooking wine or sherry

1 Heat a frying pan or wok over a high heat. Add the oils, garlic and ginger and cook for 30 seconds.

2 Add all the vegetables and cook for 3–4 minutes or until just tender.

3 Add the hoisin sauce and Chinese wine or sherry and cook for 1 further minute. Serve immediately.

Wild Rice Salad

Preparation time: 15 minutes
Cooking time: 15 minutes

SERVES 6

110 g mixed wild and long-grain rice
2 spring onions, finely sliced on the diagonal
1 red pepper, grilled, peeled, deseeded and chopped (see page 19)
1 yellow pepper, grilled, peeled, deseeded and chopped (see page 19)
¼ cucumber, deseeded and finely chopped

30 g sunflower seeds
1 small bunch of coriander, roughly chopped

For the dressing
55 g sunblush tomatoes in oil
juice of 1 lime
salt and freshly ground black pepper

1 Cook the rice according to the manufacturer's instructions. Rinse in boiling water and leave to drain well.

2 Remove the tomatoes from the oil and cut into strips. Reserve the oil.

3 Whisk the lime juice together with enough of the tomato oil to make a dressing (about 4 tablespoons). Season with salt and pepper.

4 Stir all the ingredients together with the rice and toss the salad in the dressing.

NOTE: Using peeled peppers from the deli counter saves time and if they come in oil it can also be used in the dressing.

Simmered Miso Squash

Preparation time: 15 minutes
Cooking time: 25 minutes

SERVES 4

1 large butternut squash

2 tablespoons oil

1 large onion, finely sliced

1 × 2 cm piece of fresh root ginger, peeled and finely grated

2 tablespoons miso soup paste

2 teaspoons clear honey

300 ml water

200 g bok choi, finely sliced

To prepare ahead: Cook the squash but only add the bok choi when ready to serve.

1 Peel and deseed the squash. Cut into large chunks.

2 Heat the oil in a saucepan, add the onion and fry over a low heat until soft, then increase the heat and fry until it begins to brown.

3 Add the squash and ginger and cook for 2 minutes

4 Add all the remaining ingredients except the bok choi. Cover and simmer until just cooked through (about 10 minutes).

5 Taste the liquid and if it tastes too weak, remove the vegetables from the pan and reduce the liquid by boiling rapidly. Add the bok choi and cook until just beginning to soften (1–2 minutes).

NOTE: Try to use authentic Japanese miso paste.

Thai-style Rice Salad

Preparation time: 10 minutes

SERVES 4

450 g cooked jasmine rice

1 bunch of coriander, coarsely chopped

1 bunch of mint leaves, finely chopped

1 bunch of spring onions, sliced on the diagonal

1 red chilli, finely chopped

For the dressing

grated zest of 1 lime

3 tablespoons fresh lime juice

2 tablespoons nam pla (Thai fish sauce)

1 tablespoon caster sugar

1 Mix together the dressing ingredients.

2 Stir the rice, herbs, spring onions and chilli together. Pour over the dressing and toss well.

NOTE: 40 g uncooked rice generally gives 100 g cooked rice.

VARIATIONS: Cooked shredded chicken, cooked prawns or sliced rare beef can be added to this to make it a more substantial salad. Glass noodles can be used in place of the rice.

Avocado Couscous Salad

Preparation time: 10 minutes
Cooking time: 5 minutes

SERVES 4

200 g couscous

1 large beef tomato

1 large avocado, peeled, stoned and finely chopped

1 red chilli, deseeded and finely chopped

grated zest and juice of 1 lime

2 tablespoons roughly chopped coriander

2 tablespoons extra virgin olive oil

salt and freshly ground black pepper

To prepare ahead: This salad can be made up to 24 hours in advance if the avocado is omitted. Store in the refrigerator and add the avocado just before serving.

1 Put the couscous into a bowl. Pour over boiling water or stock to cover and leave to stand for 3 minutes, or cook according to the manufacturer's instructions.

2 Meanwhile, chop the tomato finely, reserving any juice.

3 Fork the couscous through, add the chopped tomato and juice, avocado, chilli, lime zest and juice and the coriander. Add the oil and season to taste with salt and pepper.

Couscous Salad with Chickpeas, Almonds, Apricots and Coriander

Preparation time: 5 minutes
Infusing time: 10 minutes
Cooking time: 10 minutes

SERVES 4

chicken stock
1 teaspoon saffron strands (optional)
110 g couscous
1 × 400 g can of chickpeas
3 tablespoons olive oil

2 tablespoons flaked almonds, toasted (see page 17)
2 tablespoons ready-to-eat dried apricots, chopped
2 tablespoons chopped fresh coriander
salt and freshly ground black pepper

1 Heat the stock and add the saffron, if using. Remove from the heat and allow to stand for 10 minutes to infuse.
2 Pour the stock over the couscous. Cover and leave to stand according to the manufacturer's instructions. Drain and rinse the chickpeas and add to the couscous.
3 Fork through the remaining ingredients and season to taste with salt and pepper.

Fruit Couscous

Preparation time: 5 minutes
Cooking time: 10 minutes

SERVES 6

250 g couscous
chicken stock
80 g sultanas
80 g pitted dates, chopped

60 g ready-to-eat dried apricots, chopped
50 g walnuts, chopped
4 tablespoons chopped fresh coriander
salt and freshly ground black pepper

1 Cook the couscous according to the manufacturer's instructions, using stock instead of water.
2 When the couscous is ready, mix in all the other ingredients and season to taste with salt and pepper.

Herb Couscous

Preparation time: 5 minutes
Cooking time: 15 minutes

SERVES 4

2 tablespoons olive oil

1 red onion, sliced

30 g pinenuts

1 bunch of spring onions, finely sliced

1 clove of garlic, crushed

400 ml vegetable stock or water

½ glass of dry white wine

250 g couscous

1 small bunch of fresh parsley or mixed herbs, chopped

1 tablespoon balsamic vinegar

salt and freshly ground black pepper

1 Heat the oil in a saucepan, add the onion and fry over a low heat until softened. Add the pinenuts and fry until they begin to colour. Add the spring onions and garlic and cook for a further 30 seconds.

2 Add the stock or water and the wine. Bring to the boil, then simmer for 2 minutes.

3 Stir in the couscous and turn off the heat. Cover the saucepan with a lid and leave to stand for 10 minutes. Add the herbs and vinegar to the couscous, fork through and season with salt and pepper.

NOTE: Check the liquid quantity with the packet instructions: different brands of couscous require varying amounts of liquid.

Orange, Date and Carrot Couscous

Preparation time: 10 minutes
Cooking time: 10 minutes
Cooling time: 10 minutes

SERVES 6

300 ml well-flavoured chicken or vegetable stock

½ glass of dry white wine

170 g couscous

3 oranges

2 medium carrots

100 g fresh mejool dates

1 tablespoon lemon juice

2 tablespoons olive oil

1 teaspoon caster sugar

2 tablespoons chopped flat-leaf parsley

salt and freshly ground black pepper

1 Bring the stock and wine to the boil in a heavy saucepan. Stir in the couscous, turn off the heat, cover with a lid and leave to stand for 10 minutes or until all the liquid has been absorbed. Spread the couscous out on a tray to cool quickly, forking through to make sure the grains are fluffy and do not stick together.

2 Peel the oranges, making sure that all the pith is removed. Either slice the oranges crossways into slices, which should then be cut into quarters, or carefully remove the orange segments from the membrane (see page 11). Save any juice.

3 Peel and grate the carrots. Cut the dates into quarters and remove the stones.

4 Mix any reserved orange juice with the lemon juice, oil and sugar.

5 Mix together the couscous, oranges, carrots, dates and parsley. Toss in the dressing and season well with salt and pepper.

Lemon Buttered Couscous

SERVES 6–8

500 g couscous

grated zest and juice of 1 lemon

450 ml hot chicken stock or water

50 g butter

a pinch of cayenne pepper

salt

1 In a large bowl, stir the lemon zest into the couscous.

2 Add the lemon juice to the stock or water and stir into the couscous.

3 Leave to soak for about 15 minutes, then fluff the couscous up with a fork. Chop the butter into small dice and stir it into the couscous with the seasoning.

NOTES: The couscous will still be warm, but if you want it hotter you can cook it for 20 seconds in the microwave. Check the liquid quantity with the manufacturer's instructions; different brands of couscous require varying amounts of liquid.

Quick Ratatouille Couscous

Preparation time: 2 minutes

Cooking time: 15 minutes

SERVES 4–6

150 ml well-flavoured chicken stock

½ glass of dry white wine

1 × 400 g can of ratatouille

140 g couscous

a handful of fresh basil leaves

salt and freshly ground black pepper

a pinch of sugar

1 Bring the stock and wine to the boil in a heavy saucepan.

2 Using a pair of kitchen scissors, chop any large pieces of vegetable in the ratatouille into smaller pieces. Tip into the pan and bring to the boil.

3 Stir in the couscous, cover with a lid and turn the heat off. Leave for 10 minutes.

4 Fluff the couscous up with a fork, stir through the basil and season well with salt and pepper and a pinch of sugar.

NOTE: Check the liquid quantity with the manufacturer's instructions; different brands of couscous require varying amounts of liquid.

Wild Mushroom Couscous

Preparation time: 15 minutes
Cooking time: 15 minutes

SERVES 4–6

570 ml boiling vegetable stock or water

20 g dried porcini mushrooms

10 g dried shiitake mushrooms

olive oil, for frying

1 red onion, sliced

250 g oyster mushrooms, torn into pieces

250 g baby spinach leaves, washed

4 spring onions, finely sliced on the diagonal

110 g asparagus tips or fine asparagus spears

1 glass of dry white wine

140 g couscous

4 tablespoons chopped flat-leaf parsley

salt and freshly ground black pepper

To prepare ahead: Make in advance to the end of stage 4. When ready to serve, reheat the broth before adding the couscous.

1 Pour the boiling stock or water over the dried mushrooms. Allow to stand until the mushrooms are soft and rehydrated (about 15 minutes).

2 Meanwhile, heat 2 tablespoons of the oil in a heavy pan, add the onion and fry over a low heat until soft. Add the oyster mushrooms to the pan and stir well. Cover with a lid and cook until the mushrooms release liquid. Remove the lid and continue to cook until the onion and mushrooms are golden brown.

3 Add the spinach to the onion and mushroom mixture along with the spring onions and asparagus. Stir well.

4 Add the dried mushrooms, their strained soaking liquid and the wine to the mushroom mixture. Bring to the boil.

5 Stir in the couscous, turn off the heat and cover with a lid. Leave until the couscous is soft (about 10 minutes). Fluff up with a fork and season to taste with salt and pepper. Stir in half the parsley.

6 Sprinkle with the remaining parsley and serve immediately.

Mashed Potatoes

Mashed potatoes are the perfect accompaniment to dishes with delicious sauces. Try to use floury potatoes. Adding hot rather than cold milk to the potatoes prevents a gluey texture. In the basic recipe, the milk is heated without needing to use another pan. It is not possible to give a definite measurement for the milk, as different varieties of potatoes require different quantities, and personal preference as to the consistency varies. For a richer result, add double cream in place of some of the milk. Mashed potato can also be made in advance and then reheated, but be careful not to stir too vigorously when reheating as this may lead to a gluey texture. For lump-free mash a ricer is recommended but a traditional masher, sieve, or mouli can also be used. Mash can easily be reheated, covered, in the microwave, or in a conventional oven.

Basic Recipe

SERVES 4

900 g floury potatoes, peeled and cut into large even
    pieces
150–200 ml milk

60 g butter
a little freshly grated nutmeg
salt and freshly ground black pepper

1 Place the potatoes in a saucepan and add enough cold water just to cover them. Salt the water well and bring to the boil. Reduce the heat slightly and simmer for about 15 minutes, until the potatoes are tender.
2 Drain the potatoes well and mash them with a potato masher, or push through a potato ricer, mouli or sieve into the pan. Heat carefully, stirring, to allow the potato to steam-dry a little.
3 Push the potato to one side of the pan. Set the exposed part of the pan over the direct heat and pour in most of the milk. Add the butter and salt, pepper and nutmeg to taste to the milk. Tilt the pan to allow the milk to boil and the butter to melt.
4 When the milk is boiling, or near it, beat it into the potato. Check the seasoning and add a little more milk if necessary.

Variations

Mustard Mash

Stir 1 tablespoon mustard into the completed mash. Wholegrain mustard works very well, but English mustard, Dijon or a combination can also be delicious. Taste the mash and add more mustard if you prefer a stronger flavour.

Horseradish Mash

Add grated fresh horseradish to the milk when making the basic mash, or add a tablespoon or so of horseradish sauce to the finished mashed potatoes. Fresh horseradish can vary in strength, so start with a small amount and taste before adding more.

Wasabi Mash

Wasabi is a Japanese alternative to horseradish, and has a similarly strong, peppery flavour. Start by stirring 2 teaspoons into the finished mash before tasting and adding more if desired. Some chopped fresh coriander added at the end of the cooking also works well with the wasabi.

Lemon and Olive Oil Mash

Replace the butter with 4 tablespoons olive oil. Add the finely grated zest of a lemon to the finished mash. Finely chopped fresh rosemary is also delicious with lemon and olive oil mash.

Red Pepper and Garlic Mash

Use a jar of red pepper slices preserved in oil, or grill, skin and slice red peppers. If using a jar, replace the butter with 4 tablespoons of the oil from the jar; if not, use a basic olive oil instead. Once the potato is mashed, push to one side of the pan (see stage 3 of the basic recipe). Add the oil to the exposed area of the pan and add a crushed clove of garlic. Cook for 2 minutes, or until the garlic just starts to colour, taking care not to allow the potato to burn on the bottom of the pan. Add the milk to the garlic oil and follow the basic recipe. Stir in the peppers at the end, just sufficiently to heat through. Some torn fresh basil leaves or chopped flat-leaf parsley are good additions.

Cheese and Chive Mash

Stir 30–60 g grated hard cheese with a strong flavour, such as mature Cheddar, Gruyère, Parmesan or Pecorino, into the hot mashed potato, along with 2 tablespoons finely chopped fresh chives or other soft herbs.

Caramelized Onion and Thyme Mash

While the potatoes are cooking, melt the 60 g butter in a small frying pan, add a finely sliced large onion and cook over a low heat until soft, then increase the heat slightly and cook with 2 teaspoons soft light brown sugar until golden brown. Remove from the heat and add ½ tablespoon finely chopped fresh thyme. Proceed with the basic recipe (do not add more butter), then stir in the onion and thyme before serving.

Red Onion and Pancetta Mash

Finely slice a red onion and cut 100 g pancetta into small cubes, removing the rind (alternatively, use streaky bacon cut into small strips or pieces). While the potatoes are cooking, heat 4 tablespoons olive oil in a small frying pan. Cook the red onion and pancetta until the onion is soft. Then increase the heat and cook until the onion and pancetta are brown. Proceed with the basic recipe (omitting the butter), and stir in the red onion and pancetta before serving, with a tablespoon or so of finely chopped fresh parsley if liked. If preferred, cook the bacon and use raw, sliced spring onions in place of the cooked red onion.

Dill and Wholegrain Mustard Mash

Add 1 tablespoon chopped fresh dill and 1 tablespoon wholegrain mustard to the finished mashed potatoes. Taste, then add more mustard if required. Some finely grated lemon or lime zest also works well, particularly when being served with fish.

Herb Mash

Soft herbs such as basil, parsley, or chervil can be stirred into the basic mash; about a tablespoon will be enough to flavour this quantity. Either a single herb flavour or a mixture of herbs works well.

Coarse herbs or herbs with a very strong flavour such as rosemary, thyme, oregano or marjoram can be chopped extremely finely and added as above, or they can be used to make an infused olive oil which gives a more subtle flavour to the finished mash. These oils can also be used for salad dressings. Place the herb of your choice in a small saucepan and cover with olive oil (it need not be an extra virgin oil). Slices of garlic can also be added at this stage. Heat the pan gently, and when it is hot, remove from the heat and leave overnight, or for a few hours at least, to infuse. Garlic should never be left to infuse for longer than 24 hours. Strain out the herbs and the garlic, if using, and store in an airtight jar or bottle. 4 tablespoons of the herb oil can then be used in place of the butter in the basic recipe.

Pesto Mash

This is nicest made with a homemade pesto (see page 512) which can then be used in a variety of recipes, and pesto can even be made using a mixture of herbs, which can be a good way of using up leftover herbs. However, a good-quality bought pesto, either classic green or red, will also give a delicious result. Stir a tablespoon in to the finished mash, then taste and add more if required.

Mashed Potatoes with Indian Spices

While the potatoes are cooking, heat 4 tablespoons sunflower oil in a small saucepan. Add 2 teaspoons mustard seeds and cook, stirring, over a low heat until they begin to start popping. Add 1 teaspoon ground turmeric, ½ teaspoon ground cumin, ½ teaspoon ground cinnamon and a crushed clove of garlic. Stir for 1 minute, then remove from the heat. Omit the butter from the basic recipe and stir the spice mixture into the finished mash. The mixture of spices can be varied and more can be used for a stronger flavour.

Mash to Accompany Chicken or Fish

Some or all of the milk quantity can be replaced with a strong-flavoured chicken or fish stock, or milk in which fish has been poached, and some appropriate chopped herbs, such as parsley or chervil, can also be added.

Saffron Mash

While the potatoes are cooking, heat a small saucepan and add a pinch of saffron. Cook for 1 minute, moving the strands around to prevent them from burning, then add the milk and bring to the boil. Remove from the heat and allow to stand until the potatoes are cooked. Proceed with the basic recipe. Be careful not to add too big a pinch of saffron as it can taste rather overpowering and slightly medicinal. The flavour should be subtle.

Truffle Mash

Stir 1–2 tablespoons truffle oil into the finished mash, depending on the strength of the oil. More can then be drizzled over the top of the mash when it is served. Some roughly chopped fresh flat-leaf parsley can also be added.

Mash with Spinach, Rocket or Watercress

Spinach, rocket and watercress all wilt down quickly. Use a few handfuls and remove any coarse stalks. Chop roughly and wash thoroughly. Stir into the mash – the heat will quickly wilt the leaves.

Potato and Pea Mash

When the potatoes are just cooked, add 200 g frozen peas to the boiling water and simmer for 2 minutes, then continue with the basic recipe, mashing well to blend the peas with the potatoes. If you prefer to keep the peas whole, heat the milk in a separate pan, add the peas to cook them, then stir into the mashed potato.

Root Vegetable Mash

Substitute half of the potato quantity with another root vegetable such as celeriac, parsnip or carrot. The potato gives a good smooth texture (although it can be omitted entirely), but other vegetables, including butternut squash and pumpkin, can be used to provide delicious flavours. It is a good idea to cook the root vegetables in separate pans as they will take different times to cook. They can then be mashed together. Depending on the type of vegetable used, the mash may need to be of a coarser texture as not all vegetables will mash as finely as potato.

Parsnip and Crème Fraîche Purée

Preparation time: 10 minutes
Cooking time: 20 minutes

SERVES 4

450 g floury potatoes, peeled and cut into quarters
450 g parsnips, peeled, cored and cut into chunks
1–2 cloves of garlic, crushed

200 g crème fraîche
salt and freshly ground black pepper

To prepare ahead: Make in advance and reheat in a covered dish in the oven or in the microwave.

1 Boil the potatoes in salted water for 5 minutes. Add the parsnips and simmer until tender (a table knife should easily push through them).
2 Meanwhile, in a separate saucepan, mix the garlic with the crème fraîche and bring to the boil. Simmer gently for 5 minutes until reduced by half. Leave to infuse.
3 When the parsnips and potatoes are cooked, drain very well and push them through a sieve or ricer. Return them to the dry saucepan. Heat carefully, stirring, to allow the potatoes and parsnips to steam-dry.
4 Pour the crème fraîche into the parsnip and potato pan and season with salt and pepper. Beat the purée and check the seasoning before serving.

Roast Potatoes

Preparation time: 10 minutes
Cooking time: 1¼ hours

SERVES 4

900 g floury potatoes

1 tablespoon plain flour

5 tablespoons dripping or oil

salt and freshly ground black pepper

1 Preheat the oven to 200°C|400°F|gas mark 6.
2 Wash and peel the potatoes and cut them into 5 cm pieces if they are large.
3 Bring the potatoes to the boil in salted water, then simmer for 5 minutes. Drain well, return to the pan, sprinkle on the flour and shake the potatoes to roughen the surfaces.
4 Melt the dripping or oil in a roasting pan, in the oven or on the hob if the base of the pan is thick enough. When the fat is hot, add the potatoes, turning them so that they are coated all over. Season with salt and pepper.
5 Roast, basting occasionally, and turning the potatoes over halfway through cooking. It should take about 1 hour for the potatoes to be brown and crisp all over.

Sauté Potatoes

Preparation time: 10 minutes
Cooking time: 1 hour

SERVES 4

700 g even-sized floury potatoes

2 tablespoons oil

50 g butter

1 sprig of fresh rosemary

1 tablespoon chopped fresh parsley or rosemary

salt and freshly ground black pepper

1 Peel the potatoes and place them in a saucepan. Cover with cold water and add some salt. Bring to the boil, then simmer until the potatoes are tender. This will take about 15 minutes. Drain well. Break into 2.5 cm irregular chunks.
2 Heat the oil in a large sauté or frying pan, add the butter and the rosemary and wait until the foam subsides. Add all the potatoes at once.
3 Season with salt and pepper and shake the potatoes gently over the heat while they fry slowly until pale brown. Turn them only occasionally or they will break up too much. They should in any case be fairly dry and crumbly. This should take 20–40 minutes.
4 When the potatoes are brown and crisp, drain on kitchen paper, add the herbs and tip into a warmed serving dish.

Special Roast Potatoes

Preparation time: 10 minutes
Cooking time: 1 hour 45 minutes

SERVES 4

900 g floury potatoes
175 g unsalted butter

1 tablespoon finely chopped fresh herbs
salt

To prepare ahead: The potatoes can be prepared to the end of stage 5 and left for up to 4 hours before cooking.

1 Preheat the oven to 200°C|400°F|gas mark 6.
2 Wash and peel the potatoes and cut them into 3 cm chunks.
3 Bring the potatoes to the boil in a saucepan of salted water. Simmer for about 10–15 minutes, or until just cooked. Test by inserting a table knife into a potato. It should go right through the centre with no resistance.
4 Drain the potatoes very well and gently score them all over with a fork.
5 Melt the butter in a large roasting pan and turn the potatoes in the butter. Leave them to stand for 30 minutes, turning occasionally, until all the butter has been absorbed.
6 Roast in the oven, basting occasionally and turning the potatoes halfway through the cooking time. Cook for about 1 hour, or until golden brown all over, then drain off the excess butter and sprinkle with the herbs and salt.

Irish Champ

Preparation time: 10 minutes
Cooking time: 20 minutes

SERVES 4

900 g potatoes, peeled and cut into large chunks
60 g butter
225 g spring onions, sliced on the diagonal

200 ml milk
salt and freshly ground black pepper

To prepare ahead: Make the complete dish in advance, then refrigerate.

1 Boil the potatoes in salted water for about 15 minutes, until tender.
2 Meanwhile, melt the butter in a separate pan, add the spring onions and cook for 1 minute until they have slightly softened but still have some crunch. Add the milk to the pan and allow to heat through.
3 Drain the potatoes thoroughly and allow to steam-dry for a few minutes.
4 Mash the potatoes or push them through a sieve or ricer. Return them to the dry saucepan.
5 Beat the milk, butter and spring onions into the potato. Season to taste with salt and pepper.

Individual Rösti Potatoes

Preparation time: 15 minutes
Cooking time: 20 minutes

SERVES 4

2 tablespoons oil

1 Spanish onion, finely chopped

700 g large waxy potatoes, peeled

½ teaspoon very finely chopped fresh thyme or
   rosemary

30 g butter, melted

salt and freshly ground black pepper

To prepare ahead: Make the complete dish in advance, then refrigerate or freeze. Defrost thoroughly before reheating. Reheat at 200°C|400°F|gas mark 6 until crisp and heated through (about 10–15 minutes).

1 Heat the oil in a frying pan, add the onion and sweat until soft but not coloured.
2 Preheat the oven to 200°C|400°F|gas mark 6.
3 Grate the potatoes coarsely. Season with salt and leave to stand for 20 minutes.
4 Place the grated potatoes in a sieve and press out any liquid. Transfer to a bowl, stir in the onion and season with pepper, then stir in the chopped herbs.
5 Brush 2 baking sheets with some of the melted butter. Divide the mixture into 12 equal portions and press into rounds on the baking sheets, spacing them out evenly and trying to keep the potatoes as compact as possible. Brush with the remaining butter.
6 Bake in the oven for about 20 minutes, or until golden brown.

Bubble and Squeak Cakes

This is a classic leftover dish, using leftover mashed potatoes and onion and green vegetables. The title refers to the sound of the cakes frying in the pan. It can also be made as one large cake, in which case it may be easiest to turn it on to a plate and slide it back into the pan when cooking the second side.

Preparation time: 10 minutes
Cooking time: 20 minutes (using leftover mashed potatoes and cooked vegetables)

SERVES 4

450 g potatoes, mashed

450 g cooked green vegetables, such as cabbage,
   leeks or Brussels sprouts

1 egg, beaten

30 g butter

2 tablespoons oil

salt and freshly ground black pepper

To prepare ahead: Prepare the potato mixture to the end of stage 2, then refrigerate or freeze. Defrost thoroughly before reheating.

1 Mix the potatoes with the other vegetables. Season to taste with salt and pepper. Bind with the beaten egg, but the mixture must be quite firm so do not add too much.

2 Divide the mixture into 4 large or 8 small patties and shape with floured hands.

3 Melt the butter and oil in a heavy frying pan.

4 Fry the bubble and squeak cakes, pressing them down flat on the hot pan. Cook slowly to heat through and allow a crust to form on the bottom side.

5 Turn the cakes over to brown the other side. Keep warm in a low oven if it is necessary to cook a second batch.

6 Sprinkle with a little salt before serving.

Baked New Potatoes en Papillote

Preparation time: 5 minutes
Cooking time: 50 minutes

SERVES 4

700 g new potatoes
2 tablespoons olive oil
4 sprigs of fresh rosemary
4 cloves of garlic, unpeeled

1 teaspoon sea salt crystals
freshly ground black pepper
4 greaseproof paper sandwich bags

1 Preheat the oven to 200°C|400°F|gas mark 6.

2 Place the potatoes in a large bowl with the oil, rosemary, garlic and salt. Turn them lightly in the oil and season with pepper.

3 Divide the potatoes between the 4 bags and ensure each bag is sealed tightly so that the steam does not escape.

4 Bake in the oven for about 50 minutes, or until tender. When the bag browns, the potatoes will be cooked.

5 Serve the potatoes in the bags.

NOTE: Cooking bags are available from supermarkets. Alternatively, use a large sheet of greaseproof paper to make a bag, making sure all the edges are well sealed and allowing a little room for the circulation of steam. Each diner should be served their potatoes in the bag, so when they split the bag they smell the wonderful aroma that bursts out.

The potatoes can also be roasted in a large roasing tin, so that they are in a shallow layer. Turn them occasionally while cooking.

VARIATIONS: Add wedges of red onion to the potatoes in the greased bags. Add cubed pancetta at the beginning of the cooking time or wedges of onions half way through cooking time to the potatoes in the roasting tin.

Chilli Potato Wedges with Spicy Salsa

Preparation time: 10 minutes
Cooking time: 30 minutes

SERVES 2

2 tablespoons oil

2 large pinches of hot chilli powder

3 large baking potatoes

salt

For the salsa

2 spring onions, finely chopped

2 ripe plum tomatoes, finely chopped

2 tablespoons finely chopped fresh coriander

½ red chilli, finely chopped

a squeeze of lemon

To serve

soured cream

To prepare ahead: Prepare to the end of stage 5 and cook when required.

1 Preheat the oven to 200°C|400°F|gas mark 6.
2 Mix together all the salsa ingredients and set aside to allow the flavours to amalgamate.
3 Mix the oil and chilli powder in a large bowl.
4 Wash and dry the potatoes and cut them in half lengthways. Cut each half into approximately 3 wedges, depending on their size.
5 Add the potatoes to the oil and chilli powder and mix well.
6 Tip on to a baking tray with the skin side down and season with salt. Bake in the oven for 30–35 minutes, or until crisp and golden.
7 Serve the potatoes with the salsa and soured cream, either in separate dishes, spooned on to the plate or drizzled over the potato wedges.

NOTES: Grated Parmesan cheese can be sprinkled over the wedges for the last 5 minutes of cooking. The wedges are also very good made with peeled sweet potato or butternut squash and will take less time to cook.

Boulangère Potatoes

Preparation time: 10 minutes
Cooking time: 1¾ hours

SERVES 4

50 g butter

1 medium onion, sliced

700 g medium floury potatoes

chicken or vegetable stock

salt and freshly ground black pepper

To prepare ahead: Make the complete dish, then refrigerate and reheat thoroughly before serving.

1 Preheat the oven to 190°C|375°F|gas mark 5.
2 Melt the butter in a frying pan, add the onion and sweat over a low heat until soft. Then increase the heat and allow the onion to cook until golden brown, stirring regularly.
3 Transfer the onion to a roasting pan.
4 Slice the potatoes into 5 mm slices crossways, keeping the slices together. Still in their shape, flatten the potatoes slightly so that they fan out.
5 Place the potatoes on top of the onion, season well and pour in enough stock to come about a third of the way up the potatoes. Cover the roasting pan with kitchen foil.
6 Bake in the oven for 30 minutes, then remove the foil and cook for 1 further hour, basting occasionally, or until the stock has been absorbed by the potatoes and they have taken on a golden colour and are tender.

Potato and Apple Boulangère

Preparation time: 10 minutes
Cooking time: 1 hour 20 minutes

SERVES 4

30 g butter
2 medium onions, sliced
3 large potatoes
1 large Bramley apple, peeled and cored

1 tablespoon finely chopped fresh thyme
450 ml chicken stock
salt and freshly ground black pepper

To prepare ahead: Make the complete dish, then refrigerate and reheat thoroughly before serving.

1 Preheat the oven to 190°C|375°F|gas mark 5.
2 Melt the butter in a frying pan, add the onions and sweat over a low heat until soft, then increase the heat and cook until golden brown.
3 Slice the potatoes and apple finely, using a food processor if possible to save time. Mix the slices together.
4 Stir the onions and thyme into the potato and apple slices. Season with salt and pepper. Press into a casserole dish.
5 Pour over the stock. Cover with kitchen foil and bake in the oven for 45 minutes, then remove the foil and cook for a further 30 minutes, or until the potatoes are tender and beginning to brown on the top.
6 If the potatoes are cooked but not browning, heat the grill to the highest setting and grill until brown.

Dauphinoise Potatoes

Preparation time: 10 minutes
Cooking time: 1–1¼ hours

SERVES 4–6

20 g butter

1 onion, finely sliced

1 clove of garlic, crushed (optional)

450 ml mixed single and double cream, or just
   double cream for a very rich result

300 ml milk

900 g floury potatoes, peeled and finely sliced

salt and freshly ground black pepper

1 Preheat the oven to 170°C│325°F│gas mark 3.

2 Melt the butter in a frying pan, add the onions and garlic and sweat over a low heat until soft but not brown. Add the cream and milk to the pan.

3 Heat the cream and milk to scalding point, then season well with salt and pepper. Add the potatoes and simmer for 10–15 minutes, or until they begin to soften. Turn into a lightly buttered dish.

4 Bake in the oven for 1 hour, or until tender and golden brown on top.

Parsnip and Potato Dauphinoise

Preparation time: 10 minutes
Cooking time: 1–1½ hours

SERVES 4–6

1 tablespoon oil

1 medium onion, sliced

1 clove of garlic

1 teaspoon plain flour

350 g parsnips, peeled and thinly sliced

550 g floury potatoes, peeled and finely sliced

1 × 568 ml pot of double cream

salt and freshly ground black pepper

1 Preheat the oven to 170°C│325°F│gas mark 3.

2 Heat the oil in a large saucepan. Add the onion and sweat over a low heat until soft but not coloured, then add the garlic and cook for a further 45 seconds, taking care the garlic does not burn. Add the flour and cook for 1 minute, stirring.

3 Add the parsnips, potatoes and cream. Bring to the boil and season, then simmer for 5 minutes.

4 Pour the potato, parsnip and cream mixture into a large ovenproof dish.

5 Cook in the oven for 1–1½ hours, or until tender.

Artichoke Dauphinoise

Preparation time: 20 minutes
Cooking time: 40–60 minutes

SERVES 6–8

450 g Jerusalem artichokes
2 large baking potatoes
1 × 568 ml pot of double cream
¼ teaspoon freshly grated nutmeg

1 clove of garlic
2 tablespoons freshly grated Parmesan cheese
salt and freshly ground black pepper

1 Preheat the oven to 180°C│350°F│gas mark 4.
2 Peel and finely slice the artichokes and potatoes, using a food processor if possible to save time. (The skins can be left on and the artichokes and potatoes just scrubbed well if you prefer.)
3 Put the sliced artichokes into a saucepan with the cream. Bring to the boil, add the potatoes, season with nutmeg, salt and pepper and simmer for 5 minutes.
4 Cut the clove of garlic in half and rub it around an ovenproof serving dish. Tip in the artichoke and potato mixture and sprinkle with the Parmesan.
5 Bake in the oven for 40–60 minutes, or until the vegetables are soft and the top is golden brown.

NOTE: Mix the Parmesan with fresh white breadcrumbs and sprinkle on the top for a delicious gratin.

Butterbean Mash

Cooking time: 10–15 minutes

SERVES 4

150 ml water
2 cloves of garlic, peeled
1 × 400 g can of butterbeans, drained and rinsed

grated zest and juice of ½ lemon
½ tablespoon chopped fresh thyme
salt and freshly ground black pepper

1 Put the water and garlic into a saucepan, bring to the boil and add the butterbeans. Simmer until the beans are falling apart and the garlic is soft.
2 Whizz in a food processor or mash the mixture and return to the rinsed-out pan. Add the lemon zest and juice and season to taste with salt and pepper. Add the thyme. Add a little extra water if the mash is too dry.

Bean and Parsley Mash

Preparation time: 5 minutes
Cooking time: 10 minutes

SERVES 4

200 ml olive oil

1 onion, chopped

4 cloves of garlic, crushed

2 × 400 g cans of cannellini beans, drained and rinsed

grated zest and juice of 1 lemon

20 g fresh parsley, chopped

salt and freshly ground black pepper

To prepare ahead: Make the dish in advance, omitting the parsley (you might need to add a little water when reheating). Add the parsley before serving.

1 Heat the oil in a frying pan, add the onion and sweat over a low heat until soft but not coloured. Add the garlic and cook for a further 2 minutes.
2 Stir through the beans, lemon zest and juice and mash roughly with the back of a fork. Stir until piping hot.
3 Add the parsley and season to taste with salt and pepper.

Butternut Squash and Goat's Cheese Gratin

Preparation time: 15 minutes
Cooking time: 1 hour

SERVES 4–6

1 medium butternut squash

1 tablespoon extra virgin olive oil

1 teaspoon freshly chopped thyme

1 small jar of tomato and olive pasta sauce

85 g goat's cheese, broken into largeish pieces

2 tablespoons chopped fresh flat-leaf parsley

2 tablespoons pumpkin seeds, roughly chopped

2 tablespoons grated Cheddar cheese

salt and freshly ground black pepper

To prepare ahead: Complete to the end of stage 5, then refrigerate or freeze. If frozen, defrost thoroughly before reheating.

1 Preheat the oven to 200°C|400°F|gas mark 6.
2 Peel the butternut squash, scoop out the seeds and cut the flesh into even cubes.
3 Place in a roasting pan, drizzle over the oil and scatter with the thyme. Season with salt and pepper and roast in the oven for 40 minutes, turning occasionally, until the squash is just cooked and lightly coloured.
4 Mix the squash with the tomato and olive sauce, goat's cheese and parsley and pile into an ovenproof dish.

5 Mix the pumpkin seeds and cheese together and sprinkle over the top.

6 Reheat in the oven until the cheese has melted and is starting to brown. Alternatively, heat the grill to the highest setting and brown the gratin under the grill.

NOTE: This can be served on its own as a supper dish.

Bacon, Celeriac and Blue Cheese Gratin

Preparation time: 10 minutes
Cooking time: 1¼ hours

SERVES 6–8

100 g rindless smoked streaky bacon, cut into strips
1 small onion, finely chopped
1 clove of garlic, crushed
500 g waxy potatoes, peeled and finely sliced
500 g celeriac, peeled and finely sliced
100 g blue cheese, crumbled

1 tablespoon chopped fresh thyme
1 × 142 ml pot of double cream
450 ml milk
50 g fresh brown breadcrumbs
salt and freshly ground black pepper

To prepare ahead: Make the complete dish and refrigerate. Reheat in the oven at 190°C│375°F│gas mark 5 for 20–25 minutes.

1 Preheat the oven to 190°C│375°F│gas mark 5.

2 Gently fry the bacon in a dry frying pan until it just starts to colour and release its fat, then add the onion and fry until they are both golden brown. Add the garlic and cook for a further 30 seconds.

3 In an ovenproof dish, layer up the sliced potatoes and celeriac, scattering the bacon mixture, cheese, thyme, salt and pepper in between the layers – there should be about 4 layers. Reserve some cheese for the top.

4 Mix the cream and milk together and season to taste with salt and pepper (do not oversalt as the bacon and cheese may be salty). Pour over the celeriac and potato.

5 Mix the breadcrumbs with the remaining cheese and scatter over the top. Bake in the oven for 1 hour, or until a knife can be pushed all the way through the vegetables very easily.

NOTE: This dish makes a good supper dish on its own. If you have a food processor, use it to slice the potato and celeriac. Do not soak the potatoes in water when they have been peeled and sliced, as their natural starch holds this dish together.

Puy Lentils with Pancetta

Preparation time: 5 minutes
Cooking time: 20 minutes

SERVES 4

110 g Puy lentils, drained and rinsed
600 ml chicken stock
150 ml dry white wine
1 medium Spanish onion, sliced
1 sprig of fresh thyme

2 cloves of garlic, 1 bruised, 1 crushed
1 tablespoon olive oil
110 g pancetta, cut into small cubes
1 teaspoon chopped fresh thyme
salt and freshly ground black pepper

1 Put the lentils into a saucepan with the stock, wine, half the onion, the thyme and the bruised garlic. Bring to the boil, then simmer for 15–20 minutes, or until the lentils are soft.
2 Meanwhile, heat the oil in a frying pan, add the remaining onion with the pancetta and fry until the onion is soft, then increase the heat and fry until the onion and pancetta are golden brown. Add the crushed garlic and cook for 30 seconds.
3 Drain the lentils and reserve the cooking liquor. Remove and discard the bruised garlic clove, the thyme sprig and the onion. Add the pancetta and fried onion to the cooked lentils.
4 Reduce the lentil cooking liquor to 2–3 tablespoons by boiling rapidly. Stir into the lentils, add the chopped thyme and season to taste with salt and pepper.

Basmati Rice

Soaking time: 15 minutes
Cooking time: 5 minutes

SERVES 4

250 g basmati rice
salt

1 Place the rice in a bowl, cover with cold water and swirl round to wash well. Pour off the water and repeat until the water stays clear.
2 Allow the rice to soak in the water for 15 minutes. This will give a light and fluffy rice and will cut the cooking time.
3 Drain, place the rice in a saucepan and pour in just enough cold water to cover it. Bring to the boil, then reduce the heat and allow the rice to simmer for 5 minutes. The rice should then be perfectly cooked and all the water absorbed.

Thai Jasmine Rice

Cooking time: 10 minutes
Standing time: 5 minutes

SERVES 4

250 g jasmine rice
salt

1 Bring a saucepan of water to the boil. Add some salt and stir in the rice. Bring back to the boil, then reduce the heat slightly.
2 Cook the rice for 10 minutes, then drain and allow to stand for 5 minutes, covered with a lid, before serving.

Fried Rice with Pinenuts

Leftover cooked rice can be used for this recipe.

Preparation time: 2 minutes
Cooking time: 15 minutes

SERVES 4

250 g long-grain rice
4 tablespoons oil
2 spring onions, finely chopped

50 g pinenuts, toasted (see page 17)
salt and freshly ground black pepper

1 Bring a large saucepan of salted water to the boil and tip in the rice. Stir and bring back to the boil, then reduce the heat slightly and cook for 10 minutes, or until the rice is just tender.
2 When cooked, rinse the rice briefly with cold water to remove the excess starch and drain well. While the rice is draining, turn it over occasionally with a fork to allow trapped steam to escape.
3 Heat the oil in a large, heavy frying pan and add the spring onions. Add the rice, which should now be quite dry. Fry, turning all the time to brown evenly. Season to taste with salt and pepper.
4 Stir in the pinenuts before serving.

Brown Rice Pilaf with Sesame Seeds

Preparation time: 5 minutes
Soaking time: 30 minutes
Cooking time: 1 hour

SERVES 4

250 g brown rice

30 g butter

1 small onion, finely chopped

750 ml chicken or vegetable stock

3 tablespoons sesame seeds, toasted (see page 17)

1 tablespoon chopped fresh mixed herbs

paprika

salt and freshly ground black pepper

1 Soak the rice in cold water for 30 minutes, then drain thoroughly.
2 Melt the butter in a saucepan, add the onion and sweat over a low heat until soft but not coloured.
3 Add the rice and fry, stirring, for about 1 minute, until it is heated through.
4 Add the stock, salt and pepper to the pan. Bring to the boil, then cover and cook very slowly for 35–45 minutes, by which time the rice should be tender and the liquid completely absorbed.
5 Add the sesame seeds and herbs to the rice.
6 Serve sprinkled with a little paprika.

Pineapple Rice

250 g basmati or jasmine rice

150 g pineapple, chopped

1 red chilli, deseeded and finely chopped

fresh coriander leaves, roughly chopped

1 Bring a saucepan of water to the boil . Add some salt and stir in the rice. Bring back to the boil, then reduce the heat slightly.
2 Cook the rice for 10 minutes, then drain and allow to stand for 5 minutes.
3 Fork through the other ingredients and serve immediately.

NOTE: This can be made with cold cooked rice as a salad. Use the dressing for the Thai rice salad (page 354).

Egg-fried Rice with Bok Choi

Preparation time: 5 minutes
Cooking time: 10 minutes

SERVES 6

1 tablespoon oil	170 g cooked rice
1 tablespoon sesame oil	3 eggs, beaten
3 spring onions, sliced	2 tablespoons light soy sauce
2 heads of bok choi, chopped, stems and tops kept separate	freshly ground black pepper

1 Heat the oils in a large frying pan or wok over a medium heat. Add the spring onions and the chopped stems of the bok choi. Cook for about 1 minute, or until softening.

2 Add the rice and stir-fry until piping hot all the way through. Add the eggs and continue to stir-fry quickly. Season well with the soy sauce and black pepper. Reduce the heat and add the chopped tops of the bok choi, stir gently and serve immediately.

NOTE: Cooked flaked salmon or cooked prawns can be added with the bok choi to make the fried rice a meal in itself.

This is a good way of using up leftover rice. If you are using rice that has just been cooked (and is therefore still hot), stir-fry the eggs with the vegetables before adding the rice.

Chilli and Coriander Noodles

Preparation time: 15 minutes
Cooking time: 10 minutes

SERVES 4

4 sheets of medium Chinese egg noodles

2 tablespoons chilli oil

1 red pepper, cored, deseeded and diced

juice of 1 lime

110 g chopped fresh coriander

60 g cashew nuts, browned and roughly chopped (see page 17)

salt and freshly ground black pepper

1 Cook the noodles according to the manufacturer's instructions.

2 Heat the oil in a large frying pan, add the pepper and cook until soft.

3 Drain the noodles. Add the noodles, lime juice, coriander and a little salt and pepper to the frying pan. Pile into a warmed serving dish and scatter over the cashew nuts.

NOTE: Use spaghetti instead of noodles and double the remaining ingredients for a supper dish.

Sesame Noodles

Preparation time: 5 minutes
Cooking time: 5 minutes

SERVES 2

2 sheets of egg noodles

3 tablespoons sesame oil

4 spring onions, sliced

1 red chilli, deseeded and diced

1 teaspoon peeled and grated fresh root ginger

1 tablespoon sesame seeds

2 teaspoons lime juice

1 teaspoon dark soy sauce

2 tablespoon chopped fresh coriander

1 Cook the noodles according to the manufacturer's instructions. Drain and refresh in cold water. Toss the noodles in 1 tablespoon of the sesame oil.

2 Heat the remaining sesame oil in a wok or heavy frying pan and add the spring onions, chilli, ginger and sesame seeds. Cook for 1 minute.

3 Add the drained noodles to the pan and stir in the lime juice and soy sauce. Stir-fry until heated through. Finally add the coriander.

4 Check the seasoning and adjust to taste with soy sauce and lime juice. Serve immediately.

VARIATION: Add some stir-fried shredded cooked chicken to make the noodles a meal in themselves.

Fried Polenta

Cooking time: 20 minutes, plus cooling time

SERVES 4

400 ml vegetable stock

170 g polenta

30 g butter

85 g Parmesan cheese, freshly grated

2 tablespoons olive oil

salt and freshly ground black pepper

To prepare ahead: Cook, cool and cut the polenta 24 hours in advance.

1 Put the stock into a large saucepan and bring to the boil. Add the polenta and cook over a medium heat, stirring all the time, for 10 minutes or according to the manufacturer's instructions. The mixture should be very thick. Remove from the heat, season with salt and pepper, add the butter and cheese and mix well. Pour on to a wet, shallow tray and spread flat to a thickness of about 2 cm. Allow to cool completely.

2 Once cold, cut into squares, diamonds or circles. Heat the oil in a frying pan or griddle and fry the polenta on both sides, ensuring that it is hot all the way through.

NOTE: Cooked polenta can be bought in a block. Simply slice into the desired shape and fry.

Garlic Bread

150 g butter, softened

8 cloves of garlic, peeled and crushed

2 tablespoons chopped fresh parsley

2 French baton loaves or 1 baguette

To prepare ahead: This can be made well in advance of baking. It can be frozen and baked from frozen (add about 5 minutes to the cooking time).

1 Preheat the oven to 220°C│425°F│gas mark 7.

2 Mix the butter, garlic and parsley together to form a paste.

3 If using a baguette, cut in half to give 2 shorter sticks.

4 Cut the bread into slices without cutting all the way through and press the garlic butter between each slice.

5 Wrap the baguette in kitchen foil and bake in the oven for 10 minutes.

VARIATIONS: Red chilli and fresh coriander or thyme may be added in place of the parsley. Grated Cheddar cheese may be pressed on top of the baguette before baking, with the top of the foil left open so that the cheese browns. Roasting the garlic (see page 14) before mashing into the butter gives a more mellow flavour.

Oven-baked Croûtons

These croûtons work well using all sorts of bread and are a particularly good way of using up slightly stale loaves.

Preparation time: 5 minutes
Cooking time: 25 minutes

6 tablespoons olive oil
2 cloves of garlic, crushed
50 g Parmesan cheese, finely grated

150 g white bread, cut into cubes
salt and freshly ground black pepper

1 Preheat the oven to 190°C|375°F|gas mark 5.
2 Mix the oil, garlic and Parmesan together in a large bowl.
3 Add the cubes of bread and toss well so that they become covered in the flavourings. Season well with salt and pepper.
4 Spread the croûtons out on a baking sheet and bake in the oven for about 10 minutes until beginning to colour. Turn over and continue to cook for another 10 minutes until brown on all sides.
5 Remove from the oven and allow to cool completely before storing in an airtight container.

Melba Toast

Preparation time: 5 minutes
Cooking time: 35 minutes

6 slices of white bread

1 Preheat the oven to 150°C|300°F|gas mark 2.
2 Toast the bread in the toaster until just brown. It should not get too dark.
3 While still hot, quickly cut off the crusts and split the bread in half horizontally and then cut into triangles.
4 Put the toast in the oven, uncooked side up, and leave for about 30 minutes, or until golden brown.

Salad Accompaniments

A green salad is all that is needed to accompany many dishes, but it is worth experimenting with the type of leaves and ingredients used as well as varying the salad dressing itself. It is often a good idea to mix the leaves, with one leaf used to give a hint of bitterness and another to give colour. Soft herbs can also be added to the leaves to add extra flavour. It is a good idea to keep the salad fairly simple when accompanying a dish with lots of flavours, but when accompanying something quite plain, like grilled fish, the salad can be constructed to provide texture, colour and flavours.

Romaine lettuce Cos Iceberg	Crisp and mild in flavour. Use with a strong-flavoured dressing
Webbs Little Gem	Mild flavour, soft leaves. Combine with peppery leaves, crisp leaves or herbs
Oakleaf lettuce	Oakleaf adds beautifully coloured and shaped leaves
Watercress Rocket	Peppery flavour
Radicchio Chicory Curly endive/frisée	Bitter leaves. Serve with a strong-flavoured dressing or combine with milder leaves
Lamb's lettuce/mâche Baby spinach Sorrel	Stronger-flavoured leaves. Sorrel has a lemony flavour

Other Ingredients to Add to a Green Salad
Blanched French beans, cooked broad beans (pods removed), cooked peas or sugarsnaps, sliced raw mangetout, celery, cubes of cucumber, chunks of avocado, beansprouts, halved artichoke hearts, finely chopped green chillies, sliced green peppers, spring onions, shredded cabbage, shredded Chinese leaves, crisp green apple, halved green grapes

Ingredients to Add to Other Salads
Slices of coloured peppers, halved cherry tomatoes or strips of sunblush tomatoes, grated carrot, shredded red cabbage, orange or grapefruit segments, sultanas, raisins, dried apricots, dates, nectarine slices, pineapple, slices of mango, walnuts, pecans, pinenuts, mushrooms, cashew nuts, crumbled cheeses, red onion, cooked pulses, radishes, halved red grapes, sesame seeds, poppy seeds, pumpkin seeds

Salad Dressings

Most salad dressings follow a basic ratio of 1 part vinegar, or another sour ingredient, such as lemon juice, to 3 parts oil. The additional ingredients can be altered to give a huge variety of flavours. Generally, sugar or a sweetening ingredient is only added to a dressing when it is being served with a salad containing some sort of fruit.

Any well-flavoured dressing may taste overpowering. Test by dipping in some of the salad to be dressed. If it tastes too acidic, just add a little more oil. If it tastes too oily, first add a little more salt, but if that does not cure the problem, add a little more vinegar or lemon juice.

Basic French Dressing (see page 515)

Mustard Salad Dressing

1 tablespoon wine vinegar

1 teaspoon Dijon mustard

a pinch of sugar (optional)

3–4 tablespoons salad oil

salt and freshly ground black pepper

1 Mix the vinegar and mustard together in a small bowl, with a sauce whisk if you have one, or a fork. Season well with salt and pepper.

2 Gradually whisk in the oil, to form an emulsion. Adjust the seasoning if necessary.

Variations

- Vary the type of vinegar used. White or red wine vinegar does not have a particularly discernible flavour, so for a more distinctive dressing, use sherry vinegar, balsamic vinegar, a fruit vinegar such as raspberry, or a Chinese or Japanese rice wine vinegar. Alternatively, use freshly squeezed lemon or lime juice, or a combination of juice and vinegar.

- Mustard adds heat to dressings. Alternatively, use a teaspoon of grated horseradish or horseradish sauce, ¼ teaspoon wasabi paste or a little chilli oil or vinegar. Chopped fresh chilli or dried chilli flakes can also be added, or chilli dipping sauce for a sweet dressing.

- Adding sugar to a dressing gives a delicious sweet and sour flavour which is a natural partner to Asian flavourings. Try adding honey or maple syrup, being careful not to make the final flavour too sweet. Fruit juices or purées are a good way of adding sweetness without the final dressing being too sickly.

- Vary the type of oil used. Nut oils such as walnut or hazelnut are delicious. They can be used in conjunction with milder salad oil if the flavour is too strong for personal taste. Sesame oil, or part sesame oil, is delicious when dressing Asian-style salads. A really good olive oil makes a dressing on its own with just a squeeze of lemon juice and some salt and pepper.

- Other flavourings can be added to make the dressing more complex: teriyaki sauce, soy sauce, hoisin sauce or miso paste give an Asian flavour. Chopped herbs, grated citrus fruit zest, chopped nuts and crushed garlic also work well, depending on the ingredients in the salad.

Low-fat Dressings

- Put some tomato sauce into a blender or food processor with a little olive oil, balsamic vinegar and basil. Whizz until smooth, then thin down with water or vinegar depending on the flavour.
- Use low-fat yoghurt as a base and add chopped herbs, a pinch of sugar, a drop of maple syrup or honey, or a little vinegar, and mix well.
- A good-quality balsamic vinegar can dress a salad without any oil being added.

Tomato and Basil Dressing

This dressing has a very fresh flavour, but needs to be used soon after it is made as it may separate and need to be blended again.

1 tomato	a small pinch of dry English mustard
4 tablespoons oil	a small pinch of caster sugar
1 tablespoon water	a few fresh basil leaves, roughly chopped
1 tablespoon tarragon vinegar	salt and freshly ground black pepper

1 Chop the tomato and whizz in a blender or food processor with the remaining ingredients except the basil.
2 When completely smooth, push through a sieve.
3 Stir in the basil and season well with salt and pepper.

Soy and Garlic Dressing

1 small clove of garlic, unpeeled	2 teaspoons sesame oil
2 teaspoons olive oil	½ teaspoon very finely chopped fresh rosemary
30 ml plain yoghurt	salt and freshly ground black pepper
1 tablespoon light soy sauce	

1 Preheat the oven to 200°C|400°F|gas mark 6.
2 Brush the garlic with a little of the olive oil, place on a baking sheet and bake in the oven for 15 minutes. Peel the garlic and mash well.
3 Mix together the mashed garlic, yoghurt, soy sauce, seasame oil and the remaining olive oil. Stir in the rosemary and season to taste with salt and pepper.

Vegetable Accompaniments

The following table explains how to prepare and cook everyday vegetables. Quantities are based on the assumption that one farinaceous and one 'green' vegetable will be served.

Quantity for 6	Vegetable	Preparation	Suggested Cooking Method	Approximate Cooking Time
675 g	**Asparagus**	Wash, remove hard ends and peel tough outer skin if necessary. Tie in bundles	Steam or boil in unsalted water. Stems will cook slower than heads, so stand bundles upright with heads above water level (where they will cook slowly in the steam while the stems cook fast in the boiling water)	2–6 mins
			Chargrill	3–4 mins
2.3 kg	**Beans, broad**	Shell (if very young they are good boiled whole)	Boil in salted water. Remove outer skins after cooking if tough	7–10 mins
675 g	**Beans, French**	Wash, top and tail. String if necessary	Boil in salted water	5–10 mins
900 g	**Beans, runner**	String if necessary. Wash. Cut into 5 cm lengths	Boil in salted water	4–7 mins
675 g	**Beansprouts**	Wash, pick over and drain	Blanch and refresh. Stir-fry	10 secs
1.1 kg	**Beetroot, young and very small**	Wash but do not peel	Boil in salted water, then peel	1 hr
		Peel, slice or grate	Fry in butter and lemon	1–2 mins
1.35 kg	**Bok choi**	Wash and pick over. Slice if desired	Stir-fry or steam	2–5 mins
900 g	**Broccoli**	Wash. Remove tough leaves or stalks	Boil in salted water	6–8 mins
900 g	**Broccoli, sprouting**	Wash. Remove hard stalks	Boil in salted water	6–10 mins
900 g	**Brussels sprouts**	Trim off tough outer leaves. Trim stalks	Boil in salted water	6–12 mins
900 g	**Cabbage, Savoy**	Wash. Slice thinly	Boil in very little water	6 mins
900 g	**Cabbage, spring**	Wash. Shred very finely	Stir-fry or boil in salted water	Stir-fry 5 mins; boil 5 mins
900 g	**Cabbage, white**	Wash. Slice thinly	Boil in very little water	6 mins
900 g	**Carrots**	Peel and slice or cut into sticks	Boil in salted water with a pinch of sugar	5–10 mins
		Peel and grate coarsely	Stir-fry in butter or good quantity of olive oil	2 mins

1 large/2 small/ 1 mini each	**Cauliflower**	Wash. Break into florets. Remove large stalks	Boil in salted water	5–8 mins
1 head	**Celeriac**	Peel and cut into chunks	Boil or steam in salted water, purée and mash	10–15 mins
1.2–1.35 kg	**Chard**	Wash and pick over	Boil or steam	4 mins
900 g	**Chinese leaves**	Wash. Slice thickly	Stir-fry, sweat or boil very briefly	2 mins
1 each	**Courgette**	Wash and cut into 1 cm chunks	Boil in salted water or sweat in olive oil or butter	4–6 mins 5–10 mins
		Grate coarsely including skin	Stir-fry in butter or olive oil	35 secs
1 small head each 1.35 kg	**Fennel**	Trim, wash and halve lengthways. Remove woody core	Blanch, then griddle Roast	10 mins 30 mins
900 g	**Kale, curly**	Wash and remove hard stalks	Put into a covered saucepan with no extra water. Shake over moderate heat. Drain very well	6–10 mins
2 whole	**Kohlrabi**	Peel and slice thinly	Blanch	2 mins
900 g	**Leek**	Wash. Remove outer leaves and tough dark green part. Split if large. Slice	Boil in salted water or steam	6–10 mins
450 g	**Mangetout**	Wash, top and tail	Stir-fry or boil	2–4 mins
1.35 kg	**Marrow**	Wash and peel if tough-skinned. Cut into 5 cm chunks	Steam	5–10 mins
675 g	**Mushroom, button/ chestnut /field**	Do not peel unless very old and tough. Wipe and trim off any ragged stalks. Quarter if large or slice	Sweat in olive oil or butter Grill, brushed with olive oil and garlic	4–8 mins 20 mins
900 g	**Parsnip**	Peel and cut up if large	Boil in salted water or boil and mash Roast with butter or oil	10–15 mins 40 mins–1 hour
1.2 kg	**Pea**	Remove from pods	Boil in salted water with a good pinch of sugar and a sprig of mint	5–10 mins
6 large/12 small/700 g	**Potato**	Wash and scrub. If new, leave whole. Do not peel	Bake: rub with salt and prick all over Boil or steam	1 hour 10–15 mins

1.35 kg	**Pumpkin and squash**	Wash and peel. Cut into 5 cm chunks	Steam or sweat in butter	15 mins
			Roast with butter or oil	20 mins
225 g	**Sorrel**	Wash well, pick over and remove older leaves	Put into a covered pan with a few tablespoons of water. Shake over a moderate heat. Drain and squeeze dry. Chop well	2–4 mins
Cooked, 2 kg Raw, 340 g	**Spinach**	Wash well. Pull away stalks	Put into covered saucepan *without any water*. Shake over moderate heat. Drain and squeeze dry	4 mins
			Place in a colander and pour over boiling water	
24	**Spring onion**	Wash and peel	Stir-fry in oil	30 secs
2 whole/ 900 g	**Swede**	Peel and slice thickly	Sweat or steam. Mash if very wet and shake over heat to dry	20–30 mins
1.35 kg	**Sweet Potato**	Wash and leave skin on or cut into chunks	Bake	1 hour
			Roast in chunks with salt	25 mins
675 g	**Sweetcorn, baby**	Wash and trim	Boil in salted water, grill or stir-fry	5 mins
3–6 cobs	**Sweetcorn, corn on the cob**		Boil in unsalted water	8–10 mins
			Microwave in covered container with a little warm water	4 mins
			Barbecue	8–10 mins
900 g	**Turnip, small**	Peel if necessary and slice thickly	Sweat or steam. Mash if very wet and shake over heat to dry	15 mins

Potatoes

This table explains what type of potato suits different styles of cooking.

Variety	Crop	Uses	Comments
Arran Pilot	First Early	Salads, chipping, baking	White skin and flesh; waxy texture when cooked
Cara	Main	Baking, roasting	Large; oval; white skin; pink eyes; cream flesh; fluffy texture when cooked
Charlotte	Second early	Salads, steaming, boiling	Pale yellow skin and flesh; good flavour, waxy texture when cooked
Desirée	Main	Baking, roasting	Red skin; pale yellow flesh; fluffy texture when cooked
Estima	Second early	Baking, chipping, boiling, mashing	Pale yellow skin and flesh; creamy texture when cooked
Golden Wonder	Main	Salads, baking, mashing	Brown skin; pale yellow flesh; floury texture when cooked
Kerr's Pink	Main	Baking, roasting, mashing	Pale skin with pink patches; floury texture when cooked
King Edward	Main	Roasting, mashing	Large; pale skin with red eyes; creamy flesh; floury texture when cooked
La Ratte	Second early	Salads, steaming	Yellow skin; cream flesh; waxy texture when cooked
Maris Bard	First early	Salads, boiling, baking when mature	White skins and flesh; waxy texture when cooked
Maris Piper	Main	Chipping, roasting, mashing	Thin white skin; cream coloured flesh; floury texture when cooked
Nadine	Second early	Boiling, roasting	Light skin; oval; white flesh; waxy texture when cooked
Pentland Javelin	First early	Salads, boiling, steaming	Smooth white skin; white flesh; waxy texture when cooked
Pink Fir Apple	Main	Salads, boiling	Pink skin; pinky-yellow flesh; waxy texture when cooked
Romano	Main	Baking, boiling, roasting, chipping	Red skin; creamy flesh; waxy texture when cooked
Santé	Main	Boiling, chipping, roasting	White skin; creamy flesh; floury texture when cooked
Wilja	Second early	Boiling, baking, chipping	Rough yellow skin; pale yellow firm flesh; slightly dry but firm texture when cooked

NOTE: First early are harvested May–July; Second early are harvested June–September; Main are harvested September–October; Second early and maincrop potatoes are generally available from shops throughout the year.

Puddings

A lack of time and concern about the waistline are usually deterrents to making a pudding for dinner every night. The recipes in this section will probably be made when there is slightly more time to spare than usual, a need for comfort food such as at the onset of winter, or, most likely, friends round for lunch or supper.

One of the simplest and most enduring in the popularity stakes is ice cream: make your own and store it in the freezer, or buy a really good-quality variety and serve it with one of the sauces at the end of this section.

Chocolate Mousse

Preparation time: 15 minutes
Chilling time: 2 hours–overnight

SERVES 4

125 g plain chocolate
4 eggs

To decorate
grated choloate

1 Chop the chocolate into even pieces. Put into a heatproof bowl set over, not in, a saucepan of simmering water. Allow the chocolate to melt, then cool slightly.
2 Separate the eggs.
3 Whisk the egg whites until they form medium, not stiff, peaks. Stir the melted chocolate into the egg yolks and mix well. Fold in the egg whites.
4 Immediately turn the mixture into a serving dish or 4 individual pots or glasses.
5 Chill until set, preferably overnight, but for at least 2 hours. Decorate with grated chocolate before serving.

Chocolate Mousse with Marmalade Chips

Preparation time: 15 minutes
Chilling time: 2 hours–overnight

SERVES 4

110 g plain chocolate
2 tablespoons Oxford marmalade

5 eggs

1 Chop the chocolate into even pieces. Put into a heatproof bowl with the marmalade, set over, not in, a saucepan of simmering water. Allow the chocolate to melt, then cool slightly.

2 Separate the eggs. Whisk the egg whites until they form medium, not stiff, peaks. Stir the chocolate mixture into the egg yolks and mix well. Fold in the whites.

3 Turn immediately into a serving dish or 4 individual pots or glasses.

4 Chill until set, preferably overnight, but for at least 2 hours.

Mint Choc Mousse

Preparation time: 15 minutes
Chilling time: 1–2 hours

SERVES 6

1 × 300 g box of After Eight mints   500 ml double cream

1 Remove the After Eights from their wrappers and reserve 6 for decoration. Break the remainder into pieces and melt in a heavy saucepan over a very low heat with 3 tablespoons of the cream. Allow to cool slightly.

2 Lightly whisk the remaining cream.

3 Fold the mint chocolate mixture into the cream and spoon into 6 glasses. Chill before serving.

4 Remove from the refrigerator 20 minutes before serving and stick the reserved After Eights in the top of the mousse at a jaunty angle.

Chilli Chocolate Pots

Preparation time: 10 minutes
Standing time: 30 minutes
Chilling time: 1 hour

SERVES 8

1 × 284 ml pot of single cream   200 g dark chocolate, broken into pieces
2 teaspoons crushed dried chillies   2 egg yolks, beaten
15 g butter

1 Put the cream and chillies into a heavy saucepan and heat gently until it begins to steam. Turn off the heat and let the pan stand for 30 minutes.

2 Return the pan to the heat, add the butter and heat again until it steams and the butter has melted. Do not boil. Place the chocolate in a bowl and strain the hot cream on to it, to remove the chilli. Stir until the chocolate has melted, then beat in the egg yolks.

3 Pour into 8 individual pots or small coffee cups and chill for 1 hour until set. Remove from the refrigerator 20 minutes before serving.

White Chocolate and Raspberry Mousse

Preparation time: 30 minutes
Chilling time: 1 hour

SERVES 4

2 leaves of gelatine (see page 15)
200 g white chocolate, broken into pieces
500 ml double cream
1 egg white
1 punnet of fresh raspberries

To decorate

grated white chocolate

1 Soak the leaves of gelatine in cold water.
2 Meanwhile, place the chocolate and cream in a heavy saucepan over a low heat. Stir until all the chocolate has melted. Remove from the heat.
3 Squeeze out the gelatine and add to the cream mixture. Stir to dissolve.
4 Using a hand whisk, whisk the egg white until stiff but not dry. Whisk the cream mixture to cool it down further. Then add the egg white and whisk very lightly for 5 seconds.
5 Place some raspberries at the bottom of 4 tall glasses or large ramekins. Pour over the chocolate mixture, then chill until set.
6 Just before serving, scatter the grated chocolate over the mousses.

Chocolate Fondue

Preparation time: 1 minute
Cooking time: 10 minutes

SERVES 4–6

400 g chocolate, broken into pieces
1 × 284 ml pot of double cream

To serve

prepared fresh fruit such as strawberries, cherries, quartered apples and pears, segmented oranges and chunks of banana
wooden skewers

1 Melt the chocolate with the cream in a heavy saucepan over a very low heat.
2 Stir until completely smooth.
3 Place in the centre of the table and using wooden skewers, dip the fresh fruit into the chocolate.

NOTE: The zest of ½ orange or 2 tablespoons brandy or kirsch can be added to the fondue. This recipe does not specify a particular type of chocolate: it is good made with dark chocolate but can also be made with a variety of others, for example Toblerone.

Blackberry and Apple Custard Fool

Preparation time: 10 minutes
Chilling time: at least 1 hour

SERVES 4–6

3 large Bramley apples, peeled, cored and cut into
  1.5 cm chunks
225 g blackberries, washed
75 g caster sugar

1 × 142 ml pot of double cream, lightly whipped
500 g ready-made custard

To decorate
fresh blackberries

1 Put the apples, blackberries and sugar into a large saucepan and cook over a very low heat until the fruit is completely soft and the juices are syrupy. Remove from the heat and allow to cool.
2 Gently fold the cream into the custard. Add the fruit to the custard and cream mixture and gently fold through.
3 Spoon the fool into 4–6 individual glass serving dishes and chill in the refrigerator for at least 1 hour. Just before serving, decorate with the blackberries.

Gooseberry Fool

Preparation time: 15 minutes
Cooking time: 10 minutes

SERVES 4

450 g gooseberries
60 g sugar
1 × 284 ml pot of double cream, lightly whipped

To serve
sponge fingers or biscuits

1 Cook the gooseberries slowly in a saucepan with 4 tablespoons water and the sugar. Watch the pan carefully, stirring from time to time, so that it does not 'catch' on the bottom.
2 When the gooseberries are completely soft, beat them lightly with a wooden spoon and push through a sieve into a bowl. Leave to cool.
3 Stir the gooseberry purée into the whipped cream and add more sugar if necessary.
4 Pour into a serving dish. Chill, covered, or serve immediately with sponge fingers or biscuits.

Blackberry and Lime Fool

Preparation time: 30 minutes
Chilling time: 1–2 hours

SERVES 4

250 g blackberries
55 g soft light brown sugar
grated zest and juice of 1 lime
225 g plain yoghurt

225 ml double cream, lightly whipped

To serve
sponge fingers

1 Put the blackberries into a bowl. Add 1 tablespoon of the sugar and the lime zest and juice. Leave to stand for 5 minutes.
2 Meanwhile, mix the yoghurt with the cream and stir in the remaining sugar.
3 Divide the blackberries in half, with their juices. Whizz one half in a blender or food processor and pass through a sieve.
4 Mix the whole blackberries through the blackberry purée. Fold into the yoghurt and cream mixture.
5 Pile into 4 individual glass bowls and chill before serving.

Strawberry Creams

Preparation time: 20 minutes
Chilling time: 2–4 hours

SERVES 4

450 g strawberries
4 tablespoons framboise (raspberry liqueur)
3 tablespoons icing sugar
1 × 284 ml pot of double cream

To decorate
sprigs of fresh mint

1 Hull the strawberries. Choose 2 for the decoration, cut them in half and set aside.
2 Chop half the remaining strawberries into small dice. Mash the other half roughly with a fork.
3 Mix together the diced and mashed strawberries, half the framboise and 1 tablespoon of the icing sugar.
4 Put the cream into a bowl with the remaining framboise and icing sugar. Whisk until it just holds its shape.
5 Pour the strawberry mixture over the cream and fold in carefully until the mixture begins to look marbled.
6 Spoon into 4 ramekins or glasses and chill before serving.
7 Decorate with the reserved strawberries and the mint before serving.

Petits Pots de Crème

Preparation time: 5 minutes
Infusing time: 10 minutes
Cooking time: 40 minutes
Chilling time: 4 hours–overnight

SERVES 6

300 ml milk

1 × 284 ml pot of single cream

30 g caster sugar

1 vanilla pod or 2 drops of vanilla extract

4 egg yolks

1 large egg

To prepare ahead: These can be made a day in advance and kept covered in the refrigerator.

1 Preheat the oven to 150°C|300°F|gas mark 2.

2 Place the milk and cream with the sugar and vanilla pod, if using, in a saucepan and scald by bringing to just below boiling point. Allow to infuse for 10 minutes, then remove the vanilla pod. (If using vanilla extract, add it once the milk is scalded.)

3 Beat the egg yolks with the whole egg and pour on the scalded milk. Stir well, then strain the mixture through a sieve.

4 Pour the custard into 6 ramekins. Stand the ramekins in a roasting pan half filled with hot water (a bain-marie, see page 9).

5 Cover with a sheet of greaseproof paper or kitchen foil. Bake in the oven for about 35–40 minutes, or until set. Remove the covering, being careful not to let any condensed water drop on to the creams. Lift out of the water and allow to cool. Chill for at least 4 hours or overnight before serving.

VARIATION: A tablespoon of good-quality morello cherry jam may be spooned into the bottom of each ramekin before pouring on the cream.

Redcurrant and Raspberry Creams

Preparation time: 20 minutes
Chilling time: 2–4 hours

SERVES 4

100 g redcurrants
100 g caster sugar
100 g raspberries
1 tablespoon crème de cassis
1 × 284 ml pot of double cream

1 tablespoon icing sugar
150 g Greek yoghurt

To garnish
fresh raspberries
sprigs of fresh mint

1 Place the redcurrants with the sugar and 1 tablespoon water in a saucepan.
2 Simmer over a very low heat for 10 minutes, then add the raspberries and simmer for a further 2 minutes. Mash well, then pass through a sieve, pressing with a wooden spoon. Discard any pips. Add the cassis to the fruit purée.
3 Whisk the cream with the icing sugar until stiff and stir in the yoghurt. Stir in the fruit purée to give a rippled effect.
4 Pile into 4 ramekins or glasses and chill before serving. Decorate with the raspberries and mint.

Raspberry and Passionfruit Yoghurt Creams

Preparation time: 10 minutes
Chilling time: at least 1 hour

SERVES 4

150 g Greek yoghurt
1 × 142 ml pot of double cream, lightly whipped
grated zest of ½ orange

1 punnet of raspberries
3 passionfruits, halved and pulp removed
icing sugar

1 Mix together the yoghurt, cream and orange zest.
2 With the back of a fork, roughly break up one-quarter of the raspberries.
3 Combine all the raspberries and the passionfruit pulp with the yoghurt mixture and sweeten to taste with icing sugar.
4 Spoon the mixture into 4 ramekins and chill for at least 1 hour before serving.

Banoffee Cream

Preparation time: 15 minutes

SERVES 8

5 bananas, cut into 1.5 cm chunks

55 g roasted hazelnuts, roughly chopped (see page 17)

1 × 450 g jar of Dulce de Leche

1 tablespoon instant coffee powder

1 teaspoon boiling water

1 × 284 ml pot of double cream

2 tablespoons icing sugar

To decorate

cocoa powder

To prepare ahead: Complete to the end of stage 4, then refrigerate.

1 Place the bananas and hazelnuts in the bottom of a 25 cm pie dish.
2 Pour over the Dulce de Leche.
3 Make the cream: in a bowl, mix together the coffee and water to make a paste, then add the cream. Add ½ tablespoon of the icing sugar and whisk until the cream just holds its shape. Add more icing sugar to taste.
4 Spread the cream over the top of the bananas.
5 Dust with sifted cocoa powder and serve.

Passion Pudding

Preparation time: 10 minutes
Chilling time: at least 1 hour or overnight

SERVES 4

1 × 142 ml pot of double cream

150 g plain yoghurt

50–80 g raspberries

soft dark brown sugar

To prepare ahead: Make the complete pudding, then leave in the refrigerator overnight.

1 Whip the cream until it just holds its shape. Add the yoghurt and whip until soft peaks are formed.
2 Place the raspberries in the bottom of 4 ramekins. Divide the yoghurt and cream mixture between the ramekins and sprinkle sugar over the top of each to form a layer about 5 mm thick, which should completely cover the puddings.
3 Chill for at least 1 hour or overnight.

VARIATION: Any variety of chopped fresh fruit, such as bananas, grapes and pineapple, or stewed fruit may be used instead of raspberries.

Lime Syllabub

Preparation time: 10 minutes
Chilling time: 2 hours–overnight

SERVES 4

1 × 284 ml pot of double cream
grated zest of 1 lime
juice of 2–3 limes
2 tablespoons sweet white wine

4 tablespoons icing sugar, sifted, plus extra to taste

To serve
sweet biscuits

1 Place the cream in a bowl with the lime zest. Whisk until thick, gradually adding the lime juice, wine and icing sugar at intervals and allowing the mixture to thicken again between additions. Add more icing sugar if required.
2 Spoon into 4 individual glasses and chill before serving. Serve with the biscuits.

Easy Tiramisù

Preparation time: 10 minutes
Chilling time: at least 1 hour

SERVES 6

3 tablespoons boiling water
2 tablespoons instant coffee powder
3 tablespoons caster sugar
4 tablespoons dark rum
250 g mascarpone
300 g ready-made custard

2 teaspoons icing sugar, sifted
1 × 440 g Madeira cake

To decorate
cocoa powder

1 Pour the boiling water on to the coffee powder and caster sugar in a bowl. Stir well. Add the rum.
2 Mix the mascarpone, custard and icing sugar together thoroughly.
3 Cut the Madeira cake horizontally into 3 layers. Soak the cake in the coffee and rum mixture.
4 Place a sponge layer in a large serving dish or 6 individual ones, followed by a layer of the custard and mascarpone mixture. Repeat twice. Chill for at least 1 hour.
5 Just before serving, dust lightly with sifted cocoa powder.

Lemon and Honey Posset

Preparation time: 10 minutes
Chilling time: at least 1 hour

SERVES 6

500 ml double cream
100 g caster sugar
3 tablespoons clear flower-scented honey

grated zest and juice of 3 lemons

To serve
red berry fruit compote (see page 421)

1 Bring the cream slowly to the boil in a non-stick saucepan, then simmer for 3 minutes.
2 Remove the cream from the heat, then mix in the sugar and honey. Stir well, then add the lemon zest and juice. The mixture will start to set, so pour it quickly into 6 large wine or sundae glasses. Cool, then chill. Top with the fruit compote to serve.

Instant Crème Brûlée

Preparation time: 10 minutes
Chilling time: at least 1 hour

SERVES 4

500 g mascarpone
vanilla extract

icing sugar, to taste
caster sugar

To prepare ahead: The base can be prepared in advance to the end of stage 2. Only sprinkle and caramelize the sugar an hour before serving. Keep cool but do not refrigerate or the crisp layer of sugar will liquefy.

1 Beat the mascarpone lightly in a bowl. Add vanilla extract and icing sugar to taste.
2 Divide the mixture between 4 ramekin dishes and smooth the tops. Chill for at least 1 hour.
3 Sprinkle the top of the ramekins with an even layer of caster sugar.
4 Using a blowtorch, allow the sugar to melt and then caramelize.
5 Leave to cool and harden before serving.

NOTE: If you don't have a blowtorch, make a caramel in a saucepan (see page 22) and pour a thin layer over the top of the ramekins. Alternatively, use the grill.

Lemon and Raspberry Crème Brûlée

Preparation time: 10 minutes
Cooking time: 25 minutes

SERVES 6

4 eggs
1 egg yolk
150 g caster sugar
200 g Greek yoghurt

grated zest and juice of 2 lemons
225 g fresh raspberries

To finish
caster sugar

To prepare ahead: The brulée will liquefy if kept in the refrigerator. Complete to the end of stage 4. Complete the brûlées a few hours ahead of serving and leave in a cool place.

1 Preheat the oven to 180°C|350°F|gas mark 4.
2 Mix the whole eggs and yolk together briefly and stir in the sugar, yoghurt and lemon juice. Stir together carefully, taking care not to create air bubbles. Strain and stir in the lemon zest.
3 Divide the raspberries between 6 ramekins and pour the lemon mixture over the top.
4 Stand the ramekins in a roasting pan and pour in enough boiling water to come halfway up the sides. Cook in the middle of the oven for 20–25 minutes or until set. Allow to cool. Preheat the grill to the highest setting.
5 Sprinkle the tops of the brûlées with a 5 mm even layer of caster sugar.
6 Put the ramekins under the very hot grill as close as you can to the heat. The sugar will melt and caramelize before the custard underneath it boils. Watch carefully, turning the ramekins if the sugar is browning unevenly. (If you have a blowtorch, you can use this to caramelize the sugar instead of the grill, or make a caramel in a saucepan and pour over.)
7 Allow to cool completely and the caramel to set before serving.

VARIATION: Omit the brûlée topping and dust with icing sugar before serving.

Summer Fruit Tiramisù

Preparation time: 15 minutes
Chilling time: 12–24 hours

SERVES 4

110 g mascarpone
425 ml good-quality organic raspberry yoghurt
icing sugar, sifted

2 × 150 g punnets of raspberries
20 sponge fingers
4 tablespoons Muscat wine

1 Beat the mascarpone until soft. Stir in the raspberry yoghurt. Taste and if necessary sweeten with a little icing sugar. Stir in half the raspberries.

2 Place half the sponge fingers in a shallow dish and sprinkle over a little of the wine. Spread over half the yoghurt and mascarpone mixture.

3 Layer up the remaining sponge fingers and scatter over a little more wine. Spread the remaining yoghurt mixture over the top. Cover with clingfilm and chill for 12–24 hours.

4 To serve: put the remaining raspberries on the top and dust lightly with icing sugar.

NOTE: For a non-alcoholic version, use orange juice in place of the Muscat.

Ginger and Orange Tiramisù

Preparation time: 20 minutes
Chilling time: 1 hour

SERVES 10

3 eggs, separated

85 g caster sugar, plus extra to taste

450 g mascarpone

1 × 284 ml pot of double cream, lightly whipped

a few drops of vanilla extract

100 ml orange liqueur, such as Grand Marnier or Cointreau

grated zest of 2 oranges

75 ml orange juice

300 g gingernut biscuits

To decorate

cocoa powder

1 Whisk the egg yolks with 55 g of the sugar until thick and mousse-like.

2 In a separate bowl whisk the egg whites until stiff but not dry, then whisk in the remaining sugar until just combined.

3 Beat the mascarpone in a large bowl until smooth, then carefully fold in the egg yolk mixture, the cream and then the whisked egg whites. Add the vanilla extract and about 2 teaspoons sugar to taste.

4 Mix the liqueur and orange zest and juice together and pour into a shallow dish. Dip all the gingernuts briefly into the liquid and make a layer of the biscuits in the base of a serving dish.

5 Spread one-third of the cream mixture on the top and continue layering up with the gingernuts, finishing with a layer of cream.

6 Chill for 1 hour.

7 Dust with sifted cocoa powder and serve.

Gin and Tonic Jellies

Preparation time: 5 minutes
Chilling time: 4 hours

SERVES 4

4 leaves of gelatine (see page 15)
400 ml tonic water with lemon
100 ml gin

To serve

pared zest of 1 lemon, cut into fine strips

1 Soak the leaves of gelatine in cold water.
2 Heat 100 ml of the tonic water in a small pan. Remove from the heat. Squeeze the excess water from the gelatine and stir the gelatine into the warm tonic until it has dissolved. Stir in the remaining tonic water and the gin. Stir well, then pour into 4 glasses.
3 Chill until set.
4 To serve: place lemon zest strips on top of each jelly.

VARIATION: This can also be made with bitter lemon in place of tonic water.

Vodka Jellies

Preparation time: 5 minutes
Chilling time: 4 hours

SERVES 4

1 × 135 g packet of jelly, any flavour
200 ml vodka

about 300 ml water

1 Cut the jelly up into cubes and place in a bowl. Add a few tablespoons of water and heat in a microwave until melted. Do not allow to boil.
2 Remove from the microwave and add the vodka, then make up to 500 ml with the remaining water and stir well.
3 Stir, then pour into a mould or individual shot glasses. Chill until set.

Individual Apple Tarts

Preparation time: 20 minutes
Chilling time: 15 minutes
Cooking time: 20 minutes

SERVES 4

375 g ready-rolled puff pastry

4 dessert apples

caster sugar

1 egg, beaten, to glaze

3 tablespoons apricot jam

2 tablespoons water

To serve

custard, cream or vanilla ice cream

To prepare ahead: Make in advance and reheat before serving.

1 Preheat the oven to 200°C|400°F|gas mark 6.
2 On a floured surface, cut out 4 × 11 cm diameter circles from the pastry. Place on a baking sheet. Using a sharp knife, trace an inner circle about 1 cm in from the edge of each pastry circle. Do not cut all the way through the pastry.
3 Peel, core and finely slice the apples. Arrange the apple slices in concentric circles within the border of each pastry tart.
4 Sprinkle each tart lightly with caster sugar. Brush the rim of each pastry circle with beaten egg, taking care not to let it drip down the sides of the pastry. Chill for 15 minutes.
5 Bake the pastry cases on the top shelf of the oven for 20 minutes, or until golden brown.
6 Meanwhile, place the apricot jam with the water in a small pan. Warm through and stir until completely smooth.
7 Remove the tarts from the oven and leave to cool slightly, then brush liberally with the warm apricot glaze.
8 Serve the tarts warm, with custard, cream or vanilla ice cream.

VARIATION: This can also be made using shortcrust pastry instead of puff pastry.

Apple and Mincemeat Puffs

Preparation time: 10–15 minutes
Chilling time: 30 minutes
Cooking time: 15–20 minutes

SERVES 4

500 g puff pastry
1 egg, beaten with ½ teaspoon sugar

½ teaspoon ground cinnamon
grated zest and juice of ½ lemon

For the filling

1 Bramley apple, peeled, cored and cut into 1 cm chunks
120 g mincemeat

To serve

crème fraîche or brandy butter (see page 442)

1 Preheat the oven to 200°C|400°F|gas mark 6.
2 Mix the filling ingredients together in a bowl.
3 On a floured surface, roll out the pastry to the thickness of a £1 coin and cut out 4 equal squares, approximately.
4 Put a generous spoonful of the filling mixture into the centre of each square.
5 Dampen the corners of the pastry with the egg glaze and bring them up to the centre, pinching the edges tightly to seal.
6 Place the puffs on a baking sheet and brush with the remaining egg glaze. Chill for 30 minutes.
7 Bake the puffs in the oven for 15–20 minutes, or until well risen and golden brown. Serve immediately, with crème fraîche or brandy butter.

Apple and Raisin Tarts

Preparation time: 10 minutes
Chilling time: 15 minutes
Cooking time: 40 minutes

MAKES 4

For the filling

2 Bramley apples, peeled, cored and cut into 1 cm cubes
1 tablespoon Calvados or apple juice
½ teaspoon ground cinnamon
2 tablespoons raisins
caster sugar to taste
375 g ready-rolled puff pastry

For the topping

1 red dessert apple, cored and finely sliced
apricot glaze (see page 440)

To serve

vanilla ice cream

1 Preheat the oven to 200°C|400°F|gas mark 6.

2 Make the filling: put the apples and Calvados into a pan and cook over a lower heat for 20–25 minutes, or until the apples have completely broken down. Add the cinnamon and raisins to the apple purée and sweeten to taste with sugar. Allow to cool.

3 On a floured surface, cut out 4 × 10 cm circles from the pastry. Score a 1 cm border around the edge of each circle. Chill for 15 minutes.

4 Place the pastry circles on a baking sheet. Divide the filling between the tarts, placing it in the inner circle. Arrange the sliced apple on top of the filling.

5 Bake in the oven for 20 minutes, or until the pastry has risen and is golden brown.

6 Warm the apricot glaze and brush over the cooked tarts. Serve warm, with vanilla ice cream.

NOTE: To save time, you can use a ready-made apple purée.

Lemon Curd Tart

Preparation time: 20 minutes
Chilling time 15 minutes
Cooking time: 1 hour

SERVES 6–8

375 g ready-rolled sweet shortcrust pastry

For the curd

4 eggs

1 egg yolk

200 g caster sugar

1 × 142 ml pot of double cream

grated zest and juice of 2 lemons

To decorate

icing sugar, sifted for dusting

To serve

cream

1 Use the pastry to line a deep 24 cm flan ring. Chill for 15 minutes, then bake blind (see page 18). Leave to cool. Reduce the temperature to 150°C|300°F|gas mark 2.

2 Make the filling: mix the eggs and egg yolk with the sugar and whisk lightly until smooth. Add the cream and whisk again. Add the lemon zest and juice. The mixture may thicken alarmingly but do not worry.

3 Put the pastry case on to a baking sheet and spoon in the lemon filling. Bake in the oven for 40–50 minutes until almost set. Remove from the oven and allow to cool completely before removing from the flan ring.

4 Dust with icing sugar before serving the tart with cream.

NOTE: For a delicious cooked lemon pot pudding the filling mixture can be poured into ramekins and cooked in a bain-marie or a roasting tin of water at 180°C|350°F|gas mark 5 (see page 9).

Mincemeat Streusel Tart

Preparation time: 30 minutes
Chilling time: 30 minutes
Cooking time: 20 minutes

SERVES 6–8

375 g ready-rolled sweet shortcrust pastry
juice of ½ lemon
350 g very good-quality mincemeat
icing sugar

60 g butter, cut into small pieces
60 g soft light brown sugar
1 teaspoon ground cinnamon
grated zest of ½ lemon

For the topping
70 g plain flour

To serve
crème fraîche, brandy butter or vanilla ice cream

1 Preheat the oven to 200°C│400°F│gas mark 6.
2 Line a 24 cm flan ring with the pastry. Chill for 30 minutes and bake blind (see page 18). Remove from the oven and allow to cool. Reduce the oven temperature to 180°C│350°F│gas mark 4.
3 Stir the lemon juice into the mincemeat and set aside.
4 Make the topping: sift the flour into a bowl and rub in the butter until it resembles coarse breadcrumbs. Stir in the sugar, cinnamon and lemon zest.
5 Fill the flan with the mincemeat and spread over the streusel topping.
6 Return the tart to the oven and bake for 20 minutes. Check after 15 minutes and if it is beginning to get too brown, cover with kitchen foil.
7 Remove from the oven and allow to cool slightly, then dust with sifted icing sugar. Serve warm with crème fraîche, brandy butter or vanilla ice cream.

Chocolate Tart

Preparation time: 10 minutes
Chilling time: 2–3 hours
Cooking time: 25 minutes

SERVES 6

375 g ready-rolled sweet shortcrust pastry
200 g good-quality dark chocolate
1 × 284 ml pot of double cream
3 tablespoons Kahlua liqueur
a few drops of coffee essence
icing sugar

To decorate
chocolate shavings

To serve
fresh fruit

Chocolate Fondue

Chocolate Mousse

Redcurrant and Raspberry Cream

Eton Mess

Lemon and Raspberry Cheesecake Sundae

Banana and Date Puddings with Butterscotch Sauce

Lemon and Raspberry Crème Brûlée

Pear and Raisin Tarte Tatin

Apple and Mincemeat Puff

Apple and Blackcurrant Fudge Crumble

Baked Peaches with Strawberry Cream

1 Line a 20 cm flan ring with the pastry. Chill for 30 minutes and bake blind (see page 18). Remove from the oven and allow to cool.

2 Place the chocolate with half the cream and the Kahlua in a heavy saucepan over a low heat. Stir gently until the chocolate has melted, then pour into the baked pastry case and chill for 2–3 hours.

3 Just before serving, whip the remaining cream with the coffee essence. Add icing sugar to taste and spoon the cream into a bowl.

4 Sprinkle the chocolate shavings over the top of the tart. Serve a slice of the tart with the coffee-flavoured cream and fresh fruit.

Pear and Raisin Tarte Tatin

Preparation time: 20 minutes
Chilling time: 30 minutes
Cooking time: 15 minutes

SERVES 6

375 g ready-rolled puff pastry

For the filling
60 g butter
110 g soft dark brown sugar
4 large, slightly under-ripe conference pears, peeled, cored and cut into even pieces

grated zest of 1 lemon
1 teaspoon ground cinnamon
2 tablespoons large raisins

To serve
crème fraîche or vanilla ice cream

To prepare ahead: Cook to the end of stage 4. Allow the fruit and syrup to cool, then place the pastry on top and bake as required. Or make completely and reheat before serving.

1 Preheat the oven to 190°C|375°F|gas mark 5.

2 On a floured surface, cut out a 25 cm diameter circle from the pastry. Place on a baking sheet and chill for 30 minutes.

3 Melt the butter in a 25 cm frying pan with an ovenproof handle. Add the sugar and warm gently until it has dissolved and is beginning to bubble.

4 Add the chunks of pear, the lemon zest and cinnamon and cook over a low heat for 6–7 minutes. Sprinkle over the raisins.

5 Lay the pastry on top of the pears and press down lightly. Bake in the oven for 15 minutes, or until the pastry is risen and golden brown.

6 Remove from the oven and allow to cool slightly. Invert a plate over the frying pan and carefully turn out the tart.

7 Serve warm, with crème fraîche or ice cream.

Pear and Almond Tart

Preparation time: 20 minutes
Cooking time: 20 minutes

SERVES 4

375 g ready-rolled puff pastry

For the filling

1 tablespoon caster sugar
2 tablespoons ground almonds
30 g butter
2 ripe pears

30 g flaked almonds
2 tablespoons clear honey

To serve

vanilla ice cream

1 Preheat the oven to 200°C | 400°F | gas mark 6.
2 On a floured surface, cut a 30 × 20 cm rectangle from the pastry. Lay the pastry on a baking sheet and prick all over with a fork, leaving a 2 cm margin around the edge.
3 Sprinkle the sugar and ground almonds over the base, being careful not to go over the margin. Cut the butter into small dice and dot over the almonds and sugar.
4 Slice the pears and lay over the pastry, leaving the margin clear.
5 Sprinkle with the flaked almonds and drizzle with the honey.
6 Bake in the top third of the oven for 20–25 minutes.

Rhubarb Custard Tart

Preparation time: 25 minutes
Cooking time: 1 hour

SERVES 6–8

375 g ready-rolled sweet shortcrust pastry

For the filling

140 g rhubarb, sliced
75 ml water
4 eggs
1 egg yolk
170 g caster sugar

a few drops of vanilla extract
100 ml double cream

To decorate

icing sugar

To serve

Greek yoghurt, sweetened with icing sugar

1 Preheat the oven to 200°C | 400°F | gas mark 6.
2 Line a 24 cm flan ring with the pastry and chill for 15 minutes. Bake blind (see page 18). Allow to cool.
3 Reduce the oven temperature to 150°C | 300°F | gas mark 2.

4 Put the rhubarb and water into a saucepan and simmer until the rhubarb is soft. Whizz in a blender or food processor to make a smooth purée. Reduce the purée by boiling, stirring regularly to prevent it from catching on the bottom of the pan, until it measures 150 ml. Allow to cool.

5 Mix the whole eggs and egg yolk with the sugar and vanilla extract. Whisk lightly until smooth. Add the cream and whisk again. Add the rhubarb purée and beat until smooth.

6 Spoon the filling into the pastry case. Bake in the bottom third of the oven for 40–50 minutes, or until almost set. Cool on a wire rack.

7 To serve, dust with icing sugar and serve with sweetened Greek yoghurt.

Raspberry and Frangipane Tart

Preparation time: 25 minutes
Chilling time: 30 minutes
Cooking time: 55 minutes

SERVES 8

500 g sweet shortcrust pastry

For the filling
200 g butter
200 g caster sugar
2 eggs, beaten
2 yolks
4 teaspoons kirsch (optional)

4 tablespoons plain flour, sifted
200 g ground almonds
85 g good-quality raspberry jam
125 g fresh raspberries

To decorate
icing sugar

1 Preheat the oven to 200°C | 400°F | gas mark 6.

2 On a floured surface, roll out the pastry to the thickness of a £1 coin and use to line a 24 cm flan ring. Prick the base lightly all over with a fork and chill for about 30 minutes until firm.

3 Make the frangipane: cream the butter in a bowl, gradually beat in the sugar and continue beating until the mixture is pale and soft. Gradually add the whole eggs and yolks, beating well after each addition. Add the kirsch, if using, then stir in the flour and ground almonds.

4 Spread the jam evenly over the base of the chilled pastry case. Sprinkle with the raspberries so that they are evenly spaced. Pile the frangipane over the raspberries and use a spatula to smooth it out.

5 Bake the tart near the top of the oven for 10 minutes, or until the pastry is beginning to brown. Reduce the oven temperature to 180°C | 350°F | gas mark 4 and bake for a further 40–45 minutes, or until the frangipane is set.

6 Serve warm or cold. Dust with sifted icing sugar just before serving

Peach Melba Tart

Preparation time: 20 minutes
Chilling time: 15 minutes
Cooking time: 20 minutes

SERVES 4–6

375 g ready-rolled sweet shortcrust pastry

For the filling
100 ml double cream

100 ml mascarpone
225 g fresh raspberries
icing sugar to taste
2 peaches, finely sliced

1 Preheat the oven to 200°C|400°F|gas mark 6.
2 Use the pastry to line a 20 cm flan ring and chill for 15 minutes. Bake blind (see page 18).
3 Whisk the cream and mascarpone together until the mixture is smooth and holding its own shape.
4 Push 170 g of the raspberries through a sieve with a wooden spoon to remove the seeds and produce a thick coulis.
5 Fold the coulis into the cream mixture and sweeten to taste with icing sugar.
6 Pile the raspberry and cream filling into the pastry case and level out.
7 Carefully arrange the peach slices in concentric rings around the edge of the case and pile the remaining raspberries in the centre.

Pecan and White Chocolate Pie

Preparation time: 15 minutes
Chilling time: 30 minutes
Cooling time: 40–50 minutes

SERVES 8–10

500 g ready-rolled sweet shortcrust pastry

For the filling
340 g pecan nuts
4 eggs
225 g soft light brown sugar
170 g golden syrup

½ teaspoon salt
55 g butter, melted
a few drops of vanilla extract
2 tablespoons plain flour, sifted
85 g white chocolate drops

To serve
ice cream or crème fraîche

1 Preheat the oven to 200°C|400°F|gas mark 6. Heat a baking sheet.
2 Use the pastry to line a 30 cm flan case. Chill for about 30 minutes. Bake blind (see page 18).

3 Meanwhile, make the filling: chop half the nuts. The remaining nuts will be used for decoration, so chop any that are broken, reserving the best-looking ones. Whisk the eggs in a large bowl until frothy. Add the sugar, golden syrup, salt, melted butter and vanilla extract and beat well until thoroughly mixed. Whisk in the flour, making sure there are no lumps in the mixture.

4 Scatter the chopped nuts and the chocolate drops over the baked pastry case and pour over the filling. Arrange the remaining halved nuts on top.

5 Bake on the hot baking sheet in the oven for 10 minutes, then reduce the oven temperature to 170°C|325°F|gas mark 3 and bake for a further 30–40 minutes, or until the centre is just set. Serve warm or cold.

Banana, Maple and Pecan Scone Pie

Preparation time: 40 minutes
Cooking time: 25–30 minutes

SERVES 6

85 g butter
85 g granulated sugar
3 large bananas
85 g pecan nuts, chopped
2 tablespoons maple syrup

For the scone dough
225 g self-raising flour
½ teaspoon salt

1 teaspoon baking powder
55 g butter
2 tablespoons caster sugar
150 ml milk

To serve
cream

1 Preheat the oven to 200°C|400°F|gas mark 6.

2 Melt the butter in a non-stick frying pan with an ovenproof handle. When foaming, add the sugar, allow to melt and then caramelize to a golden brown. Remove from the heat.

3 Slice the bananas and arrange them in the pan. Sprinkle over the nuts. Return to the pan and cook until the caramel is a rich dark colour.

4 Remove from the heat and drizzle over the maple syrup.

5 Make the scone dough: sift together the flour, salt and baking powder in a bowl. Rub in the butter until the mixture resembles coarse breadcrumbs. Add the sugar and enough milk to bring the mixture together without kneading any more than you have to.

6 Roll the dough into a circle big enough to cover the bananas completely and press down firmly.

7 Bake in the oven for for 20–25 minutes, or until the scone topping is golden brown.

8 Remove from the oven and leave to rest for 5 minutes. Turn out on to a large round plate and serve with plenty of cream.

Millefeuilles

Preparation time: 20 minutes
Chilling time: 30 minutes
Cooling time: 20 minutes
Cooking time: 20 minutes

SERVES 6

375 g ready-rolled puff pastry

1 × 284 ml pot of double cream, whipped

icing sugar

250 g strawberries, hulled and sliced

1 Preheat the oven to 220°C|425°F|gas mark 7.

2 On a floured surface, roll out the pastry to a thin rectangle about 35 × 20 cm. Place on a baking sheet. Prick all over with a fork.

3 Leave to chill, covered, for 30 minutes. Bake in the oven until golden brown, about 20 minutes. Remove from the oven and allow to cool.

4 Carefully cut the pastry into 3 equal strips, each 12 × 20 cm.

5 Sweeten the cream with a little icing sugar.

6 Choose the piece of pastry with the smoothest base, and reserve. Then spread the other 2 strips with cream, top with strawberries and lay one on top of the other. Cover with the third, reserved piece of pastry, smooth side uppermost. Press down gently but firmly until the filling covers the pastry layer.

7 Dust the top of the millefeuilles with sifted icing sugar.

Blackberry and Pear Pancakes

Preparation and cooking time: 15 minutes

SERVES 4

225 g blackberries

3 pears, peeled, cored and cut into eighths

2 tablespoons caster sugar, plus extra if required

2 tablespoons crème de mûres or cassis

8 ready-made pancakes (or see page 519)

To serve

vanilla ice cream or cream

1 Put the blackberries and pears into a large saucepan, add 2 tablespoons caster sugar and cook over a low heat until soft. Remove the fruit from the pan, leaving the juice behind.

2 Reduce the fruit juice by boiling to a syrupy consistency.

3 Add the crème de mûres or cassis. Add more sugar to taste if necessary.

4 Heat the pancakes through. Fill them with the fruit compote and pour the syrupy sauce over the top. Serve immediately with ice cream or cream.

Pain Perdu

Preparation time: 5 minutes
Cooking time: 10 minutes

SERVES 4

4 slices of day-old white bread, 2.5 cm thick and crusts removed
50 g unsalted butter
caster sugar, for sprinkling

For the custard
1 large egg
1 egg yolk

60 g soft light brown sugar
150 ml full-cream milk

To serve
icing sugar
poached fruit, fruit compote or ice cream

1 Make the custard: put the whole egg and yolk into a large shallow dish, add the sugar and mix well, adding the milk.
2 Put the slices of bread into the custard for 5 minutes, turning them over once.
3 Melt the butter in a large frying pan and when foaming, fry the slices of bread until golden brown on both sides. Drain on kitchen paper and sprinkle with a little sugar. Keep warm until ready to serve.

VARIATION: Flavour the milk, for example with Calvados, Grand Marnier or ground cinnamon.

Lemon and Raspberry Cheesecake Sundae

Preparation time: 15 minutes
Chilling time: at least 1 hour

SERVES 6

8 digestive biscuits
55 g butter, melted
250 g mascarpone

150 g good-quality lemon curd
300 g vanilla yoghurt
200 g raspberries

1 Whizz the biscuits in a food processor or place them in bag and crush with a rolling pin.
2 Mix together the crushed biscuits and butter. Divide half the mixture between 6 tall glasses.
3 Mix the mascarpone, lemon curd and yoghurt together. Gently fold in the raspberries.
4 Divide half the mixture between the glasses. Cover with the remaining biscuit mix and spoon in the remaining cream cheese mixture. Chill for at least 1 hour before serving.

Quick Lemon and Lime Cheesecake

Preparation time: 20 minutes
Chilling time: at least 2 hours

SERVES 6–8

200 g digestive biscuits

60 g butter, melted

15 g caster sugar

1 × 397 g can of condensed milk

1 × 142 ml pot of double cream

grated zest and juice of 2 lemons

grated zest and juice of 2 limes

1 Whizz the biscuits in a food processor, or place them in a bag and crush them finely with a rolling pin. Add the butter and sugar and mix well, then press into the base of a 24 cm flan ring.

2 Pour the condensed milk into a bowl, whisk in the cream and then slowly whisk in the lemon and lime zest and juice. Whisk just until the mixture is smooth.

3 Pour the mixture on to the crumb base and chill for at least 2 hours, until set.

Baked Rum and Sultana Cheesecake

Preparation time: 25 minutes
Cooking time: 55 minutes

SERVES 8

4 tablespoons dark rum

85 g sultanas

340 g digestive biscuits

110 g butter, melted

225 g caster sugar

500 g cream cheese

1 egg, well beaten

1 teaspoon vanilla extract

1 Preheat the oven to 180°C │350°F│gas mark 4. Place the rum and sultanas in a saucepan and warm gently, or heat in a bowl in the microwave. Set aside.

2 Whizz the biscuits in a food processor or place them in a bag and crush with a rolling pin. Mix the butter with the crumbs and 3 tablespoons of the sugar.

3 Press three-quarters of the mixture into a deep 24 cm loose-bottomed cake tin.

4 Bake in the oven for 5 minutes. Leave to cool.

5 Beat the cream cheese until smooth. Beat in the remaining sugar and then the egg and vanilla extract. Drain the sultanas and fold through the mixture.

6 Pour the mixture on to the crumb base. Sprinkle with the remaining crumbs and bake in the oven for 50 minutes. Serve warm or cold.

Chocolate and Raspberry Cheesecake

Preparation time: 15–20 minutes
Chilling time: at least 3 hours

SERVES 6–8

250 g plain chocolate digestive biscuits

90 g butter, melted

3 tablespoons good-quality raspberry jam

225 g raspberries

300 g cream cheese

250 g mascarpone

150 g vanilla yoghurt

a few drops of vanilla extract

4 tablespoons icing sugar, sifted, plus extra if
required

To decorate

plain chocolate

8 springs of fresh mint

To serve

raspberries

1 Whizz the biscuits in a food processor or place them in a bag and crush with a rolling pin.
2 Place the crushed biscuits in a bowl. Stir in the butter and press the mixture into the base of a 24 cm loose-bottomed flan ring. Spread the raspberry jam over the base and scatter the raspberries on top.
3 Mix together the cream cheese, mascarpone, yoghurt, vanilla extract and icing sugar. Taste and add more icing sugar if desired. Pile the mixture on top of the raspberries and spread flat.
4 Chill for at least 3 hours, or until set.
5 To serve, grate plain chocolate over the top of the cheesecake. Place a slice of the cheesecake on individual plates. Decorate each with a sprig of mint and serve with raspberries.

Rhubarb, Orange and Gingernut Puddings

Preparation and cooking time: 20 minutes
Chilling time: 30 minutes

SERVES 4

280 g rhubarb, washed and cut into 2.5 cm slices
juice of 1 orange
60 g caster sugar
10 gingernut biscuits, crushed

30 g unsalted butter, melted
30 g demerara sugar
grated zest of ½ orange
200 ml double cream, lightly whipped

1 Place the rhubarb in a saucepan with the orange juice and caster sugar and cook over a low heat until the rhubarb is tender and cooked (about 10 minutes).
2 Mix the gingernuts together with the butter and demerara sugar. Press into the bottom of 4 glasses or ramekins.
3 Drain the rhubarb to remove any excess liquid and pulse in a food processor or mash with a fork to a rough purée. Allow to cool.
4 Stir in the orange zest, then fold in the cream. Pour over the gingernut base, then chill for 30 minutes before serving.

Blackberry and Apple Meringue Pie

Preparation time: 25 minutes
Chilling time: 30 minutes
Cooking time: 25 minutes

SERVES 6–8

375 g ready-rolled sweet shortcrust pastry
150 g blackberries, washed
2 Bramley apples, peeled, cored and diced
2 tablespoons crème de cassis or crème de mûres
caster sugar to taste

For the meringue
3 egg whites
170 g caster sugar, plus extra for sprinkling

1 Preheat the oven to 190°C|375°F|gas mark 5. Use the pastry to line a 24 cm flan ring. Chill for 15 minutes. Bake blind (see page 18). Remove from the oven and reduce the temperature to 180°C|350°F|gas mark 4.
2 Wash the blackberries and place in a small saucepan with the apples. Heat very gently until the fruit softens and becomes a thick fruit purée. Stir in the cassis or crème de mûres. Taste and add a little sugar if the mixture is very tart, but do not add too much as it should be a little sharp. Allow to cool.

3 Meanwhile, in a large clean bowl, whisk the egg whites until stiff. Add 1 tablespoon of the sugar and whisk again until very stiff and firm. Fold in the remaining sugar.

4 Spread the blackberry and apple mixture on the base of the pastry case. Pile the meringue on top, making sure that you cover all the filling. Dust with a little extra sugar.

5 Bake in the oven for 10 minutes, or until the meringue is a pale biscuit colour.

VARIATION: Other fruits such as pears or mixed forest fruits can be used, but make sure that the juices are thick and syrupy before adding to the pastry case.

Rhubarb and Custard Meringues

Preparation time: 10 minutes
Cooking time: 20 minutes

SERVES 4

450 g young rhubarb, washed and cut into 2.5 cm lengths
170 g caster sugar, plus extra for dusting
grated zest of 1 orange

500 g ready-made custard
2 egg whites

To prepare ahead: If the custard has completely cooled, the meringue can be placed on top an hour before cooking. However, if the custard is still warm, you can prepare the meringue up to an hour in advance, but do not put it on top of the custard until you are ready to cook.

1 Preheat the oven to 180°C | 350°F | gas mark 4.

2 Place the rhubarb in a pan and sprinkle over 60 g of the sugar and half the orange zest. Cover and cook over a very low heat for about 10 minutes, or until the rhubarb is soft. Divide the rhubarb between 4 large ramekins.

3 Heat the custard and stir in the remaining orange zest. Pour on to the rhubarb.

4 Whisk the egg whites until stiff but not dry.

5 Add 1 tablespoon of sugar and whisk again until very stiff and shiny. Fold in the remaining sugar. Divide the meringue between the ramekins, completely covering the custard and fruit.

6 Dust each lightly with a little extra caster sugar.

7 Place the ramekins on a baking sheet and bake in the oven for 15–20 minutes, or until golden brown on the top. Serve immediately.

Summer Fruit Alaska

Preparation time: 10 minutes
Chilling time: 30 minutes
Cooking time: 5 minutes

SERVES 6

6 generous scoops of good-quality vanilla ice cream

350 g mixed summer berries, such as raspberries,
blueberries or strawberries

2 tablespoons crème de cassis

icing sugar to taste

2 egg whites

100 g caster sugar, plus extra for dusting

To prepare ahead: The meringue will hold in the refrigerator for a couple of hours. Assemble the alaskas just before cooking.

1 Place the ice cream scoops on a baking sheet and freeze until completely solid.
2 Meanwhile, prepare the soft fruit: wash as necessary and hull and halve the strawberries, if using.
3 Divide the fruit between 6 ramekins. Add the cassis and sprinkle over a little icing sugar if the fruit is tart.
4 Preheat the oven to 230°C|450°F|gas mark 8.
5 Whisk the egg whites until stiff but not dry.
6 Add 1 tablespoon of sugar and whisk again until very stiff and shiny. Fold in the remaining sugar.
7 Place a scoop of ice cream on top of the fruit compote and then divide the meringue between the ramekins, spooning it into a dome and making sure that the meringue reaches the edges of the ramekin to cover the ice cream completely. Dust each lightly with a little extra caster sugar.
8 Place the ramekins on a baking sheet and bake in the oven for 3–5 minutes, or until golden brown on the top. Serve immediately.

Chocolate and Hazelnut Alaska

Preparation time: 10 minutes
Chilling time: 30 minutes
Cooking time: 5 minutes

SERVES 6

6 generous scoops of good-quality vanilla or
chocolate ice cream

6 ready-made chocolate brownies (or see page 454)

2 egg whites

100 g caster sugar, plus extra for dusting

60 g hazelnuts, chopped and roasted (see page 17)

6 tablespoons chocolate or butterscotch sauce (see
page 441)

To prepare ahead: Without the hazelnuts the meringue will hold in the refrigerator for a couple of hours. When ready to bake, fold the hazelnuts into the meringue and assemble.

1 Place the ice cream scoops on a baking sheet and put into the freezer until completely solid.
2 Place a piece of chocolate brownie in the bottom of each of 6 ramekins.
3 Preheat the oven to 230°C|450°F|gas mark 8.
4 Whisk the egg whites until stiff but not dry.
5 Add 1 tablespoon of sugar and whisk again until very stiff and shiny. Fold in the remaining sugar and the hazelnuts.
6 Place a scoop of the ice cream on top of each brownie and drizzle over the chocolate or butterscotch sauce. Then divide the meringue between the ramekins, spooning it into a dome and making sure that the meringue reaches the edges of the ramekin to cover the ice cream completely. Dust each lightly with a little extra caster sugar.
7 Place the ramekins on a baking sheet and bake in the oven for 3–5 minutes, or until golden brown on the top. Serve immediately.

Eton Mess

Preparation time: 10 minutes
Marinating time: at least 1 hour

SERVES 6–8

600 g fresh strawberries
grated zest and juice of 1 small orange
2 tablespoons Grand Marnier (optional)

1 × 568 ml pot of double cream
icing sugar
8 meringues nests, broken into pieces

1 Hull the strawberries, slice thickly and sprinkle with the orange zest and juice and the Grand Marnier, if using. Chill for at least 1 hour.
2 Just before serving, whip the cream until it just holds its shape and sweeten with icing sugar. Fold in three-quarters of the strawberries and the broken meringues.
3 Pile into a glass bowl and decorate with the remaining strawberries.

NOTE: This can be made using other fruit, such as raspberries or baked rhubarb. If you are short of time, omit marinating the strawberries.

Pineapple with Lime

Preparation time: 5 minutes

SERVES 6

1 large ripe pineapple
grated zest of 1 lime

To serve
6 lime wedges

To prepare ahead: Prepare completely in advance; the flavours will develop well.

1 Peel and core the pineapple and cut into wedges.
2 Sprinkle over the lime zest.
3 Serve with the lime wedges.

VARIATIONS: Very finely chop a small piece of red chilli and scatter over the pineapple with the lime. Alternatively, infuse the chilli in some sugar syrup and pour the spiced syrup over the pineapple, then sprinkle over the lime zest.

Grilled Pineapple with Ginger Mascarpone Cream

Preparation time: 10 minutes
Cooking time: 5 minutes

SERVES 6

200 g mascarpone
2 tablespoons stem ginger, chopped, plus ginger
  syrup
1 pineapple, peeled, cored and cut into wedges
icing sugar

To serve
6 lime wedges

1 Preheat the grill to the highest setting.
2 Mix together the mascarpone and chopped ginger and flavour and sweeten with a little of the ginger syrup. Chill until needed.
3 Dust the pineapple with sifted icing sugar. Place on a baking sheet and grill for about 5 minutes, or until browned on one side.
4 Serve the pineapple with the ginger mascarpone cream and lime wedges.

NOTE: A blowtorch may be used instead of the grill.

Summer Fruit Kebabs

Preparation time: 5 minutes
Marinating time: 30 minutes
Cooking time: 10 minutes

SERVES 4

grated zest and juice of ½ lime

1 tablespoon Cointreau

1 tablespoon clear honey

¼ pineapple, peeled, cored and cut into 2 cm cubes

2 bananas, cut into 2 cm slices

2 peaches, stoned and cut into chunks

4 wooden skewers, soaked in water

To serve

crème fraîche or vanilla ice cream

To prepare ahead: Thread the fruit on the soaked wooden skewers and leave to marinate for longer.

1 Mix together the lime zest and juice, Cointreau and honey.
2 Drizzle over the fruit and leave to marinate for 30 minutes.
3 Preheat the grill to the highest setting.
4 Thread the fruit on to the skewers.
5 Place the kebabs under the grill, basting occasionally with the juices.
6 Serve immediately with crème fraîche or ice cream.

Rhubarb Baked in Grenadine

Preparation time: 5 minutes
Cooking time: 30 minutes

SERVES 4

450 g rhubarb, trimmed and cut into 10 cm lengths

60 g caster sugar

seeds from 1 vanilla pod (optional)

100 ml grenadine

To serve

sweetened mascarpone and sweet biscuits

or coconut rice pudding (see page 432)

1 Preheat the oven to 180°C│350°F│gas mark 5.
2 Wash the rhubarb and place in a shallow dish. Sprinkle over the sugar and vanilla, if using, and pour over the grenadine. Bake in the oven for 30 minutes.
3 Serve warm with the mascarpone and the biscuits handed separately, or with coconut rice pudding.

Baked Apples

Preparation time: 15 minutes
Cooking time: 45 minutes

SERVES 4

4 Bramley apples
4 tablespoons mincemeat
30 g soft light brown sugar
20 g butter

To serve
custard flavoured with a little Calvados

1 Preheat the oven to 180°C|350°F|gas mark 4.
2 Wash the apples and remove the cores with an apple corer. With a sharp knife, cut a ring just through the apple skin about two-thirds of the way up each apple.
3 Put the apples into an ovenproof dish and stuff the centres with the mincemeat.
4 Sprinkle 2 teaspoons of the sugar over each apple and place a quarter of the butter on the top of each.
5 Pour some cold water into the dish to a depth of 1 cm.
6 Bake in the oven for about 45 minutes, or until the apples are soft right through when tested with a skewer. Serve with the custard.

Baked Peaches with Strawberry Cream

Preparation time: 15 minutes
Cooking time: 20 minutes

SERVES 4

150 g ripe strawberries, hulled and chopped
1 × 142 ml pot of double cream, lightly whipped
4 ripe peaches
2 tablespoons Amaretto or orange juice

a little soft light brown sugar
6 Amaretti biscuits, roughly crushed

To decorate
a few strawberries

To prepare ahead: Prepare to the end of stage 3.

1 Preheat the oven to 180°C|350°F|gas mark 4.
2 Gently stir together the strawberries and the cream. Set aside.
3 Cut the peaches in half and remove the stones. Place in a shallow ovenproof dish and sprinkle over the Amaretto and the sugar.
4 Bake in the oven for 10 minutes, or until the peaches are just beginning to soften. Stir the Amaretti biscuits into the strawberry cream.

5 Place 2 peach halves on each individual plate and drizzle over a little of the juice from the bottom of the dish. Place a large spoonful of the strawberry cream on the top or beside the peaches and decorate with the fresh strawberries.

Basic Fruit Compote

The quantities for this are approximate. If you are using a lot of juicy berries you may need less water; if using fruit such as dessert apples and pears you may need a little more. Likewise, ripe berries will need less sugar than a compote in which you use cooking apples or blackcurrants.

SERVES 4

500 g mixed fruit, peeled if necessary and cut into roughly equal pieces

50–90 g caster sugar
100 ml water

1 Put all the ingredients into a heavy saucepan and cook over a low heat until the fruit is soft and most of the liquid has evaporated.

NOTE: A wide variety of fruits can be used in compotes. Combinations that work well together are:

- Apples, pears, and blackberries
- Raspberries, strawberries and cherries
- Blackcurrants, raspberries and blueberries
- Peaches, apricots, plums
- Rhubarb and orange
- Rhubarb and ginger

Dried fruits, such as dates, raisins, prunes and apricots can be chopped and added to a fresh fruit compote at the beginning so that they absorb the other fruit flavours. They also make a delicious compote on their own without the fresh fruit, and are particularly good if some orange or apple juice is used in place of some of the water.

Compotes can be flavoured with a cinnamon stick, star anise, citrus zest, vanilla seeds or ginger. Use maple syrup, soft light brown sugar, stem ginger syrup, date syrup, elderflower cordial, crème de cassis or clear honey in place of some of the sugar.

Baked Fruit Parcels

Preparation time: 5 minutes
Cooking time: 7 minutes

SERVES 4

2 nectarines, stoned

2 fresh figs

200 g raspberries

100 g blueberries

30 g caster sugar

3 tablespoons ruby port

To serve

crème fraîche

To prepare ahead: Assemble the parcels in advance.

1 Preheat the oven to 230°C|450°F|gas mark 8.
2 Cut the nectarines into chunks and the figs into quarters and mix with the raspberries and blueberries.
3 Divide the fruit between 4 × 20 cm squares of kitchen foil and sprinkle over the sugar and port.
4 Fold up the edges of the foil to form parcels and place on a baking sheet. Bake in the oven for 7 minutes. Serve immediately with the crème fraîche.

VARIATION: The fruits in this recipe can be varied to taste. Pineapple works well.

Baked Apricots, Pistachios and Honey

Preparation time: 5 minutes
Cooking time: 15 minutes

SERVES 4

8 apricots

2 tablespoons clear honey

4 tablespoons Muscat Beaumes de Venise or other sweet white wine

85 g pistachio nuts, roughly chopped

To serve

crème fraîche or vanilla ice cream

1 Preheat the oven to 180°C|350°F|gas mark 4.
2 Cut the apricots in half and remove the stones. Place in a shallow ovenproof dish. Drizzle over the honey and wine and bake in the oven for 5 minutes.
3 Add the pistachios and bake for a further 10 minutes.
4 Serve with crème fraîche or ice cream.

Poached Pears

Preparation time: 10 minutes
Cooking time: 15 minutes

SERVES 4

100 g caster sugar
350 ml water
1 cinnamon stick (optional)
pared zest and juice of 1 orange
4 ripe pears, peeled, cored and cut into quarters or
   eighths

To serve

hot chocolate or butterscotch sauce (see page 441)
vanilla ice cream
shortbread biscuits

1 Put the sugar and water into a wide-based saucepan. Stir gently over a low heat until the sugar has dissolved. Add the cinnamon stick, if using, and the orange zest and juice.
2 Add the pears and poach gently for about 10 minutes, or until the pears are tender. This will depend on how ripe the pears are and how small they are cut.
3 Using a slotted spoon, remove the pears and place in a bowl. If necessary, bring the poaching liquor up to the boil and reduce until syrupy. Strain the syrup over the pears.
4 Serve hot or cold with the sauce, ice cream and shortbread biscuits.

Citrus Fruit Salad

Preparation time: 20 minutes

SERVES 4

2 oranges, peeled and segmented (see page 11)
1 pink grapefruit, peeled and segmented
1 white grapefruit, peeled and segmented

2 tablespoons clear honey
½ teaspoon ground cinnamon

1 Mix all the fruits together in a bowl.
2 Stir through the honey and cinnamon. Add any reserved juice from segmenting to achieve the desired consistency.

Baked Bananas with Orange and Rum

Preparation time: 15 minutes
Cooking time: 35 minutes

SERVES 4

4 large or 8 small ripe bananas

grated zest and juice of 1 large orange

4 tablespoons soft dark brown sugar

4 tablespoons dark rum

20 g butter

To serve

cream, ice cream or Greek yoghurt

To prepare ahead: Assemble the parcels in advance.

1 Preheat the oven to 180°C|350°F|gas mark 4.
2 Cut 4 pieces of kitchen foil each large enough to parcel up a banana.
3 Peel the bananas. Place 1 banana on top of each piece of foil (or 2 if using small bananas) and divide the orange zest and juice between them.
4 Sprinkle 1 tablespoon of the sugar and 1 tablespoon of the rum over each banana. Finally, cut the butter into 4 pieces and top each banana with a piece.
5 Wrap each banana securely in the foil, allowing some space for the hot air to circulate. Bake in the oven for 15 minutes, or until the banana is tender.
6 Serve with cream, ice cream or Greek yoghurt.

Soft Fruit Compote

Preparation time: 20 minutes
Marinating time: 1 hour–overnight

SERVES 4

100 g granulated sugar

seeds of 1 vanilla pod

3 tablespoons Cointreau

6 apricots, stoned and chopped

4 peaches, stoned and chopped

1 punnet of raspberries

To serve

Greek yoghurt

1 Place the sugar and a little water in a heavy saucepan. Dissolve over a low heat.
2 When the sugar has dissolved, increase the heat and boil for 5 minutes. Remove from the heat, add the vanilla seeds and Cointreau and leave to cool.
3 Place the fruits in a bowl, pour over the syrup and leave to marinate for as long as possible.
4 Serve with Greek yoghurt.

VARIATION: Omit the Cointreau and serve for breakfast.

Banana and Date Puddings with Butterscotch Sauce

Preparation time: 15 minutes
Cooking time: 15 minutes

SERVES 6

1 ripe banana	a pinch of salt
1 egg	85 g pitted dates, roughly chopped
140 g caster sugar	butter, for greasing
55 g butter, softened	
a few drops of vanilla extract	**To serve**
140 g self-raising flour	butterscotch sauce (see page 441)
½ teaspoon bicarbonate of soda	vanilla ice cream

To prepare ahead: The puddings can be made in advance and frozen, then defrosted and reheated as required.

1 Preheat the oven to 190°C|375°F|gas mark 5. Grease a 6-hole muffin tray well, and line each tin with a disc of silicone paper.
2 Whizz the banana, egg, sugar, butter and vanilla extract in a blender or food processor until smooth. Sift the flour, bicarbonate of soda and salt into a large bowl. Make a well in the centre.
3 Pour the banana mixture into the centre of the well and add the dates. Stir together with the dry ingredients. Pour the mixture into the tins. Bake in the oven for 10–15 minutes, or until well risen and golden.
4 When the puddings are cooked, remove from the oven, turn out and allow to cool slightly on a wire rack.
5 Serve the puddings warm with the butterscotch sauce poured over and around, and a scoop of ice cream on the side.

VARIATION: Bake the mixture in muffin cases and serve as a cake at teatime.

Hot Winter Fruit Salad

This is also delicious served cold, and can be served for breakfast.

Preparation time: 5 minutes
Soaking time: 4 hours–overnight
Cooking time: 30 minutes

SERVES 4

500 g good-quality mixed dried fruits, such as
    prunes, apricots, figs, pears, pineapple, mango,
    apples
1 tablespoon Calvados
Earl Grey tea
4 tablespoons fresh orange juice
2 cloves

1 × 5 cm cinnamon stick
¼ teaspoon ground mixed spice
thinly pared zest of 1 lemon
1 star anise

To serve
Greek yoghurt

1 Soak the mixed dried fruits in the Calvados and enough tea just to cover. Leave to marinate for at least 4 hours or overnight.
2 Pour the fruit and soaking juice into a heavy saucepan and add the orange juice, cloves, cinnamon, mixed spice, lemon zest and star anise. Bring to the boil, then simmer slowly for about 20 minutes, or until the fruits are soft. Add more liquid if the fruit gets too dry.
3 Remove the cloves, cinnamon, lemon zest and star anise before serving.

NOTE: 'Ready-to-eat' dried fruit is more succulent and will not need to be simmered for so long.

Instant Individual Crumbles

This is a good way of using up leftover cooked fruit.

Preparation time: 10 minutes

SERVES 4

350 g stewed or poached fruit
sugar to taste
lemon juice to taste
8 tablespoons crème fraîche

¼ teaspoon ground cinnamon
100 g crunchy oat and fruit breakfast cereal, such as
    Jordans

1 Heat the fruit gently, taste and add sugar or lemon juice.
2 Divide the fruit between 4 ramekins. Place a tablespoonful of the crème fraîche on top of the fruit.

3 Add the cinnamon to the cereal and divide the mixture over the fruit.

4 Serve with the remaining crème fraîche.

Chocolate Fondant Puddings

You will need 4 × 200 ml dariole moulds for this recipe.

Preparation time: 15 minutes
Chilling time: 30 minutes–24 hours
Cooking time: 11 minutes

MAKES 4

melted butter	95 g caster sugar
cocoa powder for dusting	3 level tablespoons plain flour
200 g dark chocolate	
95 g butter	**To serve**
3 eggs	vanilla ice cream or cream
2 egg yolks	

To prepare ahead: Make the mixture and keep in the fridge for up to 24 hours before baking.

1 Preheat the oven to 200°C|400°F|gas mark 6.

2 Brush the dariole moulds with the melted butter and dust with the cocoa powder. (To do this, pour sieved cocoa powder into the dariole moulds, tap it around the edges around and pour out.) Place the moulds in the freezer to chill while you make the mixture.

3 Put the chocolate and butter into a heatproof bowl set over a saucepan of simmering water (do not allow the bowl to touch the water). Allow the chocolate to melt.

4 In a large bowl, beat the eggs, yolks and sugar until thick and pale.

5 Fold in the melted chocolate and butter. Sieve the plain flour over the mixture and fold in.

6 Take the moulds out of the freezer and fill them with the chocolate mixture up to 1 cm below the rim, then chill for at least 30 minutes, or up to 24 hours

7 Cook in the oven for 11 minutes. Remove from the oven and leave to stand for 2 minutes.

8 Turn out on to individual plates and serve with vanilla ice cream or cream.

Raspberry Summer Pudding

Preparation time: 20 minutes
Chilling time: overnight

SERVES 4

900 g raspberries, fresh or frozen

2 tablespoons water

170 g caster sugar

4 tablespoons crème de cassis

6–9 slices of stale white bread, crusts removed

To serve

crème fraîche, sweetened with a little icing sugar

sprigs of fresh mint

1 Cook the raspberries with the water and sugar in a saucepan for 5 minutes, or until just soft but still bright in colour.

2 Drain off and reserve the juice, add the cassis and set aside.

3 Cut one slice of bread into a circle that fits snugly into the base of a pudding basin. Cut the rest into triangles.

4 Dip the triangles and circle of bread into the reserved raspberry juice and use as many as necessary to line the basin.

5 While the fruit is still just warm, pour it into the bread-lined basin. Cover with the remaining pieces of bread dipped in the fruit juice. Tip the remaining juice into a saucepan and reduce, by boiling rapidly, to a syrupy consistency. Leave to cool.

6 Stand the pudding basin on a dish. Press a saucer or plate on top of the pudding and put a weight, such as some cans of fruit, on top. Chill overnight. Remove the weight and saucer.

7 Invert a serving dish over the bowl and turn both over together. Give a sharp shake and carefully remove the bowl. Spoon over the reserved reduced raspberry juice.

8 Serve each portion with some sweetened crème fraîche, decorated with a sprig of mint.

Autumn Crumble

Preparation time: 25 minutes
Cooking time: 45 minutes

SERVES 4

3 pears, peeled, cored and cut into chunks

granulated sugar

100 g blackberries, washed

85 g hazelnuts, chopped

120 g butter

60 g granulated sugar

60 g demerara sugar

2 Bramley apples, peeled, cored and cut into chunks

For the crumble

170 g plain flour

a pinch of salt

To serve

warm custard or ice cream

To prepare ahead: The crumble mixture can be prepared in advance and kept in the refrigerator or freezer. The whole dish can also be assembled ahead of time and refrigerated until required.

1 Preheat the oven to 200°C | 400°F | gas mark 6. Preheat a baking sheet in the oven.
2 Make the crumble: sift the flour with the salt into a bowl. Rub in the butter until the mixture resembles coarse breadcrumbs, then mix in the sugars. Chill while you prepare the fruit.
3 Place half the apples and pears in an ovenproof dish and scatter over a little sugar.
4 Place the blackberries on top. Cover with the remaining apples and pears. Scatter over a little more sugar and the hazelnuts. Sprinkle the crumble mixture over the top.
5 Place on the hot baking sheet and bake in the oven for 30–45 minutes, or until hot through and slightly browned on top.
6 Serve with warm custard or ice cream.

Banoffee Crumble

Preparation time: 10 minutes
Cooking time: 30 minutes

SERVES 4

4 ripe bananas, peeled
6 tablespoons Dulce de Leche

120 g butter
60 g granulated sugar

For the crumble
170 g plain flour
a pinch of salt

To serve
vanilla ice cream or cream

To prepare ahead: Make the whole dish in advance, and refrigerate, then bake or reheat as required. The crumble topping freezes well and can be prepared and frozen separately.

1 Preheat the oven to 200°C | 400°F | gas mark 6.
2 Sift the flour with the salt into a bowl. Rub in the butter until the mixture resembles coarse breadcrumbs, then mix in the sugar.
3 Chop the bananas and place in an ovenproof dish. Spoon or drizzle over the Dulce de Leche, turning the bananas so that the toffee is distributed as evenly as possible. This can be quite difficult as the toffee is thick, so don't worry too much about it.
4 Sprinkle the crumble mixture on top and bake in the oven for 30 minutes, or until the crumble is golden.
5 Allow to cool a little before serving with ice cream or cream.

Peach Melba Crumble

Preparation time: 10 minutes
Cooking time: 40 minutes

SERVES 4–6

8 peaches, peeled and stoned

300 g raspberries

1 tablespoon soft light brown sugar

For the crumble

85 g plain flour

a pinch of salt

85 g oats

140 g butter

55 g soft light brown sugar

85 g Amaretti biscuits, crushed

To serve

vanilla yoghurt or ice cream

To prepare ahead: Assemble to the end of stage 4. The crumble topping freezes well and can be prepared and frozen separately.

1 Preheat the oven to 200°C|400°F|gas mark 6.
2 Sift the flour and salt into a bowl and add the oats. Rub in the butter until the mixture resembles coarse breadcrumbs, then stir in the sugar and Amaretti biscuits.
3 Cut the peaches into chunks and place in an ovenproof dish with the raspberries. Scatter over the sugar.
4 Sprinkle the crumble mixture over the fruit.
5 Bake in the oven for 40 minutes, or until hot and slightly browned on top. Serve with yoghurt or ice cream.

Apple and Blackcurrant Fudge Crumble

Preparation time: 15 minutes
Cooking time: 30 minutes

SERVES 6–8

900 g Bramley apples

225 g blackcurrants, destalked

60 g demerara sugar

For the crumble

225 g plain flour

a pinch of salt

140 g butter

50 g granulated sugar

250 g hard butter fudge, chopped into small pieces

To serve

custard, cream or vanilla ice cream

To prepare ahead: Complete to the end of stage 4. The crumble topping keeps well in the freezer and can be prepared and frozen separately.

1 Preheat the oven to 190°C|375°F|gas mark 6. Preheat a baking sheet.
2 Make the crumble: sift the flour with the salt into a bowl. Rub in the butter until the mixture resembles coarse breadcrumbs, then mix in the sugar. Stir through the fudge.
3 Peel and core the apples. Cut into chunks. Mix with the blackcurrants. Add the sugar and tip into an ovenproof dish.
4 Sprinkle the crumble mixture over the apples and blackcurrants.
5 Place on the hot baking sheet and bake in the oven for 30–40 minutes, or until hot through and slightly browned on top. Leave to cool for a few minutes before serving.

Bread and Butter Pudding

Preparation time: 10 minutes
Soaking time: 30 minutes
Cooking time: 25 minutes

SERVES 4

2 slices of white bread	1 rounded tablespoon caster sugar
30 g butter	300 ml full-fat milk
2 tablespoons currants and sultanas, mixed	a few drops of vanilla extract
2 teaspoons chopped mixed peel	ground cinnamon
2 eggs	demerara sugar
1 egg yolk	

1 Preheat the oven to 180°C|350°F|gas mark 4.
2 Spread the bread with the butter and sprinkle over the fruit and peel. Cut each slice into quarters. Arrange in overlapping rows in a shallow ovenproof dish, fruit side up.
3 Make the custard: mix the whole eggs and the yolk with the caster sugar and stir in the milk and vanilla extract. Strain the custard carefully over the bread and leave to soak for 30 minutes. Sprinkle with cinnamon and demerara sugar.
4 Place the dish in a roasting pan half-filled with hot water (a bain-marie, see page 9) and bake in the middle of the oven for about 45 minutes, or until the custard is set and the top is brown and crusty.

VARIATIONS: This is a basic bread and butter pudding recipe. Vary it by adding different dried fruits, such as cranberries or blueberries, to the mixture. Spread the bread with different flavourings, such as apricot or raspberry jam. Omit the fruit and use only hazelnut chocolate spread, or mincemeat at Christmas. Use different breads such as croissants, panettone or brioche.

Coconut Rice Pudding

Preparation time: 2 minutes
Cooking time: 25 minutes

SERVES 4

20 g butter
250 g arborio rice
60 g caster sugar
400 ml coconut milk

200 ml coconut cream
400 ml water

To serve
fresh fruit, such as mango, pineapple, and bananas

1 Melt the butter in a saucepan. Add the rice and stir for 30 seconds until all the grains are coated in the butter and becoming translucent.
2 Add the sugar, coconut milk and cream and the water.
3 Bring to a simmer and leave to cook for 25 minutes, stirring every 5 minutes or so.

NOTES: Once the liquids have been added, the rice can be transferred to an ovenproof dish and baked in the oven at 170°C│325°F│gas mark 3 for 35–40 minutes, stirring after 20 minutes.

This pudding can also be made using 800 ml milk and 200 ml cream, flavoured with freshly grated nutmeg, for a quick version of a traditional rice pudding.

Rice Pudding

Preparation time: 2 minutes
Cooking time: 3–4 hours

SERVES 4

a knob of butter
1 tablespoon caster sugar
60 g pudding rice

600 ml milk
a few drops of vanilla extract
freshly grated nutmeg

1 Preheat the oven to 150°C│300°F│gas mark 2.
2 Grease a pie dish with the butter. Put the sugar, rice, milk and vanilla extract into the dish. Sprinkle with nutmeg.
3 Stir, then bake in the oven for 3–4 hours, or until the pudding is soft and creamy, with an evenly coloured brown skin.

NOTE: For a quick version of rice pudding see above.

Sweet Spiced Couscous

This is good served with stewed fruit, fresh in the summer or dried in the winter. It is also a good alternative to porridge for breakfast.

Preparation time: 5 minutes
Cooking time: 5–10 minutes

SERVES 4

600 ml full-fat milk

2 tablespoons soft light brown sugar

grated zest of ½ lemon or orange

4 medjool dates, pitted and roughly chopped

85 g couscous

1 teaspoon ground cinnamon

1 tablespoon pistachio nuts, chopped and lightly toasted (see page 17)

1 Heat the milk with the sugar, citrus zest and dates. Remove from the heat and leave to stand for 5 minutes.
2 Add the couscous and the cinnamon. Bring to the boil, then simmer for 5–10 minutes, or until thick.
3 Add the pistachios and serve immediately as the couscous will continue to thicken and can become stodgy.

Affogato

Preparation time: 5 minutes

SERVES 4

4–8 scoops of good-quality vanilla ice cream

4 shots of espresso coffee

4 shots of liqueur, such as frangelico (optional)

To prepare ahead: Scoop the ice cream in advance and return to the freezer, then assemble when ready to serve.

1 Scoop the ice cream into balls.
2 Place the ice cream in individual dishes or large cups.
3 Serve the ice cream with the coffee and the liqueur, if using, in shot glasses so that your guests can pour the coffee and liqueur over the top.

Banana and Honey Ice Cream

Preparation time: 5 minutes
Freezing time: 45 minutes
Softening time: 20–30 minutes

SERVES 6

6 ripe bananas
juice of 1 lemon
6 tablespoons acacia honey
425 ml whipping cream
¼ teaspoon vanilla extract

To serve
chopped walnuts
clear honey

1 Place all the ingredients in a blender or food processor and whizz until smooth.
2 Pour into an ice-cream maker and freeze according to the manufacturer's instructions. Alternatively, pour into a freezer container and put into the freezer. When nearly solid, cut into chunks and pulse in a food processor and return to the freezer until frozen.
3 Remove from the freezer 20 minutes before serving. Serve each scoop of ice cream with walnuts scattered over the top and a drizzle of honey.

Lemon Curd Ice Cream

Preparation time: 2 minutes
Freezing time: overnight
Softening time: 1 hour

SERVES 4

400 g good-quality lemon curd (or see page 473)
400 g Greek yoghurt

1 Place the lemon curd in a bowl and stir in the yoghurt. Cover closely and freeze overnight.
2 Transfer the ice cream to the refrigerator about 1 hour before serving.

Coconut Ice Cream

Preparation time: 15 minutes
Infusing time: 30 minutes
Freezing time: 3 hours
Softening time: 20 minutes

SERVES 4

1 × 284 ml pot of double cream
200 ml coconut cream
50 ml water
60 g desiccated coconut
60 g caster sugar

4 egg yolks
2 tablespoons Malibu (optional)

To serve
hot chocolate sauce (see page 441)

1 Bring the cream, coconut cream, water and coconut to the boil in a large, heavy saucepan. Remove from the heat, cover and set aside for 30 minutes to infuse.
2 In a large bowl, whisk the sugar with the egg yolks until creamy. Add the coconut infusion and gradually mix together.
3 Return the mixture to the pan and cook over a low heat, stirring constantly with a wooden spoon, until the custard is thick enough to coat the back of the spoon. Take care not to overheat and scramble the eggs. Stir in the Malibu, if using. Leave to cool.
4 Pour the mixture into a freezer tray and freeze. When the mixture is half frozen, remove from the freezer, whisk again or pulse in a food processor and return to the freezer until firm (or alternatively use an ice-cream maker).
5 Remove from the freezer for 20 minutes before serving with chocolate sauce.

Crunchie and Brownie Ice Cream

Preparation time: 10 minutes
Freezing time: 6 hours
Softening time: 20 minutes

SERVES 8

1 × 284 ml pot of double cream
425 g ready-made fresh custard

1 Crunchie bar
110 g chocolate brownies (or see page 454)

1 Lightly whip the cream in a large bowl. Stir in the custard.
2 Bash the Crunchie bar with a rolling pin and crumble the brownies, but leave quite chunky. Stir them into the cream mixture.
3 Line a 450 g loaf tin or plastic box with clingfilm. Pour the mixture in and freeze for up to 6 hours.
4 Remove from the freezer for 20 minutes, then turn out and remove the clingfilm. Slice and serve.

Lime Sorbet

This is quite a soft-set sorbet.

Preparation time: 5 minutes
Freezing time: 3½ hours

SERVES 4

4 limes
200 g granulated sugar

600 ml water

1 Grate the zest from 2 of the limes. Put into a large, heavy saucepan with the sugar and water.
2 Place the pan over a low heat and when the sugar has completely dissolved, bring to the boil, then simmer for 5 minutes.
3 Squeeze all the limes and strain the juice into the syrup. Pour into a shallow dish and place in the freezer. When nearly solid, cut into chunks and pulse in a food processor or whisk and return to the freezer until frozen (or alternatively use an ice-cream maker).

Millionaire's Ice Cream

Preparation time: 10 minutes
Freezing time: 3 hours
Softening time: 20 minutes

SERVES 6

1 × 284 ml pot of double cream, lightly whipped
300 ml ready-made fresh custard
140 g shortbread, broken into pieces
½–¾ jar Dulce de Leche (about 225 g)

To serve

hot chocolate sauce (see page 441)

1 Mix the cream and custard together. Place in a plastic box in the freezer until half frozen.
2 Remove from the freezer and stir the shortbread and Dulce de Leche gently into the ice cream, so that there are swirls of toffee and lumps of shortbread. Return to the freezer and allow to freeze completely (or alternatively use an ice-cream maker).
3 Remove the ice cream from the freezer 20 minutes before serving, then scoop into bowls and pour over the chocolate sauce.

Pineapple Sorbet

Preparation time: 20 minutes
Freezing time: 3 hours

SERVES 4–6

1 large pineapple
170 g granulated sugar
300 ml hot water

3 tablespoons Malibu (optional)
1 egg white

1 Peel and core the pineapple and cut it into chunks. Whizz in a food processor to make a purée.
2 Dissolve the sugar in the water and bring to the boil. Simmer for 5–6 minutes, then allow to cool. (To test, place a little of the cooled syrup on a teaspoon. Dip the handle of a wooden spoon into the syrup, then rub it between your thumb and finger: it should feel oily when rubbed.)
3 Meanwhile, mix together the pineapple purée and Malibu, if using. Add the sugar syrup and stir well, then pour into a shallow container and freeze until nearly solid.
4 Cut the sorbet into cubes and place in a food processor. Whizz, using the pulse button to break up the crystals, adding the egg white at the same time. Once the egg white is incorporated, return the sorbet to the container, cover and freeze until firm.

Pineapple Yoghurt Ice Cream

Preparation time: 5 minutes
Freezing time: 3 hours
Softening time: 15 minutes

SERVES 6

½ large, ripe pineapple
200 g vanilla yoghurt

To serve

shortbread biscuits

1 Peel and core the pineapple and cut it into chunks. Whizz in a food processor to make a purée.
2 Add the yoghurt and whizz again until well blended and smooth.
3 Pour into an ice-cream maker and freeze according to the manufacturer's instructions. Alternatively, place in a plastic container, cover and freeze until nearly solid. Cut into chunks and whizz in the food processor, or whisk, then return to the freezer until firm.
4 Remove from the freezer 15 minutes before serving. Scoop into bowls and serve with the biscuits.

Seabreeze Sorbet

Preparation time: 5 minutes
Freezing time: 4 hours

SERVES 6

600 ml fresh grapefruit juice
150 ml cranberry juice cordial
30 ml vodka (optional)

grated zest of 1 lime
½ egg white, lightly beaten

1 Mix together the grapefruit juice, cranberry cordial, the vodka, if using, and the lime zest. Pour into a freezer container and freeze until nearly solid.
2 Remove from the freezer and allow to soften slightly. Cut into cubes and place in a food processor. Whizz, using the pulse button to break up the crystals, adding the egg white at the same time. Once the egg white is incorporated, return the sorbet to the container, cover and freeze until firm.

NOTE: Be sure to use undiluted cranberry cordial rather than cranberry juice.

Frozen Chocolate and Orange Cheesecake

Preparation time: 30 minutes
Freezing time: overnight
Softening time: 30 minutes

SERVES 6–8

80 g butter, melted
225 g digestive biscuits, crushed
225 g cream cheese
½ teaspoon vanilla extract
110 g caster sugar

170 g plain chocolate, melted
grated zest of 2 oranges
2 eggs, beaten
1 × 142 ml pot of double cream, lightly whipped
2 egg whites

1 Preheat the oven to 180°C|350°F|gas mark 4.
2 Mix the butter with the biscuits and press into the base of a 20 cm loose-bottomed or spring-form cake tin. Bake in the oven for 10 minutes, then leave to cool.
3 Beat the cream cheese with the vanilla extract and half the sugar. Stir in the melted chocolate, orange zest and the whole eggs. Fold in the cream.
4 Whisk the egg whites until they form medium peaks, then add the remaining sugar and whisk again for 20 seconds. Fold into the chocolate mixture. Pour this mixture on to the crumb base and freeze overnight.
5 Transfer to the refrigerator 30 minutes before serving, to soften slightly.

Meringue Ice Cream Cake

Preparation time: 20 minutes
Freezing time: at least 3 hours
Softening time: 20 minutes

8 meringue nests

200 g dark chocolate, chopped

4 tablespoons brandy

110 g flaked almonds, lightly toasted (see page 17)

1 × 284 ml pot of double cream, lightly whipped

To serve

200 g strawberries or raspberries

1 Line a 450 g loaf tin with clingfilm so that the clingfilm hangs over the edges.
2 Lightly crush the meringue nests.
3 Put the chocolate and brandy into a heatproof bowl set over, not in, a pan of simmering water and stir from time to time until melted. Allow to cool.
4 Fold the meringues, almonds, cream and chocolate mixture together and pile into the loaf tin.
5 Cover with the cling film overlap and freeze for 3 hours or overnight, until firm. Remove from the freezer 20 minutes before serving.
6 Cut the cake into slices and serve with the strawberries or raspberries on the side.

Mango and Passionfruit Sauce

2 ripe passionfruits

3 tablespoons orange juice, plus extra if required

1 large ripe mango

caster sugar (optional)

1 Cut the passionfruits in half and scoop out the pulp. Place with the orange juice in the bowl of a food processor. (A blender is not suitable for this sauce.)
2 Peel the mango, cut the flesh from the stone and roughly chop the flesh (see page 16). Add to the food processor with the passionfruits.
3 Whizz until smooth. Taste the sauce and add a little sugar if necessary. Add more orange juice if too thick. Sieve if a completely smooth sauce is required.

Raspberry Sauce

250 g fresh or frozen raspberries   icing sugar

1 Defrost the raspberries if frozen.
2 Place the raspberries in a small saucepan. If using fresh raspberries, add 2 tablespoons water. Bring to the boil, then push through a sieve with a wooden spoon to remove all the seeds.
3 Sift in icing sugar to taste. If the sauce is too thick, add a few additional spoonfuls of water. Chill before using.

Mango and Lime Coulis

1 large mango, peeled and destoned (see page 16)   icing sugar
grated zest and juice of 1 lime

1 Place the mango flesh, lime zest and juice in a processor and blend together until smooth.
2 Sieve into a bowl and add icing sugar to taste. Chill before serving.

VARIATIONS: Other fruit coulis can be made in the same way: strawberry, raspberry, blackberry or papaya work well.

Apricot Glaze

3 tablespoons apricot jam   juice of ½ lemon
1 tablespoon water

1 Place all the ingredients in a heavy saucepan.
2 Bring slowly to the boil, stirring gently (avoid beating in bubbles) until syrupy in consistency. Strain.

NOTE: Use when still warm, as the glaze becomes too stiff to manage when cold. It will keep warm standing over a saucepan of very hot water.

Blackberry Sauce

100 g granulated sugar

150 ml water

350 g frozen blackberries, defrosted

1 Heat the sugar and water in a heavy saucepan over a low heat until the sugar has dissolved. Bring to the boil. Allow to bubble for 10 minutes, or until the syrup begins to thicken and the bubbles get bigger and slower.

2 Whizz the blackberries in a blender or food processor to make a purée.

3 Pour the sugar syrup on to the blackberries and pass through a sieve. Serve hot or cold.

Hot Chocolate Sauce

170 g plain chocolate, chopped

4 tablespoons water

1 tablespoon golden syrup

1 teaspoon instant coffee powder, dissolved in

1 tablespoon boiling water

15 g butter

1 Put the chocolate into a heatproof bowl set over, not in, a saucepan of simmering water and stir from time to time until melted. Add all the remaining ingredients and stir until smooth and shiny.

Butterscotch Sauce

100 g granulated sugar

water

1 × 142 ml pot of double cream

1 Place the sugar in a large heavy saucepan and pour over enough hot water from a kettle to cover. Dissolve the sugar over a low heat without stirring or allowing the water to boil.

2 Once all the sugar has dissolved, turn up the heat and boil until it is a good caramel colour.

3 Immediately tip in the double cream (it will fizz dangerously, so stand well back). Stir until any lumps have dissolved, then simmer the sauce for 2 minutes. Remove from the heat and allow to cool.

Toffee Sauce

2 tablespoons brandy
110 g butter

60 g demerara sugar
2 tablespoons double cream

1 Place all the ingredients in a heavy saucepan, stir, and heat until melted. Bring to the boil and allow to thicken slightly.

Brandy Butter

200 g unsalted butter
200 g caster sugar

grated zest of 1 orange
4 tablespoons brandy

1 Cream the butter and sugar together until very soft and pale in colour. Mix in the orange zest and brandy to flavour fairly strongly. Serve well chilled.

Crème Anglaise (English Egg Custard)

Preparation time: 5 minutes
Cooking time: 5 minutes

300 ml milk, or milk and double cream mixed
1 vanilla pod, split lengthways, or a few drops of vanilla extract

3 large egg yolks
1 tablespoon caster sugar

1 Heat the milk and vanilla pod (if you are using vanilla extract, add in stage 3) and bring slowly to the boil.
2 Beat the egg yolks in a bowl with the sugar. Pour the milk on to the egg yolks, stirring steadily. Mix well and return to the pan.
3 Using a wooden spoon, stir over a low heat until the mixture thickens sufficiently to coat the back of the spoon (about 5 minutes). Do not allow the mixture to boil. Strain into a chilled bowl and add the vanilla extract, if using.

Cheese

Serving a cheeseboard is a great way to end a meal. You can serve it before, after or in place of pudding. It is also one of the simplest finales and only requires making a few decisions at the cheesemonger or supermarket counter.

When choosing cheeses, consider those who will be sharing the cheese. Are they adventurous or traditional? Is anyone vegetarian or allergic to cow's milk? When selecting your cheese it is also worth considering a range of textures, colours, milk types, shapes and strengths of flavour. You should have a variety of cheese on a cheeseboard to reflect different styles, textures and tastes. In its most basic form this would include a hard cheese, such as Cheddar, a soft matured cheese such as Somerset Brie, a blue cheese such as Stilton and probably a goat's cheese, either hard, such as Ticklemore, or soft, such as Capricorn. Nowadays newer cheeses such as white Stilton with fruits are growing in popularity and are often found on cheeseboards; they are less intimidating for the uninitiated cheese eater and are easier to eat than some very strong and overpowering cheeses that can be an acquired taste.

Some cheeses are seasonal: for example, Vacherin Mont d'Or is only available over the winter (particularly at Christmas) – it is delicious but extremely smelly and runny and is often served in its box with a spoon. It is so unusual that it is really best served without other cheeses, which would only act as a distraction and would also be overpowered by the Vacherin. However, if you have guests with milder palates you will need to offer an alternative.

It is better to have only a couple of large pieces of cheese rather than several small ones that will dry out, look unappetizing and will be gone after only a few guests have helped themselves. Cheese portions should not be less than 250 g in weight: anything smaller can look mean and the cheese will be more prone to drying out.

The number of cheeses on a cheeseboard depends on the number of guests, but generally it is advisable to have no more than five or six different cheeses. The amount of cheese you need depends on the occasion: if the cheese follows a heavy meal then 70–90 g per person will be sufficient. These amounts can be varied to suit the appetites of your guests.

Try to buy cheeses that are already ripe as they will not really ripen in a refrigerator. They should be stored in waxed paper and removed from the refrigerator at least 1 hour before serving.

It is also worth thinking about the shape of the cheeses on the board. You want some to have a bit of height so that they are easy to arrange on the plate. Cheeses need to be displayed so that they are easy to cut. Put the small ones in the middle, then arrange the soft ones around them. The hard cheeses that are more difficult to cut should be placed on the outside of the cheeseboard.

Choose a board appropriate to the amount and number of cheeses you have. Slate ones are becoming very popular as you can write the name of the cheese in chalk beside it. It is quite a nice idea to label the more unusual cheeses, as this will save you having to remember or your guests asking. White labels to stick in the cheese can be purchased from cheesemongers; alternatively brown parcel labels can be slipped half under the cheese.

Accompaniments for cheese are wide and varied. Some purists think only bread should be served, as biscuits mask the texture of the cheese and can be salty and affect the flavour. However, there are so many biscuits on the market that there is something to suit every palate – and cheese. Other accompaniments include: pickles, chutneys and fruit cheeses, such as quince or membrillo. Fruits such as apples, pears, figs, dates, and walnuts, brazil nuts, cherry tomatoes and celery all provide different textures to complement softer cheese, but can sometimes overpower very delicate cheese flavours.

It is traditional to serve port with cheese. Although delicious, port can often mask the flavours of all but the strongest hard blue cheeses. As a very general rule, the whiter the cheese, the whiter the wine should be, and more mature cheeses can be served with fuller-bodied wines. A light red can suit a wide range of cheeses. Sweet dessert wines often go well with cheese; the sweetness offsetting the saltiness in the cheese.

Baking

The following recipes use mainly storecupboard ingredients and so can satisfy any sudden desire for the comfort of a homebaked cake or biscuit. To test whether a large cake is cooked, press gently in the centre – it should have a spring-like texture. The cake will also be lightly browned and will shrink away from the sides slightly when cooked.

Apple and Cinnamon Cookies

Preparation time: 10 minutes
Cooking time: 10–15 minutes

MAKES ABOUT 25

110 g unsalted butter, softened, plus extra for
  greasing
170 g caster sugar
1 egg, beaten
grated zest of 1 lemon
½ tablespoon lemon juice

200 g plain flour
4 teaspoons ground cinnamon
1 teaspoon baking powder
a pinch of salt
200 g dessert apples, peeled, cored and chopped into
  small dice
icing sugar

To prepare ahead: These will keep in an airtight container for about a week.

1 Preheat the oven to 190°C│375°F│gas mark 5. Grease 3 baking sheets with butter.
2 In a large bowl, cream the butter until soft, add the sugar and beat until pale and fluffy.
3 Add the egg gradually, beating well after each addition. Add the lemon zest and juice and mix well.
4 Sift in the flour, cinnamon, baking powder and salt and mix to a stiffish dough, then stir in the apple.
5 Place large spoonfuls of the mixture on each prepared baking sheet, leaving space to allow the biscuits to spread.
6 Bake in the oven for 10–15 minutes, or until golden brown. Transfer to a wire rack and leave to cool completely.
7 Before serving, dust with a little sifted icing sugar and a little more cinnamon if desired.

Bakewell Biscuits

Preparation time: 15 minutes
Chilling time: 20 minutes
Cooking time: 18 minutes

MAKES 10–12

170 g unsalted butter, softened, plus extra for
   greasing
85 g icing sugar, sifted
1 large egg yolk
½ teaspoon almond essence
250 g plain flour, sifted

45 g ground almonds
a pinch of salt

To finish
4 tablespoons raspberry jam
icing sugar

To prepare ahead: These will keep in an airtight container for a week, unassembled. Once they have been sandwiched together the jam will begin to soften them.

1   Preheat the oven to 180°C|350°F|gas mark 4. Grease 2 baking sheets with butter.
2   In a large bowl, cream the butter until soft, add the icing sugar and beat until light and fluffy. Add the egg yolk and almond essence and beat well.
3   Fold in the flour, ground almonds and salt.
4   Shape the dough into 2 cylinders and wrap in clingfilm. Chill for 20 minutes.
5   Slice into rounds about the thickness of a £1 coin and place on the baking sheets, leaving room for the biscuits to spread. Bake in the oven for 15–20 minutes, or until a pale golden brown. Transfer to a wire rack and leave to cool completely.
6   When cool and ready to serve, sandwich the biscuits together with the raspberry jam and dust with sifted icing sugar.

Blueberry Biscuits

Preparation time: 15 minutes
Cooking time: 10–15 minutes

MAKES ABOUT 16

110 g unsalted butter, softened, plus extra for
   greasing
170 g caster sugar
1 egg, beaten
grated zest of 1 lemon

200 g plain flour
1 teaspoon baking powder
a pinch of salt
200 g dried blueberries
icing sugar

1 Preheat the oven to 190°C|375°F|gas mark 5. Grease 3 baking sheets with butter.

2 In a large bowl, cream the butter until soft, add the sugar and beat until pale and fluffy.

3 Add the egg gradually, beating well after each addition. Stir in the zest.

4 Sift in the flour, baking powder and salt and mix to a stiffish dough, then stir in the dried blueberries.

5 Place large spoonfuls of the mixture on each prepared baking sheet, leaving room for the biscuits to spread.

6 Bake in the oven for 10–15 minutes, or until golden brown. Transfer to a wire rack and leave to cool completely.

7 Before serving, dust with a little sifted icing sugar.

VARIATIONS: Dried cranberries or cherries can be used instead of the blueberries. The biscuits can be drizzled with a little melted white chocolate.

Chocolate Chip and Hazelnut Cookies

Preparation time: 20 minutes
Cooking time: 12 minutes

MAKES ABOUT 18

110 g butter, plus extra for greasing	a pinch of salt
110 g caster sugar	½ teaspoon vanilla extract
1 egg, beaten	110 g dark chocolate, chopped
170 g plain flour, sifted	60 g hazelnuts, roughly chopped

To prepare ahead: These will keep in an airtight container for about a week.

1 Preheat the oven to 180°C|350°F|gas mark 4. Grease a baking sheet with butter.

2 In a large bowl, cream the butter until soft, add the sugar and beat again until pale and fluffy. Beat in the egg, the flour, salt, vanilla extract, chocolate and nuts. Do not overstir.

3 Place large teaspoonfuls of the mixture on the prepared baking sheet, leaving room for the biscuits to spread, and bake in the oven for 10–12 minutes, or until golden brown and cooked through. Transfer to a wire rack and leave to cool completely.

VARIATION: Walnuts can be used in place of the hazelnuts.

Date and Ginger Biscuits

Preparation time: 15 minutes
Chilling time: 30 minutes
Cooking time: 15 minutes

MAKES ABOUT 15

85 g butter, softened, plus extra for greasing

85 g soft light brown sugar

1 egg, beaten

30 g dried dates, chopped

2 pieces of stem ginger, finely chopped

a pinch of salt

100 g self-raising flour, sifted

100 g medium oatmeal

To finish

extra oatmeal

To prepare ahead: These will keep in an airtight container for about a week.

1 Preheat the oven to 180°C│350°F│gas mark 4. Grease a baking sheet with butter.
2 In a large bowl, cream the butter until soft, add the sugar and beat until pale and fluffy.
3 Add the egg gradually, beating well after each addition.
4 Stir in the remaining ingredients except the oatmeal and mix to a dough.
5 Roll the dough into a cylinder about 5 cm in diameter. Roll the cylinder in oatmeal. Wrap in clingfilm and chill for at least 30 minutes.
6 Unwrap the dough, slice into 5 mm slices and arrange on the prepared baking sheet, leaving room for the biscuits to spread.
7 Bake in the oven for 15 minutes. Transfer to a wire rack and leave to cool completely.

Ginger and Orange Cookies

Preparation time: 15 minutes
Cooking time: 12 minutes

MAKES ABOUT 20

200 g butter, softened, plus extra for greasing

80 g soft light brown sugar

1 tablespoon orange juice

grated zest of 1 orange

4 pieces of stem ginger, finely chopped

200 g plain flour, sifted

a pinch of salt

To prepare ahead: These will keep in an airtight container for about a week.

1 Preheat the oven to 180°C│350°F│gas mark 4.
2 Grease a baking sheet with butter or line with silicone paper.

3 In a large bowl, cream the butter until soft, add the sugar and beat until pale and fluffy. Stir in the orange juice and zest and ginger. Stir in the flour and salt and mix to a firm dough.

4 Place balls of the mixture on the prepared baking sheet, leaving room for the biscuits to spread. Flatten lightly with the back of a fork.

5 Bake in the oven for 10–12 minutes, or until pale golden brown. Remove from the oven and allow to cool for 5 minutes, then transfer to a wire rack and leave to cool completely.

Mocha Cookies

Preparation time: 25–30 minutes
Cooking time: 15–20 minutes

MAKES ABOUT 10

80 g butter, softened
50 g caster sugar
30 g soft light brown sugar
½ egg, beaten
50 g dark chocolate chips
few drops of vanilla extract
80 g self-raising flour

pinch of salt
1 tablespoon cocoa powder
1 tablespoon finely ground fresh coffee

To finish
60 g white chocolate, melted

To prepare ahead: These will keep in an airtight container for about a week.

1 Preheat the oven to 180°C | 350°F | gas mark 4.

2 In a large bowl, cream the butter until soft, add both the sugars and beat again until pale and fluffy. Beat in the egg, then the chocolate chips and the vanilla extract.

3 Sift the dry ingredients on to the mixture and stir until smooth. Do not overstir or the dough will be very oily.

4 Place spoonfuls, spaced well apart, on 3 ungreased baking sheets. Flatten with the prongs of a fork and bake in the oven for 15–20 minutes to an even, not too dark, brown.

5 While the biscuits are still hot, ease off the baking sheets with a palette knife or fish slice, transfer to a wire rack and leave to cool completely. Drizzle with the melted white chocolate.

White Chocolate and Dried Cherry Cookies

Preparation time: 10 minutes
Cooking time: 12 minutes

MAKES ABOUT 12

150 g unsalted butter, plus extra for greasing

150 g caster sugar

½ egg, beaten

220 g self-raising flour

100 g white chocolate chunks, roughly broken

100 g dried cherries

To prepare ahead: These will keep in an airtight container for about a week.

1 Preheat the oven to 190°C|375°F|gas mark 5. Grease 2 baking sheets with butter.
2 In a large bowl, cream the butter until soft, add the sugar and beat until pale and fluffy. Gradually add the beaten egg, beating well after each addition, then add the flour, chocolate and cherries to make a dough.
3 Shape into balls and press out lightly on to the prepared baking sheets, leaving room for the cookies to spread.
4 Bake in the oven for 10–12 minutes, or until light golden. Transfer to a wire rack and leave to cool completely.

Orange Fork Biscuits

Preparation time: 15 minutes
Chilling time: 15 minutes
Cooking time: 12 minutes

MAKES ABOUT 12

110 g butter, softened, plus extra for greasing

grated zest of 1 orange

55 g caster sugar

170 g self-raising flour

a pinch of salt

To finish

icing sugar

To prepare ahead: These will keep in an airtight container for up to a week.

1 Preheat the oven to 190°C|375°F|gas mark 5. Grease 2 baking sheets with butter.
2 In a large bowl, cream the butter until soft, then add the orange zest, caster sugar and beat together until pale and fluffy.
3 Sift the flour and salt on to the mixture and stir together to form a dough.
4 Divide into balls. Arrange spaced a little apart on a baking sheet and flatten each with a wet fork. Chill for 15 minutes.

5 Bake the biscuits in the oven for 10–12 minutes, or until a light golden brown. Cool for 2 minutes, then transfer to a wire rack and leave to cool completely. Dust with icing sugar before serving.

VARIATIONS: These can be drizzled with or half dipped in dark chocolate. The flavour can be varied by using lime or lemon zest in place of the orange zest.

Smartie Cookies

Preparation time: 10 minutes
Cooking time: 20 minutes

MAKES ABOUT 10

120 g butter, softened, plus extra for greasing
60 g caster sugar
½ egg, beaten
vanilla extract

85 g self-raising flour, sifted
85 g plain flour, sifted
2 tubes of Smarties

To prepare ahead: These will keep in an airtight container for about a week.

1 Preheat the oven to 190°C|375°F|gas mark 5. Grease 2 baking sheets with butter or line with silicone paper.
2 In a large bowl, cream the butter until soft, then add the sugar and beat until pale and fluffy.
3 Gradually beat in the egg and vanilla extract to taste.
4 Stir in the flours and bring together to make a dough.
5 Divide the dough into equal portions and shape into cookies about 5 mm thick. Place on the prepared baking sheets, leaving room for the cookies to spread, and push the Smarties gently into the cookie dough.
6 Bake the cookies in the oven for 12 minutes, or until golden. Leave to cool slightly on the baking sheet, then transfer to a wire rack and leave to cool completely.

Almond Cake

Preparation time: 15 minutes
Cooking time: 35 minutes

SERVES 8

butter, for greasing
6 eggs, separated
250 g caster sugar
350 g ground almonds
1½ teaspoons baking powder
½ teaspoon almond essence

For the filling

1 × 142 ml pot of double cream
1 tablespoon Amaretto
raspberry jam
icing sugar, sifted

To prepare ahead: Make the cakes and freeze. Defrost and assemble.

1 Preheat the oven to 180°C|350°F|gas mark 4. Grease 2 × 20 cm loose-bottomed cake tins or line with silicone paper.
2 Whisk the egg yolks with the sugar until light and fluffy.
3 Whisk the egg whites until stiff but not dry.
4 Fold the egg whites into the egg yolk mixture. Fold in the almonds, baking powder and almond essence.
5 Pour into the prepared tins and bake in the oven for 35 minutes.
6 Leave to cool on a wire rack.
7 Meanwhile, whip the cream for the filling until it just holds its shape. Add the Amaretto and sweeten to taste with icing sugar.
8 When the cakes are cold, spread the top of one of the cakes with raspberry jam, then cover with the Amaretto-flavoured cream. Place the second cake on top and dust liberally with icing sugar.

Apple and Cinnamon Cake

Preparation time: 25 minutes
Cooking time: 1 hour

SERVES 8

170 g unsalted butter, plus extra for greasing
170 g caster sugar
3 eggs, beaten
170 g Bramley apples, peeled, cored and grated
170 g self-raising flour, sifted

2 teaspoons ground cinnamon
milk

To serve
crème fraîche or cream

1 Preheat the oven to 180°C|350°F|gas mark 4. Lightly grease a 20 cm cake tin with butter or line with silicone paper.

2 In a large bowl, cream the butter until soft, add the sugar and beat well until very pale and fluffy. Gradually add the eggs, beating well between each addition. If the mixture looks as though it might curdle, add a spoonful of flour.

3 Add the apple, then fold in the flour with the cinnamon. The mixture should be of reluctant dropping consistency. If it seems too thick, add a little milk.

4 Pile the mixture into the prepared cake tin and bake for 1 hour.

5 Leave the cake to cool in the tin for 10 minutes, then turn out on to a wire rack.

6 Serve warm with crème fraîche or cream for pudding or allow to cool completely and serve with tea or coffee.

Chocolate and Coconut Cupcakes

Preparation time: 15 minutes
Cooking time: 15–20 minutes

MAKES 8 LARGE CUPCAKES

110 g butter
110 g caster sugar
2 eggs
85 g self-raising flour, sifted
50 g desiccated coconut
60 g dark chocolate drops

For the topping

60 g good-quality plain chocolate
a small knob of butter
desiccated coconut

To prepare ahead: These can be frozen and then defrosted. Make the topping once defrosted.

1 Preheat the oven to 190°C|375°F|gas mark 5.

2 Line a patty tin with 8 paper cases.

3 In a large bowl, cream the butter until soft, then add the sugar and beat until pale and fluffy.

4 Mix the eggs together in a separate bowl, then gradually beat into the creamed mixture a little at a time, adding 1 tablespoon of flour if the mixture begins to curdle.

5 Fold in the flour, coconut and chocolate drops, adding enough water to bring the mixture to a dropping consistency.

6 Divide the mixture between the paper cases. Bake in the middle of the oven for about 15 minutes, or until the cakes are well risen, golden and feel spongy to the fingertips.

7 Allow the cakes to cool for a few minutes in the tins, then turn out on to a wire rack and leave to cool completely.

8 For the topping: melt the chocolate carefully with the butter, spoon over the cupcakes and scatter with a little desiccated coconut. Allow the chocolate topping to cool.

Carrot Cake

Preparation time: 20 minutes
Cooking time: 1 hour

SERVES 8–10

170 ml vegetable oil

225 g caster sugar

2 large eggs

225 g plain flour

1 teaspoon bicarbonate of soda

½ teaspoon salt

1½ teaspoon, ground cinnamon

1 teaspoon vanilla extract

170 g carrots, peeled and grated

For the icing

110 g cream cheese

225 g icing sugar, sifted

grated zest of ½ orange

To prepare ahead: Make the cake and freeze. Defrost and ice.

1 Preheat the oven to 170°C | 325°F | gas mark 3. Grease a 27 × 20 cm cake tin with a little of the vegetable oil.
2 Combine the remaining oil and the sugar, then mix in the eggs.
3 Sift the flour, bicarbonate of soda, salt and cinnamon together and add to the mixture. Mix thoroughly.
4 Add the vanilla extract and the carrots. Pour the mixture into the prepared cake tin. Bake in the oven for 1 hour. Leave to cool on a wire rack.
5 Make the icing: beat together the cream cheese, icing sugar and orange zest and then spread over the carrot cake.

Chocolate Brownies

These can be served at teatime or with hot chocolate sauce (page 441) and ice cream for pudding.

Preparation time: 20 minutes
Cooking time: 30 minutes

MAKES 16

140 g unsalted butter, softened

200 g dark chocolate, chopped

225 g sugar

1 teaspoon vanilla extract

a pinch of salt

2 large eggs, at room temperature, beaten

1 large egg yolk, at room temperature

85 g plain flour, sifted

To prepare ahead: The brownies freeze well.

1 Preheat the oven to 180°C|350°F|gas mark 4. Line a 20 cm square tin with silicone paper.

2 In a bowl set over, not in, a pan of simmering water, melt the butter and the chocolate together. Remove the pan from the heat and allow to cool slightly. Whisk in the sugar and then the vanilla extract and salt. The mixture will be somewhat grainy.

3 Whisk in the eggs and the egg yolk until well mixed. Add the sifted flour and stir well until thick and smooth. Pour into the prepared tin and bake for 30–35 minutes, or until a knife inserted in the middle comes out with moist crumbs (not wet batter) clinging to it.

4 Allow the cake to cool before cutting into squares with a sharp knife.

Christmas Cupcakes

Preparation time: 10 minutes
Cooking time: 15 minutes

MAKES 8 LARGE CUPCAKES

110 g butter, softened
110 g soft dark brown sugar
2 eggs, beaten
110 g self-raising flour, sifted
½ teaspoon ground cinnamon
1 teaspoon ground mixed spice
a large pinch of freshly grated nutmeg

6 glacé cherries, chopped and dusted with a little of the flour
40 g raisins
40 g mixed peel

To finish
2 tablespoons icing sugar, sifted

To prepare ahead: These can be made in advance and frozen.

1 Preheat the oven to 190°C|375°F|gas mark 5. Line a patty tin with 8 paper cases.

2 In a large bowl, cream the butter until soft, then add the sugar and beat until pale and fluffy.

3 Add the beaten eggs into the creamed mixture a little at a time, adding 1 tablespoon of flour if the mixture begins to curdle.

4 Fold in the flour and spices, adding enough water to bring the mixture to a dropping consistency. Stir in the cherries, raisins and mixed peel.

5 Divide the mixture between the prepared cases. Bake in the middle of the oven for about 15 minutes, or until the cakes are well risen, golden and feel spongy to the fingertips.

6 Mix together the icing sugar with a very little boiling water and drizzle over the top of the cakes.

Apple Crumble Muffins

Preparation time: 25 minutes
Cooking time: 25 minutes

MAKES 8 LARGE MUFFINS

250 g self-raising flour

½ teaspoon bicarbonate of soda

1 teaspoon ground cinnamon

140 g soft light brown sugar

1 Bramley apple, peeled, cored and chopped into
   1 cm dice

1 large dessert apple, peeled, cored and chopped into
   1 cm dice

85 g butter, melted

2 large eggs

150 ml milk

For the crumble topping

2 tablespoons plain flour

½ teaspoon ground mixed spice

30 g butter

4 tablespoons soft light brown sugar

1 Preheat the oven to 190°C|375°F|gas mark 5.

2 Line a muffin tin with 8 paper cases.

3 Make the topping: sift together the flour and mixed spice and rub in the butter until the mixture resembles breadcrumbs. Stir in the sugar. Refrigerate until required.

4 In another bowl sift together the flour, bicarbonate of soda and cinnamon. Stir in the sugar and apples. Make a well in the centre.

5 Mix the butter, eggs and milk together.

6 Pour the wet ingredients into the apple, sugar and flour mixture and stir in quickly.

7 Divide the mixture between the muffin cases. Sprinkle the crumble mixture on the top and bake in the oven for 20 minutes.

Cheese and Bacon Muffins

Preparation time: 15 minutes
Cooking time: 20–25 minutes

MAKES 12

½ tablespoon oil

110 g streaky bacon, diced

225 g plain flour

½ teaspoon salt

2½ teaspoons baking powder

2 eggs

4 tablespoons olive oil

250 ml full-fat milk

110 g strong Cheddar cheese, coarsely grated

To prepare ahead: These can be frozen, defrosted and reheated to serve.

1 Preheat the oven to 190°C|375°F|gas mark 5. Oil the muffin tins or line with paper cases.
2 Heat the oil in a frying pan, add the bacon and cook until golden brown and the fat is rendered. Remove from the pan with a slotted spoon and leave to drain on kitchen paper.
3 Sift the flour, salt and baking powder into a large bowl. In a separate bowl, beat together the eggs, oil and milk. Stir in the cheese and bacon.
4 Quickly stir the wet ingredients into the flour. Spoon the batter into the muffin cases and bake for 20–25 minutes. Allow the muffins to cool for a few minutes in the tin.
5 Serve warm or cold with soups or for breakfast.

Chocolate and Peanut Muffins

Preparation time: 15 minutes
Cooking time: 25 minutes

MAKES 6 LARGE MUFFINS

170 g plain flour

a pinch of salt

1½ teaspoons baking powder

55 g caster sugar

1 egg

125 ml milk

55 g butter, melted

4 tablespoons crunchy peanut butter

55 g dark chocolate drops

For the topping

100 g plain chocolate, chopped

10 g butter

2 tablespoons water

To prepare ahead: The muffins can be frozen and the topping made once defrosted.

1 Preheat the oven to 190°C|375°F|gas mark 5. Line a large muffin tin with 6 paper cases.
2 Sift the flour, salt and baking powder into a bowl. Stir in the sugar and make a well in the centre.
3 In a separate bowl, beat the egg, milk, butter and peanut butter together.
4 Stir the wet mixture into the dry one and fold in the chocolate drops.
5 Divide the mixture between the muffin cases. Bake in the oven for 25 minutes. Remove from the oven and allow to cool slightly, then turn out on to a wire rack and leave to cool completely.
6 Make the topping: put the chocolate, butter and water into a heatproof bowl set over, not in, a saucepan of simmering water and leave until melted. Allow to cool slightly, then spoon over the cakes. Leave to cool completely.

Chocolate Drop Scones

Preparation time: 10 minutes
Cooking time: 20 minutes

MAKES 25

225 g self-raising flour
½ teaspoon salt
2 eggs, separated
300 ml milk

1 tablespoon butter, melted and cooled
110 g chopped chocolate or drops, white, plain or milk
butter, for greasing

To prepare ahead: These can be made in advance and kept warm. Cover when reheating to prevent them from drying out.

1 Sift the flour and salt into a large bowl. Make a well in the centre and add the egg yolks and a quarter of the milk.
2 Mix with a wooden spoon, gradually drawing in the flour from the sides of the bowl to make a smooth batter. Add the remaining milk gradually until the batter is the consistency of thick cream.
3 Fold in the butter and chocolate drops.
4 Whisk the egg whites until stiff but not dry and fold into the batter.
5 Meanwhile, lightly grease a heavy frying pan or griddle iron and heat it. When really hot, drop 2 spoonfuls of batter on to the surface, keeping them well separated.
6 Cook for 2–3 minutes. When the undersides of the pancakes are brown, bubbles rise to the surface. Lift the pancakes with a fish slice, turn over and brown on the other side.
7 Keep warm, covered with a clean tea-towel.

VARIATIONS: The chocolate can be omitted for plain scones to serve with jam. Alternatively, replace the chocolate with grated lemon zest and 85 g raisins.

Apricot Scones with Ginger Cream

Preparation time: 25 minutes
Cooking time: 10–15 minutes

MAKES 6–8

225 g self-raising flour, plus extra for dusting
½ teaspoon salt
55 g butter
30 g caster sugar
85 g dried apricots, chopped
150 ml milk

To glaze
beaten egg or milk

To serve
2 pieces of stem ginger, finely chopped
2 tablespoons stem ginger syrup
1 × 142 ml pot of double cream, lightly whipped

To prepare ahead: The scones freeze well. Defrost and reheat gently before serving.

1 Preheat the oven to 220°C|425°F|gas mark 7. Flour a baking sheet.

2 Sift the flour with the salt into a large bowl.

3 Rub in the butter until the mixture resembles coarse breadcrumbs. Stir in the sugar. Add the apricots.

4 Make a deep well in the flour, pour in the milk and mix to a soft, spongy dough with a knife.

5 On a floured surface, knead the dough very lightly until just smooth. Roll or press out to about 2.5 cm thick and stamp into 5 cm rounds with a pastry cutter. Knead any scraps together to make extra scones.

6 Brush the scones with beaten egg for a glossy crust, sprinkle with flour for a soft one or brush with milk for a light gloss and soft crust.

7 Bake the scones on a baking sheet at the top of the oven for 10 minutes, or until well risen and brown and the bases golden brown. Transfer to a wire rack and leave to cool.

8 Stir the chopped ginger and ginger syrup into the whipped cream.

9 To serve: cut the scones in half horizontally and sandwich together with the ginger cream.

Flapjacks

Preparation time: 15 minutes
Cooking time: 30 minutes

MAKES 16

170 g butter

100 g soft light brown sugar

4 tablespoons golden syrup

½ teaspoon ground cinnamon

250 g rolled oats

3 tablespoons seeds, such as pumpkin seeds, sesame seeds, sunflower seeds, poppy seeds

To prepare ahead: These will keep in an airtight container for about 5 days.

1 Preheat the oven to 190°C|375°F|gas mark 5. Grease a 30 × 24 cm tin.

2 Melt the butter in a saucepan.

3 Add the sugar and syrup to the warm melted butter and heat through. Stir in the cinnamon.

4 Remove the pan from the heat and stir in the oats and seeds.

5 Pour the mixture into the tin and spread evenly.

6 Bake in the oven for about 30 minutes, until golden brown.

7 Remove from the oven, mark immediately into bars and leave to cool in the tin.

Cranberry Scones with Orange and Brandy Butter

Preparation time: 20 minutes
Cooking time: 10 minutes

MAKES 6–8

For the orange and brandy butter

85 g unsalted butter, softened

grated zest of 1 orange

4 tablespoons icing sugar

2 tablespoons brandy

For the scones

225 g self-raising flour

a pinch of salt

55 g butter

30 g caster sugar

55 g dried cranberries

grated zest of 1 orange

150 ml milk

1 egg, beaten

To prepare ahead: The scones can be made in advance and frozen. Defrost and reheat gently to serve.

1 Preheat the oven to 220°C | 425°F | gas mark 7.

2 Make the orange and brandy butter: beat the butter until soft, then beat in the orange zest, icing sugar and brandy. Taste and sweeten further with icing sugar if necessary. Transfer to a serving dish, cover and chill.

3 Make the scones: sift the flour and salt into a large bowl. Rub in the butter until the mixture resembles coarse breadcrumbs. Stir in the sugar and add the cranberries and orange zest.

4 Make a deep well in the centre and pour in the milk. Mix to a soft, spongy dough with a knife.

5 On a floured surface, knead the dough very lightly until just smooth. Press out to 2.5 cm thickness and cut into rounds, using a 5 cm pastry cutter. Knead together any scraps of dough to make extra scones. Place on a baking sheet.

7 Brush the scones with the beaten egg and bake in the oven for 10 minutes, or until golden brown. Transfer to a wire rack and leave to cool.

8 To serve: cut the scones in half and serve with the brandy butter.

Jaffa Jam Tarts

Preparation time: 5 minutes
Cooking time: 10 minutes

MAKES ABOUT 24

375 g sweet shortcrust pastry

shredless Seville orange marmalade

200 g plain chocolate, chopped

20 g butter

1 Preheat the oven to 200°C|400°F|gas mark 6.
2 On a floured surface, roll out the pastry to 6 mm thickness. Cut into rounds and use the pastry to line a 2 × 12 hole patty tin.
3 Spoon a teaspoon of marmalade into each tart case.
4 Bake in the oven for 10 minutes.
5 Meanwhile, place the chocolate and butter in a heatproof bowl set over, not in, a saucepan of simmering water and leave until melted.
6 Spoon the chocolate on to the tarts and allow to cool.

Hazelnut and Cinnamon Pastries

Preparation time: 20 minutes
Chilling time: 10 minutes
Cooking time: 15 minutes

MAKES 16

30 g butter, plus extra for greasing

55 g soft light brown sugar

½-1 teaspoon ground cinnamon

grated zest of 1 orange

1 × 240 g tube of ready-made croissant dough

55 g hazelnuts, roughly chopped

For the glacé icing

2 tablespoons icing sugar

boiling water

1 Preheat the oven to 200°C|400°F|gas mark 6. Grease a baking sheet.
2 Melt the butter in a saucepan and add the sugar, cinnamon and orange zest.
3 Unroll the croissant dough, but keep as one sheet, do not separate into triangles. Using a pastry brush, spread the sugar and butter mix over the croissant dough.
4 Scatter the hazelnuts over the sugar layer.
5 Roll the dough up into a sausage shape along the length of the rectangle.
6 Cut the roll into 16 slices and gently flatten each round slightly to 1 cm thickness. Place on the greased baking sheet and chill for 10 minutes, or until firm.
7 Bake the pastries in the oven for 10 minutes, or until golden brown. Transfer to a wire rack and leave to cool.
8 Make the icing: mix the icing sugar together with a little boiling water so that it is just runny, then drizzle over the pastries.

VARIATIONS: 30 g of the hazelnuts may be replaced with 30 g dried apricots, chopped. The pastries may be brushed with warm melted apricot jam or marmalade to replace the icing.

Sweet Almond Straws

Preparation time: 20 minutes
Chilling time: 15 minutes
Cooking time: 15 minutes

MAKES 20

500 g puff pastry

plain flour, for rolling

30 g butter, melted

1 egg, beaten

nibbed almonds

sugar crystals

ground cinnamon

1 Preheat the oven to 200°C | 400°F | gas mark 6.
2 Roll out the pastry on a floured surface to the size of an A5 sheet of paper.
3 Brush with the melted butter and then the beaten eggs. Sprinkle liberally with some of the nibbed almonds, sugar crystals and cinnamon. With a floured rolling pin, roll the pastry out to A4 size.
4 Turn it over and brush with the remaining butter and egg glaze.
5 Sprinkle over more sugar, cinnamon and almonds. Roll out again until the pastry is about 5 mm thick.
6 Trim the edges and cut into strips about 1.5 cm wide.
7 Twist each pastry straw a few times, as you would cheese straws, and place on a baking sheet. Chill for 15 minutes.
8 Bake in the oven for 15 minutes, or until brown and crisp.
9 Transfer to a wire rack and leave to cool. These straws are particularly good served warm.

Soda Bread

Preparation time: 10 minutes
Cooking time: 40 minutes

MAKES 1 LOAF

225 g wholemeal flour

225 g plain white flour, plus extra for rolling and dusting

1½ teaspoons salt

2 teaspoons bicarbonate of soda

1 tablespoon sugar

45 g butter, plus extra for greasing

1 × 284 ml pot of buttermilk

extra milk for mixing

1 Preheat the oven to 190°C | 375°F | gas mark 5. Grease a baking sheet with butter.
2 Sift the dry ingredients into a warmed large mixing bowl.

3 Rub in the butter until the mixture resembles coarse breadcrumbs, then add the buttermilk and mix to a soft dough. (Add more milk if necessary.)

4 Place the dough on a floured surface and shape with a minimum of kneading into a large circle about 5 cm thick. Dust lightly with flour. With the handle of a wooden spoon, make a cross 2 cm deep on the top of the loaf.

5 Place on the prepared baking sheet and bake in the oven for 35–40 minutes, or until risen and golden brown. Transfer to cool on a wire rack and leave to cool.

NOTE: If buttermilk is not available, use ordinary milk and add 2 teaspoons of cream of tartar with the flour.

Olive and Basil Bread

Preparation time: 20 minutes
Proving time: 2 × 35 minutes
Cooking time: 35 minutes

MAKES 1 LOAF

1 × 280 g packet of bread mix
6 tablespoons ready-made basil pesto (or see page 512)

3 tablespoons plain flour
110 g good-quality black olives, pitted and roughly chopped

1 Preheat the oven to 200°C|400°F|gas mark 6.

2 Make up the bread following the manufacturer's instructions, but adding the pesto in place of 6 tablespoons of the water called for. Add the flour.

3 Knead the dough well until smooth. Place in a lightly greased bowl covered with lightly greased clingfilm and leave in a warm place to rise until doubled in size. This will probably take about 35 minutes.

4 Knead in the olives. Shape into a loaf and place on a greased baking sheet, cover and again leave to rise. After 20 minutes make slashes across the top of the bread with a sharp knife. When the dough has doubled in size again, after about 35 minutes, bake in the oven for 35 minutes. The loaf is cooked when it is nicely browned and sounds hollow when the base is tapped.

5 Transfer to a wire rack and leave to cool.

NOTE: This can also be made in a breadmaker, following the manufacturer's instructions.
VARIATION: Use sundried tomatoes in place of half of the olives.

Fruited Soda Bread

Preparation time: 10 minutes
Soaking time: 30 minutes
Baking time: 45 minutes

MAKES 2 LOAVES

150 g mixed dried fruits, such as dried apple,
sultanas and raisins
2 tablespoons maple syrup
225 g wholemeal flour
225 g plain white flour
2 teaspoons ground mixed spice
1½ teaspoons salt

50 g butter, plus extra for greasing
100 g caster sugar
2 teaspoons bicarbonate of soda
50 g hazelnuts, roasted and chopped
1 × 284 ml pot of buttermilk
extra milk for mixing

1 Place the dried fruits in a bowl, pour over boiling water to cover and stir in the maple syrup. Grease 1 large or 2 small baking sheets with butter.
2 Preheat the oven to 190°C|375°F|gas mark 5.
3 Sift the flours with the mixed spice and salt into a bowl. Rub in the butter until the mixture resembles coarse breadcrumbs. Add the sugar and bicarbonate of soda. Stir in any bran left in the sieve.
4 Strain the fruit, discard the liquid and add the fruit, with the nuts, to the flour.
5 Add the buttermilk and any extra milk to make a soft but not sticky dough. Shape into 2 round, slightly domed loaves.
6 With the floured handle of a wooden spoon, mark a cross 2 cm deep on the top of the loaves.
7 Bake in the oven for 40–50 minutes. Transfer to a wire rack and leave to cool but serve while still warm.

Toffee Marshmallow Crisp

Preparation time: 15 minutes
Cooling time: 30 minutes

MAKES ABOUT 24

120 g butter, plus extra for greasing
150 g butter toffees

200 g marshmallows
150 g Rice Krispies

1 Melt the butter, toffees and marshmallows together in a heavy pan over a low heat, stirring gently.
2 Lightly grease a 30 × 20 cm shallow tin.
3 Remove the pan from the heat and stir in the Rice Krispies so that they are all coated well.
4 Pour into the tin, press down and allow to cool. Cut into squares.

Malteser Cake

Preparation time: 15 minutes
Chilling time: 2 hours

SERVES 10

85 g butter

2 tablespoons golden syrup

2 tablespoons cocoa powder

170 g digestives biscuits, crushed

175 g Maltesers, half crushed and half left whole

1 Melt the butter and golden syrup in a small, heavy pan. Stir in the cocoa powder, biscuits and crushed Maltesers until well combined.

2 Allow to cool slightly, then stir through the whole Maltesers.

3 Line a 450 g loaf tin with clingfilm. Pour in the mixture and press down well, but try not to crush the whole Maltesers.

4 Chill for 2 hours, or until set.

5 Slice the cake and serve.

Double Chocolate Crispy Cakes

Preparation time: 20 minutes
Chilling time: 30–40 minutes

MAKES 10–15

225 g white chocolate, broken into squares

110 g Coco Pops

55 g raisins

1 Bring a small pan of water to the boil. Remove from the heat. Place the chocolate in a heatproof bowl set over, not in, the pan of water. Stir until melted, then remove the bowl from the hot pan.

2 Stir in the coco pops and raisins. Quickly divide between paper cases, then chill for at least 30 minutes before serving.

Chocolate Crispy Cakes

Preparation time: 10 minutes
Cooling time: 30 minutes

MAKES 8–10

45 g butter

2 tablespoons golden syrup

30 g cocoa powder

45 g Rice Krispies or Cornflakes

1 Melt the butter slowly with the golden syrup. Add the cocoa powder and stir until completely mixed. Allow to cool slightly.

2 Stir in the Rice Krispies and mix until they are coated in the chocolate mixture.

3 Divide between paper cases and allow to cool completely.

Chocolate Biscuit Cake

Preparation time: 10 minutes
Chilling time: 2 hours

SERVES 8

110 g butter, plus extra for greasing

110 g caster sugar

2 teaspoons cocoa powder

1 egg, beaten

170 g digestive biscuits, broken

1 × 200 g bar of plain or milk chocolate

1 Put the butter, sugar and cocoa powder into a heavy saucepan. Place over a low heat and allow to melt.

2 Meanwhile, grease a 20 cm square cake tin with a little butter.

3 Remove the saucepan from the heat and allow to cool slightly, then beat in the egg.

4 Gradually stir in the biscuits. The mixture should be quite firm by the time all the biscuits have been added.

5 Pile into the prepared tin and press down firmly. Chill for 2 hours.

6 To turn out the cake, place the bottom of the tin in a bowl of very hot water for a few seconds, then turn out on to a plate.

7 Meanwhile, melt the chocolate in a heatproof bowl set over, not in, a pan of simmering water.

8 Pour the chocolate over the cake and leave to set.

VARIATIONS: Oaty biscuits such as HobNobs can be used in place of the digestives. Melt 100 g each of white and plain chocolate, pour on to the top of the cake and marble together.

Chocolate Orange Crisps

Preparation time: 10 minutes
Chilling time: 30 minutes

MAKES 50 PIECES

400 g good-quality dark chocolate, evenly chopped   200 g demerara sugar
grated zest of 1 orange

1 Place the chocolate and the orange zest in a heatproof bowl set over, not in, a saucepan of simmering water. Stir occasionally so that the chocolate melts evenly.
2 Allow the mixture to cool until it is no longer warm to the touch, but still fluid.
3 Stir in the sugar. Spread the mixture thinly over a large piece of silicone paper. Place another piece of paper over the top and roll with a rolling pin to an even thinness.
4 Chill until set.
5 When the chocolate is firm but not brittle, cut into shapes, then chill again until completely cold.

VARIATIONS: The orange zest can be replaced with lime zest, a couple of teaspoons of peppermint essence or very strong coffee.

Chocolate Truffles

Preparation time: 10 minutes
Cooling and chilling time: 3 hours

MAKES 24

250 g 70% cocoa solids chocolate, roughly chopped   **To finish**
100 ml double cream   cocoa powder, sifted
1 vanilla pod, split lengthways
20 g unsalted butter

1 Melt the chocolate in a heatproof bowl set over, not in, a saucepan of simmering water. Remove from the heat and leave to cool but not set.
2 Put the cream into a saucepan, add the vanilla pod and bring to scalding point (just below boiling). Remove from the heat and leave to cool. Remove the vanilla pod.
3 Beat the butter until very soft. Mix it into the chocolate, beat in the vanilla cream and chill until firm.
4 Shape into small balls and roll lightly in cocoa powder. Chill again before serving.

VARIATIONS: Roll the truffles in chopped nuts or crushed Amaretti biscuits, or drizzle with melted chocolate.

Hard Fudge

Cooking time: 40 minutes

110 g hard margarine or unsalted butter, plus extra for greasing
450 g granulated sugar

150 ml evaporated milk
a pinch of cream of tartar
a few drops of vanilla extract

1 Grease a 17.5 cm square tin well with margarine or butter.

2 Melt the margarine or butter in a heavy saucepan over a low heat.

3 Add the sugar, evaporated milk, cream of tartar and vanilla extract. Stir gently but continuously until the sugar has dissolved. This should take about 15 minutes. Bring to the boil slowly and allow to boil for 15–20 minutes, still stirring gently so that the mixture does not stick to the bottom of the pan. If using a sugar thermometer, it should reach a temperature of 240°F, when a small amount of the fudge dropped from the spoon into a bowl of cold water will form a soft ball.

4 Take the pan off the heat and beat the fudge for 2 minutes. Pour into the tin and allow to cool for 10–15 minutes before marking squares on the top. Allow to cool completely before turning out of the tin and cutting into squares.

Toffee Apples

Preparation time: 10 minutes
Cooking time: 25 minutes

MAKES 8

butter, for greasing
8 medium eating apples
700 g caster sugar

200 ml water
wooden skewers

1 Lightly butter a baking sheet or line with silicone paper. Thoroughly wash the apples and dry well.

2 Place a wooden skewer vertically almost completely through the centre of each apple.

3 In a large, heavy saucepan dissolve the sugar and water over a low heat, stirring gently. When the sugar has dissolved, stop stirring and then bring to the boil until the sugar has reached the hard crack stage (155°C|300–310°F on a sugar thermometer), when it has become a dark golden colour and a small amount dropped into cold water sets hard.

4 Holding the skewers firmly, dip the apples into the sugar and twirl around for a few seconds to coat thoroughly and evenly. Leave the apples with the sticks pointing upwards on the baking sheet to cool.

Lemon Curd Tart

Pain Perdu with Fruit Compote

Seabreeze Sorbet and Pineapple Sorbet

Affogato

Coconut Rice Pudding and Rhubarb Baked in Grenadine

Frozen Chocolate and Orange Cheesecake

Crunchie and Brownie Ice Cream

(From top) Chocolate Biscuit Cake, White Chocolate and Dried Cherry Cookies, Chocolate Chip and Hazelnut Cookies, Bakewell Biscuits, Mocha Cookies, Apricot and Ginger Scones

Apricot Scone with Ginger Cream

Apple and Rum Punch

Rich Hot Chocolate

Iced Berry Smoothie

Lime Squash

Granola

Fruit Compote and Yogurt

Drop Scones with Bacon, Fried Eggs and Maple
Syrup

Boiled Eggs and Soldiers

Preserving

Preserving is not generally thought of as an everyday skill, and certainly it might not feature as part of a busy evening when the challenge is to find time to cook dinner at all amid all the other chores. However, preserving is simple and a wonderfully satisfying way of utilizing a glut of vegetables and fruit. Preserves will keep for up to a year without deteriorating and can be used in a number of recipes in this book. Chutneys, which are always sweet and sour mixtures, somewhere between a pickle and a jam, are the easiest preserves to make.

Put preserves, whilst still hot, straight into sterilized jars. This can be done by boiling the jars in a pan of water, or washing them well and placing them in a low oven (100°C|200°F|gas mark ½) until dry and hot. Cover the preserves immediately, either with special waxed discs, or cut greaseproof paper to fit and dip in vodka. Next, seal with non-metallic tight-fitting lids, or special cellophane circles, and secure with elastic bands. Cellophane covers are best used when the chutney is to be eaten within a few months; lids are suitable for longer storage.

Banana Chutney

Preparation time: 10 minutes
Cooking time: 2 hours

MAKES 500 G

4 bananas, roughly chopped
2 onions, finely chopped
300 ml malt vinegar
120 g pitted dates, chopped
300 ml water
1 × 2.5 cm piece of root ginger, peeled and grated

½ teaspoon dried chilli flakes
½ teaspoon ground cinnamon
½ teaspoon ground allspice
170 g soft light brown sugar
½ teaspoon salt

1 Place all the ingredients except the sugar and salt in a large, heavy saucepan and simmer gently for about 1½ hours, stirring occasionally, until all the ingredients are soft and the liquid has almost evaporated.
2 Add the sugar and salt and stir over a low heat until the sugar has dissolved.
3 Bring to the boil and boil rapidly, stirring, until thick.
4 Pour into dry sterilized jars and cover (see above).

Pear and Date Chutney

Preparation time: 15 minutes
Cooking time: 1 hour

MAKES 1 KG

900 g pears, peeled, cored and chopped

225 g onions, chopped

225 g tomatoes, roughly chopped

110 g pitted dates, roughly chopped

225 g celery, chopped

600 ml white wine vinegar

½ teaspoon cayenne pepper

1 teaspoon salt

350 g soft light brown sugar

1 Place the pears, onions, tomatoes, dates and celery in a large, heavy saucepan. Add the vinegar and cook over a low heat, stirring occasionally, until all the ingredients are tender and the liquid has almost evaporated.

2 Add the cayenne, salt and sugar and continue to cook, stirring, until the sugar has dissolved and the mixture is thick.

3 Pour into dry sterilized jars and cover (see page 469).

Apple and Ginger Chutney

Preparation time: 20 minutes
Cooking time: 1¼ hours

MAKES 1 KG

450 g Bramley apples, peeled, cored and roughly chopped

450 g onions, roughly chopped

450 g firm pears, peeled, cored and roughly chopped

1 clove of garlic, finely chopped

300 ml cider vinegar

1 × 2 cm piece of fresh root ginger, peeled and grated

1 × 250 g pack of ready-to-eat dried pears, roughly chopped

170 g soft light brown sugar

grated zest and juice of 2 lemons

1 Place all the ingredients except the dried pears, sugar and lemon zest and juice in a large, heavy saucepan. Simmer very gently, stirring occasionally, for 45 minutes, or until soft and the liquid has almost evaporated.

2 Add the remaining ingredients and stir until the sugar has dissolved.

3 Continue cooking over a low heat until the mixture is thick and the apples, pears and onions are soft.

4 Pour into dry sterilized jars and cover (see page 469).

Plum and Orange Chutney

Preparation time: 30 minutes
Cooking time: 1¾ hours

MAKES 1 KG

450 g Bramley apples, peeled, cored and chopped
450 g onions, finely chopped
450 g plums, stoned and chopped
1 clove of garlic, peeled and finely chopped
2 teaspoons yellow mustard seeds
1 stick of cinnamon
1 star anise
300 ml cider vinegar
85 g soft light brown sugar
85 g soft dark brown sugar
grated zest and juice of 1 orange

1 Place all the ingredients except the sugars and the orange zest and juice in a large, heavy saucepan and simmer gently, stirring occasionally, for 1 hour, or until soft and the liquid has almost evaporated.
2 Add the sugar and orange zest and juice and stir over a low heat until the sugar has dissolved.
3 Bring to the boil and boil rapidly, stirring, until thick. Remove the cinnamon stick and star anise.
4 Pour into dry sterilized jars and cover (see page 469).

Spiced Tomato Chutney

Preparation time: 30 minutes
Cooking time: 3 hours

MAKES 1.5 KG

1.75 kg tomatoes, peeled and sliced (see page 22)
250 g onions, sliced
6 fresh or dried red chillies, chopped
450 g granulated sugar
1 tablespoon salt
300 ml red wine vinegar

1 Place all the ingredients except for the vinegar in a large saucepan.
2 Bring to the boil and simmer, stirring from time to time, for 1½ hours.
3 Add the vinegar and simmer for a further 1½ hours, or until very thick and syrupy. Stir every so often to prevent the chutney from catching on the base of the pan.
4 Pour immediately into dry sterilized jars and cover (see page 469).

Raspberry Jam

Preparation time: 10 minutes
Cooking time: 20 minutes

MAKES 1.8 KG

900 g fresh raspberries
75 ml water
juice of 1 lemon

450 g jam sugar, warmed in a low oven
450 g granulated sugar, warmed in a low oven

1 Leave 4 or 5 small plates to chill in the refrigerator before making the jam. These can be used to test for the setting point.

2 Place the raspberries, water and lemon juice in a preserving pan or large saucepan and simmer for 5 minutes, until the raspberries are soft and beginning to break up. Crush them gently with the back of a wooden spoon.

3 Remove the pan from the heat and add the sugars. Stir until the sugar has dissolved. Return the pan to the heat and boil without stirring for about 6 minutes, then begin testing for the setting point: remove the pan from the heat, and put a small spoonful of the jam on to one of the cold saucers. Return it to the refrigerator for 2 minutes. Push your finger through the puddle of jam. If a slight skin has formed, setting point has been reached, so proceed to the next step. If no skin has formed, return the pan to the heat and boil for another few minutes before testing again.

4 Skim any scum from the surface of the pan and allow to stand for 10 minutes, then stir to ensure the pieces of raspberry are distributed evenly through the mixture.

5 Pour into dry sterilized jars and cover (see page 469). Store in a cool, dark, airy place.

NOTE: This recipe can be used for strawberries as well, in which case use all jam sugar.

Lemon Curd

Preparation time: 10 minutes
Cooking time: 15 minutes

MAKES 450 G

2 large lemons
85 g butter

225 g granulated sugar
3 eggs, lightly beaten

To prepare ahead: This will keep in the refrigerator for about 3 weeks.

1 Grate the zest of the lemons on the finest gauge on the grater, taking care to grate the zest only, not the pith.
2 Squeeze the juice from the lemons.
3 Place the lemon juice, butter, sugar and eggs in a heavy saucepan or double boiler and heat gently, stirring all the time, until the mixture is thick.
4 Pass through a sieve, then stir in the lemon zest.
5 Spoon into dry sterilized jars and cover (see page 469).

Drinks

In this section we have given recipes that can be made very easily every day, as well as those for special occasions. Making your own smoothie can be a healthy and delicious way to start the day – without spending a fortune in juice bars. They are also a clever way of getting children to consume some of their 'five-a-day'.

Mulled Wine

Preparation time: 20 minutes

MAKES 3 LITRES

4 × 75 cl bottles of full-bodied red wine
600 ml orange juice
300 ml water
1 orange, studded with 12 cloves

150 ml orange liqueur, such as Cointreau
2 cinnamon sticks, broken in half
225 g granulated sugar, or to taste

1 Place all the ingredients in a large saucepan and stir over a low heat to dissolve the sugar.
2 Bring to simmering point and add more sugar to taste if necessary.
3 Keep warm, but do not boil or the alcohol will evaporate.

White Mulled Wine

Preparation time: 30 minutes

MAKES ABOUT 2½ LITRES

150 ml brandy
1 litre medium-dry sparkling cider
2 × 75 cl bottles of dry white wine
300 ml water

60 g granulated sugar, or to taste
1 apple, cored and sliced
2 oranges, sliced
1 cinnamon stick

1 Place all the ingredients in a large saucepan and stir over a low heat to dissolve the sugar.
2 Bring to simmering point and keep warm for 15 minutes. Do not boil or the alcohol will evaporate.

NOTE: The quantities of brandy and sugar can be varied to taste.

Mulled Cider

Preparation time: 30 minutes

MAKES 2 LITRES

170–200 g granulated sugar

425 ml water

1 pouch of mulled cider mix

1½ litres dry cider

apple slices (optional)

1 Mix together the sugar, water and spice mixture in a saucepan. Heat gently to dissolve the sugar, then increase the heat and boil for 5 minutes. Remove from the heat and leave to infuse.

2 Add the cider to the mixture and heat gently, then strain and add the apple slices, if using. Serve hot.

Apple and Rum Punch

Preparation time: 30 minutes

MAKES 1 ½ LITRES

pared zest of 1 lemon

6 cloves

6 juniper or allspice berries

3 cinnamon sticks

½ nutmeg

1.1 litres medium cider

150 ml orange juice

150 ml water

225 g soft light brown sugar

150 ml dark rum

To decorate

pared zest of 1 orange and 1 lemon

1 Tie the lemon zest, cloves, juniper or allspice berries, cinnamon sticks and nutmeg together in a small piece of muslin.

2 Pour the cider, orange juice and water into a large saucepan, add the bag of spices and heat very gently to simmering point, then remove from the heat, add the sugar and stir to dissolve. Remove the spice bag.

3 Add the rum and the orange and lemon zest and serve immediately.

Cider Punch

If a sweeter punch is preferred, use a medium-dry cider.

Preparation time: 5 minutes

MAKES 1.1 LITRES

150 ml brandy, chilled

1 litre dry sparkling cider, well chilled

2 dessert apples, cored and sliced

1 orange, sliced

a few sprigs of fresh mint

1 Pour the brandy into a jug. Add the cider, fruit and mint and stir well.

Champagne Cocktails

These cocktails call for Champagne, but they work just as well with sparkling white wine. The Champagne or sparkling wine must only be added to the glass at the last moment.

Basic Champagne Cocktail

sugar lumps

Angostura bitters

brandy

Champagne or sparkling wine, chilled

1 Place a sugar lump in each glass and add a couple of drops of Angostura bitters and 1 teaspoon brandy.

2 Just before serving, pour on the chilled Champagne or sparkling wine to fill the glass.

Red Sparkling Cocktail

Grand Marnier or Cointreau

cranberry juice

Champagne or sparkling wine, chilled

1 Place a teaspoon of Grand Marnier or Cointreau in a Champagne flute and half fill with cranberry juice. Just before serving, top up the glass with Champagne or sparkling wine and stir gently.

Amaretto and Champagne Cocktail

Amaretto

Champagne or sparkling wine, chilled

1 Place 1–2 teaspoons Amaretto in a Champagne flute, top up with Champagne or sparkling wine and stir gently.

Kir Royale

1 part crème de cassis

5 parts chilled Champagne or sparkling wine, chilled

1 Pour the crème de cassis into a Champagne flute. Top up with Champagne or sparkling wine and stir gently.

Bucks Fizz

orange juice

Champagne or sparkling wine, chilled

1 Half fill a Champagne flute with orange juice, top up with Champagne and stir gently.

Non-alcoholic Drinks

Lime Squash

Preparation time: 5 minutes
Infusing time: overnight

580 g granulated sugar
grated zest and juice of 6 limes
½ teaspoon citric acid

½ teaspoon tartaric acid
2 teaspoons Epsom salts
300 ml boiling water

1 Place all the ingredients together in a large bowl and leave overnight.
2 Strain into clean glass bottles and store in the refrigerator until required.

Sparkling Elderflower

Preparation time: 10 minutes, plus 24 hours dissolving time
Maturation time: 2 weeks

MAKES 4.5 LITRES

2–4 elderflower heads, in full bloom and undamaged
pared zest and juice of 1 lemon
675 g caster sugar

2 tablespoons white wine vinegar
4.5 litres cold water

1 Place the elderflower heads in a large bowl with the lemon zest and juice, sugar and vinegar.
2 Add the water, cover with a clean tea-towel and leave for 24 hours, stirring occasionally, until the sugar has dissolved.
3 Strain the liquid and pour through a funnel into strong sterilized screwtop or wire-top bottles. Seal the bottles immediately and store in a cool, dark place for 2 weeks.
4 Serve chilled.

NOTE: You will need clean, strong screwtop bottles or well-sealing bottles. Grolsch beer bottles are ideal. Open the bottles over a sink as the fizz has a tendency to rush out.

Elderflower Cordial

Preparation time: 5 minutes
Infusing time: up to 24 hours

MAKES 1½ LITRES

1.2 litres boiling water
15 elderflower heads
1 orange, sliced

1 lemon, sliced
900 g sugar
30 g citric acid

1 Pour the water over all the other ingredients in a bowl. Cover and stir. Leave to infuse for up to 24 hours, stirring from time to time. Strain into a clean jug and bottle.
2 Dilute to taste with still or sparkling water.

NOTE: This cordial will keep for a year in airtight bottles stored in a cool, dark place. Elderflowers are best picked during the day in sunlight, to ensure all the flower heads are open. Try to choose bushes that are not too close to main roads where possible.

Iced Berry Smoothie

1 × 500 g bag of frozen forest fruits   200 ml orange juice

1 Put the forest fruits into a food processor and whizz until smooth.
2 Add the orange juice as necessary to bring it to the desired consistency. Serve.

Strawberry Smoothie

100 ml orange juice   2 kiwi fruits, peeled and sliced
2 bananas, peeled and chopped   110 g strawberries, hulled

1 Put all the ingredients into a food processor and whizz until smooth. Push through a sieve if desired.
2 Chill until ready to serve.

NOTE: This is a basic recipe; vary by using different combinations of fruit and fruit juice.

Banana Milkshake

4 scoops of vanilla ice cream   400 ml milk
3 bananas, sliced   4 ice cubes

1 Put all the ingredients into a food processor and whizz until smooth. Add more milk if necessary to achieve the desired consistency.
2 Serve immediately.

NOTE: A variety of fruit, such as raspberries, strawberries, peaches, blueberries or a combination of all, can be used in milkshakes.

Iced Coffee

Preparation time: 10 minutes
Chilling time: 1 hour

SERVES 4

6 teaspoons sugar
8 shots of espresso coffee
1 litre milk

ice cubes
4 scoops of vanilla ice cream

1 Stir the sugar into the espresso to dissolve, then chill.

2 Divide the coffee between 4 large glasses. Stir 250 ml milk into each glass. Add 3 ice cubes to each.

3 Place a scoop of vanilla ice cream on the top of each glass and serve with a long spoon.

NOTE: This can be whizzed in a blender to give a smoother, thicker drink.

Rich Hot Chocolate

1 × 284 ml pot of double cream
150 g dark 70% cocoa solids chocolate, chopped
   into small pieces
500 ml milk

sugar, to taste, if required

To serve

marshmallows or grated chocolate (optional)

1 Pour the cream into a medium saucepan and bring gently to the boil. Remove from the heat and stir in the chocolate until it has completely melted.

2 Add the milk and stir over a low heat until hot but not boiling. Add a couple of spoonfuls of sugar to taste, if desired.

3 Pour into individual mugs and top with marshmallows or grated chocolate, if using. Serve immediately.

VARIATIONS: Add the grated zest of 2 oranges or a teaspoon of instant coffee powder.

Breakfasts

Weekday breakfast should be quick and easy to prepare, but some of the following recipes can be at least semi-prepared the night before. Other recipes that take a little longer are designed for weekends or whenever there is time to enjoy what should be the most important meal of the day.

Granola

Preparation time: 5 minutes
Cooking time: 25 minutes

MAKES ABOUT 600 G

350 g rolled jumbo oats
2 tablespoons sunflower seeds
2 tablespoons pumpkin seeds
100 g skinned hazelnuts
75 g flaked almonds
60 g demerara sugar
8 tablespoons apple juice

2 tablespoons clear honey
30 g dried cherries
30 g dried blueberries
4 dried figs, roughly chopped

To serve

milk or yoghurt
fresh fruit (optional)

1 Preheat the oven to 180°C|350°F|gas mark 4.
2 In a large bowl, mix together the oats, seeds, nuts and sugar.
3 Mix the apple juice and honey together and warm through in a saucepan or in the microwave. Pour over the oat mixture. Stir well.
4 Spread the mixture over a large baking sheet and bake in the centre of the oven for 20–25 minutes, stirring occasionally, until crisp and beginning to brown. It is important to check from time to time to prevent the mixture from burning.
5 Remove from the oven and allow to cool completely.
6 When cold, stir in the dried fruit and transfer to an airtight container until required.
7 Serve with cold milk or yoghurt and stir through fresh fruit if desired.

VARIATIONS: Any variety of dried fruit can be added to this granola mixture. A little cinnamon added to the honey is also delicious.

Porridge

Cooking time: 35 minutes

SERVES 4

1 litre water or water and milk mixed
salt or sugar

100 g medium oatmeal

To prepare ahead: Porridge keeps for up to 1 hour in a cool oven if covered with a lid, although it may need to have extra milk added to it before serving.

1 Bring the liquid to the boil in a saucepan and add salt or sugar to taste.
2 Sprinkle in the oatmeal, keeping the liquid on the boil and stirring all the time.
3 Simmer for 30 minutes, stirring occasionally. If necessary, add a little more water.

VARIATIONS: As well as seasoning with salt or sugar, or a little of each, honey or maple syrup can be drizzled over the top of the porridge. The type of sugar used, from white caster sugar to rich dark muscovado, can vary the taste too.

Muesli

Muesli keeps well in an airtight container.

Preparation time: 10 minutes
Cooking time: 30 minutes

MAKES ABOUT 1 KG

45 g golden linseeds
45 g sunflower seeds
45 g pumpkin seeds
85 g flaked almonds
350 g rolled jumbo oats
100 g rice flakes or wheat bran

300 g mixed dried fruit, such as cranberries, sour cherries, jumbo raisins, chopped dates, apples, pears, mango

To serve

milk
fresh fruit, such as bananas, raspberries, blueberries, strawberries

1 Preheat the oven to 190°C | 375°F | gas mark 5.
2 Place the seeds and nuts in a large roasting pan. Bake for 10–15 minutes, or until well toasted, stirring occasionally to prevent the nuts from burning.
3 Remove from the oven and allow to cool. Stir in the oats, rice flakes or wheat bran and dried fruit.

4 When the mixture is absolutely cold, store in an airtight container until required.

5 To serve: soak a portion of the muesli in a bowl in milk, fruit juice or water overnight in the refrigerator. The following morning, serve with a little extra fresh milk or juice, and fresh fruit.

NOTE: The quantity of fruits and nuts can be varied, and chopped hazelnuts and pecan nuts are also delicious. The sweetness of the dried fruit means that you should not need to add extra sugar.

Yoghurt and Fruit Compote

No quantities are given for this recipe as they depend on taste. The nuts and seeds can be toasted in quite large batches as they will keep in an airtight container.

fruit compote, homemade (see page 421) or good-quality bought compote, such as Yeo Valley
vanilla or plain yoghurt
fresh fruit, such as raspberries, strawberries, chopped banana, blueberries

toasted nuts, such as hazelnuts, flaked almonds
toasted seeds, such as sunflower, pumpkin, golden linseed
clear honey (optional)

1 Place the fruit compote in a bowl and spoon over the yoghurt. Scatter over the fruits and seeds and drizzle with honey, if liked.

Boiled Eggs

2 eggs per person, at room temperature

To serve
buttered toast

1 Bring a saucepan of water to the boil. The eggs should be at room temperature, but if they are taken straight from the refrigerator, add 30 seconds to the cooking time.

2 Carefully lower the eggs into the water, using a slotted spoon.

3 Keep the water simmering or boiling gently, not too vigorously, which tends to crack the shells and toughen the whites. Cook for 4½ minutes (or see page 13).

4 Remove from the water with the slotted spoon. Place in egg cups and serve with buttered toast.

English Breakfast

There is not a great deal of skill involved in cooking a good English breakfast, but it is quite difficult to ensure that everything is cooked perfectly at the same time. Here is an order of work that will ensure success.

Preparation time: 20 minutes
Cooking time: 30–40 minutes

1 good-quality sausage per person
1 tomato per person
fresh herbs, such as parsley, chives or basil, chopped
butter and oil, for frying
1 large field mushrooms per person
2–3 rashers of bacon per person

1 small can of baked beans per person (optional)
1–2 eggs per person
salt and freshly ground black pepper

To serve
tomato ketchup

1 Preheat the oven to 190°C|375°F|gas mark 5. Preheat the grill to the highest setting.

2 Separate the sausages, place in a small roasting pan and place in the oven for about 30 minutes, or until cooked, turning them regularly to ensure an even colour.

3 Prepare the remaining ingredients once the sausages are in the oven. Remove the tomato stalks with the tip of a small sharp knife. Cut the tomatoes in half horizontally, place cut side up on half of a baking tray and season well with salt and pepper. Sprinkle with some of the herbs and then drizzle with oil, or top with a knob of butter.

4 Trim the stalks from the mushrooms and place stalk side up on the baking tray with the tomatoes if there is room. If not, prepare a separate tray. Drizzle a little oil or place a knob of butter on each mushroom, sprinkle with herbs and a little water and season with salt and pepper. Place the tomatoes and mushrooms in the oven with the sausages.

5 The bacon can either be grilled or fried. Start cooking it when the sausages just need a little more browning. If grilling, lay out all the bacon on a baking sheet with a lip. Grill until brown and crisp on both sides, then keep warm in the oven. If frying, heat a large frying pan. Streaky bacon will not need any extra fat in the pan, but if using back bacon, add a little oil. Add the bacon in one layer only. The bacon will shrink as it heats, so if all of it will not fit initially, add it gradually to the pan. Reduce the heat once the first side has started to brown. Brown well on both sides, then drain off any excess grease on a piece of kitchen paper.

6 Once the sausages are cooked and brown, turn the oven right down to its lowest temperature, so all the other ingredients can be kept warm once they are cooked. The tomatoes and mushrooms should be cooked until soft and kept warm in the oven.

7 Heat up the baked beans, if using, and warm the plates.

8 Cook the eggs only when everything else is ready. Heat some oil in a frying pan. Some people prefer a crisp egg, in which case only add enough oil to cover the base thinly. If a softer white is preferred, add about 1 cm oil to the pan and heat it up. A knob of butter can also be added to the oil. Crack the eggs one at a time into a small bowl and then lower into the hot oil. As soon as the white has begun to set, reduce the heat of the pan.

Cook until the white is set but the yolk is still runny. If using more oil, baste the hot oil over the top of the egg with a spoon. Use a palette knife or a fish slice to ensure the eggs do not stick to the base of the pan.

9 Divide the ingredients between the warmed plates and serve immediately.

Drop Scones with Bacon, Fried Eggs and Maple Syrup

Preparation time: 10 minutes
Cooking time: 10 minutes

SERVES 4

110 g plain flour

½ teaspoon mustard powder

¼ teaspoon salt

1 egg, separated

150 ml milk

1 tablespoon melted and cooled butter

oil

4 eggs

8–12 slices honey or maple cured bacon

To serve

very good-quality maple syrup

To prepare ahead: The drop scones can be made a day in advance, kept covered and reheated before serving.

1 Sift the flour, mustard and salt into a bowl. Make a well in the centre and add the egg yolk and half the milk. Mix well and gradually draw in the flour, adding the remaining milk as you go. Add the butter.

2 Whisk the egg white and fold it into the batter.

3 Preheat the grill to the highest setting.

4 Grease a large, heavy frying pan with a lid with oil and cook the drop scones in 2 tablespoon-size portions. They are ready to turn over when small air bubbles appear on the surface. When cooked, keep warm.

5 Grill the bacon until just crisp.

6 Meanwhile, add a little more oil to the pan. Crack the eggs into the pan and place a lid on top. Cook until the white is set.

7 Arrange the drop scones on individual plates, top with the bacon and eggs and drizzle with the maple syrup.

Poached Eggs on Toast

Cooking time: 2–3 minutes

SERVES 4

1 teaspoon white wine vinegar (optional)

4 very fresh cold eggs

4 slices of toast, buttered

salt and freshly ground black pepper

1 Fill a large saucepan with water and the vinegar, if using, and bring to simmering point. Stir the pan so the water moves round in a circular fashion.

2 Crack an egg into a cup and slide gently into the centre of the pan, holding the cup as near to the surface of the water as possible. Raise the temperature so that the water bubbles gently. Using a slotted spoon, draw the egg white close to the yolk.

3 Poach each egg for 2–3 minutes, or until the white is set but the yolk is still soft.

4 Lift out with a slotted spoon, drain the base of the spoon on kitchen paper and trim the egg whites if they are very ragged at the edges.

5 Place each egg on a piece of toast and sprinkle with salt and pepper. Serve immediately.

NOTE: Alternatively, use an egg poacher (see page 13).

Baked Mushrooms and Eggs

It is important that you choose mushrooms with a lip so that the egg is held in the bowl of the mushroom.

Preparation time: 10 minutes
Cooking time: 30 minutes

SERVES 4

4 Portobello or field mushrooms with a lip

1 clove of garlic, crushed

2 rashers of bacon, chopped

olive oil

4 eggs

chopped fresh parsley

salt and freshly ground black pepper

1 Preheat the oven to 200°C|400°F|gas mark 6.

2 Remove any stalks from the mushrooms and make a little hollow in the centre of each mushroom with a spoon. Chop the stalks and any removed flesh and set aside. Place the mushrooms skin side down on a baking sheet and divide the garlic, bacon and the chopped mushroom between them. Drizzle over a little oil and season.

3 Cook in the oven for 20–25 minutes, or until tender. Remove from the oven, crack an egg into each mushroom and return to the oven for 5 minutes, or until the white is set but the yolk is still soft.

4 Sprinkle with parsley and serve immediately.

Kedgeree

This is an excellent dish for using up leftover rice or cooked fish.

Preparation time: 2 minutes if using leftovers, 30 minutes if preparing all the ingredients
Cooking time: 10–15 minutes

SERVES 6

60 g butter

300 g cooked long-grain or basmati rice

400 g smoked haddock or fresh salmon fillet,
   cooked, skinned and boned

3 hardboiled eggs, roughly chopped

cayenne pepper

salt and freshly ground black pepper

To garnish

chopped fresh parsley

To prepare ahead: Have the eggs boiled and the fish and rice cooked in advance and combine as described when required.

1 Melt the butter in a large, shallow saucepan and add all the remaining ingredients.

2 Stir gently until very hot, being very careful not to break up the pieces of fish too much or to mash the rice. It is important that cooked rice is reheated to a very high temperature.

3 Serve sprinkled with the parsley.

NOTE: If making large quantities, heat in the oven instead of on top of the stove. Kedgeree will not spoil in a low oven (130°C|250°F|gas mark 1). Stir occasionally.

Kedgeree can also be cooked in the microwave. Transfer all the ingredients into a dish, cover well and microwave until hot through. Stir gently halfway through cooking.

VARIATION: Smoked trout can also be used in kedgeree.

Huevos Rancheros

Preparation time: 5 minutes
Cooking time: 10 minutes

SERVES 4

8 tablespoons arrabiata pasta sauce
4 flour tortillas
1–2 tablespoons vegetable oil
4 eggs

4 tablespoons finely crumbled Lancashire,
   Wensleydale or grated Cheddar cheese
chopped fresh coriander (optional)
salt and freshly ground black pepper

1 Heat the arrabiata sauce in a heavy saucepan. Bring to the boil, then allow to simmer and reduce until very thick, stirring occasionally to prevent it from catching on the bottom of the pan as it thickens.
2 Place a non-stick frying pan with a lid over a medium–high heat. Add the tortillas one at a time and fry for 15 seconds on each side or until warm. Put on to a plate and keep warm.
3 Heat a little oil in the pan and crack in the eggs. Allow the eggs to cook until set, sunny side up. Cover the pan for a minute or so to ensure even cooking. Season with salt and pepper.
4 Place each tortilla on a warmed plate, spoon over the arrabiata sauce and top with an egg. Sprinkle over the cheese and the coriander, if using. Serve immediately.

French Toast

Preparation time: 3 minutes
Cooking time: 3 minutes

4 slices of white bread
2 eggs
150 ml milk

55 g butter
oil
salt and freshly ground black pepper

1 Cut the slices of bread in half on the diagonal.
2 Beat the eggs, milk and a little salt and pepper together in a bowl.
3 Melt half the butter with a tablespoon of oil in a heavy frying pan.
4 Dip the bread into the egg mixture and make sure that it is well coated.
5 When the butter is foaming, fry the bread in it until golden brown on both sides. Drain on kitchen paper. Continue to fry until all 8 pieces of bread have been cooked.

NOTE: You can serve French toast with bacon and maple syrup, with strawberries, with marmalade or sprinkled with caster sugar. Omit the pepper from the mixture with sweet accompaniments.

Waffles

Waffles are best made in a waffle iron, but if you do not have one they can be made like drop scones in a large frying pan.

Preparation time: 15 minutes
Cooking time: 2 minutes

MAKES 15

3 eggs, separated
45 g unsalted butter, melted
350 ml milk
a few drops of vanilla extract
340 g plain flour
a pinch of salt

2 teaspoons bicarbonate of soda
3 tablespoons icing sugar, plus extra for dusting

To serve

maple syrup and crispy smoked bacon, or butter and jam

1 Place the egg yolks, butter, milk and vanilla extract in a jug and mix together.
2 Sift the flour, salt, bicarbonate of soda and icing sugar into a large mixing bowl. Make a well in the centre and gradually add the egg, butter and milk mixture, to make a smooth batter.
3 Place the egg whites in a separate bowl and whisk to medium peaks. Fold the egg whites into the batter, using a large metal spoon.
4 Cook the waffles in a waffle iron according to the manufacturer's instructions.
5 Dust with sifted icing sugar and serve with maple syrup.

NOTE: The first waffle often sticks to the waffle iron and should be discarded.

VARIATION: Ground cinnamon or ginger can be added to the batter.

Quick Canapés

These canapés can be put together in minutes, often from storecupboard ingredients, for an impromptu celebration. They can also be served instead of a first course for casual entertaining.

Quick Canapé Ideas

- Smoked salmon parcels: take narrow (2–3 cm) strips of smoked salmon, place a little smoked trout or salmon pâté at one end and roll up a couple of times
- Mini poppadoms topped with tandoori chicken and either raita (see page 495) or mango chutney. Garnish with a coriander leaf
- Pieces of toasted naan bread topped with coronation chicken and garnished with snipped chives
- Pieces of melon or fig wrapped in Parma ham and secured with a cocktail stick
- Cooked tiger prawns, with tails left on, served with garlic mayonnaise
- Cocktail sausages with mustard mayonnaise or a soft mash (see page 358)
- Cooked asparagus tips wrapped in Parma ham with hollandaise sauce to dip
- Hardboiled quails' eggs served with flavoured salts
- Crudités or crisps and dips
- Chinese pancakes with shredded duck and plum sauce
- Grissini with Parma ham wrapped around one end
- Crostini or bruschetta (see page 491)
- Mini pitta bread filled with a slice of lamb, some lettuce and sweet chilli sauce
- Halved mini balls of mozzarella and halved cherry tomatoes threaded alternately on cocktail sticks
- Leaves of little gem lettuce with a small spoonful of prawn cocktail and sprinkled with paprika
- Leaves of chicory with a small spoonful of blue cheese mixed with cream cheese and garnished with a quarter of a walnut

You can buy many items ready-made:

- Tartlet cases can be filled with all sorts of savoury mixtures, as for bruschetta toppings: smoked chicken, coriander and mango; finely chopped tomato, onion and mint; crème fraîche and mascarpone topped with feta; poached salmon and dill mayonnaise; smoked trout pâté; chopped mozzarella, Parma ham and pesto; smoked duck or venison with chilli jelly
- Sweet tart filling suggestions: lemon curd; crème fraîche and raspberries; mascarpone sweetened and flavoured with coffee, dusted with cocoa

- Bought blinis provide a good base for smoked salmon or fish roe. Using a small pastry cutter, you can also make good canapé bases from potato scones, pumpernickel bread and rye bread. Croûtes can also be made from thin white toast
- Cheese straws
- Charcuterie
- Marinated olives and feta on cocktail sticks
- Fish pâtés can be beaten with a little cream cheese, crème fraîche or mayonnaise to get a dipping consistency

A Selection of Bruschetta

The following selection of bruschetta or crostini make good canapés, snacks or first courses. The bread can be either toasted French or Italian bread.

1 French stick

1 clove of garlic, halved

2 tablespoons extra virgin olive oil

To prepare ahead: These can be stored for several days in an airtight container.

1 Preheat the oven to 180°C|350°F|gas mark 4.
2 Cut the bread into 1 cm slices on the diagonal. Rub with the cut side of the garlic and drizzle with oil. Bake in the oven for 10 minutes, or until crisp.
3 Spread with any form of paste: pesto (see page 512), aïoli, mayonnaise (see page 513), tapenade (see page 513), fruit chutney, crème fraîche, tzatziki (see page 495), pâté. Then top with one of your chosen ingredients:

- Smoked salmon, gravad lax (see page 183)
- Parma ham, honey roast ham, chorizo sausage
- Roast chicken, tandoori chicken
- Goat's cheese, mozzarella, brie. Cheese-topped bruschetta can then be grilled
- Roasted pepper strips, sunblush tomatoes, artichoke hearts

Honey-glazed Sausages with Celeriac Mash

Preparation time: 5 minutes
Cooking time: 20 minutes

60 cocktail sausages
2 tablespoons wholegrain mustard
2 tablespoons clear honey

For the celeriac mash
250 g celeriac, cooked and mashed
80 ml crème fraîche
1 tablespoon wholegrain mustard
salt and freshly ground black pepper

To prepare ahead: Make the mash in advance and reheat before serving.

1 Preheat the oven to 200°C|400°F|gas mark 6.
2 Put the sausages into a roasting pan and stir through the mustard, then drizzle with the honey. Bake in the oven for 20 minutes, or until the sausages are beginning to brown, shaking the roasting pan at intervals to prevent them from sticking together. They should also be stirred around to prevent those on the edges getting browner than those in the middle.
3 Make the mash: cook the celeriac in a large saucepan of boiling salted water until tender. Remove from the heat and drain. Mash well, add the crème fraîche and mustard and season to taste with salt and pepper.
4 Serve the sausages on a large plate, with the celeriac mash in a small bowl and cocktail sticks to hand.

Avocado Dip

Preparation time: 5 minutes

2 avocados, mashed
1 clove of garlic
1 tablespoon chopped fresh chives

juice of ½ lemon
salt and freshly ground black pepper

1 Combine all the ingredients, beat well, and season to taste with salt and pepper.

NOTE: Try not to prepare too far in advance as this dip may discolour. Store with the avacodo stones in the dip as this can prevent discolouration.

Cream Cheese Dip

Preparation time: 5 minutes

200 g cream cheese
1 tablespoon soured cream
2 tablespoons chopped fresh chives

a little milk
salt and freshly ground black pepper

1 Mix the cream cheese with the soured cream and chives, season with salt and pepper and add enough milk to bring the dip to the required consistency.

Blue Cheese Dip

Preparation time: 5 minutes

225 g blue cheese
1 shallot, very finely chopped
1 teaspoon white wine vinegar

4 tablespoons soured cream
salt and freshly ground black pepper

1 Beat the cheese with a wooden spoon and mix in the shallot and vinegar. Beat in the soured cream and season to taste with salt and pepper.

Mustard Dip

Preparation time: 5 minutes

150 ml ready-made mayonnaise (or see page 513)
1 × 142 ml pot of soured cream

2 tablespoons wholegrain mustard

1 Combine all the ingredients together.

Cream Cheese and Sweet Chilli Dip

Preparation time: 5 minutes

400 g cream cheese
1 tablespoon milk (optional)
chopped fresh chives or coriander (optional)
sweet chilli dipping sauce

To serve
tortilla chips

To prepare ahead: Complete to the end of stage 3 and chill. Remove from the refrigerator well before serving to allow the dip to soften up.

1 Beat the cream cheese in a bowl until soft and smooth (if very thick, let it down with a tablespoon of milk). Stir in the herbs, if using.
2 Pile the mixture into a wide bowl, making a mound in the centre of the dish.
3 Pour the sweet chilli dipping sauce in quite a thick layer around the cream cheese.
4 Serve tortilla chips separately.

Guacamole

Preparation time: 15 minutes

1–3 fresh green chillies
2 ripe avocados
1 large clove of garlic, crushed
1 teaspoon salt
3 tablespoons chopped fresh coriander leaves
1 large tomato, quartered, deseeded and diced

1–2 spring onions, finely sliced on the diagonal
juice of 1 lime

To serve
crudités or tortilla chips

To prepare ahead: Although this cannot be prepared too far in advance as it is likely to discolour, placing the avocado stone back in the centre of the guacamole and covering well with clingfilm will keep discoloration to a minimum.

1 Wearing rubber gloves, cut the chilli in half, remove the seeds and chop the flesh finely.
2 Peel and stone the avocados. Place the avocado flesh in a mixing bowl and mash to a rough-textured purée with a fork. Stir in the chilli, the garlic, salt and coriander and mix well.
3 Stir the chopped tomato into the avocado mixture with the spring onions and add lime juice to taste. Serve with crudités or tortilla chips.

Hummus

Preparation time: 5 minutes

1 × 400 g can of chickpeas
½ teaspoon ground cumin
2 tablespoons tahini (optional)
2 cloves of garlic, roasted (see page 14)
juice of 1 lemon
4 tablespoons olive oil
a pinch of cayenne pepper
salt and freshly ground black pepper

To garnish
a pinch of paprika
good-quality olive oil
flat-leaf parsley

To serve
toasted pitta bread, crudités or crisps

1 Drain and rinse the chickpeas and tip into a food processor. Whizz until smooth.
2 Add the remaining ingredients, and whizz again, adding a little water if necessary, to produce a soft cream.
3 Serve on a plate or in a bowl, sprinkled with a little paprika and drizzled with a little oil. Garnish with the parsley. Serve with toasted pitta bread, crudités or crisps.

NOTE: Raw garlic can be used, but roasting it will give a more mellow flavour. Reserve a tablespoon of the chickpeas and stir into the blended hummus with some toasted pinenuts for a more textured dip.

Quick Tzatziki or Raita

Serve with crisps as a dip or as an accompaniment to spicy dishes.

1–2 teaspoons mint sauce or mint jelly
150 g plain yoghurt
1 × 5 cm piece of cucumber, deseeded and chopped
   or grated

caster sugar (optional)
salt

To prepare ahead: This can be kept covered in the refrigerator until required.

1 Stir the mint sauce or jelly into the yoghurt and mix well. Stir in the cucumber and season to taste with salt and a little caster sugar, if liked.

VARIATION: This can also be made using chopped fresh dill in place of the mint sauce.

Quick Babaganoush

Preparation time: 5 minutes
Cooking time: 20 minutes

2 medium aubergines (about 630 g), peeled and cut into 2 cm cubes
4 cloves of garlic, peeled and halved
½ tablespoon chopped fresh thyme
a pinch of sweet paprika (optional)
50 ml good-quality olive oil

juice of ½ lemon
1 tablespoon chopped fresh parsley
salt and freshly ground black pepper

To serve
pitta bread

1 Place the aubergine, garlic, thyme and paprika, if using, in a ceramic microwave dish. Season with salt and pepper. Cover with a tight-fitting lid or clingfilm.
2 Cook on full power in the microwave for 5 minutes. Remove the lid and stir well. Replace the lid and cook for a further 10 minutes. Remove the lid carefully – there will be a lot of steam.
3 Place the contents of the dish in a sieve, allowing excess liquid to drain away. Allow to cool.
4 Place in a blender or food processor and whizz, gradually adding the olive oil in a steady stream with the motor running.
5 Add the lemon juice and parsley. Season to taste with plenty of salt and pepper and pile into a serving dish. Serve with plenty of hot pitta bread.

Smoked Salmon Canapés with Dill Crème Fraîche

Preparation time: 15 minutes

MAKES 12

3 slices of rye bread
85 ml crème fraîche
1 tablespoon chopped fresh dill
150 g smoked salmon, cut into strips

freshly ground black pepper

To garnish
sprigs of fresh dill

1 Using a small pastry cutter, cut 4 rounds from each slice of rye bread.
2 Mix together the crème fraîche and dill and season with pepper.
3 Place a small teaspoon of the crème fraîche mixture on top of the rye bread and arrange the smoked salmon on top. Place a sprig of dill on top of the salmon.
4 Arrange on a large plate to serve.

VARIATION: Irish potato farls or blinis can be used instead of rye bread.

Blinis with Mascarpone and Salmon Roe

Preparation time: 10 minutes

MAKES 30

250 g mascarpone

30 blinis

1 small jar of salmon roe

To garnish

sprigs of fresh dill

1 Beat the mascarpone lightly.

2 Spoon a little of the mascarpone on to the blinis and top with a little salmon roe.

3 Garnish each blini with a small sprig of dill.

Sesame Prawn Toasts

Preparation time: 10 minutes

Cooking time: 5 minutes

MAKES 20

140 g raw tiger prawns, peeled and deveined (see page 20)

1 tablespoon egg white

1 heaped teaspoon cornflour

a squeeze of lemon juice

a large pinch of salt

5 slices of white bread

2–3 tablespoons sesame seeds

oil, for deep-frying (see page 12)

To serve

sweet chilli dipping sauce

To prepare ahead: Complete to the end of stage 2, then refrigerate.

1 Put the prawns, egg white, cornflour, lemon juice and salt into a food processor. Whizz to a paste.

2 Cut the crusts off the bread. Spread the prawn paste evenly over the slices of bread and press a generous quantity of sesame seeds on top. Cut the slices of bread in half, then cut each half into 4 triangles or short fingers.

3 Heat the oil in a deep fryer or heavy saucepan, until a crumb will brown in 15 seconds.

4 Fry the sesame seed toasts, prawn side down, a few at a time, in the hot oil for 10–15 seconds, then flip them over and fry for a further 10–15 seconds until golden brown. Make sure the oil does not get too hot. Drain on kitchen paper and serve immediately with the dipping sauce.

VARIATION: These can also be made with chicken: use 140 g chicken, ½ red chill and 1 tablespoon chopped fresh coriander. Whizz to a paste with the cornflour and lemon juice and continue from stage 2.

Filo Tartlets with Crab, Ginger and Lime

Preparation time: 15 minutes
Cooking time: 20 minutes

MAKES 25 TARTLETS

For the tartlets

1 × 200 g pack of filo pastry

30 g butter, melted

For the crab filling

1 × 170 g can of white crabmeat

1 tablespoon mayonnaise

2 spring onions, finely sliced on the diagonal

1 × 2 cm piece of fresh root ginger, peeled and grated

grated zest and juice of 1 lime

1 Preheat the oven to 180°C|350°F|gas mark 4.

2 Cut the filo pastry sheets into 6 cm squares, and press into tartlet moulds, brushing each square of pastry with melted butter as you go. You will need 3 layers of pastry per tartlet: try to place the sheets at alternating angles, to resemble a star shape.

3 Place another tartlet tray on top of the prepared one, and bake in the oven for 8–10 minutes, or until nicely browned and crisped on top.

4 Mix together the crab, mayonnaise, spring onions, ginger and the lime zest and juice. Use the juice of the lime sparingly and to taste – if the mixture seems too runny, add a little more mayonnaise.

5 Fill the tartlet cases 30 minutes before serving.

NOTE: You can buy ready-made tartlet cases to fill with the mixture.

Leiths Basic Recipes

This book is written with the intention of saving time in the kitchen and so ready-prepared ingredients have been recommended throughout the recipe sections. This section is for the purists who prefer to start every dish from scratch, or for those who have always wanted to know how to make the ingredients they have hitherto been buying. At Leiths we believe that homemade will always taste better, but that some compromise has to be made by those who, unlike professional chefs, do not have all day to spend in the kitchen.

Stock

Homemade stocks will add a much better flavour to dishes than bought stocks, but can be time-consuming to make. However, all stocks can be reduced to a concentrate by boiling once they have been strained: the concentrate can then be stored in the refrigerator for 2 days, or frozen until needed. It can then be diluted and used as required. It can be a good idea to freeze stock in an ice cube tray. When frozen, turn into a bag and store in the freezer.

Chicken Stock

Preparation time: 5 minutes
Cooking time: 3–4 hours

1–2 kg raw chicken bones
1 onion, sliced
1 carrot, sliced
2 sticks of celery, sliced

a small handful of fresh parsley stalks or leaves
2 sprigs of fresh thyme
1 bay leaf
10 black peppercorns

1 Put all the ingredients together into a saucepan. Cover generously with cold water and bring to the boil slowly. Skim off any fat and/or scum.
2 Simmer for 3–4 hours, skimming frequently and topping up the water level so that it covers all the ingredients throughout the cooking time.
3 Strain the stock and then reduce by boiling to the required strength. The liquid should reduce to about half the original quantity.
4 Remove any remaining fat. Cool, then refrigerate or freeze until needed.

Chicken or Turkey Stock with Cooked Bones

This recipe uses the leftover bones from the roast bird, which are often more readily available than raw bones.

Preparation time: 5 minutes
Cooking time: 2–3 hours

cooked chicken or turkey bones

1 onion, sliced

1 stick of celery, sliced

1 carrot, sliced

a few fresh parsley stalks

2 sprigs of fresh thyme

2 bay leaves

10 black peppercorns

1 Put all the ingredients into a large saucepan. Cover generously with cold water and bring slowly to the boil. Skim off any fat and/or scum.
2 Simmer slowly for 2–3 hours, skimming frequently and topping up the water level if necessary so that all the ingredients are covered.
3 Strain and if the flavour is not strong enough, reduce by boiling rapidly. Cool, then refrigerate or freeze until needed.

Fish Stock

Preparation time: 5 minutes
Cooking time: 20–30 minutes

½ onion, sliced

1 carrot, sliced

1 stick of celery, sliced

1 kg bones, skins, fins, heads or tails of white fish

a few fresh parsley stalks

1 bay leaf

a pinch of chopped fresh thyme

6 black peppercorns

1 Put all the ingredients together into a saucepan, with cold water to cover, and bring to the boil. Turn down to a simmer and skim off any scum.
2 Simmer for 20 minutes if the fish bones are small, 30 minutes if large. Strain and reduce as necessary.
3 Cool, then refrigerate or freeze until needed.

Shellfish Stock

Preparation time: 5 minutes
Cooking time: 30 minutes

1 onion, sliced
1 carrot, sliced
1 stick of celery, sliced
about 1 kg crustacean and mollusc shells, such as
    prawn shells, mussel shells, lobster shells or crab
    shells (a mixture can be used)

1 bay leaf
1 sprig of fresh thyme
6 black peppercorns

1 Put all the ingredients into a saucepan. Cover with cold water and bring to the boil, then reduce the heat and simmer for 30 minutes. Skim regularly.
2 Strain and reduce to two-thirds of the original quantity by boiling rapidly. Cool, then refrigerate or freeze until needed.

Vegetable Stock

Preparation time: 5 minutes
Cooking time: 40 minutes

4 tablespoons oil
1 onion, chopped
1 leek, chopped
1 large carrot, chopped
2 sticks of celery, chopped
a few cabbage leaves, shredded
a few mushroom stalks

2 cloves of garlic, crushed
a few fresh parsley stalks
6 black peppercorns
1 large bay leaf
6 tablespoons dry white wine
pinch of salt

1 Heat the oil in a large saucepan. Add the vegetables, cover and cook over a low heat for 5 minutes, or until softening.
2 Add the garlic, parsley stalks, peppercorns, bay leaf, wine, salt and enough cold water to cover. Bring to the boil, then lower the heat and simmer for 30 minutes or until the liquid is reduced by half.
3 Strain the stock through a sieve, pressing hard to remove as much of the liquid as possible. Discard the vegetable pulp. Allow to cool and skim off any oil.
4 Reduce by boiling to the required strength of flavour. Cool, then refrigerate or freeze until needed.

Gravies and Sauces

Onion Gravy

Preparation time: 5 minutes
Cooking time: 20 minutes

30 g butter
2 medium onions, sliced
2 tablespoons soft dark brown sugar
1½ tablespoons plain flour

150 ml red wine
300 ml chicken or beef stock
2 sprigs of fresh thyme
salt and freshly ground black pepper

1 Melt the butter in a saucepan, add the onions and cook over a low heat until very soft.
2 Add the sugar and turn up the heat. Allow the onions to caramelize and turn a rich golden brown.
3 Add the flour and cook for 30 seconds. Add the wine and allow to reduce by half, stirring well, then add the stock and the thyme.
4 Bring to the boil and reduce until the mixture has a good gravy consistency. Taste and season with salt and pepper. Remove the thyme before serving.

White Sauce

This sauce is extremely useful once mastered as it is very versatile and has a huge number of variations. It can be used to accompany chicken or fish, as part of a fish or chicken pie, with pasta or to bind together other ingredients. The key is to start slowly when adding the milk and make sure the lumps have been beaten out after each addition. Alternatively, buy a good-quality white sauce which can also be adapted to the variations below.

Basic Recipe

MAKES 300 ML

20 g butter
a pinch of dry English mustard or ½ teaspoon made
   English mustard

20 g plain flour
300 ml milk
salt and freshly ground white pepper

1 Melt the butter in a heavy saucepan with a thick base to prevent the sauce from catching.
2 Remove the pan from the heat and stir in the flour and dry mustard. Return to the heat and cook, stirring, for 1 minute.
3 Remove the pan from the heat and add a little of the milk. Stir well to beat out any lumps, then add a little more milk. Beat out any lumps again. When the mixture has

become a thick liquid rather than a lump of dough, return to a low heat and little by little add the remaining milk, stirring all the time.

4 When all the milk has been incorporated, increase the heat and bring the sauce to the boil. Lower the heat and simmer for 2 minutes, stirring occasionally.

5 Season to taste with salt, pepper and the made mustard, if using.

Variations

- **Cheese sauce:** Add a pinch of cayenne pepper with the dry English mustard. Add 50–80 g grated cheese to the finished hot sauce. Do not boil the sauce once the cheese has been added or it may become greasy and have a grainy texture. Mature Cheddar or Gruyère are the classic cheeses to use, but the addition of a little Parmesan or even some blue cheese can also work well.

- **Quick béchamel sauce:** Add a bay leaf, a couple of slices of onion, a blade of mace and some fresh parsley stalks to the sauce while it is simmering. Allow to infuse for a few minutes before sieving out the solid ingredients and reheating the sauce to serve.

- **Parsley sauce:** Wash a handful of fresh parsley leaves and chop as finely as possible. Stir into the finished sauce. This is traditionally served with fish, poached chicken, or ham. Serve immediately as otherwise the sauce will discolour.

- **Onion sauce:** Melt 30 g butter in a saucepan and add a very thinly sliced onion. Cook over a low heat until soft but not brown. Add the flour and proceed following the basic recipe. This sauce can be puréed in a blender if a smooth sauce is preferred and a tablespoon of double cream can be added at the end for a richer result. This is traditionally served with lamb, but works well with a variety of vegetable dishes.

- **Watercress sauce:** Increase the mustard quantity to a heaped teaspoon. Wash a bunch of watercress and remove any coarse stems. Chop the watercress well and add to the finished sauce. Liquidize for a vibrant green sauce. Serve immediately.

- **Chicken and mushroom sauce:** Melt 30 g butter in a saucepan and add a very finely diced shallot and 100 g finely chopped mushrooms. Cook over a low heat until soft. Substitute some strong chicken stock for half the milk and add a dash of white wine. Proceed following the same method as the basic recipe.

- **Fish cream sauce:** Melt 20 g butter in a saucepan and add a very finely chopped shallot. Cook over a low heat until soft. Add the flour as in the basic recipe, but then in place of the milk use a mixture of well flavoured fish stock (see page 500), dry white wine or vermouth and milk. 2 tablespoons double cream added at the end will give a richer result. Add 1 tablespoon finely chopped fresh herbs, such as chervil, dill, basil or parsley when ready to serve.

Fresh Tomato Sauce

This recipe is for a very smooth sauce. Leave the sauce unwhizzed or unsieved if a chunkier texture is preferred.

Preparation time: 10 minutes
Cooking time: 35 minutes

3 tablespoons oil
1 large onion, finely chopped
10 tomatoes, roughly chopped
a pinch of caster sugar

150 ml chicken or vegetable stock
1 teaspoon chopped fresh thyme
salt and freshly ground black pepper

1 Heat the oil in a saucepan, add the onion and cook for 3 minutes, or until just beginning to soften. Add the tomatoes, salt, pepper, sugar and stock and cook for a further 30 minutes.
2 Whizz the sauce in a blender or food processor, then push it through a sieve to remove the tomato skins and seeds. It may be necessary to do this in 2 batches.
3 If the sauce is too thin, reduce by simmering to the desired consistency.
4 Add the thyme. Taste and adjust the seasoning if necessary.

Tomato Sauce

Preparation time: 10 minutes
Cooking time: 40 minutes

3 tablespoons olive oil
1 small onion, chopped
1 small carrot, chopped
1 stick of celery, chopped
½ clove of garlic, crushed
1 × 400 g can of chopped tomatoes
1 bay leaf

fresh parsley stalks
juice of ½ lemon
a dash of Worcestershire sauce
1 teaspoon caster sugar
1 teaspoon chopped fresh basil or thyme
salt and freshly ground black pepper

1 Heat the oil in a large saucepan, add the onion, carrot and celery and sweat over a low heat for about 10 minutes, until beginning to soften. Add the garlic and cook for 1 further minute.
2 Add all the remaining ingredients, seasoning well with salt and pepper. Cover and simmer over a medium heat for 30 minutes. Remove the bay leaf.
3 Whizz the sauce in a blender or food processor and sieve it if a smooth sauce is required: make sure as much of the vegetable pulp as possible is pushed through the sieve.
4 If the sauce is too thin, return to the rinsed-out pan and reduce by boiling rapidly. Check the seasoning, adding more salt, pepper and sugar if necessary.

Red Pepper Sauce

Preparation time: 10 minutes
Cooking time: 30 minutes

1 tablespoon oil
1 onion, finely chopped
1 stick of celery, finely chopped
1 red pepper, cored, deseeded and cut into strips
2 tomatoes, chopped

1 clove of garlic, crushed
1 sprig of fresh thyme
6 tablespoons water
salt and freshly ground black pepper

1 Heat the oil in a saucepan, add the onion, celery and pepper and sweat over a low heat until just beginning to soften. Add the tomatoes, garlic, thyme and water and season lightly with salt and pepper. Cover and cook over a low heat for about 20 minutes, or until the pepper is completely soft. Remove the sprig of thyme.
2 Whizz in a blender or food processor until smooth, then sieve, making sure as much of the vegetable pulp as possible is pushed through the sieve. Check the seasoning and the consistency of the sauce and add a little more water if too thick. Reheat to serve.

Plum Sauce

Preparation time: 5 minutes
Cooking time: 5 minutes

1 tablespoon sesame oil
1 × 2.5 cm piece of fresh root ginger, peeled and sliced
2 tablespoons miso paste

200 g plum jam
1 teaspoon chilli powder
30 g caster sugar

1 Heat the oil in a small saucepan, add the ginger and fry for 2 minutes to flavour the oil lightly.
2 Remove the ginger with a slotted spoon and discard. Add the miso paste, plum jam, chilli powder and sugar to the oil and heat gently, stirring, until smooth.

Mint Sauce

Preparation time: 5 minutes
Infusing time: 1–2 hours

a large handful of fresh mint
2 tablespoons caster sugar

2 tablespoons hot water
2 tablespoons white wine vinegar

1 Wash the mint and shake it dry. Remove and discard the stalks and chop the leaves finely. Place in a bowl with the sugar.
2 Pour on the hot water and leave for 5 minutes to dissolve the sugar. Add the vinegar and leave to infuse for 1–2 hours.

Horseradish Cream

Preparation time: 5 minutes

1 × 142 ml pot of double cream
1–2 tablespoons finely grated fresh horseradish
2 teaspoons white wine vinegar

½ teaspoon made English mustard
sugar to taste
salt and freshly ground white pepper

1 Put all the ingredients into a bowl and whisk to the required consistency. Taste and add more horseradish if required. The sauce will thicken further when chilled.

Cumberland Sauce

Preparation time: 10 minutes
Cooking time: 10 minutes

2 oranges
1 lemon
150 ml port
½ teaspoon Dijon mustard

225 g redcurrant jelly
1 shallot, chopped
a pinch of cayenne pepper
a pinch of ground ginger

1 Peel 1 of the oranges and the lemon with a potato peeler, removing only the outer zest. Cut the zest into fine shreds.
2 Squeeze the juice from all the fruit and strain into a small saucepan. Then add the remaining ingredients with the citrus shreds. Simmer for 10 minutes, then cool.

Apple Sauce

Preparation time: 5 minutes
Cooking time: 10–15 minutes

450 g Bramley apples
grated zest of ¼ lemon

3 tablespoons water
2 teaspoons sugar

1 Peel, quarter, core and chop the apples.
2 Place in a heavy saucepan with the lemon zest, water and sugar. Cover and cook over a very low heat until the apples are soft, stirring occasionally. Add extra sugar if required. Serve hot or cold.

Bread Sauce

Preparation time: 5 minutes
Standing time: 30 minutes
Cooking time: 5 minutes

500 ml full-fat milk
½ onion, thickly sliced
6 cloves
2 bay leaves
5 peppercorns, or a pinch of freshly ground white pepper

a pinch of freshly grated nutmeg
100 g fresh white breadcrumbs (see page 10)
100 g butter
60 ml cream (optional)
salt

1 Place the milk in the saucepan with the onion, cloves and bay leaves.
2 Add the peppercorns, nutmeg, and a good pinch of salt. Bring to the boil very slowly. Remove from the heat and leave to stand.
3 Strain the milk on to the breadcrumbs in a bowl. Add the butter and the cream, if using. Mix and return to the saucepan.
4 Reheat the sauce carefully without boiling.
5 If the sauce becomes too thick, beat in more hot milk until creamy. Bread sauce can be served hot, cold or at room temperature.

Red Onion Marmalade

Preparation time: 5 minutes
Cooking time: 20 minutes

2 tablespoons oil

3 medium red onions, chopped

1 clove of garlic, crushed

3 tablespoons soft dark brown sugar

300 ml red wine

1 tablespoon clear honey

salt and freshly ground black pepper

1 Heat the oil in a heavy saucepan, add the onions and sweat over a low heat until very soft. Add the garlic and stir for 30 seconds.

2 Add the sugar, turn up the heat and allow the onions to caramelize.

3 Add the wine and reduce until there is almost no liquid left in the pan.

4 Stir in the honey, then season to taste with salt and pepper. This can be served hot or cold.

Salsas

Salsas – the Spanish word for sauce – are made from a variety of ingredients including fruits and vegetables, spices and, traditionally, chillies. They are used all over Mexico and are served at the table with almost any dish, not unlike a relish or chutney.

Salsas can be fresh or cooked, and can have a wide variety of textures, from chunky to smooth. Many types of good-quality cooked salsas – most often with a tomato base – are now available in jars. The following fresh salsas are great for livening up a plain piece of grilled chicken, fish or even a steak.

Fresh salsas are easy to make: the prepared ingredients are simply stirred together and a little oil or dressing added if desired. They can be made in advance as long as they contain no ingredients that will discolour, such as apple or avocado. Making the salsa in advance allows the flavours to develop, often giving a softer rather than a crunchier texture.

Mango Salsa

Preparation time: 10 minutes

½ red onion, finely sliced or finely chopped

1 mango, peeled, stone removed and finely diced

1 bunch of finely chopped fresh coriander

1 tablespoon lime juice

1 tablespoon olive oil

1 red chilli, chopped (optional)

salt and freshly ground black pepper

1 Mix together all the salsa ingredients and season with salt and pepper.

Lime and Cucumber Salsa

Preparation time: 10 minutes

½ cucumber

2 tablespoons oil

1 tablespoon chopped fresh dill

1 tablespoon lime juice

grated zest of ½ lime

½ teaspoon caster sugar

salt and freshly ground black pepper

1 Mix together all the salsa ingredients and season with salt and pepper.

Citrus Salsa

Preparation time: 10 minutes
Standing time: 30 minutes

1 red onion, very finely chopped

3 tablespoons olive oil

1 lemon

1 orange

½ grapefruit

1 lime

1 red chilli, very finely chopped

2 tablespoons chopped fresh coriander

salt and freshly ground black pepper

1 Mix the onion and oil together and leave to stand for 30 minutes.
2 Segment all the citrus fruits (see page 11) and roughly chop the membrane-free segments. Add the citrus fruits and the remaining ingredients to the onion and season to taste with salt and pepper.

Tomato and Mint Salsa

Preparation time: 10 minutes
Standing time: 10 minutes

1 shallot, finely sliced

1 tablespoon wine vinegar

3 tablespoons olive oil

4 tomatoes, quartered, deseeded and finely chopped

1 clove of garlic, crushed

1 tablespoon chopped fresh mint

salt and freshly ground black pepper

1 Mix together the shallot, vinegar and oil and allow to stand for 10 minutes.
2 Add the tomatoes, garlic and mint and season to taste with salt and pepper.

Spicy Tomato Salsa

Preparation time: 10 minutes

2 spring onions, finely chopped
2 ripe plum tomatoes, finely chopped
2 tablespoons finely chopped fresh coriander

½ red chilli, finely chopped
a squeeze of lemon

1 Mix together all the salsa ingredients and season with salt and pepper.

Cherry Tomato and Dill Salsa

Preparation time: 10 minutes

½ red onion, finely chopped
1 tablespoon red wine vinegar
3 tablespoons olive oil

12 ripe cherry tomatoes, chopped into eighths
1 tablespoon chopped fresh dill
salt and freshly ground black pepper

1 Mix together all the salsa ingredients and season with salt and pepper.

Apricot Salsa

Preparation time: 10 minutes

225 g ripe apricots, halved and stoned
2 spring onions, finely sliced
2 tablespoons chopped fresh coriander
1 clove of garlic, crushed
1 red chilli, deseeded and chopped

1 × 2.5 cm piece of fresh root ginger, peeled and grated
1–2 tablespoons rice wine vinegar
salt and freshly ground black pepper

1 Mix together all the salsa ingredients and season with salt and pepper.

Salsa Verde

Preparation time: 10 minutes

½ cucumber, deseeded and finely diced
½ green chilli, finely diced
1 shallot, finely chopped
grated zest and juice of 1 lime

1 teaspoon caster sugar
1 tablespoon chopped fresh coriander
salt and freshly ground black pepper

1 Mix together all the salsa ingredients and season with salt and pepper.

Warm Red Salsa

Preparation time: 10 minutes
Cooking time: 15 minutes

1 red pepper, halved, cored and deseeded
1 large tomato, quartered, deseeded and finely diced
1 tablespoon chopped fresh basil
1 tablespoon olive oil

juice of ½ lemon
juice of ½ orange
salt and freshly ground black pepper

1 Grill and skin the peppers (see page 19).
2 Dice the pepper flesh finely and mix with the remaining ingredients. Season to taste with salt and pepper.
3 Just before serving, heat through very gently until just warm.

NOTE: Use bought skinned peppers if preferred. Use some of the oil in which they are preserved in place of the olive oil.

Basil Pesto

Pesto can also be made in a pestle and mortar. A little warm water or stock can be whisked into the finished pesto to create a coating sauce to serve with grilled fish or chicken.

Preparation time: 10 minutes

2 cloves of garlic

2 large cups of fresh basil leaves

60 g pinenuts

60 g Parmesan cheese, freshly grated

150 ml olive oil

salt

1 Whizz the garlic, basil and pinenuts together in a blender or the small bowl of a food processor to make a paste. You may need to add a little of the oil to help the blades to purée the mixture.

2 Add the Parmesan, then gradually blend in the oil and season well with salt. Cover and chill until required.

NOTE: Classic pesto can be adapted by changing the herbs, nuts and cheese used. The nuts can be toasted if preferred (see page 17). The garlic can also be roasted for a more mellow flavour (see page 14).

VARIATIONS:

- **Coriander pesto**: Use coriander instead of the basil and blanched almonds, roughly chopped, instead of the pinenuts.
- **Chilli and coriander pesto**: Use coriander instead of the basil and add 2 chopped green chillies to the mixture with the coriander.
- **Dill pesto**: Use a large handful of fresh dill instead of the basil and blanched almonds instead of the pinenuts.
- **Red pesto**: Add 60 g chopped sundried tomatoes to the mixture with the basil. Use Pecorino cheese instead of Parmesan.
- **Rocket pesto**: Use 60 g rocket instead of the basil and blanched almonds instead of the pinenuts.
- **Parsley pesto**: Use a large handful of fresh parsley instead of the basil, blanched almonds instead of the pinenuts, and grated Cheddar cheese instead of the Parmesan.
- **Goat's cheese pesto**: Use 60 g toasted sunflower seeds instead of the pinenuts and 60 g hard goat's cheese instead of the Parmesan.

Black Olive Tapenade

Preparation time: 5 minutes

100 g black olives, pitted

2 tablespoons capers, drained and rinsed

1 clove of garlic, chopped

75 ml olive oil

salt and freshly ground black pepper

1 Put the olives, capers and garlic into a food processor and process until smooth. You may want to add a little oil to help the blender purée the mixture.

2 With the motor is still running, pour in the oil. Season with salt and pepper. Cover and chill until required.

Mayonnaise

Mayonnaise can also be made quickly in a food processor or blender, but the quantity must be sufficient for the blades to be in contact with the egg yolks before the oil is added. The variations below can be made with either homemade or bought mayonnaise.

Preparation time: 20 minutes

2 egg yolks

1 teaspoon dry English mustard

1 tablespoon white wine vinegar

300 ml olive oil, or 150 ml each olive and salad oil

a squeeze of lemon

salt and freshly ground black pepper

1 Put the egg yolks into a bowl with a pinch of salt, the mustard and some of the vinegar. Beat well with a wooden spoon.

2 Add the oil, literally drop by drop, beating all the time, ensuring the mixture is thickening before adding the next drop. The mixture should be very thick by the time half the oil is added.

3 Beat in the lemon juice.

4 Resume pouring in the oil, going more quickly now, but alternating the dribbles of oil with small quantities of the remaining vinegar. Season to taste with salt and pepper.

NOTE: If the mixture curdles, another egg yolk should be beaten in a separate bowl, and the curdled mixture beaten into it drop by drop.

VARIATIONS:
- Tartare sauce: Add chopped fresh parsley, gherkins and capers.
- Garlic mayonnaise: Add crushed garlic or chopped roast garlic (see page 14).
- Herby mayonnaise: Add 2 tablespoons chopped, mixed fresh herbs.
- Lemon or lime mayonnaise: Add the grated zest of a lemon or lime.
- Marie Rose sauce: Add tomato ketchup and a splash of Worcestershire sauce.

Hollandaise Sauce

Hollandaise sauce will set too firmly if allowed to get cold and it will curdle if overheated. It can be made in larger quantities in either a blender or a food processor: simply put the egg yolks and salt into the blender or food processor and blend lightly. Add the hot reduction and allow to thicken slightly. Set aside. When ready to serve, pour in hot melted butter, slowly allowing the sauce to thicken as you do so. The quantity must be sufficient for the blades to be in contact with the egg yolks before the oil is added.

Preparation time: 5 minutes
Cooking time: 20 minutes

3 tablespoons white wine vinegar
6 black peppercorns
1 bay leaf
1 blade of mace
2 egg yolks

3 tablespoons double cream
a knob of butter
100 g unsalted butter, softened
lemon juice
salt and freshly ground white pepper

1 Place the vinegar, peppercorns, bay leaf and mace in a small, heavy saucepan and reduce by simmering to 1 tablespoon. Strain this reduction into a bowl immediately or the remaining liquid may evaporate.

2 Fill a roasting pan with water about 4 cm deep. Place on the hob and heat so that one side of the pan is bubbling and the other is not bubbling at all.

3 Cream the egg yolks with a pinch of salt, the cream and a knob of butter in a small bowl. Set the bowl in the roasting pan on the side that is not bubbling. Using a wooden spoon, beat the mixture until slightly thickened, ensuring that the water immediately around the bowl does not boil. The mixture should have the consistency of Greek yoghurt.

4 Add a little of the vinegar reduction. Mix well. Stir over the heat until slightly thickened. The mixture should be warm. Beat in the softened butter piece by piece, increasing the temperature slightly as the sauce thickens and more butter is added. Take care that the water does not boil. The sauce should thicken after each addition of butter. If it suddenly looks very greasy, whisk in a teaspoon of the reduction or cold water.

5 When the sauce has become light and thick, remove from the heat. Taste for seasoning and if necessary add lemon juice or more reduction, salt and pepper. Keep warm by standing the bowl in warm but not boiling water.

VARIATIONS:

- **Béarnaise sauce:** Add a chopped shallot, a sprig of fresh thyme and a sprig of chervil to the vinegar. When the sauce is complete, add 1 teaspoon chopped fresh tarragon, 1 teaspoon chopped chervil and 1 teaspoon concentrated beef stock.
- **Mustard hollandaise:** Add 1 teaspoon mustard, either wholegrain or made English, to the completed sauce.
- **Herby hollandaise:** Add 4 tablespoons chopped fresh herbs and a pinch of cayenne pepper to the finished sauce.
- **Roast garlic hollandaise:** Add 2 crushed roast garlic cloves (see page 14) and 1 teaspoon chopped fresh parsley to the finished sauce.

French Dressing (Vinaigrette)

Preparation time: 5 minutes

1 tablespoon wine vinegar
½ teaspoon mustard
1 teaspoon chopped fresh herbs

3–4 tablespoons oil
salt and freshly ground black pepper

1 Place the vinegar with the mustard, the herbs, a pinch of salt and a few grindings of pepper in a small bowl.

2 Gradually whisk in the oil to form an emulsion. Store in the refrigerator.

NOTE: French dressing can also be made successfully by putting all the ingredients in a jam jar with a tight fitting lid. Screw the lid on securely and shake all the ingredients together well.

VARIATIONS: See page 382.

Pastries and Batters

The following recipes are for making pastry by hand. If a food processor or mixer is available, it is good idea to rub the butter into the flour until they resemble breadcrumbs in the machine, then tip the mixture into a bowl and add the liquid by hand. This will prevent the pastry from becoming tough.

Rough Puff Pastry

While there is no place for puff pastry in a 'simple' book, a good rise can be achieved with the easier rough puff pastry, for those who would prefer to make and not buy their pastry.

Preparation time: 30 minutes
Chilling time: 1 hour

85–135 ml very cold water, to mix
225 g plain flour, plus extra for rolling

a pinch of salt
150 g butter, cut into sugar-cube sized pieces

1 Measure the water into a jug and place in the refrigerator to chill.
2 Sift the flour with the salt into a bowl. Stir in the pieces of butter. Do not rub them into the flour.
3 Add enough chilled water just to bind the flour to a paste. Mix first with a knife, then with one hand, to bring the dough together. (The butter should still be in lumps.)
4 Chill, wrapped, for 10 minutes.
5 On a floured surface, roll the pastry into a strip about 30 × 10 cm long. Take care not to overstretch and break the surface of the pastry.
6 Fold the strip into 3 and turn so that the folded edge is to your left, like a closed book.
7 Again roll out the pastry into the same sized strip, fold in 3 again and chill for 15 minutes.
8 Roll and fold the pastry again and chill for 15 minutes.
9 Roll and fold again, by which time the pastry should be ready for use, with no signs of streakiness. If it is still streaky, roll and fold once more.
10 Roll into the required shape.
11 Chill again before baking.

Rich Shortcrust Pastry

Preparation time: 10 minutes
Chilling time: 30 minutes

very cold water, to mix
170 g plain flour
a pinch of salt

100 g butter, cut into small cubes
1 egg yolk

1 Place a jug of water in the refrigerator to chill.
2 Sift the flour with the salt into a large bowl.
3 Rub in the butter until the mixture resembles coarse breadcrumbs.
4 Mix the egg yolk with 2 tablespoons of the water and add to the mixture.
5 Mix to a firm dough, first with a knife, and finally with one hand. It may be necessary to add more water, but the pastry should not be too damp. (Though crumbly pastry is more difficult to handle, it produces a shorter, lighter result.) Press the pastry into a flat disc shape.
6 Chill, wrapped, for 30 minutes before using. Allow the rolled-out pastry to relax before baking.

Sweet Shortcrust Pastry

Preparation time: 10 minutes
Chilling time: 30 minutes

very cold water, to mix
170 g plain flour
a pinch of salt
100 g butter, cut into small cubes

1 tablespoon caster sugar
1 egg yolk
a few drops of vanilla extract

1 Place a jug of water in the refrigerator to chill.
2 Sift the flour with the salt into a large bowl.
3 Rub in the butter until the mixture resembles coarse breadcrumbs. Stir in the sugar.
4 Mix the egg yolk with 2 tablespoons of the water and the vanilla extract. Add to the mixture.
5 Mix to a firm dough, first with a knife and then with one hand. It may be necessary to add more water, but the pastry should not be too damp. (Though crumbly pastry is more difficult to handle, it produces a shorter, lighter result.) Press the pastry into a flat disc shape.
6 Chill, wrapped, for 30 minutes before using. Allow the rolled-out pastry to relax before baking.

Wholemeal Pastry

Preparation time: 5 minutes
Chilling time: 30 minutes

very cold water, to mix
110 g wholemeal flour
110 g plain white flour

a pinch of salt
140 g butter, cut into small cubes

1 Place a jug of water in the refrigerator to chill.

2 Sift the flours with the salt into a large bowl and add the bran from the sieve. Rub in the butter until the mixture resembles coarse breadcrumbs.

3 Add 2 tablespoons of the water and mix to a firm dough, first with a knife and then with one hand. It may be necessary to add more water, but the pastry should not be too damp. (Although crumbly pastry is more difficult to handle it produces a shorter, lighter result.) Place the pastry into a flat disc shape.

4 Chill, wrapped, for at least 30 minutes before using. Allow the rolled-out pastry to relax before baking.

NOTE: All wholemeal flour may be used if preferred.

VARIATION: To make sweet wholemeal pastry, mix in 2 tablespoons sugar once the fat has been rubbed into the flour.

Pancakes (Crêpes)

Preparation time: 10 minutes
Chilling time: 30 minutes
Cooking time: 20–25 minutes

MAKES ABOUT 12

100 g plain flour

a pinch of salt

1 egg, beaten

1 egg yolk

300 ml milk, or milk and water mixed

1 tablespoon oil

oil, for cooking

To prepare ahead: Layer up the pancakes with strips of greaseproof paper between them to prevent them from sticking together. They can be frozen like this, well wrapped, then defrosted as required.

1 Sift the flour with the salt into a bowl and make a well in the centre, exposing the bottom of the bowl.

2 Put the whole egg and the yolk with a little of the milk together into the well.

3 Using a wooden spoon or whisk, mix the egg and milk and then gradually draw in the flour from the sides as you mix. Add more milk to the central well little by little as required to prevent it from becoming too thick and dough-like.

4 When the mixture reaches the consistency of thick cream, add the remaining milk and stir in the oil.

5 The consistency should now be that of thin cream. (The batter can also be made by placing all the ingredients together in a blender for a few seconds, but take care not to overwhizz or the mixture will be bubbly.)

6 Cover the bowl and chill for about 30 minutes, to allow the starch cells to swell, giving a light result.

7 Prepare a pancake pan or frying pan by heating well and wiping with oil. Pancakes are not fried in fat – the purpose of the oil is simply to prevent sticking.

8 Pour enough batter into the hot pan to coat the base of the pan thinly. Swirl the pan to help the batter spread across the base.

9 Place over medium heat and, when the pancake is pale brown on the underside, use a palette knife and your fingers to turn the pancake over. Cook the other side until brown. (Pancakes should be extremely thin, so if the first one is too thick, add a little extra milk to the batter. The first pancake is unlikely to be perfect, and is often discarded.)

10 Make up all the pancakes, turning them out on to a plate.

NOTE: This batter can also be used for Yorkshire puddings.

Index

A Note on the Authors

Viv Pidgeon read Geography at Bristol University and then completed the Diploma in Food and Wine at Leiths School of Food and Wine. After graduating she cooked in the UK and abroad and worked as a caterer in London before returning to the School in 1998 as part of the staff. She has written for *House and Garden* magazine, contributed to *Leiths Cookery Bible* and coordinated and wrote for the Leiths *Daily Mail* recipe column. Viv lives in London.

Jenny Stringer was the principal of Leiths School of Food and Wine from 2002 to 2007. She has contributed to *Leiths Cookery Bible* and the Leiths *Daily Mail* recipe column. Jenny began her cookery training following a degree in English and Publishing. After training at Leiths School of Food and Wine, she worked for HRH the Prince of Wales at Highgrove and St James's Palace as well as doing a variety of freelance cooking jobs, before returning to Leiths as a teacher, where she worked for ten years. Jenny lives in Bromley with her husband and their two sons.